Sino-Enchantment

EDINBURGH STUDIES IN EAST ASIAN FILM
Series Editor: Margaret Hillenbrand

Forthcoming titles

Independent Chinese Documentary: Alternative Visions, Alternative Publics, Dan Edwards

The Cinema of Ozu Yasujiro: Histories of the Everyday, Woojeong Joo

Eclipsed Cinema: The Film Culture of Colonial Korea, Dong Hoon Kim

Moving Figures: Class and Feeling in the Films of Jia Zhangke, Corey Kai Nelson Schultz

Memory, Subjectivity and Independent Chinese Cinema, Qi Wang

Hong Kong Neo-Noir, Esther C. M. Yau and Tony Williams

'My' Self on Camera: First Person Documentary Practice in an Individualising China, Kiki Tianqi Yu

Worldly Desires: Cosmopolitanism and Cinema in Hong Kong and Taiwan, Brian Hu

Tanaka Kinuyo: Nation, Stardom and Female Subjectivity, Irene González-López and Michael Smith

Killers, Clients and Kindred Spirits: The Taboo Cinema of Shohei Imamura, David Desser and Lindsay Coleman

Sino-Enchantment: The Fantastic in Contemporary Chinese Cinemas, Kenneth Chan and Andrew Stuckey

www.edinburghuniversitypress.com/series/ESEAF

Sino-Enchantment

The Fantastic in Contemporary
Chinese Cinemas

Edited by
Kenneth Chan and Andrew Stuckey

EDINBURGH
University Press

Edinburgh University Press is one of the leading university presses in the UK.
We publish academic books and journals in our selected subject areas across the
humanities and social sciences, combining cutting-edge scholarship with high editorial
and production values to produce academic works of lasting importance. For more
information visit our website: edinburghuniversitypress.com

© editorial matter and organisation Kenneth Chan and Andrew Stuckey, 2021, 2023
© the chapters their several authors, 2021, 2023

Edinburgh University Press Ltd
The Tun – Holyrood Road
12(2f) Jackson's Entry
Edinburgh EH8 8PJ

First published in hardback by Edinburgh University Press 2021

Typeset in 10/13 Chaparral Pro by
IDSUK (DataConnection) Ltd

A CIP record for this book is available from the British Library

ISBN 978-1-4744-6084-2 (hardback)
ISBN 978-1-4744-6085 9 (paperback)
ISBN 978-1-4744-6086-6 (webready PDF)
ISBN 978-1-4744-6087-3 (epub)

The right of Kenneth Chan and Andrew Stuckey to be identified as the editors of this
work has been asserted in accordance with the Copyright, Designs and Patents Act
1988, and the Copyright and Related Rights Regulations 2003 (SI No. 2498).

Contents

List of Figures vii
Acknowledgements ix
Notes on the Contributors x
Note on Romanisation xiii

1 Introduction: The Fantastic as Sino-Enchantment in Contemporary Chinese Cinemas 1
   Kenneth Chan and Andrew Stuckey

PART I   VISUALITY/VIRTUALITY

2 Heroic Human Pixels: Mass Ornaments and Digital Multitudes in Zhang Yimou's Spectacles 27
   Jason McGrath

3 The Spectacle of Co-Production in *The Great Wall* 49
   Dan North

4 The Blockbuster Breakthrough: The Fantastic in *Hero* 71
   Li Yang

PART II   GENRES OF SINO-ENCHANTMENT

5 The Restrained Fantastic in Hou Hsiao-hsien's *The Assassin* 95
   Andrew Stuckey

6 An Auteurist Journey through the Fantastic Mode: A Case Study of Ho Meng-hua 112
   Shi-Yan Chao

7 Tracing the Science Fiction Genre in Hong Kong Cinema 128
   Tom Cunliffe

8   Chick Flick Fantasy and Postfeminism in Chinese Cinema:
    20 Once Again as a Transnational Remake   149
    Elaine Chung

9   The Sacred Spectacle: Subverting Scepticism in Tsui Hark's
    Detective Dee Films   166
    Ian Pettigrew

PART III ETHICS

10 Almost Wild, But Not Quite: The Indexical and the Fantastic
    Animal Other in China-Co-Produced (Eco)Cinema   185
    Yiman Wang

11 Domesticity, Sentimentality and Otherness: The Boundary of
    the Human in *Monster Hunt*   203
    Mei Yang

12 Transforming Tripitaka: Toward a (Buddhist) Planetary Ethics
    in Stephen Chow's Adaptation of *Journey to the West*   222
    Kenneth Chan

    Coda: Sino-Enchantment in a Time of Crisis   245
    Kenneth Chan and Andrew Stuckey

Selected Filmography   249
Bibliography   255
Index   277

Figures

Figure 2.1	Moon fights Snow. Source: *Hero* (2002).	31
Figure 2.2	Qin army ranks. Source: *Hero* (2002).	33
Figure 2.3	Terracotta warriors. Source: David J. Davies.	34
Figure 2.4	Beijing Olympic opening ceremony (2008). Source: US Olympic Committee officially licensed DVD release.	38
Figure 3.1	Sets built at Qingdao Oriental Movie Metropolis for *The Great Wall*. Source: *The Great Wall* VFX Breakdown, Base FX (2017).	50
Figure 3.2	Fan Bingbing as shapeshifting Daji in *League of Gods*, shot against greenscreen. Daji's deadly tails added in postproduction. Source: *League of Gods* (2016).	60
Figure 3.3	Traditional Chinese designs incorporated into the anatomy of the Taotie. Source: *The Great Wall* (2016).	63
Figure 3.4	A 'digital multitude' of Taotie attacks the Great Wall. Source: *The Great Wall* (2016).	64
Figure 4.1	Moon fights Snow. Source: *Hero* (2002).	84
Figure 4.2	Nameless. Source: *Hero* (2002).	85
Figure 4.3	Nameless and Snow amidst arrows. Source: *Hero* (2002).	87
Figure 4.4	Underwater shot of Sword. Source: *Hero* (2002).	88
Figure 5.1	Natural scenery. Source: *The Assassin* (2015).	107
Figure 6.1	Temptations of the flesh. Source: *Princess Iron Fan* (1966).	117
Figure 6.2	Luo Yin seducing Xu Luo. Source: *Black Magic* (1975).	125
Figure 7.1	Flying with grapple hook and rope. Source: *Butterfly Murders* (1979).	137
Figure 7.2	*Kung fu* fight involving technology and technological flaws. Source: *Health Warning* (1984).	143
Figure 7.3	Workers sleeping in cages. Source: *The Final Test* (1987).	145
Figure 8.1	A rejuvenated Malsoon banters with Park at the waterpark. Source: *Miss Granny* (2014).	156

Figure 8.2	Mengjun transformed into an attractive young woman. Source: *20 Once Again* (2015).	158
Figure 11.1	Illustration of *Dijiang*. Source: Hu Wenhuan, *Xin ke Shanhai jing* ([1593] 2013).	206
Figure 11.2	Song dances with Wuba. Source: *Monster Hunt* (2015).	210
Figure 12.1	Bereaved mother battles giant fish demon. Source: *Journey to the West: Conquering the Demons* (2013).	235
Figure 12.2	Luminous Buddha looms over Planet Earth. Source: *Journey to the West: Conquering the Demons* (2013).	238

Acknowledgements

We are very grateful to Margaret Hillenbrand (the series editor), Gillian Leslie (senior commissioning editor), Richard Strachan (assistant commissioning editor) and the copyeditor and staff at Edinburgh University Press for seeing us through the production of this book. We also wish to thank the anonymous peer reviewers for their helpful comments and suggestions. Most of all, we are grateful to our contributors for their unflagging intellectual labour. Chapter 2 is a revised version of Jason McGrath's essay, originally published in *Modern Chinese Literature and Culture* 25, 2, Fall 2013, 33–61. We thank MCLC for granting Edinburgh University Press permission to include the essay in its revised form within this volume.

Notes on the Contributors

Kenneth Chan is Professor of English at the University of Northern Colorado. His publications include *Yonfan's Bugis Street* (Hong Kong University Press, 2015) and *Remade in Hollywood: The Global Chinese Presence in Transnational Cinemas* (Hong Kong University Press, 2009), and his essays have appeared in numerous edited books and academic journals. His latest project focuses on the fantastic and the posthuman in contemporary cinema.

Shi-Yan Chao is Research Assistant Professor at the Academy of Film at Hong Kong Baptist University. He holds a PhD in Cinema Studies from New York University, and was an INTERACT postdoctoral fellow in the Weatherhead East Asian Institute at Columbia University. His latest publications include *Queer Representations in Chinese-Language Film and the Cultural Landscape* (Amsterdam University Press, 2020) and articles on transnational media, independent cinema, film history and vocal performance.

Elaine Chung is Lecturer in Chinese Studies at the School of Modern Languages, Cardiff University. She recently completed her PhD thesis on South Korean screen stardom in China at SOAS, University of London. Her research focuses on the transnational politics of East Asian popular cultures. Her essays on Chinese–Korean film and TV co-productions have appeared in various edited volumes, including *The Rise of K-Dramas* (McFarland, 2019) and *Asia-Pacific Film Co-Productions* (Routledge, 2019).

Tom Cunliffe recently completed his PhD at the Centre for Media and Film Studies at SOAS, University of London. His project focuses on the films directed by Lung Kong (1934–2014) as a means of rethinking the industrial conditions, stylistic traits, political concerns and reception of Hong Kong cinema made in the period 1966–77. His essays have appeared in journals including *Framework* and *Screen*, and he has taught film studies at SOAS, Goldsmiths, University of London and King's College London.

Jason McGrath is an Associate Professor in the Department of Asian and Middle Eastern Studies at the University of Minnesota – Twin Cities, where he also serves on the graduate faculty for Moving Image and Media Studies. He teaches modern and contemporary Chinese literature, film and media, and his research interests include theories of film realism, slow cinema, digital culture, ecocriticism and Taiwan studies. His book *Postsocialist Modernity: Chinese Cinema, Literature, and Criticism in the Market Age* was published by Stanford University Press in 2010, and his current project is a history of realism in mainland Chinese fiction film.

Dan North is an independent scholar based in China. For more than ten years, he taught film studies at the University of Exeter, UK, followed by teaching posts at Leiden University and Webster University in the Netherlands. Now teaching film history, theory and practice at Qingdao Amerasia International School, he is the author of *Performing Illusions: Cinema, Special Effects, and the Virtual Actor* (Wallflower Press, 2008) and co-editor, with Bob Rehak and Michael S. Duffy, of *Special Effects: New Histories, Theories, Contexts* (Palgrave/BFI, 2015).

Ian Pettigrew received his PhD in Film and Media Studies from the University of Miami. His book *The Cine of Ermanno Olmi* is published by McFarland in 2021. He has published articles on Chinese cinema, Italian cinema, and religion and cinema in *Asian Cinema, Journal of Religion and Film, Cinej: Cinema Journal, Journal of Popular Film and Television* and *Quarterly Review of Film and Television*.

Andrew Stuckey has taught at Kalamazoo College, the Ohio State University, the University of California at Irvine and the University of Colorado at Boulder. His publications include *Old Stories Retold: Narrative and Vanishing Pasts in Modern China* (Lexington Books, 2010) and *Metacinema in Contemporary Chinese Film* (Hong Kong University Press, 2018), as well as journal articles appearing in periodicals such as *Modern Chinese Literature and Culture, Journal of Chinese Cinemas* and *Asian Cinema*.

Yiman Wang is Professor of Film and Digital Media at the University of California, Santa Cruz. She is the author of *Remaking Chinese Cinema: Through the Prism of Shanghai, Hong Kong and Hollywood* (University of Hawaii Press, 2013). She has guest-edited a special issue for *Feminist Media Histories* on Asian feminist media and has published numerous articles in journals and edited volumes. She is currently completing a monograph on Anna May Wong, the best-known early twentieth-century Chinese–American screen-stage performer.

Li Yang holds a PhD in Comparative Literature from the University of Texas at Austin. Having previously worked as Assistant Professor of Chinese at Lafayette College, she is currently an independent scholar based in Austin, Texas. Her research interests include contemporary Chinese cinema, popular culture, globalisation theories, gender and sexuality, and digital humanities. She is the author of *The Formation of Chinese Art Cinema: 1990–2003* (Palgrave, 2018).

Mei Yang is Associate Professor of Chinese in the Department of Languages, Cultures and Literatures at the University of San Diego. Her areas of research include Chinese literature, cinema and culture. Her recent publications about Chinese independent films have appeared in *Modern Chinese Literature and Culture*, *China Media Research*, *China Review International* and *American Journal of Chinese Studies*. Currently, she is working on a book manuscript about the representation of subjectivity located in different types of spaces, as seen in contemporary Chinese-language cinemas.

Note on Romanisation

Romanisation of Chinese names, places and terms follows the standard Hanyu pinyin format, with the exception of place or personal names which already have a widely recognised non-pinyin romanisation: for example, Taipei, Tsui Hark or Ho Meng-hua. English names are used for text titles throughout the book, although, on their first appearance in any chapter, original titles and their English translation are given for all works of film, television, literature and other written texts. Complete information – including Asian characters and their romanisation – can also be found in our Selected Filmography or Bibliography for film and book titles that receive more than passing attention in the analyses presented in the following chapters.

Chapter 1

Introduction: The Fantastic as Sino-Enchantment in Contemporary Chinese Cinemas

Kenneth Chan and Andrew Stuckey

In recent years, the Chinese cinema industries have increasingly featured elements of the fantastic in their productions. It is not that films displaying fantastical images or narratives of fantasy were unprecedented in Chinese film history. It is, rather, that as the Chinese film market (in the People's Republic of China, PRC) has turned into the second-largest globally (a feat it achieved in 2012)[1] and is on its way to becoming the largest (as projected to occur in 2020),[2] a noticeably significant proportion of the total film production output is now devoted to movies that tap into the increasing popularity of fantasy genres or, in one way or another, exploit cinema's capacity and propensity to offer spectacular images of fantastic events, grotesque creatures, magical abilities, martial prowess and/or spiritual encounters. This volume of essays is a collective and concerted effort to grapple with a rapidly growing body of contemporary cinema featuring the fantastic. The chapters focus on case studies of individual auteurs, important films, innovative technologies and iterative themes, all of which arise out of the national/transnational Chinese cinematic industrial triangle of Hong Kong, Taiwan and the PRC.

More specifically, as editors of this volume, we rely on the theoretical concept of 'Sino-enchantment' as a critical tool, not only to corral these exciting essays of varied interpretive approaches and foci into a coherent collection, but also to envision a hermeneutical boundary that is flexible and porous enough for this wild thing one calls the fantastic in Chinese cinemas to run free, while also being solid enough to demarcate the critical and theoretical range the fantastic presents. In unpacking this particular theoretical turn of phrase, which we do in detail later in this introductory chapter, we argue that analysing the fantastic as Sino-enchantment unveils the cultural, political and ideological complexities, contradictions and complicities that the fantastic harbours, as it is located within the intersections of Chinese tradition and modernity. However, we also defend the potentialities that the fantastic, as genre and modality, can bring not only to Chinese cinemas aesthetically, but also to Chinese cultural politics in an ethically energising and transformative way. Therefore, Sino-enchantment, as a theoretical framework, is our means of productively capturing these cultural tensions that characterise the fantastic we see in contemporary Chinese cinemas.

This introductory chapter features four sections, providing historical context and critical theory. The first section situates this volume within the definitional and discursive parameters of fantasy as a genre and as a modality in filmmaking and film studies generally. Zeroing in on Chinese films, the second section provides a brief survey of the history of the fantastic in Chinese cinemas, as well as a preliminary examination of the roles the fantastic has played in Chinese society and culture. We argue that fantastic films, throughout cinematic history, have relied on what Tom Gunning has called a cinema of attractions to engage and solidify audiences. This process, as a consequence, has transformed and hybridised the genres that are specifically popular to Chinese film-viewing audiences. As entrée to the chapters within this volume, the third section theorises the fantastic in Chinese cinemas as Sino-enchantment. We contend that the fantastic, in spite of its ideological problems, continues to resonate with audiences because of its capacity to re-enchant modern life with ethical possibilities for wonder and amazement. We conclude this introduction with the fourth section, which pulls and tugs at the theoretical threads that run through the various chapters of this book.

The Fantastic as Genre and Mode in Cinema

Our use of the term 'the fantastic' naturally requires definition. But we do see this process of delimiting terminological boundaries as transcending the usual scholarly convention and obligation. In fact, ascertaining the critical semantics of the term helps position 'the fantastic in contemporary Chinese cinemas' within a Venn diagram (or as part of a series of overlapping concentric circles) that involves the fantasy film and its modalities in Hollywood and global cinema and the place the fantastic occupies within film studies in general. This definitional discourse, on one hand, points to the overdetermined nature of the cultural construct that is the fantastic, an overdetermination that includes the transnationality and the globality of film as a cross-cultural commodity – in other words, the fantastic in Chinese cinemas is not a hermetically sealed cultural phenomenon. On the other hand, it also suggests, in apparent contradistinction, the notion that the fantastic in Chinese cinemas brings its own set of cultural specificities that deserve identification and analysis. This oppositional tension, and the cultural anxieties that it evokes, ultimately leads us to our theoretical conception of Sino-enchantment as a critical device to provide, hopefully, some interpretive legibility.

To begin, we see 'the fantastic' as a broad umbrella term encompassing the fantasy film as a legitimate genre (with its subcategories and other related genre types) and fantasy elements as a genre mode permeating other non-fantasy genre categories. In her important essay on genre and melodrama, Christine Gledhill observes that the notion of film genre, as a cultural construction, is complex in its constitution and evolution. For instance, she argues that 'the life of a genre is cyclical, coming round again in corkskrew [sic] fashion, never quite in the same place'.[3] She uses the word 'modality'[4] to argue not only that genre changes through time and in different cultures, but also that the boundaries of genre are porous. In other words, genre conventions and expectations shift throughout film history. Genres interpenetrate one another to create hybrid genres. Genres, to varying degrees, appropriate the modes and elements of other genres in the shifting processes of evolution and hybridisation. This fluidity and malleability of cultural and aesthetic conventions, as they relate to the fantastic, understandably generate anxieties among genre purists and, at times, audiences at large (which is a testament to how well Hollywood and other global mainstream film industries have trained their consumers). We devote the remainder of this section to examining some of these anxieties as a means toward highlighting the significance of these definitional discourses to the fantastic Chinese film.[5]

By conceptualising the fantastic as inclusive of fantasy as genre and mode, we are cognisant of the strategic taxonomy this binarism relies upon. But we are also aware that this theoretical structuring has had the benefit of foundational debates from literary and film scholars over the last five decades. By no means is this chapter able to replay in detail all the nuances of these debates, but some critical plot-points deserve cursory mention because of their resonance for this volume. For instance, film scholars have argued that cinema, as a whole, is a fantastical medium. The beginning of French cinema was narrated as a battle between documentary realism (as championed by the Lumière brothers with their *actualités*) and fictional films of narrative fantasy (magically created by Georges Méliès). As this drama of film history plays out, Méliès clearly won the fight. But what this agonistic tale of narrative cinema's birth does not tell us is the notion that cinema, as a medium, is intrinsically fantastical in its propensity for spectacular images and stories, and fantastical in its very technological mechanism. Joshua Bellin makes this general point about cinema's roots in the fantastic by arguing that

> fantasy film, as a genre and an idea, is inseparable from the birth, development, and identity of the cinema. Not only were some of the earliest narrative films works of fantasy, but the history of film more generally is a history of the fantastic, the illusion, the unreal.[6]

What Bellin is suggesting, then, is that cinema, even realist and documentary films, relies on a fantastical sleight of hand to construct or reconstruct cinematic imagery to serve its narrative function. Making this point for us is Chapter 10 of our book, where author Yiman Wang foregrounds the deployment of the fantastic in Chinese ecocinema through examples from a wildlife documentary and the use of realistic footage of wild animals in a fictional feature film.

But to stop at this definitional premise of all cinema being fantastical, or being inherently fantastical in its structural processes, is to deny the fantastic its more incisive usefulness. Brian Attebery correctly concludes that 'a term broad enough to include both *Conan the Barbarian* and *Cosmicomics* threatens to become meaningless'.[7] James Donald extends this argument further by suggesting that an overly expansive 'category of fantasy becomes virtually useless as a means of distinguishing between different types of film',[8] a notion that would clearly unsettle audiences' expectations of genre conventions and mainstream studios' slavish attempts, through a vicious feedback loop, at catering to those conventions – one thinks of the overwrought superhero franchises like the Marvel and DC cinematic universes, or of the seemingly endless adaptations of the writings of J. R. R. Tolkien and J. K. Rowling. Like the term 'realism', it is the complex vastness of the fantastic that has led many literary and film scholars to struggle with its definitional problematics by offering taxonomic solutions. For instance, in his foundational structuralist text *The Fantastic: A Structural Approach to a Literary Genre*, Tzvetan Todorov splits what one would generally consider to be fantasy or the fantastic into three subgenres: the uncanny, the fantastic and the marvellous, with the fantastic floating between the other two categories and possessing the 'hesitation experienced by a person who knows only the laws of nature, confronting an apparently supernatural event'.[9] The limitations of Todorov's categories, as Rosemary Jackson accurately surmises, rest on the notion that his work 'fails to consider the social and political implications of literary forms',[10] hence diminishing its usefulness to a contemporary film studies project like ours (a point we will return to in greater detail later in this chapter).

What Todorov's structuralist formulation does reveal, however, is not just the shortcomings of dogmatising categorical boundaries in genre studies, but also the cultural, political, aesthetic and academic anxieties exposed in the attempts to pin down this slippery object that is the fantastic. Another illustrative example can be seen in Brian Attebery's similarly tripartite configuration of mode, genre and formula. While he sees 'the fantastic mode' as 'a vast subject, taking in all literary manifestations of the imagination's ability to soar above the merely possible', Attebery argues that, on the other end of the spectrum, lies 'fantasy-as-formula, which is essentially a commercial product', whose 'success depends on consistency and predictability', and whose commercialism 'tends toward triviality'. He then lands on the compromise of fantasy-as-genre to suggest that this 'in-between category' is 'something varied and capable of *artistic* development'.[11] This distinction between formula as commercial and genre as art serves to pre-empt the lack of cultural, critical, aesthetic and academic respect that the fantastic (in both literary and filmic forms) and studies of the fantastic often suffer. Steve Neale observes how adult audiences would deny their consumption of the fantastic by dismissing them as children's films,[12] while David Butler bemoans the fact that the genre does not command academic and intellectual attention for precisely that reason.[13] Built into the rationality of this marginalising of the fantastic is the genre's exemplification of cinema as a mode of 'escapism without any meaningful content or social function',[14] enabled by the presence of cinematic spectacles through special effects[15] (as if escapist spectacles and special effects automatically diminish or are inherently devoid of cultural and intellectual significance). Katherine Fowkes has so insightfully teased out the ideological assumptions of this dismissive logic, that escapist fantasy films invite 'audiences to abandon real-world problems and solutions for (usually) nostalgic and conservative illusions'[16] and the triviality of play and playfulness is antithetical 'to a world of rationality, work, and conformity'.[17] In fact, playfulness is, precisely, one of the elements of the genre/mode that presents the fantastic with its potential for cultural and political subversion, which our conception of Sino-enchantment incorporates.

Obviously, we strongly believe in the cultural, aesthetic and political significance of the fantastic; hence this particular volume of essays on fantastic Chinese films. However, we do not seek to idealise the fantastic and are not blind to the pitfalls that the fantastic presents, including formulaic and unimaginative recycling of themes, plotlines and genre conventions, which one witnesses in Hollywood summer blockbusters, remakes and movie series. At the same time, we do disavow the cultural and intellectual elitism that characterises perceptions of the fantastic, especially in its B-movie format, as a genre that is unworthy of scholarly enquiry. For the study of the fantastic, in its varied and heterogeneous formulations, encompassing a range of cinematic quality and taste, and catering to a wide swath of diverse audiences, can teach us about the identities that we embrace, the desires that drive us and the ideologies that define us as a culture, a society and a species. Or as Joshua Bellin so aptly puts it, the fantastic 'provoke[s] a perspective, provide[s] a context, produce[s] a way of seeing' the world.[18] This collection of essays, therefore, tackles a broad range of films, from the B-movie Hong Kong archive of Shaw director Ho Meng-hua (Shi-Yan Chao's Chapter 6), to the spectacular computer-generated imagery (CGI)-filled, mainstream Chinese co-productions of recent years (Jason McGrath's Chapter 2 and Dan North's Chapter 3), to the dipping of the fantastic into the intellectual Taiwanese art cinema of Hou Hsiao-hsien (Andrew Stuckey's Chapter 5).

This subject of the qualitative range of the fantasy film provides a convenient point for us to pivot to the quantitative range of the genre's typology, as we close this section of the introduction. The elasticity of the fantasy film troubles film critics and scholars into proliferating an entire taxonomy of subgenres and adjacent genres as part of fantasy cinema's remit. When one thinks of the Hollywood fantasy film, the adaptations of Tolkien's *The Hobbit* and *The Lord of the Rings* and Rowling's *Harry Potter* and *Fantastic Beasts* series come quickly and easily to mind. These films, in part, establish magic as the fantastical quality defining the diegetic worlds of the genre. But, obviously, the magical fantasy film is only one of many genre types that scholars have identified as occupying the larger umbrella category of the fantastic, a list that includes the following: monster films (*King Kong*, *The Fly*, *Clash of the Titans*, the *Godzilla* films, *Jurassic Park*),[19] science fiction, horror, wonder films (Raoul Walsh's *The Thief of Bagdad*, *The Lost World*, Fritz Lang's *Die Nibelungen*, *A Matter of Life and Death*),[20] epics and spectacles (*Ben-Hur*, *Spartacus*, *The Ten Commandments*, *Cleopatra*, *The Greatest Show on Earth*, *The Towering Inferno*, *Earthquake*, *Apocalypse Now*),[21] sword and sorcery (*Excalibur*, *Conan the Barbarian*, *The Dark Crystal*, *The Lord of the Rings*),[22] film blanc or the supernatural romantic comedy (*It's a Wonderful Life*, *A Matter of Life and Death*, *Bruce Almighty*),[23] the fairy-tale film (*Snow White and the Seven Dwarfs*, *Pinocchio*, *Splash*, *The Princess Bride*, *Shrek*)[24] and magic realism (*The Tin Drum*, *Orlando*).[25] The purpose of this short and cursory catalogue is, obviously, not meant to be exhaustive or prescriptive; its intent is to demonstrate the multiplicity of definitional nomenclature that has emerged out of critical work done on the fantastic, and to show how porous these subcategories are in their intersecting and overlapping characteristics.

Ultimately, the lessons we can draw here for the fantastic Chinese film are twofold. First, an understanding of the fantastic in American (and European) cinema reinforces the notion that Chinese films are not culturally insulated; the fantastic in Chinese cinemas is affected and inflected by the global cross-pollination of cinematic cultures, trends and influences. For instance, in the sword and sorcery category, David Butler describes *A Touch of Zen* (*Xianü*, King Hu, 1971) as 'an extreme example' with 'cultural and spiritual depth',[26] hinting at an international connectivity. Stephen Teo echoes this point by highlighting how 'the swashbucklers of Douglas Fairbanks, Sr . . . were popular with Chinese audiences' and that 'Chinese filmmakers [of the Shanghai era] attempted to cash in on the popularity by creating a Chinese equivalent of these same genres.'[27] It is crucial to observe that these cross-cultural connections are not one-way streets. Illustrating this point, in the late 1990s and the 2000s, is Hong Kong director Yuen Woo-ping, who was then in high demand as a martial arts choreographer, working on big-budget studio productions like *The Matrix* trilogy and Quentin Tarantino's *Kill Bill* films and, hence, having an impact on how Hollywood films stage action and martial arts sequences.[28]

In underscoring this trans-Pacific feedback loop between Hollywood and Chinese cinemas, we are not diminishing in any way the cultural specificities that Chinese cinemas bring to the fantastic, which is the second lesson we can take away from the genre typologies of the Hollywood fantasy film. It is inevitable that Hollywood's construction of fantasy films shapes the taste of audiences globally. But the fantastic Chinese film brings to the table culturally specific elements and, thus, redefining and reconfiguring Hollywood genre narratives and conventions for viewers of Chinese cinemas. Drawing on the animation techniques from Disney and DreamWorks in depicting monstrous creatures on screen, *Monster Hunt* (*Zhuoyao ji*, Raman Hui, 2015) generates imagistic energy from its Chinese classical literary sources, as Mei Yang notes in Chapter 11. Tom Cunliffe, in Chapter 7, traces the unique history of the rare Hong Kong science fiction film by acknowledging the mimicry of Hollywood trends while bringing the Hong Kong cultural and political context to bear on these films. And, as Elaine Chung analyses in Chapter 8, the film blanc assumes Chinese guise (via the remaking of a South Korean film, which remade Hollywood versions of the body-swap tale), all enabled by an East Asian cinematic regionalism. Aside from appropriating and hybridising Hollywood forms, fantastic Chinese films also offer culturally unique subgenres, such as the martial arts film, which (in addition to Stephen Teo's contention that it is a genre trend Hollywood has helped fan in the 1920s) has a long and distinguished history that originated from Chinese classic literature and opera.[29] Chapters 2, 3, 4, 5 and 9 in this volume all deal with the martial arts genre in some shape or form, while Kenneth Chan's Chapter 12 closes our book with a case study of the cinematic adaptation of the literary epic *Journey to the West* (*Xiyou ji*, c. sixteenth century), which has become a Chinese filmic institution of its own. Following in this vein, the next section of this introduction maps in greater detail the fantastic in Chinese cultural traditions and cinematic history.

The Fantastic in Chinese Culture and Cinemas

As a narrative mode, the fantastic has a long precedence, hailing from some of the earliest stories still extant in cultures around the world. Of course, at the time of their initial narrative occurrence, these stories may not necessarily have been perceived as fantastic (though certainly unusual and awe-inspiring), but rather as factual recounting of actual events and individuals. From the viewpoint of the broadest understanding of the fantastic as a narrative mode, Aesop's fables (talking animals), religious and social mythologies (Biblical stories, Greek mythology, the Hindu epics), literary epics (like *Beowulf* and *Gilgamesh*) and fairy tales can all be considered fantastic narratives. Chinese storytelling is no different in this regard. To name merely two examples, the earliest sections of *The Classic of Mountains and Seas* (*Shanhai jing*) have been dated to the fourth century BCE while surreal portions of the *Zhuangzi* also hail from the Warring States period (476–221 BCE). In its earliest form, *The Classic of Mountains and Seas* integrated shamanistic practices connecting the human world with various gods and spirits, as well as knowledge of medicinal, mineral and animal anomalies.[30] Early Chinese histories, likewise, often incorporate legends with fantastic elements. But it is really in the medieval period, with the advent of anomaly tales (in both the shorter, epigrammatic *zhiguai* and the more fully realised *chuanqi* versions), that fantastic storytelling comes into its own in Chinese literary history.[31] After this point, fantastic elements can be found across the spectrum of narrative forms, and it is also at this time that notions of fictionality began to develop into sophisticated systems.[32] Whether it be the resurrection of Du Liniang at the heart of *The Peony Pavilion* (*Mudan ting*), the pervasive ghost and fox spirit stories that take up such a large proportion of *Strange Stories from a Chinese Studio* (*Liaozhai zhi yi*), or the heavenly stone which finds human incarnation in *Dream of the Red Chamber* (*Hongloumeng*), the fantastic continued to play a significant role in Chinese literary narratives.

Confucius famously said that he kept his distance from ghosts and spirits (*jing guishen er yuan zhi*),[33] and so the most respectable literary forms – poetry and history – generally avoided discussions of supernatural personages or events.[34] Indeed, one of the defining features of anomaly tales is precisely the fact that they are not verifiable history.[35] Nevertheless, despite its original low ranking – in cultural regard – especially of *xiaoshuo* (literally, 'small talk' or 'hearsay', though by the modern period the term means 'fiction') – much of this literature over time has come to be among the most highly esteemed literary work from China.

In the early twentieth century, the literary revolution promoted by such figures as Liang Qichao, Hu Shih, Chen Duxiu and Lu Xun (among many others) reversed the longstanding literary hierarchies and promoted narrative fiction as the foremost of literary forms. In large part, this shift was understood as an anti-traditional step that would help propel China into the modern period, undoing its insular focus on its own literary and artistic traditions and instead reorienting outwards to the global literary community.[36] However, in its emphasis on realist modes and styles, the new literature and art of the twentieth century, perhaps ironically, echoed Confucius's leeriness towards spirits (and, by extension, the fantastic or other unverifiable phenomenon). Even so, in a certain parallel to earlier Chinese literary history, fantastic literature, especially of martial arts derring-do, persisted and even thrived in the newly created mass market of print publications. Literary reformers, however, continued to denigrate these works as lower art forms that were included in the catchall slur of Mandarin Ducks and Butterfly literature.[37]

This understanding of the general state of literary and artistic reception of fantastic modes and forms in China in the early twentieth century allows us to locate early Chinese film within the hierarchical spaces of artistic and cultural forms during this time. Certain scholars of early Chinese film have emphasised the element of 'shadowplay' (*yingxi*) as the ontological basis for early Chinese film.[38] Shadowplay is understood to emphasise display and performativity over representations of the profilmic world. And in its emphasis on play, early Chinese film, like early cinemas elsewhere in the world, engaged in what Tom Gunning has termed a cinema of attractions.[39] This mode of film highlights exhibition – including sight gags, novelties, slapstick and other performances relying on physicality, optical illusions and other cinematic trickery – while disregarding narrative immersion – continuity, psychological character development or other aspects of what came to constitute classical cinema. That is to say, the cinema of attractions is a mode of filmmaking that revels in amazing displays and seems to invite the audience (rather than immerse it in a continuous story) to acknowledge and admire the skill that has been presented in the film.[40]

It is worth emphasising that this early Chinese cinema developed as part of what Alexander Des Forges, adapting the term from Régis Debray, calls a mediasphere: a unified textual system constituted by a wide variety of (not necessarily aligned) discrete units – newspapers, dramatic performances both traditional and new, film, novels, radio programmes and tea house culture – that is characterised by overlapping mutual reference and influence.[41] The discontinuous but coinciding nature of this mediasphere, like serialised fiction, is reflected in the attraction of early cinema that emphasises separate spectacles united in one film. Likewise, Chinese cinemas developed as one portion of an entertainment culture, including amusement venues such as Shanghai's Great World that capitalised on distorted visions created by the ha-ha mirror and trick photography.[42] In such an environment, the cinema of attractions was merely one among many of such entertainments that gained audiences because of the amazing (and fantastic) images it displayed.

Chris Berry and Mary Farquhar argue that operatic film, the earliest genre of Chinese film, is especially inclined to a cinema of attractions.[43] Likewise, the craze for martial arts extravaganzas (which Berry and Farquhar include as an outgrowth of opera films), beginning in the late 1920s, was in no small part spurred and sustained by special effects that displayed martial arts masters flying across the sky and possessing other amazing powers.[44] Still, it was also at about this same time that classical narrative cinema was cementing its dominance. And in a certain alignment of interests, a cohort of younger filmmakers, influenced by the May Fourth Movement and the new literature that it spawned, entered the industry and began to promote the modern and wholesome attributes that they presumed to adhere in realist modes.[45] Nearly simultaneously, in 1931, in the lead-up to the implementation of the New Life Movement, the censorship bureau of the Nationalist Party's government (which, as a revolutionary party, even if right-wing, was also committed to the modernisation of China) banned *wuxia shenguai* (martial arts and spirits) movies as feudal and immoral.[46]

After martial arts, ghost movies are perhaps the most obvious examples of fantastic films in Chinese cinemas. Though technically not a ghost movie, and by the end the causes underlying the surreal images are revealed to be thoroughly mundane (if terrible), Maxu Weibang's *Song at Midnight* (*Yeban gesheng*, 1937) can be seen to inaugurate the prominence of striking imagery and surreal events in Chinese horror films.[47] This remake of the 1925 *The Phantom of the Opera* (Rupert Julian) accentuates the (horrifying) image of the scarred visage as both narrative device and marketing tool.[48] The vast treasure trove of Chinese ghost and demon stories, especially drawn from *Strange Stories from a Chinese Studio*, then went on to inspire the development of horrific images and narratives in Chinese film. Stephen Teo notes that Maxu himself was one of the most important directors who instigated this mode of filmmaking in the early postwar Hong Kong film industry.[49] Moreover, in its emphasis on folk religious beliefs, primarily of Daoist and Buddhist origins, there is a certain crossover between this genre of film and that of martial arts.[50]

All the same, even if realist modes, especially in Shanghai's left-wing cinema of the 1930s, and the narrative immersion of classical cinema were dominant, elements of a cinema of attractions persisted. To give just two brief examples, the short scene of the children's talent show in *The Goddess* (*Shennü*, Wu Yonggang, 1932) displays the same sorts of dancing or other skills of movement in which a cinema of attractions indulges.⁵¹ Perhaps even more to the point, *Street Angel* (*Malu tianshi*, Yuan Muzhi, 1937) takes special pleasure not only in displaying magic tricks and other optical illusions but also in revealing how those tricks work. Here the display of the fantastic is enjoyed even as it is revealed to be based in mundane causes.⁵²

The political exigencies of the Second Sino-Japanese War and then the Chinese Civil War that followed it, as well as a continued emphasis on realist narrative forms, left little room for fantastic films or other modes of the cinema of attractions during this period. Likewise, after the wars, in both the Communist Party-controlled mainland and in the Nationalist Party-controlled Taiwan, the continued emphasis on modernity (whether it be socialist or capitalist) and realist forms meant a sharp de-emphasis on fantastic imagery or storytelling in the films produced in these regions. Thus, in its commitment to establishing a socialist society, nearly all artistic work in the PRC went into reflecting on China's recent historical past or else its contemporary moment of transformation employing the mode of socialist realism. Of course, attractions persist in, for example, the exhilarating action sequences of military battles, but fantastic films, as such, were notably repressed. And in Taiwan, the government promotion of Healthy Realism (an outgrowth and extension of the earlier New Life Movement) similarly served to downplay fantastic modes in favour of modern, realist filmmaking. There are some exceptions, naturally, such as China's first animation feature film *Princess Iron Fan* (*Tieshan gongzhu*, Wan Laiming and Wan Guchan, 1941), which relates an episode from the classic Chinese novel *Journey to the West*.⁵³ This film was produced within Japanese-controlled Shanghai and thus was not strictly subject to anti-feudal concerns. More important than this, though, is the fact that animation as a technology that represents characters and events but which is in no way restricted either to perspectival realism, to biology (such as the fact that nonhuman animals do not speak) or to Newtonian physical laws is an especially conducive form through which to consider fantastic filmmaking. Likewise, in Taiwan, the continued salience of market factors, as well as a commitment to traditional Chinese culture that helped demarcate the Nationalist Party's claim to represent the Chinese nation in contrast to the Communist Party, mitigated the modernising and realist demands of Healthy Realism. Hence, on the one hand, the classic martial arts film, *A Touch of Zen*, which is adapted from a story in *Strange Stories from a Chinese Studio*, was produced in Taiwan. On the other hand, in the PRC, the continuation of operatic film in the form of model opera – especially inasmuch as that form revels in hyperboles of individual bravery and commitment – likewise marks the continuation of a cinema of attractions that can easily be thought of in terms of the fantastic.⁵⁴

If, for the most part, the film industries in Taiwan and the PRC eschewed fantastic modes and images, the Hong Kong industry continued making many films in this vein. Again, a focus on the operatic mode (and its outgrowths, the martial arts film and costume drama [*guzhuang pian*]) is quite useful here.⁵⁵ All three of these film genres were popular and financially rewarding for the studios which set up shop in Hong Kong during and after the Second Sino-Japanese War. If, in the 1940s and 1950s, the opera film, especially of the *huangmeidiao* style, was in vogue, this overlapped with costume dramas (often recounting Chinese history or famous fictional or dramatic works) and martial arts, which dominated this slice of the market by the 1960s and 1970s. A particularly interesting example, from our point of view, is *The Love Eterne* (*Liang Shanbo yu Zhu Yingtai*, Li Han-hsiang, 1963).⁵⁶ The film retells the famous folktale of lovers who, unable to be together in life, are transformed into butterflies. For most of the film, though sung and accompanied with traditional dramatic gestures that engage the attractions of what Weihong Bao calls 'technologies of the body',⁵⁷ the story is related in a thoroughly mundane manner. The final moments of the film, however, exploit a mechanically based special effect when Liang Shanbo's grave is ripped asunder, which then cuts to an animation of the two lovers transformed into butterflies fluttering together through the air. The era of martial arts films which soon afterwards dominated the cinema of Hong Kong, whether the historical–culturalist films of King Hu or the masculinist films of Chang Che,⁵⁸ elaborated on this trend for intricate costumes and premodern customs with fantastic spectacles of martial prowess and supernatural skills.

These trends continued and developed into Hong Kong cinema's New Wave. Tsui Hark is perhaps the most prominent New Wave director building on fantastic elements. Stephen Teo describes his innovations in this way:

> Thus beginning with *The Butterfly Murders* [*Diebian*, 1979], Tsui based his postmodern agenda on mutating *wuxia*'s fantasy tradition. This formula was applied to *Zu: Warriors of the Magic Mountain* [*Xin Shushan jianxia*, 1983], based on the old school fantasy of Huanzhu Louzhu's 'Shu Shan' series. Tsui inducted the genre into the age of *Star Wars* by using that movie's special effects experts to bring the conceptual fantasy world of *Zu* into life on the big screen. The film's incorporation of 1980s state-of-the-art special effects technology and its association with science-fiction meant that fantasy was integrated into the genre without inducing the kind of debates about its harmful or superstitious aspects that affected its development in Shanghai during the late 1920s.⁵⁹

Teo seems to indicate, here, that, to a certain extent (at least in terms of the martial arts genre), the fantastic filmmaking in Chinese cinemas has come full circle. Indeed, there is much truth to this notion, especially with regard to the reliance on attractions achieved by means of special effects to engage and address the audience. For, as Dan North, Bob Rehak and Michael Duffy rather artfully theorise about special effects, 'Encoded in any film is a metanarrative about its own production, but this is rendered more starkly when the material traces of that production are written into the image in the form of ostentatious technique and marketable spectacle.'[60]

As these technologies for filmic special effects advance and as they continue to play a major role in box-office receipts, it is inevitable that Tsui Hark's first forays into fantasy martial arts would translate effectively into Chinese transnational co-productions, with titles like Ang Lee's *Crouching Tiger, Hidden Dragon* (*Wohu canglong*, 2000), Zhang Yimou's *Hero* (*Yingxiong*, 2002), Chen Kaige's *The Promise* (*Wuji*, 2005), John Woo's *Red Cliff* (*Chibi*, 2008), Peter Chan's *Dragon* (*Wuxia*, 2011) and Wong Kar-wai's *The Grandmaster* (*Yidai zongshi*, 2013), extending the attractions-based – and special effects-fuelled – appeal of martial arts film in the creation of fantastic images and stories.

Simultaneous with the Hong Kong New Wave's reinvigoration of martial arts filmmaking is a similar revival of horror (or at least ghost and monster) movies. As Ackbar Abbas notes, Hong Kong cinema always works within and between genres.[61] The Hong Kong horror film has typically centred on ghosts, revivified corpses (though distinct from zombies in the Hollywood style) and demons drawn from Buddhist or Daoist representations of the underworld.[62] To pick up where we left off earlier, Maxu Weibang's relocation enabled him to continue making horror films in the Hong Kong industry, and a few others followed his example, often adapting tales from *Strange Stories from a Chinese Studio*. As with martial arts cinema, the efforts of the New Wave filmmakers also revivified the horror genre, with *A Chinese Ghost Story* (*Qiannü youhun*, Ching Siu-tung, 1987), though not the first in this trend, setting the standard for later examples. Stephen Teo notes that Tsui Hark, as producer of the *Chinese Ghost Story* series and director of a few other horror films himself, also made his influence felt in this genre, as he did with the martial arts film. Indeed, through an emphasis on state-of-the-art special effects and the incorporation of martial arts-style action sequences, Tsui – and other directors who followed his example – ensured that the horror and martial arts genres remained firmly bound together.[63]

As we proceed into the post-1997 era, and as the production and especially the financing of movies have migrated to the PRC, these thematic elements – folk religious beliefs, loosely tied to Buddhist and/or Daoist practices, underlying fantastic ghost or demon films – are transposed into the contemporary moment. Just as with the example of martial arts films, it is easy to see the influence that these Hong Kong horror films from the 1980s and 1990s have on contemporary Chinese co-productions, such as *Monster Hunt*, *The Great Wall*

(*Changcheng*, Zhang Yimou, 2016) and *League of Gods* (*Fengshenbang*, Koan Hui, 2016), all of which incorporate elements of martial arts-style action with monsters or spirits drawn from folk beliefs and literary sources.

A few key points can be drawn from this historical overview of fantastic Chinese cinemas. First, the two main genres of fantastic filmmaking, horror and martial arts, while distinct, simultaneously also exhibit a self-reinforcing mutual influence that serves to draw them together, as well as bringing other related genres (costume/period films, opera films and literary adaptations of premodern texts) into their orbit. Second, the spectacles that constitute a cinema of attractions have relied (and continue to rely) on technical aspects of filmmaking that enable audiences to perceive impossible events, actions and creatures. If, in earlier moments, these effects were created through optical and editing techniques, in the contemporary moment they are increasingly composed from computer-generated effects and images. This, in turn, begs the question of what constitutes the nature of animation, especially its ontological relationship both to film and specifically to fantastic filmmaking. It also complicates the notion of indexicality, the relationship between the cinematic image and its correlative profilmic subject, in this era of digital filmmaking and what D. N. Rodowick describes as the virtual life of film.[64] Third, and finally, it would be remiss on our part to ignore the jarring absence (in our historical mapping above) of certain genres that are usually associated with fantastic Hollywood film production, such as science fiction, a genre which is now making its mark in the rapidly expanding Chinese co-production industries, as a result of the accessibility and affordability of digital animation technologies. Recent Chinese science fiction titles include *Bleeding Steel* (*Jiqi zhi xue*, Leo Zhang, 2017), *Shanghai Fortress* (*Shanghai baolei*, Teng Huatao, 2019) and *The Wandering Earth* (*Liulang diqiu*, Frant Gwo, 2019), the last of which is adapted from the work of Liu Cixin, who is best known for his Hugo Award-winning science fiction novel *The Three-Body Problem* (*Santi*, 2008).[65]

Sino-Enchantment

The brief overview sketched out above is by no means comprehensive. Instead, our goal is to map out fantastic filmmaking's constitutive presence in Chinese cinema history, as well as to outline a few of the more prominent branches it has developed over time. We have also confined our account to mainstream cinemas and have focused primarily on martial arts and horror films. Of course, and as several of the chapters in this volume demonstrate, fantastic filmmaking has not been, nor is it currently, restricted to mainstream films. The boundaries separating mainstream popular cinema and art/experimental film are much more porous than most anticipate, allowing for a dialectical dynamic to occur between the two. The fantastic as a cultural cinematic practice often crosses these boundaries, making it one of the central genre modalities in Chinese film.

Although it seems obligatory to cite Tzvetan Todorov in any discussion of the fantastic (film or literature, East or West), we are not the only ones who have found his structural analysis wanting, as we have noted earlier. One could further argue that Todorov's structuralism leads to a 'totalizing' approach,[66] or that his fundamentally European and modern outlook translates poorly to the (premodern) Chinese context.[67] While these are certainly valid criticisms, more important is the fact that his intriguing definition of the fantastic as 'that hesitation experienced by a person who knows only the laws of nature, confronting an apparently supernatural event'[68] is of limited value in actually analysing cultural texts. That is to say, if, as the subtitle to Todorov's book seems to indicate, the fantastic constitutes its own distinctive genre, there are almost no texts which either strive for or actually achieve maintaining the fundamental ambiguity between the 'laws of nature' and 'an apparently supernatural event' from beginning to end. Instead, and we can think of almost no examples to the contrary,[69] such texts inevitably either resolve into a straightforward account of a supernatural event or reveal the natural causes that led to the misapprehension of a mundane occurrence as supernatural. That is, in Todorov's own terms, these texts become in the end either uncanny, 'the supernatural explained', or marvellous, 'the supernatural accepted'.[70] At best, then, Todorov's notion of the fantastic describes a mood which may characterise certain moments or portions of a narrative but cannot delineate a defining characteristic of a unique genre.

In our opinion, Bliss Cua Lim offers a more fruitful direction for a consideration of the fantastic film. Lim examines the fantastic in the context of the modern(ist) disenchantment of the world.[71] She argues that the fantastic persists as vulgar – popular, devalued, disreputable – or primitive in the midst of an Enlightenment-derived, disenchanted and scientific modern outlook that scorns the fantastic as backward, superstitious, unsophisticated and gullible.[72] That is, the fantastic serves the modernising discourse of rationality as a negative example of what must be transcended, superseded and left behind in the course of a universal process of modernisation. Modernity is supposed to have displaced and replaced the fantastical enchantment of religion and mystical beliefs, for instance.[73] But for Lim, 'what is most provocative about the fantastic is its capacity to insinuate the *failure* of modern disenchantment to completely supplant nonmodern worlds'.[74] In other words, the fact that the fantastic persists indicates the incompleteness of modernity as a global project.

Lim's study examines this incompleteness from the perspective of temporality: the fantastic bears a temporality which is incompatible with modern temporality based in homogenous, empty time.⁷⁵ She argues that the fantastic marks 'immiscible temporalities' because of their incompatibility with modern, disenchanted life.⁷⁶ This is a valuable insight, especially with regard to the horror films on which Lim focuses in her study. However, we do not think we need to be limited to temporal considerations of the fantastic. In addition to temporal recursions, the fantastic is also capable of striking more general blows against the ongoing process of disenchantment and in support of a certain re-enchantment of society and culture.

Indeed, rather than the failure, per se, of a fully implemented modernism, the recent collection *The Re-Enchantment of the World*, edited by Joshua Landy and Michael Saler, has intriguingly argued that re-enchantment is an integral part of modernity's disenchantment of the world.⁷⁷ If the rationality of the bureaucratic administration of society in concert with the scientific exploration and explanation of natural cycles, events and processes has led to the loss of traditional opportunities for wonder and mystification in human experience, these scholars argue that this disenchantment simultaneously opens up other, newer modes of wonder. Landy and Saler identify three modes in which re-enchantment may operate. First is the binary: 'the notion that any lingering enchantment within Western culture must of necessity be a relic, a throwback, a corner of unenlightened atavism yet to be swept clean [by modern society]'. Second is the dialectical: 'the notion that modernity is itself enchanted, unbeknown to its subjects, in a deceptive and dangerous way'. Third is the antinomial: 'the fact that modernity embraces seeming contraries, such as rationality and wonder, secularism and faith . . . which simultaneously enchants and disenchants, which delights but does not delude'.⁷⁸

Lim's approach, though valorising to be sure, seems to work within this first mode, the binary. She sees fantastic narratives as ways of resisting the homogenising forces of enlightenment and colonialism. The second mode, the dialectical – as in the Frankfurt School, perhaps especially Adorno, or as in Guy Debord – emphasises the arbitrary and ultimately human-centred and human-controlled nature of so-called 'scientific' truths. Landy and Saler urge us to reject both the binary and the dialectical versions of enchantment within modern life, and their volume naturally focuses on the possibilities for clear-eyed and hard-nosed awe in response to modern life, that embraces both the materialism of the world in which we live, as well as the possibilities for curiosity, exploration and discovery enabled by modernity.

While we agree that the antinomial approach to re-enchantment has the best potential to be intellectually stimulating, we cannot accept Landy and Saler's dismissal of the other two. The nearly exclusive focus their collection puts on Western (especially French and German) notions of re-enchantment probably blinds them to the political – localising and potentially liberating – uses that can be made of re-enchantment, which Lim brings out in her work. Moreover, in light of the huge resurgence of religious practices across China and of a large variety of denominations since Opening and Reform, practices which have persisted in Hong Kong and Taiwan even in the face of the development of capitalist modernity, we hesitate simply to dismiss religious faith (even if we may not share that faith) as these editors do:

> When we speak here of re-enchantment, we do not have in mind the periodic resurgence of traditional ideas and practices (for example, the survival in some quarters of exorcism rites), or again the sporadic generation of new creeds, such as spiritualism, that have sought to replace the old. As Camus would say, to embrace such a creed is not to solve the problem of disenchantment but rather to change its terms on the sly.[79]

The tone here (and elsewhere in the book) smacks of the worst sort of smug intellectual elitism. Beyond that, it is also blind to the resistant politics that religious faith may enable that works against modern disenchantment in similar ways to that which Lim describes. The Chinese state's fear of the Falun Gong sect, and even more appalling the recent wholesale repression of Uighur Muslim faith that has been called cultural genocide, are evidence for the truth of this statement. Even if, in practice, such a politics seldom emerges or is, in fact, diverted by the modern enchantment of capitalist society that the dialectical mode critiques, the potential for such a politics stemming from religious faith remains, and we think it important to acknowledge that potential.

In our attempt to draw into an, at times, conflictual, contradictory and/or contestatory approach to understanding the fantastic Chinese film in the context of the multiplicity and heterogeneity of Chinese modernities[80] – forms of modernity that permit traditional Chinese cultures, ideologies and religions to co-exist with technologised, hybrid and diversely politicised modernities – we bring together the binary, the dialectical and the antinomial into what we term 'Sino-enchantment' to engage the fantastic that we see in contemporary Chinese cinemas. Our use of the 'Sino' prefix is not intended to be reductive in its cultural attribution – that is, referring solely to the PRC and its drive to dominate what it means to be Chinese; it is also meant to echo Shu-mei Shih's theorisation of the Sinophone, which taps into 'a network of places of cultural production outside China and on the margins of China and Chineseness, where a historical process of heterogenizing and localizing of continental Chinese culture has been taking place for several centuries'.[81] The Sinophone of Sino-enchantment 'frustrates easy suturing . . . while foregrounding the value of difficulty, difference, and heterogeneity'.[82] The cultural hybridity and heterogeneity of Hong Kong in the years just preceding its retrocession to China seem also to have come to characterise China as a whole, hence impacting the film culture of Chinese co-productions. 'Socialism with Chinese characteristics', the market economy sustained within an authoritarian regime and the condition of postsocialism are all quick shorthand versions with which we might indicate the contradictions inherent in such hybridity and diversity.[83] Moreover, though differences exist between Hong Kong, the PRC, Taiwan, Singapore and other Sinophone communities, to be sure, the aspect of being caught in between surely also applies to each in its own way. Fantastic films, in their invocation of traditional practices, beliefs and possibilities for transcendence by means of advanced special effects, mark a certain recognition of how Sino-enchantment brings tradition and modernity into confluence with each other.

Finally, we aspire to heighten the theoretical play that Sino-enchantment brings to our understanding of the fantastic by envisioning the ethical potentialities and possibilities the concept can generate. In her illuminating consideration of enchantment in modern society, Jane Bennett contends that 'the mood of enchantment may be valuable for ethical life', because it can 'be deployed to propel ethical generosity'.[84] The fantastic as enchantment can induce in us 'a condition of exhilaration or acute sensory activity',[85] whose material affect may evoke joyful playfulness that 'spills over into critical consciousness and tempers it, thus rendering its judgments more generous and its claims less dogmatic'.[86] The implications here for our engagement with the fantastic Chinese film is profound, in that Sino-enchantment teaches us not only to care for the aesthetic development of Chinese cinema as a whole, but also to reach ethical positions that value human connectivity and concern, that care for life in all its forms, and that mobilise a global politics of protection and preservation of this planet we call home.

The Chapters: Sino-Enchantment Deployed

The chapters in this book are distributed into three segments. The opening part, entitled 'Visuality/Virtuality', foregrounds the significant growth and popularity of the fantastic Chinese film as a consequence of digital cinema's dominance in the new millennium. All three chapters direct their attention to the work of Fifth Generation auteur Zhang Yimou and his place in the digital era. Originally published in *Modern Chinese Literature and Culture* and specially revised for this book, Jason McGrath's important essay (Chapter 2) on director Zhang's spectacles demonstrates how enchantment with his CGI-driven creations can lead to ideologically problematic readings. Taking a different approach is Dan North's examination, in Chapter 3, of the technological–industrial complex that supports a major production such as *The Great Wall* (2016). Rounding off the section is Chapter 4, where Li Yang revisits Zhang's critically well-worn *wuxia* classic, *Hero* (2002), to study how the fantastic infuses the genre with a sufficient degree of spectacle for it to attain blockbuster status.

The biggest portion of the book focuses on 'Genres of Sino-Enchantment', where various contributors handle a diverse array of fantastic cinema. The part opener features an illuminating analysis of how fantastical elements can redefine the visual experience of art/experimental film – Andrew Stuckey illustrates this in his examination of the critically acclaimed *wuxia* entry *The Assassin* (*Cike Nie Yinniang*, Hou Hsiao-hsien, 2015) in Chapter 5. Chapter 6 brings readers back in time to the Shaw Brothers archive, where Shi-Yan Chao tracks director Ho Meng-hua's work in different fantastical subgenres. This brief historical turn demonstrates the impact that Ho's dabbling in the fantastic had on contemporary Chinese films, in particular in his series of four films adapting *Journey to the West*. Tom Cunliffe's Chapter 7 fills a significant historical lacuna (as illustrated in this introductory chapter) by cataloguing the rare instances of Hong Kong science fiction films, hence showing how these films lay the groundwork for the current rise of the Chinese science fiction blockbuster today. Chapter 8 analyses *20 Once Again* (*Chongfan ershisui*, Leste Chen, 2015), a body-swap tale that could potentially be categorised as a film blanc title. Elaine Chung approaches this 'chick flick fantasy' through a postfeminist lens. The section ends with Ian Pettigrew's Chapter 10, which takes on the 'sacred spectacle' in the recent Detective Dee films by director Tsui Hark, hence examining the place religion, superstition and mysticism occupy in the newly reconfigured *wuxia shenguai pian*.

The final three chapters constitute the last part of the book, entitled 'Ethics'. In Chapter 10, Yiman Wang criss-crosses the documentary–fantasy boundary to extract an analysis of the fantastic in two ecocinematic titles, thereby illustrating the expansive terrain that Sino-enchantment traverses, beyond the genres that one usually associates with the fantastic. Mei Yang shows, in Chapter 11, the classical origins of the popular mainstream film *Monster Hunt* and connects the traditional Chinese notions of family and domesticity to contemporary conceptions of modern Chinese life and its ethics. Closing the section is Kenneth Chan's Chapter 12, which not only places Stephen Chow's adaptation of *Journey to the West* in the context of the long history of filmic adaptations of the religious classic, but also rethinks the film's notions of enchantment and disenchantment as two sides of the same discursive coin in an expanded Buddhist ethics of planetary connections. Finally, we offer a brief coda to close out the book and point to the rich potentialities that

Sino-enchantment and the fantastic can offer in this difficult era of political, economic and health crises across the globe.

Notes

1. 'China becomes world's second-biggest movie market' (last accessed 28 November 2019). For a scholarly study tracking China's rise and domination of the film market in the twenty-first century, see Michael Curtin, *Playing to the World's Biggest Audience*.
2. Paul Bond, 'China film market to eclipse U. S. next year' (last accessed 28 November 2019).
3. Christine Gledhill, 'Rethinking genre', 227.
4. Ibid., 223.
5. For the sake of brevity and convenience, and from this point on in the main text, we refer to 'the fantastic in contemporary Chinese cinemas' as 'fantastic Chinese films', unless noted otherwise.
6. Joshua David Bellin, *Framing Monsters*, 196.
7. Brian Attebery, *Strategies of Fantasy*, 1.
8. James Donald, 'Introduction', 10.
9. Tzvetan Todorov, *The Fantastic*, 25.
10. Rosemary Jackson, *Fantasy*, 6.
11. Attebery, *Strategies of Fantasy*, 2. Emphasis added.
12. Cited in Alec Worley, *Empires of the Imagination*, 10; originally from Steve Neale, *Genre and Hollywood*, 36. It is fascinating and ironic that in Neale's wide-ranging study of genre, the fantasy film and the fantastic are not granted their own chapter or section, but are embedded in his study of epics and spectacles, horror and science fiction, and teen pics.
13. David Butler, *Fantasy Cinema*, 2.
14. Ibid., 3.
15. Ibid., 4–5.
16. Katherine A. Fowkes, *The Fantasy Film*, 6.
17. Ibid., 7.
18. Bellin, *Framing Monsters*, 9.
19. Ibid.
20. Butler, *Fantasy Cinema*, 34–6.
21. Neale, *Genre and Hollywood*, 85–92.
22. Butler, *Fantasy Cinema*, 70–6. According to Butler, the term 'sword and sorcery' originated from author Fritz Leiber (Butler, *Fantasy Cinema*, 70–1).
23. Ibid., 45–8.
24. Ibid., 48–58.
25. Worley, *Empires of the Imagination*, 84.
26. Butler, *Fantasy Cinema*, 70.
27. Stephen Teo, *Chinese Martial Arts Cinema*, 24.
28. For more details on Yuen's role, see Leon Hunt, *Kung Fu Cult Masters*, 181.

29. This is also a history that Teo traces in his book. Teo, *Chinese Martial Arts Cinema*.
30. Richard E. Strassberg, *A Chinese Bestiary*, 3–13.
31. Robert Ford Campany, *Strange Writing*; Sarah M. Allen, *Shifting Stories*.
32. For accounts of a similar – but markedly later – process in Europe, see Nicholas Paige, 'Permanent re-enchantments', 159–80.
33. *Lunyu* 6.22. CHANT (Chinese Ancient Text Database), (last accessed 28 November 2017). An English translation is available in Confucius, *The Analects*, 84.
34. There are exceptions, of course. As Strassberg notes, the poetry collection *Songs of Chu* (*Chuci*, c. Warring States Period) also incorporates shamanistic traditions of human interaction with supernatural forces (*A Chinese Bestiary*, 11–12). Another famous example is Cao Zhi's poem 'Luo shen fu' ('Rhapsody on the Goddess of the Luo River', c. third century CE).
35. Campany, *Strange Writing*; Allen, *Shifting Stories*. In later periods, historiographical issues are sometimes deliberately raised within fantastic stories, creating a sophisticated exploration of the relationship between fact and fiction; see Judith T. Zeitlin, *Historian of the Strange*.
36. Accounts of this change are legion. One of the best is Theodore Huters, *Bringing the World Home*.
37. E. Perry Link, Jr, *Mandarin Ducks and Butterflies*; Rey Chow, *Woman and Chinese Modernity*, 34–83.
38. Zhang Zhen, *An Amorous History of the Silver Screen*; Chen Xihe, 'Shadowplay'. This article was originally published in 1986, roughly contemporaneously with Gunning (see the next note). For a critical view of shadowplay as an overhasty generalisation of the differences between East and West that ignores early Chinese film theorists' own recognition of the importance of the image as well as of play, see Victor Fan, *Cinema Approaching Reality*, 23–30.
39. Tom Gunning, 'The cinema of attraction[s]'. This article was originally published in 1986. Zhang, *An Amorous History of the Silver Screen*, 12–16, is explicit in drawing the connection between shadowplay and Gunning.
40. Gunning, 'The cinema of attraction[s]'.
41. Alexander Des Forges, *Mediasphere Shanghai*.
42. See Christopher Rea, *The Age of Irreverence*, especially 63–73.
43. Chris Berry and Mary Farquhar, *China on Screen*, 47–74.
44. Zhang, *An Amorous History of the Silver Screen*, 199–243; Weihong Bao, *Fiery Cinema*, 39–90.
45. Zhang, *An Amorous History of the Silver Screen*, 246–54; Yingjin Zhang, *Chinese National Cinema*, 63–71.
46. Berry and Farquhar, *China on Screen*, 58; Zhang, *An Amorous History of the Silver Screen*, 235–43. See also Yingjin Zhang's more general account in *Chinese National Cinema*, 62–3.
47. For detailed discussions of *Song at Midnight*, see Zhang, *An Amorous History of the Silver Screen*, 319–44, and Yiman Wang, *Remaking Chinese Cinema*, 119–28. Zhang notes that the films Maxu made prior to *Song at Midnight* emphasise strangeness

and other sorts of uncanny personages and events, while Wang goes on to discuss a 1995 Hong Kong-produced remake of *Song at Midnight*.
48. Zhang, *An Amorous History of the Silver Screen*, 300.
49. Stephen Teo, *Hong Kong Cinema*, 221–2.
50. Both Zhang, *An Amorous History of the Silver Screen*, 332, and Teo, *Hong Kong Cinema*, 219–29 note the mutual influence exerted and felt between martial arts and ghost films. For the intersections between the *wuxia pian* and horror film conventions in recent Hong Kong–China co-productions, see Kenneth Chan, 'Tsui Hark's *Detective Dee* films'. Chan's essay is a part of a collection examining the Hong Kong horror film trend: Gary Bettinson and Daniel Martin, *Hong Kong Horror Cinema*.
51. Explaining the ideas of Gu Kenfu, Weihong Bao calls these skills 'technologies of the body'; see her *Fiery Cinema*, 54. See also Laurent Guido, 'Rhythmic bodies/movies', 139–56.
52. Many of the essays collected in Joshua Landy and Michael Saler (eds), *The Re-Enchantment of the World*, also note the typical manœuvre of self-reflexivity and a propensity to debunk the supernatural by marking the mundane basis for seemingly fantastic events.
53. For discussions of *Princess Iron Fan* and the Wan brothers, see Bao, *Fiery Cinema*, 359–74; Daisy Yan Du, 'Suspended animation'.
54. Berry and Farquhar, *China on Screen*, 58–66.
55. Ibid., 66–74.
56. An excellent close reading of the film's display of gender fluidity can be found in Tan See-Kam and Annette Aw, 'The Love Eterne'.
57. Bao, *Fiery Cinema*, 54.
58. These characterisations follow Teo, *Chinese Martial Arts Cinema*, 84–139.
59. Ibid., 157–8.
60. Dan North, Bob Rehak and Michael S. Duffy, 'Introduction', 5.
61. Ackbar Abbas, *Hong Kong*, 27–8.
62. The characterisations and overview that follow are generally summarised from Teo, *Hong Kong Cinema*, 219–29. Tying the horror film to the mysteries of traditional Chinese medicine are Hong Kong directors Peter Chan's and Fruit Chan's short film entries in the genre. Emilie Yueh-yu Yeh and Neda Hei-tung Ng, 'Magic, medicine, cannibalism'.
63. Teo, *Hong Kong Cinema*, especially 226–9.
64. D. N. Rodowick, *The Virtual Life of Film*.
65. The role of science fiction is really quite fascinating in this regard. Chinese-language science fiction literature (both translated and original) has enjoyed a high tide of popularity in the new century (with roots going back even further). And science fiction films, such as *Avatar* (James Cameron, 2009) and the *Transformers* series (Michael Bay, 2007, 2009, 2011, 2014, 2017), have been exceptionally strong performers with Chinese audiences. But to date, there have been few successful science fiction films produced in China. Science fiction, like the other mainstream industrial genres we have discussed, martial arts and horror, also relies on fantastic images

and narratives. Given the dearth of domestically produced science fiction films, we have not addressed its impact in this chapter. But it is surely relevant and important to track the ways in which fantastic science fiction films intersect with the trends described here.
66. Campany, *Strange Writing*, 22–3.
67. Zeitlin, *Historian of the Strange*, 7.
68. Todorov, *The Fantastic*, 25.
69. The one example that Todorov himself relies on is *Le Diable amoureux* (1772) by Jacques Cazotte. Nicholas Paige endorses this view and extends it to other examples as well, though we admit we remain sceptical. See Paige, 'Permanent re-enchantments'.
70. Todorov, *The Fantastic*, 41–2.
71. The term 'disenchantment' is usually attributed to Max Weber, as coined in the early twentieth century, but as Andrea Nightengale, Linda Simon and Michael Saler show in their respective contributions to the collection Landy and Saler (eds), *The Re-Enchantment of the World*, 15–71, the basis for this understanding of modern life goes back much further in history and has also elicited a wide variety of responses in philosophy, literature and practice.
72. Bliss Cua Lim, *Translating Time*, 21–5.
73. Landy and Saler, 'Introduction', 1–2.
74. Lim, *Translating Time*, 110. Original emphasis.
75. Lim bases her argument mostly on Bergson's philosophy, but the phrase 'homogenous, empty time' comes from Walter Benjamin.
76. Lim, *Translating Time*.
77. Landy and Saler (eds), *The Re-Enchantment of the World*.
78. Landy and Saler, 'Introduction', 3.
79. Ibid., 2.
80. Jenny Kwok Wah Lau (ed.), *Multiple Modernities*.
81. Shu-mei Shih, *Visuality and Identity*, 4.
82. Ibid., 5.
83. A good introduction to the discourse of postsocialism in the Chinese context is Jason McGrath, *Postsocialist Modernity*.
84. Jane Bennett, *The Enchantment of Modern Life*, 3.
85. Ibid., 5.
86. Ibid., 10.

PART I
VISUALITY/VIRTUALITY

Chapter 2

Heroic Human Pixels: Mass Ornaments and Digital Multitudes in Zhang Yimou's Spectacles

Jason McGrath

During NBC's live US television broadcast of the opening ceremonies of the 2008 Beijing Olympics, Bob Costas remarked that the thousands of drummers who kicked off the ceremony performed with 'almost *fierce* precision' (his emphasis). A little later in the broadcast, commentator Matt Lauer observed:

> Bob, a nation of 1.3 billion putting on a show like this, and people at home are not alone if they're saying it's both awe-inspiring and perhaps a little intimidating, but they told these drummers earlier in a rehearsal to smile more, and that's taken some of the edge off of it . . . *some* [dry laughter].

What exactly was 'fierce' or 'intimidating' about the performances hardly needed to be spelled out, nor was the metonymic relation of the performers to their 1.3 billion Chinese compatriots questioned. While NBC's narration of the spectacle – staged by renowned film director Zhang Yimou – mostly hewed to the themes of harmony and openness ('one world, one dream') that were the official script of the ceremonies, moments like these clearly activated a dark yet familiar alternative image of the Chinese as an undifferentiated, highly disciplined mass, a threatening 'yellow horde' that comes from an imagination fuelled by longstanding Western racism as well as Cold War fantasies of communism. As a television critic for the *Orlando Sentinel* bluntly put it, the opening ceremony 'reduced performers to cogs in a machine' and aimed 'to celebrate Chinese militarism' to the extent that 'a dance to Mao and Cultural Revolution . . . would have been in keeping with the military themes'.[1]

The threat invoked is that of the loss of freedom through the total subsumption of the individual by the collective, a sense that is rhetorically emphasised by describing the performers' precision not just as *fierce* or *intimidating* but as downright *military*. None the less, the NBC commentators themselves mostly attempted to present such issues in a polite, politically correct, culturally relativist frame. For example, as a vaguely traditionally costumed performer danced upon a surface held aloft by a multitude of people below her, the commentators remarked on 'the symbolism of this one dancer being supported by these many beneath her', explaining that

> it's a fundamental issue in the nature of Chinese culture about the relationship between the one and the many, and Zhang Yimou, who's a master of visual symbolism, obviously here sending a message that great accomplishments – great individual accomplishments – particularly in this society rely on much more than the individual alone.

Indeed, the Western imagination activated here is one overdetermined not just by the threat of communism but by past stereotypes ranging from patriarchal Confucian family values to 'Oriental despotism'; as Daniel Vukovich has argued, the demonisation of Chinese communism is deeply imbricated in the broader orientalist discourse about China in the West.[2] There is, in fact, a fundamental irony to any Western fears of an overly unified and thereby threatening Chinese society. As Tong Lam has shown, the very concept of *society* did not exist in China until around the beginning of the twentieth century, and it was introduced into Chinese discourse mainly as a lamented *lack*, in that 'many Chinese writers contended . . . that China did not have a real society'.[3] The fear was rather that, as Sun Yat-sen himself put it, China was merely '"a heap of loose sand" (*yipan sansha*) made up of four hundred million individuals' rather than 'a cohesive "national social body" (*minzu tuanti*) as solid as a rock', and that it was thus unable to stand up to imperialist aggression from more economically and militarily advanced nations.[4]

A century later, of course, in the context of China's emergence as an economic powerhouse within a precarious global capitalist system, any Western paranoia over a Chinese society so solidified as to lack individual granularity contrasts with the ongoing fear within China of social disintegration in the face of the massive forces transforming the country. Westerners' suspicious comments on the Olympic ceremony, in fact, are perhaps motivated equally by fears of uncontrollable global economic forces. The anxiety they reveal has to do not so much with Confucian tradition or Maoist ideology but rather with the idea that the Chinese economic machine, fuelled by a vast, disciplined social workforce, will overcome Western economic hegemony. Such conditions are additionally relevant to NBC anchor Jim Lampley's description of the Olympic ceremony as 'a spectacle without equal in

Olympics history – 15,000 cast members in a futuristic production that exceeds even the most lavish of Hollywood blockbusters'. Specifically, cinematic spectacle has become one of the areas in which competition from China offers both a threat and an opportunity, just as the Olympic festivities themselves were judged at least somewhat negatively according to liberal Western criteria even as they were packaged and consumed abroad for the profit of global media corporations such as NBC.

It is at least partly in this context that we should understand the by-now-familiar story of the transition of director Zhang Yimou himself from being lauded in the West as a dissident artist to being criticised for selling out to an oppressive Chinese government. In this chapter I will look in particular at how Zhang has reimagined traditional Chinese culture and history through the use of CGI in special-effects blockbusters in the latter stage of his career, as well as through his work on the opening and closing ceremonies for the Beijing Olympics. One issue I will examine is the claim that Zhang Yimou's talents have been thoroughly co-opted by the Chinese communist authorities. In particular, his 2002 film *Hero* (*Yingxiong*) and his Olympic ceremonies choreography have been accused of promoting what is at best the crass nationalism of a Chinese state on the rise and at worst a downright totalitarian or fascist aesthetic that celebrates mindless submission of the individual to state power. I will consider such views through selected Western and Chinese criticism, as well as through the critiques of fascist aesthetics offered by Susan Sontag and Siegfried Kracauer. More importantly, however, I seek to complicate such a perspective by reference to a set of theoretical terms that enable an approach to the aesthetics of human figures in these works. These terms include the 'digital multitude', as conceived by Kristen Whissel in her analysis of special-effects blockbusters, as well as Kracauer's divergent discussions of the 'mass ornament' as a manifestation either of fascism or of capitalist modernity. I will suggest that the sorts of mass spectacles organised by Zhang Yimou in the end say more about the 'harmony' of contemporary China with globalised capitalism than about either totalitarian aesthetics or nationalist propaganda. In fact, of much more interest than their ostensible capitulation to Chinese nationalism is their demonstration of the logic of digital labour in a globalised economy, including the surplus value offered by Chinese workers within a system of global labour arbitrage.

CGI and the Cultural Imaginary

The CGI-enabled Chinese martial arts cinema that has come to prominence since around the turn of the twenty-first century often draws on funding and talent from across 'greater China' and beyond. Special effects of one kind or another have been an important aspect of martial arts films since the silent era of Shanghai cinema, but shortly after the turn of the century the use of CGI in particular was featured in global blockbusters in the resurgent genre such as *Crouching Tiger, Hidden Dragon* (*Wohu canglong*, Ang Lee, 2000), *Hero* (2002), *House of Flying Daggers* (*Shimian maifu*, Zhang Yimou, 2004), *Kung Fu Hustle* (*Gongfu*, Stephen Chow, 2004) and *Red Cliff* (*Chibi*, John Woo, 2008). In such films, digital techniques were enlisted to create spectacular illusory effects corresponding to stories and images from the Chinese narrative tradition – from the Buddha's palm motif in *Kung Fu Hustle* to the trick torching of Cao Cao's armada in *Red Cliff*'s adaptation of the *Romance of the Three Kingdoms* (*Sanguo yanyi*) story. The virtual reality of CGI enables an expressionistic illusionism that frees the filmmaker from the ontological realism of traditional photography and enables a remediation in particular of the *wuxia* (martial arts) tradition in Chinese vernacular narrative.[5]

A striking example of the use of CGI to achieve aesthetic effects (and emotional affects) that favour expressionism over photographic realism is the scene in *Hero* in which, just after Flying Snow defeats Moon in a swordfight, all the leaves in the surrounding birch forest change within seconds from yellow to a deep blood red. The scene makes no pretence to prosaic realism but rather allows Zhang Yimou, who, from his earliest films, could be numbered among the most painterly of contemporary directors, to become so almost literally – at least in so far as, according to the hyperbolic assertion of new media theorist Lev Manovich, in the digital age cinema 'is no longer an indexical media technology but, rather, a subgenre of painting'.[6] In fact, the technological challenges of the scene in the birch forest introduce many of the issues we will be considering here, including the complicated relationship between the actual photographic realism of on-location shooting and the photo-realist illusionism of CGI added in postproduction, but also the more specific issue of the challenge of scale in generating images of massive numbers of the same things – in this case, the leaves themselves.

Mary Farquhar has detailed how the scene was put together.[7] The shooting location was a real birch forest in Mongolia, and the original yellow colour of the leaves results from filming the scene at exactly the right moment in the autumn when the leaves were changing colour and beginning to fall. The further change in colour to blood red, of course, was achieved by CGI in postproduction, but the filmmakers had another problem, which was that the leaves in the forest – though carefully selected by colour and gathered to form swirling masses during the original shoot – were not nearly great enough in number to achieve the desired effects, and they were falling so quickly that the trees had become too bare by the late stages of on-location

Figure 2.1 Moon fights Snow. Source: *Hero* (2002).

shooting. Both problems were solved through compositing, by creating computer models from the original leaves and then adding texture, variation and swirling effects to achieve the masses of leaves in the final images in the film – in which digital leaves mix seamlessly with the 'real' leaves in the forest from the original photographic footage (Fig. 2.1). The leaves thus became one incidental version of the 'digital multitudes' we will be examining here, even carrying the sense of danger that such multitudes generally represent (to be discussed shortly), in that 'the whirlwind of golden leaves becomes Flying Snow's weapon' as she fatally defeats Moon.[8] Particularly with their spectacular transition from yellow to blood red, the leaves additionally are relatively straightforward as a 'painterly' effect in that, 'unusually, the after-footage makes the special effects transparent or "visible" in a celebration of colour, movement, and death'; the painterly use of CGI does not just play a supporting role but ends up being the main focus of the scene's last few shots.[9]

Digital Multitudes in Martial Arts Films

A more explicit example of a digital multitude in recent Chinese martial arts cinema can be found in John Woo's *Red Cliff*. In an especially spectacular 'tracking' shot (in which the camera movement is not real but virtual), a released dove flies from one military encampment across the Yangzi river to another one, passing in the process a giant armada of ancient warships. Not only is the camera movement an animated illusion, but most of what we see in the image is computer-generated. The multitude of ships is a composited image; there were only a few boats of different sizes actually built as physical models, while all the others were created digitally out of the photographic information from the actual ones. In an interview included as a special feature on the film's overseas DVD release, director John Woo confirms that, for most of the shot, the bird, the ships and the river are all computer-generated, and he further asserts that his producer warned him that it might be the most expensive shot in film history – though he proceeded with it anyway, helping to make *Red Cliff* the highest-budget film ever produced in Asia up to that time. The result, in the case of this shot, is an unprecedentedly awe-inspiring visualisation of Cao Cao's vast armada, helping to renew the cultural imagination of this legendary historical event vividly for contemporary audiences both in China and abroad.

Cao Cao's digital armada recalls the one in the Hollywood epic film *Troy* (Wolfgang Petersen, 2004), the armada of which is first introduced in a spectacular shot that tracks backward rather than forward, revealing an ever-greater expanse of sailing ships. Kristen Whissel mentions this shot as one example of what she labels digital multitudes, or 'massive CG armies, swarms, armadas, and hordes composed of as many as hundreds of thousands of digital beings'.[10] Exemplified by such images as the seemingly infinite armies of orcs and Uruk-hai in the *Lord of the Rings* trilogy (Peter Jackson, 2001/2002/2003), the digital multitude evokes the sublime fear of a threat that appears overwhelming, portending apocalyptic, epochal historical change. Often, as in the case of the allies facing down Cao Cao's force in *Red Cliff*, the narrative leads up to a massive battle pitting a grossly outnumbered minority, led by the film's protagonists, against a vastly superior force. Whissel mentions Zhang Yimou's *Curse of the Golden Flower* (*Mancheng jindai huangjinjia*, 2006) as among the films employing digital multitudes, but she does not linger much on that case – perhaps because it lacks some of the elements that she finds in other films such as the *Lord of the Rings* trilogy and *The Mummy* (Stephen Sommers, 1999). While *Curse of the Golden Flower* employs CGI in several shots to multiply into vast armies the few hundred People's Liberation Army soldiers who were actually used as extras, those armies represent not so much an ultimate threatening *other* but rather rival factions loyal to different members of the royal family in a palace intrigue. A better example from among Zhang Yimou's films, more akin to Cao Cao's vast armed force in Woo's *Red Cliff*, would be the army of China's first emperor, Qin Shihuang, as depicted in *Hero*.

That army in *Hero* – based on the actual historical force immortalised in the form of the terracotta warriors that the Qin Emperor had placed in his tomb – is represented as a vast, threatening multitude from the perspective of the colourful array of assassins who hope to eliminate the Qin ruler before he can militarily overwhelm their home states and subordinate them to a newly unified China. These fictional assassins – Nameless (Jet Li), Broken Sword (Tony Leung Chiu-Wai) and his apprentice Moon (Zhang Ziyi), Flying Snow (Maggie Cheung) and Long Sky (Donnie Yen) – must confront the massive army of the conquering Qin forces.[11] In an early sequence, for example, the Qin army advances on a tiny settlement in the state of Zhao, housing a calligraphy school where some of the assassins are staying. Throughout the sequence, dozens of shots show tight bunches of foot soldiers and archers, their density strongly accentuated by the use of telephoto lenses. Whereas these shots employ hundreds of extras, there are repeated shots of a computer-generated multitude in a type of composition described by Whissel – high-angle extreme long shots that accentuate the army's lateral extension along the x-axis, filling the frame and spilling off the wide screen into offscreen space, as well as its depth along the z-axis, extending all the way to the horizon formed by distant mountains (Fig. 2.2). As with the digital multitudes Whissel examines, such a composition serves to spatialise time, with the vast army dramatically suggesting an epochal transition in which massive destruction will lead to a new order. At the same time, such images of the Qin soldiers in *Hero* seem to reference directly the familiar iconography of the terracotta army that protected the actual Qin Emperor's tomb (Fig. 2.3).

The digital army in *Hero* unleashes a deadly metonymic digital multitude when its archers begin firing their arrows en masse toward the calligraphy school, a symbol of, among other things, the independence of the state of Zhao, which the Qin ruler is determined to conquer. The thousands of arrows that the Qin archers rain down upon the school are represented as digitally generated swarms in several types of shots. Shots from the perspective of the Qin army itself show the arrows being launched into the sky in great numbers. Extreme long shots from the perspective of the settlement show the masses of arrows rising from the distant army and then taking up ever more of the screen as they race towards the 'camera', thus beginning as an array of specks in the distance

Figure 2.2 Qin army ranks. Source: *Hero* (2002).

Figure 2.3 Terracotta warriors. Source: David J. Davies.

and ending by almost filling the screen. A brief but spectacular 'tracking' shot early in the sequence shows the arrows approaching the settlement, seemingly from the perspective of one of the arrows in flight.[12] More conventional ground-level shots show them being shot by the army or landing at the settlement, which then bristles ever more densely with fallen arrows. During part of the sequence, Nameless and Flying Snow go outside on the roof of the calligraphy school to fend off the arrows acrobatically and protect the school. These shots often reach such a degree of expressionism that the images seem to come less from photographed reality than from a cartoon fantasy, with the arrows forming almost abstract patterns of lines that are implausibly scattered this way and that by the heroic characters. Indeed, Flying Snow in particular is shown as fending them off with little more than her long sleeves. The digital swarms of arrows thus reinforce the impression of the overwhelming numbers of the Qin forces, while the small band of assassins appear somewhat like the members of the 'Fellowship of the Ring', a tiny force romantically and heroically resisting a great army against all odds.

Scenes at the Qin imperial palace further emphasise the Qin army's size and discipline, either through tightly framed telephoto shots showing dense groups of soldiers or, again, through extreme long shots of digitally generated multitudes. In the film's climactic closing sequence, in which Nameless is executed by a gigantic firing squad after he spares the life of the Emperor, a flying mass of arrows again appears as a digital multitude, shot from similar angles as in the earlier sequence at the calligraphy school. The effect is, as Farquhar has put it, 'like a swarm of black locusts' which 'symbolise the King's power as they kill Nameless'.[13]

Through scenes such as these, the Qin army is shown to be an awesome and formidable force, always dressed in black, contrasting with the colourful costumes of the assassins. In her insightful analysis of *Hero*, Wendy Larson has argued convincingly that the film's dramatic colour schemes serve partly to help contrast the vibrant world of the assassins with the regimented, grim world of the Qin ruler.[14] The assassins come from the rich traditional imagination of *jianghu*, or 'rivers and lakes' – the *wuxia* milieu not just of warrior prowess but of love, passion, individuality and spiritual culture, as represented by themes such as calligraphy in addition to the balletic beauty of the martial artists' fighting styles. The Qin Emperor's palace complex, in contrast, is a place committed only to military and political power, where even some decorative green curtains must be torn down after they are realised to be a place where assassins might hide. The King's black-clad forces achieve victory not through beautiful displays of graceful movements and gravity-defying acrobatics but through rigid, ruthless discipline combined with sheer numbers.[15] At different points in her discussion of colour in *Hero*, Margaret Hillenbrand describes them as the 'mechanically massed ranks' of the 'Qin military machine', consisting of 'militarised automaton[s]' moving with 'robotic precision', further noting that it is such depictions of the Qin army that 'helped earn Zhang the comparison with [Leni] Riefenstahl', the notoriously talented filmmaker who helped propagandise the German Nazi Party.[16]

Fascist Aesthetics and the Mass Ornament

In this context we can turn to the questions *Hero* raises about the decision of Nameless, the greatest of the film's fictional would-be assassins, to spare the future Emperor's life just when he finally has the opportunity to kill him, on the rationale that a greater good will be achieved by the King's plan to conquer all the rival kingdoms and unite 'all under heaven' (*tianxia*) – under not just singular political rule but also standardised measures, a unified writing system and so on. The willing abrogation of the romantic individualism of the *wuxia* world in favour of submission to state power under Qin rule has been taken by critics both in and out of China as a thinly veiled gesture of ideological support for China's current leadership, with its emphasis on harmony over individual rights and national unity over autonomy for diverse regions including Tibet, Xinjiang, Hong Kong and Taiwan. Bloggers in China accused Zhang Yimou of stimulating 'viewers' desire for domination', 'directing totalitarian group calisthenics' and following 'fascist aesthetics'.[17] Beijing Film Academy professor Cui Weiping referred directly to Susan Sontag's classic 1975 essay about Riefenstahl, including the latter's infamous documentary on Hitler's 1934 Nazi rally at Nuremberg, *Triumph of the Will* (1935). Sontag's essay was also the reference point for J. Hoberman's review of *Hero* in the *Village Voice*, which concluded as follows:

> *Hero*'s vast imperial sets and symmetrical tumult, its decorative dialectical montage and sanctimonious traditionalism, its glorification of ruthless leadership and self-sacrifice on the altar of national greatness, not to mention the sense that this might somehow stoke the engine of political regeneration, are all redolent of fascinatin' fascism.[18]

Certainly, there is evidence to support this argument. Aside from the final decision of Nameless to negate himself in the service of a totalitarian ruler, the film employs many other tropes that recall *Triumph of the Will*. Soldiers chant in seemingly impossible unison; compositions, particularly within the magnificent palace grounds of the Qin ruler, are relentlessly symmetrical; one shot of the Qin army, in which Nameless walks through a multitude of soldiers toward his audience with the Emperor, even recalls a specific shot in Riefenstahl's film. Parts of Sontag's analysis of *Triumph of the Will* could well be applied to *Hero*:

> Fascist aesthetics . . . flow from (and justify) a preoccupation with situations of control, submissive behavior, and extravagant effort; they exalt two seemingly opposite states, egomania and servitude. The relations of domination and enslavement take the form of a characteristic pageantry: the massing of groups of people; the turning of people into things; the multiplication of things and grouping of people/things around an all-powerful, hypnotic leader figure or force . . . . Fascist art glorifies surrender; it exalts mindlessness: it glamorizes death.[19]

The references to submissive behaviour, a combination of both egomania and servitude, surrender to an all-powerful leader and the glamourisation of death all resonate with the sacrifice of Nameless, while the references to 'the massing of groups of people', 'the turning of people into things' and 'the multiplication of things' all recall the depictions of the massive Qin army, including digital multitudes in which the 'things' that 'people' are turned into include the pixelated representations generated by computer simulation and animation programs. Indeed, the digital multitudes analysed by Whissel – the armies of evil creatures in *The Lord of the Rings* and the clone army in *Star Wars: Attack of the Clones* (George Lucas, 2002), for example – embody the fascist ideal of 'a multiplicity that functions as one, a heterogeneous mass that functions homogeneously'.[20]

Whissel herself mentions *Triumph of the Will* as one of the predigital forerunners to the digital multitude, in which enormous masses of Nazi Party members are organised to present a 'visual uniformity' that renews national identity and suggests that a new era is dawning.

The massed formations of real people in Riefenstahl's film, through their highly disciplined bodies and visual uniformity as a group, anticipate digital multitudes in the specific form that Siegfried Kracauer labelled 'mass ornaments'. In *From Caligari to Hitler: A Psychological History of the German Film*, Kracauer finds that 'absolute authority asserts itself by arranging people under its domination in pleasing designs', resulting in 'the complete triumph of the ornamental over the human'.[21] Addressing mass rallies such as that in *Triumph of the Will*, Kracauer asserts, Hitler 'surveyed not so much hundreds of thousands of listeners as an enormous ornament consisting of hundreds of thousands of particles'.[22] Kracauer also notes how groups of Nazis 'were trained to speak in chorus', a disconcerting effect echoed by the beastly Uruk-hai soldiers chanting in unison in *The Lord of the Rings*, as well as both the soldiers and retainers of the Qin Emperor repeatedly doing the same in *Hero*.[23] According to Kracauer, such 'living ornaments . . . symbolically presented the masses as instrumental superunits' – anticipating Whissel's description of the digital multitude as 'a multiplicity that functions as one'.[24] Kracauer argues that Hitler and his staff must have appreciated the mass ornaments 'as configurations symbolising the readiness of the masses to be shaped and used at will by their leaders', while the film's spectators would have been captivated by their aesthetic qualities and led 'to believe in the solidity of the swastika world'.[25]

We already have seen that mass ornaments and digital multitudes co-exist and reinforce each other in *Hero*; closer shots show Qin army soldiers, played by extras, doing things in unison – chanting, shooting arrows, raising banners and so on – while extreme long shots feature digital multitudes that emphasise not just the uniformity but also the vastness of Qin Shihuang's force. Such masses of soldiers serve as 'instrumental superunits' serving 'absolute authority', as in the Nuremberg rallies described by Kracauer.

Not long after making *Hero* and *Curse of the Golden Flower*, Zhang Yimou would employ human mass ornaments to an almost unprecedented degree in the opening and closing ceremonies of the 2008 Beijing Olympics. The ceremonies were actually a series of spectacles, with symbolic vast numbers of performers (exactly 2,008 drummers, for example) creating precise stadium-friendly living ornaments of immense proportions. Of particular interest here are the instances in which the human units of the ornaments invoked the pixels of a digital display. In the opening sequence with drummers, for example, each drum was a square that lights when struck. In the final countdown to the beginning of the Olympics (at precisely 8:08:08 p.m. on 8 August 2008 or 08/08/08), each drummer appeared as a pixel in a living digital display as the final sixty seconds were counted down, ending in the explosions of fireworks celebrating the fact that the time – which had been counted down across China for years, often in digital displays placed prominently in provincial capitals, for example – had finally arrived.

Later in the ceremony, a wondrous electronic screen in the shape of a giant scroll showed digital images while further human mass ornaments were assembled on top of it. A key sequence featured what appeared to be an oversized, mechanised moveable-type printing press, highlighting China's pioneering role in the history of printing technology. In the Olympics ceremony, the giant blocks of the press rippled to create human waves and settled into various patterns, most notably repeated variations of the character *he*, or 'harmony' (Fig. 2.4). The final effect came in a spectacular reveal of the 'Mechanical Turk' nature of the whole sequence's technology: the tops of the printing blocks suddenly popped open to show that each one had a person inside, and that the machine-like precision of the spectacle had been achieved not by high-tech programmers but by a collection of individuals who must have drilled for countless hours to achieve it.[26] As the NBC commentator gushed at the point of reveal, 'And how did they do it? They do it with people, not with computers' – each person being a modular agent in achieving the overall effect.

Figure 2.4 Beijing Olympic opening ceremony (2008). Source: US Olympic Committee officially licensed DVD release.

Zhang Yimou's drumming and printing press sequences of the Olympics opening ceremonies are thus particularly notable for their imitation of digital display screens, despite the fact that they were mass ornaments created with real people. The pixel is the smallest unit of information in a digital image, but it has meaning only as part of a larger constellation of pixels, the meaning or overall impression of which is clear only by means of viewing the totality. In arranging dynamic human bodies into arrays of pixel-like units, Zhang Yimou refers to the dominant mode of visuality of new media in the digital age – and, indeed, new media played a key role throughout his ceremonies' choreography. However, at the same time, Zhang's human pixels mimic the aesthetics of the mass ornament, as described by Kracauer and as employed elsewhere in the same ceremonies. As in the early twentieth-century mass ornaments observed by Kracauer, in the Beijing Olympics opening pageant 'people become fractions of a figure', 'clusters whose movements are demonstrations of mathematics'.[27]

What Does the Mass Serve?

Here, however, I am quoting not Kracauer's critique of the Nuremberg rallies featured in *Triumph of the Will*, but rather his original landmark essay 'The Mass Ornament', written in 1927, well before the rise of Hitler, which took as its main example not the fascist masses but the British popular dance troupe the Tiller Girls, akin to the American precision dance company the Rockettes. Kracauer had reacted much more ambivalently to *these* mass ornaments, seeing in them a true aesthetic reflection of the capitalist mode of production: 'The mass ornament is the aesthetic reflex of the rationality to which the prevailing economic system aspires.'[28] The pleasure taken in such ornaments by the public was thus, according to Kracauer, 'legitimate', and superior at least to a reactionary bourgeois appreciation of the noble forms of high art from a pre-Fordist/Taylorist society. Here Kracauer's rhetoric anticipates Walter Benjamin's welcoming of the loss of art's 'aura' in the age of technological reproducibility, with a similar argument that the way to genuine human liberation lies through and beyond the current mode of production, not by a turning back to try to regain some romanticised lost state of nature or purity.[29]

The digital multitudes of contemporary special effects cinema serve partly to update the aesthetics of the mass ornament, but in a way that uses real bodies, if at all, only as information that gets processed and multiplied into 'ornaments' on a potentially unprecedented scale. The monster armies in the *Lord of the Rings* trilogy are, in an important sense, the aesthetic descendants of the Nazi masses captured by Riefenstahl, but with their sublime appeal morally inverted since the film does not celebrate the invincible force their discipline seems to imply but uses it as a vehicle of both awe and dread – indeed, drawing in part on the historical memory of Hitler's war machine. The human mass ornaments of the Olympics ceremonies, on the other hand, are the descendants of the Tiller Girls, in that they are consumed primarily as superficial entertaining spectacle (even if they still can be turned into objects of dread by Western commentators, as we have seen).

Despite the similarities of their aesthetics, if not their media, an interesting paradox arises in the comparison between mass ornaments and digital multitudes. The former, in trying to achieve the mathematical precision noted by Kracauer, essentially aim to turn human bodies, or parts thereof, into machine-like collections of identical parts – whether the simultaneously moving, identically costumed legs of the Tiller Girls or the identically choreographed swinging arms of the Olympic ceremony drummers. That is, mass ornaments take what are organic and different – individual human bodies – and attempt to make them look as much as possible mechanised and identical. Digital multitudes, on the other hand, begin with sameness – the exact multiplication of visual information from a single leaf into a swarm of leaves, or from a few dozen model boats into an armada of thousands – and, in order to make it visually 'realistic', intentionally introduce some level of difference. Thus, programs such as MASSIVE (Multiple Agent Simulation System in Virtual Environment, used to create the digital multitudes in *The Lord of the Rings*) apply fuzzy-logic-based algorithms to information from either live photography or hand animation to program each 'agent' within a multitude to respond to its immediate environment in ways that add a further level of complexity to what would otherwise too obviously be a mere cut-and-paste multiplication of identical visual images. (In fact, some of the vastest digital multitudes presented in *Hero* appear, in freeze frame, to lack the level of complexity that MASSIVE had lent to the *Lord of the Rings* multitudes, weakening the realism of the effect.)

Keeping in mind the similar aesthetic effect – though, in a sense, coming at it from opposite directions – of mass ornaments and digital multitudes, in the context of the Beijing Olympics as well as *Hero* it is important to distinguish Kracauer's descriptions of the purpose and audience of the mass ornament in his original essay, as compared to his revival of the term in *From Caligari to Hitler*. In the latter work, he makes clear that the living ornaments of the Nuremberg rally exist to serve the gaze of authority, in particular the Führer himself. Riefenstahl's film depicts just such an organisation of visuality through cuts from the masses of soldiers and party members to low-angle shots of Hitler looking out over them. In one sequence, such a cut interrupts a slow pan across the crowd, so that, with the insertion of the shot of Hitler, we are invited to interpret the panning view as a point-of-view shot from his perspective as his eyes scan the ornamental mass.

In the Olympic ceremonies, the gaze of the Chinese leader, Hu Jintao, is briefly invoked in so far as he is shown being seated and waving to the crowd before the ceremonies begin. However, he appears in the frame equally with International Olympic Committee President Jacques Rogge and, in any case, is rarely shown after the ceremonies begin. The NBC broadcast of the event equally features George W. and Laura Bush being seated, while the CCTV broadcast skips that detail, instead cutting from the seating of Hu to multiple shots of the anonymous crowd in the stadium. Such shots invoke the source of the gaze through which the original mass ornaments described by Kracauer were appreciated: 'The regularity of their patterns is cheered by the masses, themselves arranged by the stands in tier upon ordered tier.'[30] In the televisual age, of course, even the massive crowd in the stadium is dwarfed by the vast audience viewing the spectacle from homes across the planet. For those viewers, the pleasure of viewing Zhang Yimou's elaborate ornaments lies partly in the frequent cut-ins, in both the CCTV and NBC broadcasts, through which the totality is periodically abandoned in order to view the atomic units at work creating the ornaments. These closer shots of the vigorous bodies and smiling faces of the individuals making the patterns help to glorify their voluntary role in the display.

As we have seen, the ceremonies were widely taken as displays of a nationalistic China on the rise, and, of course, it is true that the various spectacles Zhang Yimou deployed, which go far beyond the few I have highlighted here, seek to demonstrate China's illustrious past and point to its future prominence. However, in the end, it is quite a stretch to equate the posture of the current Chinese government with the fascist movement in the 1930s or Zhang Yimou with Leni Riefenstahl. As the introduction to a volume of essays on narratives of the Beijing Olympics puts it, 'China intended the "One World, One Dream" theme to project a benign, harmony-seeking China emerging as a powerful yet positive global force'.[31] The character for 'harmony' may be selectively interpreted as a warning to Taiwan or Tibet, but it was first and foremost an acknowledgement that an increasingly powerful China was none the less now fully integrated with the world economy. In short, if the masses of Red Guards gathered in Tiananmen Square under the appreciative gaze of Mao in the late 1960s represented real resistance to global capitalism, the mass ornaments of the 2008 Olympics represented quite the opposite.

Armies of Mass Production

Taking our cue from Kracauer, then, we might reconsider the aesthetics of the Olympic ceremonies in light of the system they idealistically express. For Kracauer, mass ornaments like the Tiller Girls were the aesthetic reflections of the factory assembly line:

> Everyone does his or her task on the conveyer belt, performing a partial function without grasping the totality. Like the pattern in the stadium, the organization stands above the masses, a monstrous figure whose creator withdraws it from the eyes of its bearers, and barely even observes it himself. – It is conceived according to rational principles which the Taylor system merely pushes to their ultimate conclusion. The hands in the factory correspond to the legs of the Tiller Girls.[32]

Such a connection is still highly relevant when interpreting the mass ornaments of Beijing in 2008, given China's transformation into the 'workshop of the world', where ever more millions of young people from farming families leave the countryside to labour in the gigantic factories that feed Walmart's shelves and Amazon.com's warehouses, in a case that 'looks something like Fordism on Steroids'.[33] Take Foxconn, for instance, the Taiwan-based company that manufactures high-end components for many of the leading computer and mobile phone companies and was for a time China's largest private employer. Its Longhua factory campus – the one in Shenzhen that became infamous for worker suicides – 'houses and employs an army of 400,000' in a system 'redolent of the Taylorism of the early twentieth-century assembly lines'.[34] Indeed, in the context of China's central role in the production chain of today's global capitalist economy, the harmonious patterns of the Olympic mass ornaments, rather than arousing fear, might well reassure foreign observers of the skill and precision of the anonymous Chinese who make their iPhones, while demonstrating to Chinese audiences the beauty of the system and the honour of their place in it. In reality, of course, the labourers in factories such as those of Foxconn submit, for lack of better options, to being on the receiving end of a system of corporate exploitation through global labour arbitrage, in which the transnational mobility of capital – yet relative immobility of labour – in an integrated world economy permits the swift relocation of production to any locales where labour is both adequate and cheapest: thus, Foxconn's and similar companies' recent large-scale migration of operations from Chinese coastal locations like Shenzhen to interior sites like Chongqing and Chengdu, where both land and people are bought more cheaply.

None the less, if the mass ornaments of the Beijing Olympic ceremonies in some ways echo those of the early twentieth century in their evocation of factory labour, the specifically digital form in which Zhang Yimou cast some of his spectacular arrays of human bodies calls for an updated explanation in light of the rise of the global digital economy. The new situation has spurred entirely new methods of value extraction that rely upon individual users of computers, tablets and smartphones to generate profit for corporations. These range from the value of aggregated information from individual users' web browsing and Facebook 'likes' to more systematic forms of crowdsourcing such as Amazon's Mechanical Turk (named after the fake chess automaton mentioned earlier), a system whereby workers throughout the world can perform human intellectual labour for US-based companies on a piecemeal basis.[35] Such digital labour often pays only a few cents per task completed, and the companies enjoy complete freedom from payroll taxes, minimum wage laws or the need to provide benefits, job security, overtime pay, workers' compensation and so on.

Zhang Yimou's heroic human pixels encapsulate the new digital logic of the human web-browser as a producer of surplus value. As commonly understood, 'a pixel is an atomic visible element of an image, a picture element or picture cell', but more technically a pixel is defined as 'a sample of the visual properties of an image that may be representative of a point or a region within the image'.[36] In other words, what is important about a pixel is not that it is an individual point, but that it provides a certain small parcel of information which, when combined with a vast array of other pixels providing slightly different parcels of information, will become useful as a component within some totality. Similarly, when I 'like' a product on Facebook or produce a particular browsing history in a computer session, that information is not of particular interest in itself (thus digital-age paranoia based on more traditional fears of being personally spied on are often misplaced), but when treated as an aggregated 'pixel' within a much larger array of information, the information produces value for whatever company has the power to aggregate it. Thus, Zhang Yimou's groupings of human bodies evoke simultaneously the Fordist–Taylorist regime of factory labour (still quite predominant in Chongqing, even if largely vanished from Detroit) through their functions as mass ornaments, as well as the newer logic of digital labour in the global economy through their representation of humans as pixels. Indeed, the human pixels of the Olympics ceremonies, like the individual 'agents' making up a digital multitude in a special effects film, may appear to be at least slightly autonomous individuals but actually are carefully arrayed to serve a higher function.

Globalised Spectacle

From the perspective of the home television viewer/consumer, the Olympic ceremonies in fact were not totalitarian displays but manifestations of the society of the spectacle, and if they represent a threat from China, it is not a political or military threat but merely a threat to the Western-centrism of the spectacle. As Guy Debord writes, 'The society which carries the spectacle does not dominate the underdeveloped regions by its economic hegemony alone. It dominates them *as the society of the spectacle*.'[37] Zhang Yimou shows that China too can carry the spectacle and assert its own hegemony, but more or less within the terms of global commerce and media exhibitionism already set by capitalism.

Here we have perhaps come a long way from the images of despotic rule in *Hero*, but really the charges of totalitarian ideology in that film are equally spurious. The displays of mindless obedience and military might in *Triumph of the Will* are clearly celebrated, but, as Wendy Larson has emphasised, those by the Qin army in *Hero* take place in contrast to the colourful, romantic, cultural and individualistic *wuxia* world of the assassins, who thus represent the kind of nostalgic turn Kracauer scorns, a world of nature and beauty that seeks an implausible autonomy from a globalising system.[38] Nameless only recognises the futility of this dream, but that does not mean that he, or the film narration as a whole, glorifies the conquering power of the system. At the end of the film, even the Emperor himself appears to be saddened and yet incapable of resisting the structure of power that he embodies, as he yields reluctantly to the retainers who demand in unison that he execute the would-be assassin who has just spared his own life and whom he has called his *zhiji* (true friend).

As Gary D. Rawnsley argues, 'rather than celebrating the authoritarianism of Qin, *Hero* is in many ways a depressing and desolate representation of society at that time'.[39] Haizhou Wang and Ming-Yeh T. Rawnsley have documented that the film actually frustrated the expectations of martial-arts film fans in Chinese communities precisely in so far as the codes of morality and justice of the legendary *jianghu* are jettisoned in favour of the logic of the state, which the *jianghu* by definition exceeds and opposes.[40] Thus, while Western commentaries have tended to read Nameless as the eponymous 'hero', Wang and Rawnsley cite a poll in which more than twice as many Chinese saw Flying Snow (the one assassin character who holds out against the Qin Emperor until her dying breath) as the film's hero.[41] The dissatisfaction with *Hero* among mainland Chinese critics and audiences presents a conundrum since the film none the less broke box-office records in China. Sabrina Qiong Yu has, however, extensively documented the possibility that one of the main explanations for this was that the film was consumed avidly in China as laughable camp.[42] Its reception in the United States also was far from uniform, with some critics and scholars arguing forcefully against the view of the film as a rationale for authoritarianism.[43] Robert Eng, for example, sees the Qin army represented as a repulsive Nazi-type force in the same way that we have described the digital multitudes in *The Lord of the Rings* ('The Qin army's unison cry of "Feng! Feng!" is chillingly similar to the Nazi salute "Sieg heil!"'), and he remarks that 'the film ends not in a surge of patriotic feeling but on a pronounced mournful note of contingency and skepticism'.[44]

Zhang Yimou himself has said the following of *Hero*: 'My hope in this film, as I have tried to make clear, was to help give Chinese cinema greater international influence in the realm of big-budget entertainment movies – the main trend in the movie industry right now.'[45] Again, rather than a sinister totalitarianism, we have a more benign effort to measure up to the West in the offering of spectacles within the harmonious totality of global capitalism. In fact, given the globalisation of film production and CGI technology, the national boundaries suggested by terms like 'Hollywood' or 'the Chinese film industry' are, in many ways, obsolete. Most of the high-end CGI work in *Hero* was done in Sydney by the Australian- and US-based company Animal Logic. Meanwhile, again taking advantage of global labour arbitrage, Hollywood special effects blockbusters are increasingly likely to outsource much of their digital wizardry to East Asia, or to take on Chinese production companies as co-producers of the film as a whole.[46] For example, *Cloud Atlas* (Tom Tykwer, Andy Wachowski and Lana Wachowski, 2012) was co-produced by the Hong Kong-based Media Asia Group, while Digital Domain, a leading Hollywood special effects company founded by James Cameron, the director of the mega blockbusters *Titanic* (1997) and *Avatar* (2009), was purchased in 2012 by the Chinese company Galloping Horse, which teamed with an Indian firm for the acquisition. Such examples of industrial interpenetration are plentiful, but suffice it to say that, while the branding of films as Chinese or American, Asian or Western, may matter a great deal to critics, fans or nationalists of various sorts, national and regional boundaries are increasingly irrelevant to media conglomerates in either location that stand to make millions of dollars from a global blockbuster. Here again, in this context of global productive forces, the strikingly efficient mass ornaments of Zhang Yimou's Olympic opening ceremonies and the digital multitudes of his film *Hero* do not so much take on a nationalist, Sinocentric meaning but rather suggest a more genuinely global sense of the forces that, in fact, rule 'all under heaven'; the modular units of technical labour that create the digital effects of global blockbusters are themselves spread globally, competing to exceed each other's technological prowess in creating convincing illusions while undercutting each other's costs. This remains true, even though the film, as Margaret Hillenbrand shows, markets itself globally through an appeal that is as regional as it is national, given Zhang Yimou's clear aesthetic debt to Akira Kurosawa, particularly a flamboyant use of colour that, in part, signifies a certain contemporary pan-Asian aesthetic.[47]

Whereas the foreboding digital multitudes of Hollywood action films ultimately are defeated by colourful individuals in an assertion of the ideology of personal freedom, *Hero* takes a much darker view; rather than claiming the ongoing relevance of rugged individualism, it shows the homogenising force of a globalising power as ultimately irresistible. Far from being a celebration of authoritarianism, unlike a Hollywood blockbuster, it simply refuses to provide any utopian sugarcoating or romantic reassurance that the brutal and seemingly irresistible globalising power can be magically stopped by the romantic individual (Luke Skywalker blowing up the Death Star; Frodo destroying the Ring of Power). The film's last shots reveal the final image of the ostensible 'hero', showing not Nameless himself but his empty profile left by the hail of arrows that killed him, while in the reverse shot the Emperor stands helpless in the kind of oppressively symmetrical extreme long shot that has been Zhang Yimou's speciality at least since *Raise the Red Lantern* (*Dahong denglong gaogaogua*, 1991), an individual reduced, like the erased Nameless, to a mere location in a structure, the totality of which exists as an end in itself.

Acknowledgements

My thanks to the *MCLC* editors and anonymous readers for their very helpful suggestions, to David J. Davies for key reading recommendations and the use of his photograph, and to Daniel Morgan for feedback and encouragement.

Notes

1. Hal Boedeker, 'Olympic opening ceremony', (no longer accessible as of 14 March 2020).
2. Daniel Vukovich, *China and Orientalism*.
3. Tong Lam, *A Passion for Facts*, 9.
4. Ibid., 9.
5. Around the turn of the millennium, for example, Chinese critic Chen Xihe celebrated how the 'virtual realism' of CGI had freed Chinese filmmakers from the ontological realism of live-action film. Chen Xihe, 'Xuni xianshizhuyi he houdianying lilun' (Virtual realism and post-filmic theory).
6. Lev Manovich, *The Language of New Media*, 295.
7. Mary Farquhar, 'Visual effects magic', 191–3.
8. Ibid., 193.
9. Ibid., 193.
10. Kristen Whissel, 'The digital multitude', 91.
11. The film is often said to have a *Rashomon*-like structure, but the comparison is fairly weak since Akira Kurosawa's film from 1950 much more radically leaves the 'true' story in question, whereas *Hero* narrates several stories later shown to be false, ending with a version acknowledged as 'true' within its fictional world.
12. Such 'arrow POV shots' would be derided as cliché by the time Ridley Scott used them in 2010 in his *Robin Hood*. See Mandi Bierly, '*Robin Hood* and the great arrow POV shot debate' (last accessed 2 November 2020).

13. Farquhar, 'Visual effects magic', 193.
14. Wendy Larson, *Zhang Yimou*, 283.
15. While *Hero* takes many liberties with the actual history of the Qin Emperor – in so far as that history is known through such sources as Sima Qian's *Historical Records (Shiji)* – its portrayal of the extreme regimentation of the Qin army is based on historical fact. See Lothar Ledderose, *Ten Thousand Things*, for an account of how the ancient armed force itself was organized, as well as how a veritable army of regimented craftsmen mass-produced the terracotta facsimile of the army to protect the emperor after death.
16. Margaret Hillenbrand, '*Hero*, Kurosawa and a cinema of the senses', 131, 132.
17. Comments are by Liu Hongbo, Zhu Dake and Cui Weiping, respectively, from translations posted in Sophie Beach, 'Zhang Yimou and state aesthetics' (last accessed 2 November 2020).
18. J. Hoberman, 'Man with no name tells a story of heroics, color coordination' (last accessed 15 March 2020).
19. Susan Sontag, 'Fascinating fascism', (last accessed 15 March 2020).
20. Whissel, 'The digital multitude', 103.
21. Siegfried Kracauer, *From Caligari to Hitler*, 94.
22. Ibid., 95.
23. Ibid., 301; Whissel, 'The digital multitude', 98.
24. Kracauer, *From Caligari to Hitler*, 301; Whissel, 'The digital multitude', 103.
25. Kracauer, *From Caligari to Hitler*, 302.
26. The Mechanical Turk was the fake chess-playing machine that amazed audiences in Europe in the late 1700s. A mechanised Turkish-looking automaton connected to a large box with a chess board on top appeared to be able to defeat human opponents at the game. In fact, a *real* human hiding inside the box determined the 'Mechanical Turk's' moves.
27. Siegfried Kracauer, *The Mass Ornament*, 76.
28. Ibid., 79.
29. Walter Benjamin, 'The work of art in the age of its technological reproducibility – second version'.
30. Kracauer, *The Mass Ornament*, 76.
31. Monroe E. Price, 'Introduction', 6.
32. Kracauer, *The Mass Ornament*, 78–9.
33. Andrew Ross, 'In search of the lost paycheck', 28.
34. Ibid., 28, 29.
35. Ayhan Aytes, 'Return of the crowds'.
36. Steven L. Tanimoto, *An Interdisciplinary Introduction to Image Processing*, 5–6.
37. Guy Debord, *Society of the Spectacle*, sec. 57.
38. Larson, *Zhang Yimou*, 271–304.
39. Gary D. Rawnsley, 'The political narrative(s) of *Hero*', 23.
40. Haizhou Wang and Ming-Yeh T. Rawnsley, '*Hero*', 98–9. For a rich overview of martial arts cinema in the context of the *wuxia* literary tradition, including the concept of *jianghu*, see Stephen Teo, *Chinese Martial Arts Cinema*.

41. I have long suggested such a view to students in classes when using *Hero* (a word which lacks both gender and number in Chinese). Flying Snow's resistance calls our attention to the gendered nature of the fascist celebration of submission to the state. In contrast to what Klaus Theweleit calls the 'ideal man of the conservative utopia' – a veritable 'robot' with a 'machinelike' exterior and no interior life, Flying Snow embodies an almost stereotypically deconstructive femininity in so far as she passionately resists to the bitter end any totalising authority, no matter how rationally beneficial it may claim to be for 'all under heaven'. Theweleit, *Male Fantasies*, vol. 2, 162.
42. Sabrina Qiong Yu, 'Camp pleasure in an era of Chinese blockbusters', 135–51.
43. These include Wendy Larson as cited above, as well as Robert Y. Eng, "Is *Hero* a paean to authoritarianism?', and Taylor, '*Hero*' (both last accessed 15 March 2020).
44. Eng, 'Is *Hero* a paean to authoritarianism?'.
45. Bert Cardullo, *Out of Asia*, 140.
46. See Dan North's Chapter 3 in this volume, for more on the globalised visual effects industry in film.
47. Hillenbrand, '*Hero*, Kurosawa and a cinema of the senses'.

Chapter 3

The Spectacle of Co-Production in *The Great Wall*

Dan North

In September 2013, at the ground-breaking ceremony for the Qingdao Oriental Movie Metropolis studios in China's Shandong Province, a coterie of Hollywood stars was paraded before the cameras: Leonardo DiCaprio, Nicole Kidman, Ewan McGregor, John Travolta, Christoph Waltz and Kate Beckinsale, alongside local megastars Zhang Ziyi, Jet Li, Tony Leung, Donnie Yen, Zhao Wei and Huang Xiaoming. This show of transnational glamour and goodwill signalled a plan by the Chinese media and leisure conglomerate Dalian Wanda to attract Hollywood talent to live, work and make films in China. Targeting the super-rich as guests and investors, the blueprints incorporated a 300-berth yachting marina, two international schools, a theme park, a mall, hotels and retail outlets built around the centrepiece of one of the world's largest film production facilities, spread across a site of more than 5 million square metres. It contained thirty soundstages, including one billed as the biggest ever built: although it was modelled on, and accredited by, Pinewood Studios in the UK, the promotional rhetoric invoked a Hollywood scale.[1] All of this investment was a gesture of confidence that film projects co-produced between China and the USA were viable and sustainable. Wanda's chairman, Wang Jianlin, stated in a speech at the ceremony that the studio was 'a major measure to implement the national policy of building a cultural power, a major strategy for Wanda's cultural industry development, and a major attempt to create China's global cultural brands'.[2] The strategy was to build the material resources for every stage of a film's production, populate it with a professional filmmaking community and promote its productions through the film-cultural efforts of a newly established Qingdao International Film Festival. Wanda even promised to lay on extra direct flights between Qingdao and Los Angeles to cater to the expected influx of Hollywood talent.[3]

The scale of Wanda studios suggested that its co-produced films would be similarly monumental, but it also positioned the business itself as spectacular in its scope and ambition. Ahead of the studios' official opening in April 2018, the first film to shoot at the Qingdao studios was *The Great Wall* (*Changcheng*), in March 2015, directed by one of China's most respected auteurs, Zhang Yimou. The soundstages were not yet completed, but some of the film's exteriors were shot on reconstructions of the Great Wall of China in four sections, the largest stretching almost 150 metres, against enormous green screens.[4] This footage would then be heavily augmented with CGI to 'key out' much of the landscape, replacing the construction-site backdrop and the smoggy skies with digital extensions of the Wall stretching across the mountains into the distance. An ersatz Great Wall would serve as proof of concept for Wanda's actual architectural developments (Fig. 3.1).

Set at some point during the Song Dynasty (CE 960–1279), the story of *The Great Wall* follows Matt Damon's William Garin and his sidekick Pero Tovar (Pedro Pascal), who have entered China in search of the explosive 'black powder' they might bring back to the West and sell as a weapon of war. As captives of the Nameless Order, an army stationed on the Great Wall of China, they discover that the Wall is under siege from the Taotie, four-legged beasts of legend that swarm across the land, devouring all in their path and feeding their semi-digested food to their queen. William and Pero must decide whether to stand and fight alongside their Chinese hosts, or to use the next attack as a cover for their escape. Meanwhile, William develops a tentative relationship with Commander Lin Mei (Jing Tian), the brave and principled warrior who soon finds herself at the head of a mission to destroy the Taotie and prevent them from reaching the capital city of the kingdom, Bianliang.

Figure 3.1 Sets built at Qingdao Oriental Movie Metropolis for *The Great Wall*. Source: *The Great Wall* VFX Breakdown, Base FX (2017).

The film opens with the Legendary Pictures logo superimposed over an extreme long shot of Planet Earth, which displaces onscreen the Celtic shield-knot insignia of Legendary Pictures and the planetary logo of Universal Pictures, the film's main production companies. The camera pushes in on the world until the Great Wall becomes visible, continuing through the clouds for a fly-by shot of the Wall that seamlessly composites the practical sets with computer-generated environments. It is an eloquently calculated opening, not only because it plays upon the popular misconception that the Great Wall is visible from space, but also because the studio logos form a symbolic map of their own: Legendary! Universal! These are statements of grandiose intent that imbricate the business of film production into the graphic rhetoric of visual spectacle. Legendary Entertainment is an American media corporation that has been co-producing films for Warner Bros and Universal since 2005, but which has also been a wholly owned subsidiary of Wanda Group since 2016.[5] It has become an exemplar of transnational franchise-building, using its Chinese connections to enhance access to the distribution and exhibition channels in China, guarded as they are by economic and political protectionism; its recent slate includes *Warcraft: The Beginning* (Duncan Jones, 2016), a fantasy film based on the popular video game, which earned more than half of its global box office in China,[6] and the ongoing marquee-monster franchise instalments *Godzilla* (Gareth Edwards, 2014), *Kong: Skull Island* (Jordan Vogt-Roberts, 2017) and *Jurassic World: Fallen Kingdom* (J. A. Bayona, 2018). But *The Great Wall* was Legendary's first project built around Chinese–US co-operation.

Co-produced films need shared material bases of production, and stories that can resonate with audiences across cultural boundaries. By telling a story about representatives of two nations learning to co-operate in defiance of a common threat, *The Great Wall* neatly matched its narrative structure to the larger meta-narrative of its making. This chapter offers a case study of *The Great Wall* and the way it came to stand in for debates around co-productions between China and other filmmaking nations (especially the USA). Principally, it analyses the way that visual effects are used to present fantastic imagery that shapes the visual identity of the film around a blend of Chinese and Hollywood conventions. Looking at the production history of the film provides numerous points of entry for thinking about the role played by visual effects as narrational agents and as promotional structures: by examining how visual effects are used as tools that ostensibly conceal the mechanics of a film's construction but simultaneously point to the traces of manufacture, we can add nuance to discussions of how spectacle might become a marketable commodity, and about the relationship between fantasy and technology.

The Hollywood Model with Chinese Characteristics

The Great Wall was widely reported as a bellwether for the viability of Hollywood/China co-productions, placing traditional Chinese iconography inside the familiar trappings of a Hollywood blockbuster.[7] The rising costs of producing movies on an epic scale (or rather, the willingness of producers to allocate vast sums to single productions) mean that studios demand extra security for their investments, in the form of reliably profitable film properties or franchises, usually driven by 'knowable' quantities such as star performers and state-of-the-art visual effects. While Hollywood has made few compromises to tailor its product to the tastes of Chinese audiences, Chinese studios have regularly attempted to make films in the Hollywood style, a term used as a metonym for large-scale spectacular films. As Yingjing Zhang has pointed out, 'the rush to produce Chinese blockbusters has been motivated by the leading producers' conviction that high-budget (or Hollywood-style "high-concept") films are the only way to secure financial returns in a risky business environment'.[8]

Behind Wanda's infrastructural building project lies a range of negotiating strategies between Hollywood and China over what constitutes the 'Hollywood model'. Zhang Yimou has suggested that Hollywood has

> gone through many years of tempering to form a typical Hollywood style, to set up a mainstream model for world commercial film. As for [Chinese] mainland film, because it hasn't developed any fixed pattern, each director relies upon his or her own mode of thinking to tell a story.[9]

Elsewhere, he has described 'the Hollywood approach' taken by *The Great Wall* as inherently commercial: 'Merchandise tie-ins – everything from porcelain tea sets to cellphone cases and even a fashion range – are already saturating the shops. It's the sort of activity that would impress any studio head from America.'[10]

Recent efforts to strengthen systems of co-production show us two industrial bases (each containing many other industries and teams of personnel) feeling their way towards compromises and common ground. Hollywood looked to China because the domestic film market was unreliable in its tastes: access to a vast audience abroad would offset some of the risk involved in expensive film productions, even as US share in Chinese box office was decreasing.[11] China looked to Hollywood as a model of successful, rationalised studio production and technical expertise.

The Chinese government's adoption of a Hollywood model, letting the market lead production and reducing some government restrictions over distribution, has led to a resurgence in the domestic film industry in recent years.[12] But the authorities' position has been, says Xiaoqun Zhang, 'paradoxical', eager to adopt Hollywood production methods, while at the same time fearful of a cultural invasion from abroad. Since co-production policies in the PRC invite films to apply for approval during preproduction, foreign producers 'have strong market incentives to follow Chinese co-production policy from the beginning of a project to secure market access'.[13] In the context of Xi Jinping's China, this kind of soft power follows the President's instruction to 'give a good Chinese narrative, and better communicate China's messages to the world'.[14] According to David Shambaugh, part of the propaganda focus of the Xi era has been in smoothing out the image of the state-owned international news agency Xinhua, 'trying to alter its stilted and propagandistic flavour and package its content in more viewer-friendly formats'.[15] In other words, the strategy involves retaining control of the media, but giving it the feel of a free commercial press. This approach extends to the realm of popular cinema in China, which looks like a mainstream commercial industry, for the most part, but remains heavily regulated for content by the state.

The kinds of visual spectacle offered by CGI may be tied up with a sort of scopic soft power, displaying fiscal strength through the internationally recognised language of technological attractions. Visual effects provide an example of what Rey Chow calls '[transcultural] modes of fascination', means of engaging audiences 'in ways independent of their linguistic and cultural specificities'.[16] The technologies needed to create digital visual effects overlap considerably with the consumer electronics and artificial intelligence that Chinese companies want to advertise and sell in global markets. As Aynne Kokas states, 'Intense special effects meet the demands for infrastructure outlined in the twelfth five-year plan, which stipulates "cultural innovation, video production, publication, printing and reproduction, performing and entertaining arts, digital contents, and animation".'[17] Visual effects are therefore a shop window for displaying the state of the local art, a marker of scientific sophistication.

The visual effects industry in China has been expanding rapidly since around 2010 to meet an accelerating demand for technically advanced visual media. However, Chinese visual effects are sometimes denigrated by critics and audiences as cheap and inferior symptoms of a cycle of fantasy film production that outpaces the capabilities of the local technology providers, catching visual effects (VFX) creators 'between money-grubbing producers and disappointed audiences as they work under tight schedules with limited budgets'.[18] Visual effects supervisor Guan Mingjie even suggests that the damning insult of *wumao texiao* (fifty-cent visual effects) 'put much pressure on VFX companies [and] . . . pushed the industry onto a path of continuous progress'.[19]

Recent revisionist scholarship on visual effects has made the case that special/visual effects, rather than offering interruptions to narrative, are communicative agents in film texts, making meaning by adding to a film's semiotic vocabulary. However, we cannot ignore the contexts of material production in which they are created since, even though the promotional rhetoric of digital visual effects is that they can now blend harmoniously with a film's profilmic content, they remain perhaps the most visible bridge between the diegesis and the industrial bases of the medium. As Aynne Kokas suggests, 'the production ecosystem is a place-based network of media labor and capital, structured by hierarchies of industrial power and influenced by ethnicity, language, culture and citizenship'.[20] The 'digital turn' may have made it seem as though computers can be used to summon any imagery demanded by a film's screenplay, but the affordances of that technology remain subject to budgetary concerns, ever-tightening release schedules and the human labour relations that allow them to function. Hye Jean Chung has argued that contemporary films are frequently produced in transnational contexts with digital workflows that connect workers from disparate locations and then efface the material conditions of those labour relations behind a rhetoric of seamless composition. It takes a strategy of critical reading that she dubs 'heterotopic perception' to unpick those seams and examine the production contexts that are masked when visual effects strive to hide the traces of their manufacture.[21] Similarly, Bob Rehak notes that we need to study 'the social and cultural dynamics around effects work'[22] through an understanding of their production contexts, as documented in paratextual accounts (behind-the-scenes disclosures such as 'making of . . .' documentaries), but also by looking at 'the types of storytelling that have emerged in tandem with special effects' development: inherently transmedial, world-based, and populated by characters whose augmented nature grants them unusually extended and expansive screen presence'.[23] By reading into the production contexts of *The Great Wall*, via its extensive use of visual effects, we can better appreciate the role of visual spectacle in enunciating the stories of art and industry that underpin their manufacture.

Aynne Kokas compares Xi Jinping's professed ideal of a 'Chinese Dream' (*Zhongguo Meng*), 'a vision of China's global power through media branding',[24] to the concept of Hollywood as a 'dream factory', a phrase which combines the representational fluidity of dreams with the pragmatics of production-line factory labour. Collaborations with film industries outside China, whether sharing audiences or ideas, are part of 'a systematic, policy-driven attempt to enhance investment in the Chinese culture industries as a way of increasing the PRC's international influence'.[25] President Xi urged Chinese cultural producers to 'tell Chinese stories well, broadcast Chinese voices, and explain Chinese characteristics properly'.[26] As David Shambaugh has argued, 'Beijing is assertively promoting its culture and society abroad through sports, fine arts, music, film, literature, and architecture'.[27] A. T. McKenna and Kiki Tianqi Yu have written about how the PRC privileged certain types of film when selecting its submissions to the Oscars, seeking nationalistic affirmation through international awards,[28] and Zhang Yimou's films have been China's official entry to the Academy Award for Best Foreign Language film on an unrivalled seven occasions.[29] A central prop in the promotion of *The Great Wall* was the director Zhang himself, revered in China and respected abroad as a director whose filmography straddles prestige historical drama and period martial arts film. It is interesting to observe the interactions between the auteurist discourses of *The Great Wall*'s presentation and the relatively anonymous contributions of its visual effects artists. Zhang has located in his own films, and those of other Fifth-Generation directors, 'the awakenings of cultural reflection and cultural awareness'.[30] Zhang established the Fifth-Generation visual style as director of photography for his film-school colleague Chen Kaige's *Yellow Earth* (*Huang tudi*, 1984) through 'his way of filming the land, his sense of a people immured in tradition' and, with Chen, recounting 'the story of what it is like to live under a stifling, oppressive society'.[31] His films have often focused on the minute details of a single environment or community, such as the distillery at the centre of *Red Sorghum* (*Honggaoliang*, 1988) or the walled gentry mansion in *Raise the Red Lantern* (*Dahong denglong gaogaogua*, 1991) that houses and imprisons Gong Li's concubine, Songlian, with an aesthetic of confinement that allegorises Zhang's concern with China's 'historical legacy of extinguishing human desire'.[32] While critics posit divisions between Zhang's culturally serious historical films and his popular *wuxia* releases such as *Hero* (*Yingxiong*, 2002) and *House of Flying Daggers* (*Shimian maifu*, 2004), it has often been noted that Zhang blends authentic Chinese costumes and production design with stylised sets and 'invented rituals' that stack the visual deck in favour of his allegorical leanings.[33] *The Great Wall* blends that focus on the themes of environmental confinement, depicting the Great Wall as a stoic military garrison that confines its soldiery so that the imperial masters can play lavishly in the capital city it defends, and on the overdetermined props and costumes that signify an alternate historical vision of China.[34] Sheldon Hsiao-peng Lu argues that Zhang's films

> have attracted a large international audience precisely because they are regarded as authentically 'national', 'Chinese', and 'Oriental'. Thus, an indigenous cultural critique through the medium of national cinema becomes at the same time a cultural sellout of the Chinese nation in the international film market.[35]

Similarly, Lu says that Zhang 'has been taken as an exemplary instance of the willful surrender of Third World cinema to the Orientalist gaze, as a classic case of the subjugation of Third World culture to Western hegemony'.[36]

In *The Great Wall*, Zhang Yimou stages elaborate battles that employ a battery of inventive and improbable war machines, turning warfare into a floorshow of gymnastic violence, complete with armies divided into teams, colour-coded uniforms and rhythmic accompaniment from a troupe of traditional *tanggu* (ceremonial drummers). The Wall's battlements bristle with military contraptions, including giant scissors, catapults and gantries of bungee cords that launch spear-wielding women in long blue capes into the thick of a Taotie attack before pulling (some of) them back up to safety. The costumes, based on medieval Chinese armoury, were devised by Mexican designer Mayes C. Rubio, known for her work on fantasy and science fiction films including *Avatar* (2009), *John Carter* (2012) and *Warcraft: The Beginning* (2016). Zhang Yimou has experience with marshalling cultural styles and artefacts for spectacular display. For his 2008 staging of *Turandot* at Beijing's Forbidden City, he replaced the Italian operatic elements of the performance with a collage of Chinese traditional motifs, applying his 'notable and costly insistence on period detail'[37] to produce 'a kind of cultural ambassador between East and West'.[38] The lavish production, packaging Chinese traditions in Zhang's signature colourful style, became one proving-ground for Zhang's opening ceremony at the Beijing Olympics. Jason McGrath has drawn parallels between the spectacles of the Beijing Olympics 2008 opening ceremony, which included the co-ordinated rhythms of 2,008 Chinese drummers, and the digitally augmented crowds of soldiers in Zhang's *Hero* and *Curse of the Golden Flower* (*Mancheng jindai huangjinjia*, 2006),[39] seeing in both 'the logic of digital labor in a globalized economy, including the surplus value Chinese workers offer within a system of global labor arbitrage'.[40] The armies of *The Great Wall* combine human extras with ranks of digital figures to fill out their numbers.

At stake here may be the way that visual effects submit human subjects to their own logic, leading viewers to understand people in digital terms and activating or enculturing metaphors of regimentation, order, control or the loss of individual identity. Technologies invite people to adopt their themes, metaphors, workflows and structures, and visual effects technologies are no different. McGrath notes that the direction of crowds of live drummers is ontologically distinct from the digital multitude. The drummers aim for perfect co-ordination as a mass, submitting their individual bodies to the bigger picture of a spectacular unison, and the audience interprets the performance as a feat of corporeal control. The digital crowd is programmed to express aspects of randomness in order to simulate the imperfections of human masses and belie its algorithmic origins.[41] In a comment that chimes with Hye Jean Chung's heterotopic perspective, McGrath observes that 'the modular units of technical labor that create the digital effects of global blockbusters are themselves spread globally, competing to exceed each other's technological prowess in creating convincing illusions while undercutting each other's costs'.[42] He finds, then, a compact summary of the dual logic of the visual effects business, striving to simulate the look of costliness and thus enhance the marketable, connotative power that costly spectacle carries, while reducing the actual labour costs of that work. What we see in Zhang Yimou's digitally enhanced martial action scenes is the technological remediation of his distinctive deployment of Chinese cultural iconography for narrative and/or commercial ends, which extends to the depiction of the Wall itself, and to the film's monsters.

The Great Wall makes little historico-geographical sense: its images of the Wall are based on the most popularly recognisable sections, with their crenellated battlements and guard towers, built during the Ming Dynasty around six centuries ago (and long after the Song Dynasty, during which the film is set); it depicts the Wall as close to both Bianliang and the painted mountains of Gansu Province, when in reality they are 1,000 kilometres apart. Itself a kind of composite in the public imagination, the Great Wall is marketed as one massive feat of architectural engineering, but was in reality built in different styles, with many gaps and disputed structures, by multiple dynasties over thousands of years. In place of historical precision, the film offers a collage of agglomerated Chinese tourist sites and signifiers. Returning to the film's opening shot, we can see what a purposeful statement of intent it is, displaying its signature image, a symbol of architectural and military prowess, not as a record of a real place but in the form of a visual effect assembled from profilmic and digital sources. The composited elements are seamlessly intertwined as a graphic analogue for the labour relations and the infrastructural supports that have been pulled together to make the image possible. The shot is, significantly, an aerial fly-by, assembled as if filmed by drones flying over the Wall. A key visual trope of promotional videos for architectural projects, the fly-by offers a disembodied, abstracted perspective that surveys vast areas from above to show off their scale and range. To promote the opening of the Oriental Movie Metropolis, Wanda partnered with DJI, the Shenzhen-based manufacturers of drone-mounted cameras, capturing aerial footage of the site that was used in a short video narrated by Matt Damon and featuring Zhang Yimou talking about his hopes for the studios' international productions.[43]

As Lisa Purse has argued, cinema has always amalgamated elements from various sources (profilmic action, edited to create the illusion of spatiotemporal continuity, layers of sound effects, music and so on), but the promise of digital imaging technologies is to render the lines between composited elements invisible, giving a seamlessly blended view inside the world of the film. Purse's discussion of what she terms the 'disaggregate digital composite' focuses on self-reflexive uses of CGI that foreground the layering of the digital image.[44] She also suggests that 3D is one driver of the rise in self-conscious digital compositing because of its emphasis on 'novel commodity spectacles'. She notes that 'many films released in Digital 3D feature moments at which extended push-ins past different planes of the image or the expansion of a movement or object into its constituent layers assert the novelty of the Digital 3D experience'.[45] One shot in *The Great Wall*, for example, flies over the ranks of the Nameless Order, between spears and swords that push out into negative parallax (that is, they appear to thrust out of the screen at the audience) showing off the deft integration of costumed extras with CGI backgrounds and digital set extensions, even as attention is drawn to the complexity of their combination. The mobile camera, as opposed to continuity edits that stitch together a semblance of the spatial relationships between the different elements of the scene, emphasises the shot as an act of compositing that relies on the interdependence of each layer of the image.

Visual effects are one particular site of visual representation where the sites of co-production, of transnational labour, are most clearly displayed, but Purse describes this as a tension between

> a visual rhetoric of cohesion that allows digital objects a presence and function within the film world, and a visual rhetoric of fragmentation that, while it might extend into the diegetic world, points to the digital object's technological construction and artifice.[46]

The experience of watching visual effects is most often associated with the showcase attractions of action and spectacle, with synthetic bodies and fantasy worlds, but the processes of visual effects can incorporate all of the technologies that augment and manipulate profilmic space and hide the joins between them, a sophisticated play between ostentation and concealment.

Visual Effects and the Monstrous Multitude

Visual effects permeate the fabric of fantasy cinema and, even as they ostensibly strive for integration into the diegetic worlds for which they are designed, they inevitably interrupt the story and invite contemplation of the mechanisms of the films' production. As Robert Stam and Toby Miller once put it, capital-intensive visual effects production in films is responsible for 'fetishising innovation and difference, pointing out the fallacy in mimesis to the audience as part of its product differentiation'.[47] As Bob Rehak writes, even visual effects designed to simulate an impression of reality simultaneously serve to showcase 'the limitless capabilities of an entertainment industry prolix with its powers of illusion'.[48] Moreover, visual effects are used not just to brand the film as innovative and technically advanced, but in textually productive ways that emblematise a film's core themes and solidify its aesthetic profile. By aiming to replicate the Hollywood mode of spectacular CGI, *The Great Wall* was positioning itself in contrast to an aesthetic of surplus and excess that often characterises digital effects in Chinese fantasy blockbusters.

In Chinese fantasy films, the primary uses of visual effects are for character animation and environments, but digital effects houses are called upon for a range of tasks, divided up into specialist practices such as motion capture, modelling, compositing, lighting or matte painting. All of these distinct processes are connected by their common processing through digital workflows, combining to form a unified aesthetic design that belies its status as a multi-sourced collage of elements.

In the fantasy–martial arts film *The Thousand Faces of Dunjia* (*Qimen dunjia*, Yuen Woo-Ping, 2017), a remake of Yuen's *The Miracle Fighters* (*Qimen dunjia*, 1982), almost the entire climactic battle is a contest between digital demon figures. If director Yuen Woo-Ping's reputation was made on choreographing intensely physical combat scenes, it has been remediated in *Dunjia* by a different form of confrontation that showcases the operations of diligently applied software, not trained human bodies. The rapidly growing visual effects industry in China is serving this remediation process by offering increased control over every stage of a film's workflow, but it is also being fed by the desire to emulate the Hollywood model, with visual effects production seemingly its most readily imitable feature.

John Dietz,[49] a veteran of the Harry Potter films, acted as visual effects supervisor for *League of Gods* (*Fengshenbang*, 2016), a frenetic gods-and-demons fantasy which was planned as the first part of a franchise but which, at time of writing, has no sequel in production. The film is saturated with digital animation of characters, creatures, backgrounds, sets and props: almost all of it is shot in front of greenscreens, allowing live foreground action to be composited with digitally generated (or separately shot) backdrops, and augmented with digital extensions and embellishments of characters' bodies (Fig. 3.2). Dietz summarises his work on *League of Gods* in terms of its comparisons to Hollywood production pipelines: 'A lot of the action, particularly the VFX set-pieces, are very much in the line of a western VFX tentpole film. . . . People in the west will be like, "Holy shit, they did that for how much money?!".'[50] If the elements are not carefully blended to confirm their co-presence in the frame, the imagery can appear strangely synthetic: it might be suitable for a depiction of battles between gods, demons and mythical warriors, but it also makes plain the collaging processes of a film produced rapidly at workstations around the globe, bodies and places 'beamed into' the frame remotely and unable to erase the traces of their manufacture completely.

Figure 3.2 Fan Bingbing as shapeshifting Daji in *League of Gods*, shot against greenscreen. Daji's deadly tails added in postproduction. Source: *League of Gods* (2016).

Additionally, as Jason McGrath suggests, 'given the globalization of film production and CGI technology, the national boundaries suggested by terms such as "Hollywood" or "the Chinese film industry" are in many ways obsolete'.[51] Indeed, Melis Behlil has argued that 'rather than being a specific geographic location, Hollywood functions as a network of production, distribution and exhibition across the world, spreading through local involvement'.[52] Consider the complexities of the origins of visual effects: for all the talk of a Hollywood effects style, or a Chinese aesthetic, the visual effects for *League of Gods* were co-produced by multiple effects houses in India, Canada, South Korea and the USA.[53] *The Thousand Faces of Dunjia* credits ten effects houses (plus several more for stereoscopic conversion), including teams from China, South Korea, Ukraine, India and Thailand: 60 per cent of the film's shots used greenscreen. *Zhong Kui* (*Zhong Kui fumo: xueyao moling*, Peter Pau and Tianyu Zhao, 2015) names twenty-six effects houses in its end credits, including creature designs by New Zealand's Weta (the workshop behind Peter Jackson's *Lord of the Rings* franchise, which recently contributed to another Chinese production, *Animal World*), South Korean studios Macrograph, StudioMG, Digital Idea, M2, IOFX, Realade, Madman Post, D4CUS, Pix, Magnon Studio, Pretzeal and Giant Step. Pixomondo, founded in Germany but now operating across multiple locations including Los Angeles, Beijing and Shanghai, provided about three minutes of computer-generated animation.[54] These houses may have relationships with studios, but also compete on a film-by-film basis for contracts to work on shots and sequences that are parcelled out to companies with specialist experience. It makes little sense to try to locate a unified 'local aesthetic' at work in these kinds of productions, though we can observe how digital workflows have made it possible to make films like this across borders and time zones so fluidly. In this sense, branding films as 'Hollywood films' or 'Chinese films' might be a way to appeal to particular audiences, and the nationalities of films in China are used to decide exhibition quotas, but these are labels that have little identificatory or interpretive value. Instead, we can observe, in the creation of spectacular imagery for a co-production like *The Great Wall*, a complex commingling of tropes, techniques and citations from disparate sources, echoing the globalised structures of their assembly lines.

Visual effects for *The Great Wall* were managed at Industrial Light and Magic (ILM)'s facility in Singapore, the first time ILM had based a feature film at its Asian branch. The most prestigious effects house in the world, ILM usually uses its San Francisco base as the hub of production, farming out particular sequences to its other studio locations and managing other contributing effects houses.[55] About half of the film's visual effects shots were completed by Beijing-based Base FX, founded by Christopher Bremble in 2006. Initially working on outsourced material for Hollywood films and TV (they won awards for prestigious TV shows *The Pacific* and *Boardwalk Empire*),[56] Base soon began to corner a market for visual effects in China, thanks to lower labour costs and the ready availability of trained digital artists. They specialised in science fiction films but ended up working on domestic Chinese films such as Zhang Yimou's *Flowers of War* (*Jinling shisanchai*, 2011), since there was a growing demand for visual effects for Chinese productions. In a familiar refrain, Bremble promised in 2012 to bring to China 'the Hollywood way, a collaborative pipeline that helps to circulate brilliant ideas'.[57] At the 2013 Beijing Film Festival, where Lucasfilm's Kathleen Kennedy was a keynote speaker, Base signed a pact with ILM (for whom they were already a subcontractor) to work exclusively with them on their Hollywood films.[58]

ILM oversaw the creation of the film's primary assets: digital models of the armies, creatures, mountains, buildings and the Wall itself. Once these assets were built at ILM, they could be shared with all the different effects houses and ingested by their workflows.[59] The production team used photogrammetry (collecting photographic reference material from real-world locations that can then be mapped on to digital models, affording them photorealistic textures and surfaces) of Chinese architecture, basing its version of Song era Bianliang on Beijing's Forbidden City and compiling a bible of images that could be accessed by animators working on the film from anywhere in the world. It seems relevant to Zhang Yimou's fascination with period detail that *The Great Wall* figuratively dragged and dropped digital images of present-day architectural artefacts to stand in for ancient locations.

Julie Turnock has argued that ILM's predominance in the visual effects business makes it seem as if their visual style, modelled on a cinematographic style inherited from the highly situated cameras of American New Hollywood cinema but promoted as photorealism, is the natural state of the industry, the template for all forms of visual effects.[60] ILM's involvement in a supervisory capacity inscribes *The Great Wall* with that signature aesthetic, and differentiates it from other Chinese fantasy films. The film's action and demonology stand in sharp contrast to the spectacles of *League of Gods*, for example, which is filled with transmogrifying beings that defy gravity and physics. It is a fantasy film without any supernatural events (once we accept the possibility of the Taotie themselves), opting for a more stately aesthetic derived from historical and physical realism, albeit a highly stylised and exaggerated realism. Every instance of flight in *The Great Wall* is explained with mechanical engineering: the swooping dives that the spear-wielding, bungee-jumping team of warriors take from the battlements, and the giant sky lanterns that carry the army to the imperial palace for the film's finale. The film's monsters similarly blend mythic concepts with physical, biological traits. Extensive and expensive visual effects suffuse the film's vision of a monstrous horde threatening a mythicised version of Song era China, supplemented by colourful and ornate sets, props and costumes to depict the serried ranks of the Nameless Order, who make for an arresting chromatic spectacle when the vibrant soldiery clash with their jade-coloured Taotie opponents, pitting one massed, hierarchical population against another. Visual effects supervisor Samir Hoon noted that Zhang Yimou wanted the film's colours to 'pop': that is, to stand out to a point that 'straddled a fine line between reality, and hyper-real, fantasy looking stuff', another way in which visual effects might point to the layered, composite nature of the image by accenting certain elements rather than blending them into the diegetic space.[61]

The designs for the film's computer-generated Taotie drew on a range of sources. The creatures are described in the *Shan hai jing* (*The Classic of Mountains and Seas*), a sort of mythical geography of China dating back as far as the fourth century BCE, as having the body of a goat, tigers' teeth, a human face, but eyes in their armpits.[62] The Taotie are derived from a motif found on ritual bronze vessels from ancient China (showing only the creature's head, since they are greedy enough to eat their own bodies), which can be seen on their heads when they lurch into close-up, rebranding the CGI horde with a traditional Chinese appearance incorporated in their design (Fig. 3.3).

Even more than the Wall itself, the Taotie are the film's 'digital effects emblem', defined by Kristen Whissel as a visual effect that 'gives stunning (and sometimes) allegorical expression to a film's key themes, anxieties, and conceptual obsessions – *even as it provokes feelings of astonishment and wonder*'.[63] Whissel's concept of the

Figure 3.3 Traditional Chinese designs incorporated into the anatomy of the Taotie. Source: *The Great Wall* (2016).

emblem asks us to consider visual effects as key semiotic actors in the film's diegesis (that is, they are designed to embody something significant to our interpretation of the ideas and concepts behind the movie): these are attractions that do not halt or distract from the narrative, but instead crystallise its meaning(s) in intensively visual terms. It also offers taxonomic models for identifying effects that turn into what Bob Rehak calls 'micro-genres', whereby particular visual effects or applications of effects are repeated across a range of films and 'ownership of a kind can still be established at the level of stylistic signature and a form of brand consciousness'.[64] Micro-genres are formed often because they articulate a 'conceptual obsession' that is widely recognised.[65] The Taotie rushing towards the Great Wall as a ravenous mass of toothed mouths is an example of what Whissel terms the 'digital multitude', a recurrent image used to 'emblematize [films'] protagonists' relationships to sudden, often apocalyptic change' (Fig. 3.4).[66]

Just as Jason McGrath analysed the connotations of co-ordinating human movement in Zhang Yimou's live and filmed work, Whissel suggests that the digital multitude is a visual exploration of 'the relationship between the individual and the collective',[67] and in *The Great Wall* the connotative burden of the Taotie is made plain during Strategist Wang's (Andy Lau) explanation of their origins. He describes how the Taotie came from a meteorite that broke open the Jade Mountain. When the Emperor greedily took the opportunity to mine all of the exposed jade, the creatures were unleashed. They are therefore positioned as a moralistic pestilence, a reminder of the consequences of unchecked avarice, and the Wall itself is reimagined as an armed response to an external threat rather than a divisive signifier of military might and ethnic factionalism. The emblem of the digital multitude serves its own purpose in this film, but it is also put into intertextual

Figure 3.4 A 'digital multitude' of Taotie attacks the Great Wall.
Source: *The Great Wall* (2016).

dialogue with other films bearing iconographic similarities and, in many cases, which use the same MASSIVE software package to generate vast crowds of figures from motion-captured or computer-generated actors: MASSIVE was developed for the *Lord of the Rings* series, and was also licensed for use on *I, Robot* (Alex Proyas, 2004), *John Carter* (Andrew Stanton, 2012) and *Game of Thrones* (2011–19). Even though digital multitudes can be deployed in films with any historical setting, they are united by the way they articulate diegetically an overwhelming threat, and extradiegetically the awesome potential of technology to mediate the relationships between humans and systems of global finance, culture and representation. As the computer-generated creatures charge the Wall's battlements, they are metaphorically attacking the line that separates the profilmic moment from the digital workspace. Visual effects supervisor Samir Hoon has discussed the challenges of 'trying to balance and marry everything, to get them to live in the same world'.[68] So much of the spectacular imagery in the film relies upon the diligent work of compositors, match-movers, rotoscopers, painters and animators, who might be working in different countries and time zones, to remove the graphic traces of compositing and give the impression of a unified diegetic space. The visible ostentation of all the resources we can see deployed in the image is matched by the need to occlude all of the labour relations that made it possible.

In the tradition of the contemporary Hollywood blockbuster, *The Great Wall* is politically non-committal, diplomatically gesturing towards intercultural solidarity and critiquing the excesses of imperial rule only in passing: the Taotie could signify any kind of rapacity (imperial power, consumerism and so on), and their image is one of terrifying uniformity that can be met only with an equal and opposite degree of stoic unity. The Great Wall itself is a dividing line between states, a symbol of stasis and control, an immoveable barrier against the headlong rush of the Taotie. This is the classic visual rhetoric of disaster movies: a terrible force of nature assails a mighty man-made structure. While the human ranks of the Chinese military are differentiated by their colour-coded armour, the Taotie are a sickly grey–green swarm, a frenzied tsunami of flesh. Whissel sees this 'hypergenerative' aspect in many digital multitudes: we never see them breed, but their numbers always return replenished as easily as pixels on a screen. She also notes the 'deadly vitality' of digital creatures, which are loaded with a surplus of the characteristics of organic life in an effort to 'overcome the ontological differences' between these synthetic beasts and the human actors with whom they share the screen.[69] The Taotie are, for instance, given the evolutionary advantages of several different species: the size, speed and strength of rhinos, spliced with the hive-minded intelligence and swarming instincts of insects.

The Nameless Order are, in turn, aestheticised not as a mass, but as a beautifully symmetrical array of different parts working together to beat back the Taotie horde. The Taotie's mindless conformity in the service of their queen is therefore differentiated from the collaborative conformity of the Wall's guardians, who submit to their duties in service of the Emperor because it is a noble purpose, not their inbred instinct. Although there are shots in the film when human armies are supplemented with digital extras, the Nameless Order are coded in backstage disclosures such as the promotional featurettes discussed earlier, as human performers in order to set up an ontological clash between analogue and digital, human and alien. This differentiation is crucial to the function of the digital multitude as a way to distinguish between the superorganism of the Taotie, and the individual characters who have dutifully chosen to take their place inside a regimented, self-abnegating order. This is obviously germane to debates around the role of the individual in any society, but particularly so in China, where citizens must find their places without dissent under an authoritarian regime. William's conversion from the classical trope of a reluctant hero to acceptance of his calling to fight – as he says, 'for something worth fighting for' – comes from his encounters with the noble and selfless Chinese army, particularly Lin Mei: their mutual respect is played out like a chaste romantic attraction, corralling the Classical Hollywood romantic paradigm towards a propagandist purpose. It is hard to resist interpreting this as an allegory of co-production, one that ends with Lin Mei staying in China while William rides off into the sunset like the classical hero in a Hollywood western, each of them having expanded their horizons and vanquished the enemy, but nevertheless returning to their original roles.[70] Reportedly, however, the 'Hollywood ending' of the early version of the screenplay was to have seen William stay behind to marry Lin Mei, until Zhang Yimou insisted that it be changed.[71] Without this formulaic conclusion, the film reads less like a 'white saviour' narrative than one in which a foreigner slips into China to steal its knowledge and resources, and ends up joining forces with the Chinese military to solve a shared problem and learn lessons in personal integrity, trust and courage. He then goes home, morally (if not materially) enriched by his co-operative encounter with the Chinese empire. The film's metanarrative of international co-production has operated on three key levels: *industrial* (the film is produced across nations and production contexts), *diegetic* (the film dramatises a crisis that can be solved only by shared knowledge and action by people of different nations) and *aesthetic* (the film incorporates visual motifs and effects derived from the artistic conventions of different cultures). We can find in *The Great Wall* an unusually tight enmeshing of diegetic narrative and cultural–industrial context, where visual spectacle serves as a shop window for the corporate structures behind it and the national interests inspiring it, even as they complete their own tasks of compositing elements of disparately sourced imagery into a cohesive act of narration.

Conclusion: The Business of Spectacle

The Great Wall fared poorly at the box office, incurring huge losses for its producers, and shaking the confidence of other potential investors in US–Chinese co-productions.[72] Government officials, perhaps unnerved by the slowing growth in China's domestic box office, blamed the film's financial failure on negative reviews that threatened the future of the Chinese film industry, pushing review aggregators Douban and Maoyan to remove the lower scores of some professional critics from their sites.[73] If *The Great Wall* was not intended as a franchise film, it was surely a testing ground for the workflows and visual style of future co-produced franchises. Building franchises takes the combined work of many companies many years to achieve. The Disney-owned Marvel Cinematic Universe (MCU), for instance, has been constructed into a matchstick cathedral of intersecting narratives that flatter attentive, loyal fandom and commit viewers to a continuous story world. One of the common threads of that franchise is the visual effects work provided predominantly by ILM, who provide the 'house style' that gives the MCU a branded visual template. The MCU is not easily imitable, but what can be emulated is the aesthetic of ILM, which has spent more than four decades building its brand, honing its expertise and training new artists and technicians. Visual effects are thus treated as metonyms of the film business, marshalling in their spectacular compositions the imagery of unity, stitching together disparately produced elements into a seamless whole (or at least working towards that goal) and serving as a showroom for their makers' 'industrial prolixity', to paraphrase Rehak.

The Oriental Movie Metropolis was officially opened on 28 April 2018, its leisure facilities (mall, theme park, water-slide park) emblazoned with images of Charlie Chaplin, Marilyn Monroe, Bruce Lee and Ingrid Bergman. At the Spring Festival in February 2019, when Chinese blockbusters compete for a share of the holiday audience, two films, *The Wandering Earth* (*Liulang diqiu*, Frant Gwo) and *Crazy Alien* (*Fengkuang de waixingren*, Ning Hao), both of which were shot predominantly at Qingdao, topped the box office. This raised the profile of the Movie Metropolis, but it has so far hosted only domestic productions. Amid rising debts and investigations into Wang Jianlin's finances, Wanda sold its interest in the studios it had built, retaining only a management role.[74] One of its most prominent productions, *Godzilla: King of the Monsters* (Michael Dougherty, 2019), produced by Wanda's own acquisition, Legendary Pictures, relocated shooting from Qingdao to Atlanta, Georgia, to reduce costs, undermining their own efforts to attract foreign productions to use the Chinese facilities. The facilities at Qingdao are relatively expensive for domestic productions, which can shoot more cheaply at an established lot such as Hengdian World Studios in Zhejiang Province. The promised international film festival appeared as the SCO Film Festival, an offshoot of the political conference of the Shanghai Co-operation Organisation (hosted for the first time in Qingdao in June 2018), screening films from the participating countries. The SCO indicated Qingdao's serious intent as a newly promoted Tier 1 city, but also its obeisance to Beijing.

The Great Wall might be a prototype for a kind of international co-production that bows respectfully to China, its traditional culture and its vast market of air-conditioned IMAX theatres. But it might just as easily be a warning against the mass production of delocalised event movies whose rough edges have been focus-grouped to a smooth, featureless surface that offends no national sentiments but excites little cultural pride or fervour in the process. The infrastructural underpinnings of a film's manufacture are usually 'keyed out' of our viewing experience like so much greenscreen and replaced with a more suitable background. Studio production facilities and visual effects houses represent the material infrastructure of fantasy visualisation, the systems through which national myths may be processed into consumable imagery. Through them we can read the representational discourses of national culture and the aesthetics of entertainment, always inflected by the shifting foundations of state power.

Notes

1. 'Pinewood presents accreditation to Wanda Studios Qingdao' (last accessed 4 October 2018).

2. Wang Jianlin, 'Welcome remarks' (last accessed 7 September 2018).
3. As a result of these efforts, and the city's claim to having the first cinema ever built in China (1907), Qingdao was designated a UNESCO City of Film in November 2017. Mo Hong'e, 'Qingdao set for "city of film"' (last accessed 2 October 2018).
4. Mark Dillon, 'Production slate', 21.
5. When this chapter was nearing completion, Universal cut its ties with Legendary, announcing that following the international success of the *Fast and the Furious* franchise, they no longer needed the help of Legendary to access the Chinese market. Trey Williams, 'Universal no longer needs Legendary's help in China' (last accessed 8 November 2018).
6. Scott Mendelson, 'Box office: *Warcraft* bombs in America, is huge in China' (last accessed 14 January 2018). See also Brent Lang, '*Warcraft* opens to massive $46 million in China' (last accessed 14 January 2018).
7. Patrick Brzeski, 'China box office' (last accessed 14 January 2018). For a quantitative analysis of the press coverage of the film, see Xiaoqun Zhang, 'Business, soft power, and whitewashing'.
8. Yingjin Zhang, *Cinema, Space, and Polylocality in a Globalizing China*, 176.
9. Zhang Yimou, quoted in Chun Chun, 'Ten years of suppressed energy: the creative path of Zhang Yimou', *City Entertainment: Film Biweekly* 394, 19 May 1994, reprinted in Frances Gateward (ed.), *Zhang Yimou: Interviews*, 52.
10. James Mottram, 'Zhang Yimou talks *The Great Wall*' (last accessed 6 September 2018).
11. Between 2012 and 2017, the US share of the Chinese box office decreased from 49 per cent to 32 per cent. Hannah Beech, 'How China is remaking the global film industry' (last accessed 27 February 2019).
12. Xiaoqun Zhang, 'Business, soft power, and whitewashing', 318–19.
13. Aynne Kokas, *Hollywood Made in China*, 23.
14. Xi Jinping, quoted in David Shambaugh, 'China's soft-power push' (last accessed 3 November 2020).
15. Shambaugh, 'China's soft-power push'.
16. Rey Chow, 'Film and cultural identity', 171.
17. Kokas, *Hollywood Made in China*, 24.
18. Yin Yijun, 'Building the industry behind China's unbelievable TV shows' (last accessed 2 November 2020).
19. Quoted in ibid.
20. Kokas, *Hollywood Made in China*, 136.
21. Hye Jean Chung, *Media Heterotopias*. See also Hye Jean Chung, 'Media heterotopia and transnational filmmaking'.
22. Bob Rehak, *More Than Meets the Eye*, 197.
23. Ibid., 198.
24. Kokas, *Hollywood Made in China*, 4.
25. Ibid., 2.
26. Xi Jinping's speech is widely quoted in English translation. See, for example Associated Press, 'China's state broadcaster CCTV rebrands international networks as CGTN in global push' (last accessed 2 March 2019).

27. Shambaugh, 'China's soft-power push'.
28. A. T. McKenna and Kiki Tianqi Yu, 'Internationalising memory'.
29. These were for *Red Sorghum* (1988), *Ju Dou* (1990, co-directed with Yang Fengliang), *The Story of Qiu Ju* (*Qiu Ju da guansi*, 1992), *Hero* (2002), *House of Flying Daggers* (2004), *Curse of the Golden Flower* (2006) and *The Flowers of War* (2011).
30. Sheldon Hsiao-peng Lu, 'National cinema, cultural critique, transnational capital', 110.
31. Joan Dupont, 'Zhang Yimou, keeping cool in the face of censorship' (last accessed 7 September 2018).
32. Zhang Yimou, quoted in Lu, 'National cinema, cultural critique, transnational capital', 110.
33. Radha O'Meara, 'Inventing rituals' (last accessed 5 October 2018).
34. Weta handled much of the visual effects work, and also provided props in the form of thousands of weapons. See the *Great Wall* page at Weta's website, <https://www.wetaworkshop.com/projects/the-great-wall/> (last accessed 10 September 2018).
35. Lu, 'National cinema, cultural critique, transnational capital', 105.
36. Ibid.
37. Chi-ming Yang, *Performing China*, 189.
38. Ibid., 191.
39. Jason McGrath, 'Heroic human pixels'. Ching Siu-tung, director of *A Chinese Ghost Story* (*Qiannü youhun*, 1987) and *The Heroic Trio* (*Dongfang sanxia*, 1993), choreographed action for Zhang Yimou's Hero and for the opening ceremony of the 2008 Olympic Games in Beijing.
40. McGrath, 'Heroic human pixels', 54.
41. Ibid., 66.
42. Ibid., 74.
43. 'Qingdao Wanda Studio - Narrated by Matt Damon', *DalianWandaGroup*, YouTube.com, 1 November 2016, available at <https://youtu.be/hGebewDk-aI> (last accessed 17 October 2018). See also the live demonstration of DJI cameras at the opening of the Movie Metropolis, 7 June 2018, available at <https://youtu.be/_IX3ZnT1FGM> (last accessed 4 February 2019).
44. Lisa Purse, 'Layered encounters'.
45. Ibid., 154.
46. Ibid., 152.
47. Robert Stam and Toby Miller, *Film Theory*, 97.
48. Rehak, *More Than Meets the Eye*, 2.
49. Chiefeditor (pseudonym), 'A foreign film producer's experience in China' (last accessed 11 June 2018).
50. Colman, '"Feng Shen Bang"' (last accessed 2 June 2018).
51. McGrath, 'Heroic human pixels', 73.
52. Melis Behlil, *Hollywood Is Everywhere*, 14.
53. These houses were Azure VFX (India), Dexter Studios (Seoul, South Korea), Fido, Blur (Culver City, California), Gimpville (Oslo, Norway), Mokko Studio (Montreal, Canada), Tippett Studio (USA, founded in 1984 by Phil Tippett, a puppeteer with Industrial Light and Magic; in the same year as *League of Gods*, they were working on

visual effects for *Gods of Egypt* [Alex Proyas, 2016], the closest American counterpart to that film). The motion capture for the final action sequence was produced at House of Moves in California.
54. Graham Edwards, '*Zhong Kui* VFX Q&A' (last accessed 3 November 2020).
55. Dan Sarto, 'ILM Singapore hubs its first feature with Zhang Yimou's *The Great Wall*' (last accessed 8 November 2018).
56. Laurie Burkitt, 'Made in China: visual effects for big-budget movies' (last accessed 27 February 2019).
57. 'Emmy winner taps Chinese film market' (last accessed 14 June 2018). Base FX extended their operations to facilities in Wuxi, Xiamen and a visual effects training centre in DaChang Film and Media Centre. They also set up Base Pictures to produce their own films.
58. Variety Staff, 'ILM teams with China's Base FX' (last accessed 13 June 2018); Clifford Coonan, 'ILM to pact with China's Base FX' (last accessed 13 June 2018).
59. Samir Hoon, quoted in Sarto, 'ILM Singapore hubs its first feature'.
60. Julie Turnock, *Plastic Reality*.
61. Samir Hoon, quoted in Sarto, 'ILM Singapore hubs its first feature'.
62. Zhang Qian, 'The "Four Evils" are still out there' (last accessed 21 February 2019).
63. Kristen Whissel, *Spectacular Digital Effects*, 6. Original emphasis.
64. Rehak, *More Than Meets the Eye*, 174.
65. The alternative viewpoint here is that, rather than paraphrasing a culturally resonant idea, certain effects are repeated because they conveniently match the affordances of the most commonly available software: that is to say, effects may be used because they are readily available and attractively voguish.
66. Whissel, *Spectacular Digital Effects*, 60.
67. Ibid., 60.
68. Samir Hoon, quoted in Sarto, 'ILM Singapore hubs its first feature'.
69. Whissel, *Spectacular Digital Effects*, 92.
70. Sarto, 'ILM Singapore hubs its first feature'.
71. Yiwen Wang, 'An analysis of the cultural elements and international reach of *The Great Wall*', 312.
72. Pamela McClintock and Stephen Galloway, 'Matt Damon's *The Great Wall* to lose $75 million; future US–China productions in doubt' (last accessed 24 March 2018).
73. Clarisse Loughrey, 'China responds to poor performance of its films by censoring bad reviews' (last accessed 24 March 2018).
74. Pei Li and Adam Jourdan, 'China's Hollywood romance sours amid trade war, debt fears' (last accessed 14 July 2018).

Chapter 4
The Blockbuster Breakthrough: The Fantastic in *Hero*

Li Yang

Introduction

Since China started to import Hollywood's contemporary commercial hits at the end of 1994, the crisis-stricken Chinese film industry viewed the production of local blockbusters as a ticket out of financial gloom. Illustrated by imported titles including *The Fugitive* (Andrew Davis, 1993), *True Lies* (James Cameron, 1994) and *Titanic* (James Cameron, 1997), the concept of the 'blockbuster', (*dapian* in Chinese, literally meaning 'big picture') is generally understood as the type of film originating in Hollywood with 'big budget, big production, big marketing and big market'.[1]

Even amidst doubting industry voices, Chinese films that sought to emulate the Hollywood blockbuster model mushroomed. With the necessary adjustment of scale, increasing budgets was the first and relatively easy step forward. While the average budget for a Chinese film in the 1980s was capped at around 2.5 million yuan ($312,500),[2] Zhang Yimou's *Shanghai Triad* (*Yao a yao, yaodao waipoqiao*, 1995) reached 10 million ($1.25 million), Chen Kaige's *Temptress Moon* (*Fengyue*, 1996) 30–40 million ($3.75–5 million), Zhou Xiaowen's *The Emperor's Shadow* (*Qinsong*, 1996) 40 million ($5 million) and Chen Kaige's *The Emperor and the Assassin* (*Jing Ke ci Qinwang*, 1998) 70–80 million ($8.75–10 million). In particular, Xie Jin's *The Opium War* (*Yapian zhanzheng*, 1997) made headlines with its unprecedented budget of over 100 million yuan ($12.5 million). Unfortunately, a higher budget did not automatically translate into audience appeal. Neither *The Opium War* nor the films listed above managed either to recoup their investments at the box office or to become the captivating pop cultural event expected of a movie blockbuster.

Then, Zhang Yimou's *Hero* (*Yingxiong*, 2002) exploded on to the scene. *Hero* raised the financial stakes even higher by assembling an astonishing budget of 250 million yuan ($31.25 million), even though it was still fairly modest compared to Hollywood blockbusters. Although the film's reception was polarising, *Hero* attracted a storm of media attention and became the highest-grossing Chinese film up to that time. More importantly, *Hero* initiated a new chapter for the Chinese film industry as the first successful homegrown blockbuster. Since 2002, the Chinese film industry has reversed its financial decline, entering a period of miraculous growth that has continued to the present day. By 2012, merely a decade later, the Chinese film market had managed to become the second largest in the world, with an astounding average annual growth rate of 33.9 per cent.[3] The endless stream of locally grown blockbusters inspired by *Hero*'s commercial success played a definitive role in resuscitating the ailing Chinese film industry and leading the way for industrial revival and prosperity.

What made *Hero* a historic blockbuster success? Because of the unpredictable cultural consumption patterns and risk-inducing nature of the contemporary filmmaking business, an all-encompassing answer remains elusive. Many elements – textual, industrial and cultural – necessarily interacted during that particular historical moment to make *Hero* successful. The drive to create China's breakthrough blockbuster, however, demands more focused attention: what aesthetic changes are required by the exponentially augmented film budget? In other words, what exactly are the 'big' aesthetics that burn big money and can attract audiences large enough to sustain this financial loop? This chapter focuses on one previously neglected area – the fantastic – and explores how it contributes to *Hero*'s success as a blockbuster. Jenny Kwok Wah Lau has already invoked the concept of the 'blockbuster' in her analysis of *Hero* in an article published in 2007. While generally sceptical of the impact of *Hero*'s blockbuster strategy on Chinese cinema, Lau specifies the budget, as well as the stellar cast and crew, as crucial measures taken by Zhang to achieve the blockbuster outcome;[4] these elements, while absolutely essential, are commonly identified.

By shedding light on the fantastic in *Hero* in conjunction with its blockbuster status, this chapter contributes to the ongoing scholarship on the film and, more significantly, to an understanding of this watershed moment in the development of contemporary Chinese commercial cinema. As an outgrowth of the media frenzy it instigated back in 2002–4, *Hero* has also spawned numerous critical studies. The bulk of previous scholarship emphasises *Hero*'s ideological orientation from the perspectives of nationalism, authoritarianism, transnationalism and empire-building against a new globalising world order.[5] These political readings intersect with another set of scholarship that focuses on the film's status as the first global hit made in China.[6] Indeed, one critical anthology devoted to *Hero* is explicitly entitled *Global Chinese Cinema*.[7] *Hero* needed the international market to recuperate its unprecedented production cost, and its successful globalising aesthetic and marketing strategies deserved every bit of the critical attention they garnered. However, the same level of international success has yet to be duplicated by another Chinese film, not even Zhang's own martial arts follow-ups like *House of Flying Daggers* (*Shimian maifu*, 2004) and *Curse of the Golden Flower* (*Mancheng jindai huangjinjia*, 2006), or the current highest grosser *Wolf Warrior 2* (*Zhanlang 2*, Wu Jing, 2017). *Hero* was not quite the start of a global Chinese cinema that can rival Hollywood's transnational reach; rather, it catalysed the emergence of the local blockbuster cinema – a feat equally significant. In today's burgeoning Chinese film market, initially boosted by *Hero* and other local blockbusters, international popularity is not necessarily a requisite for commercial success, since domestic hits such as *Wolf Warrior 2* and *The Wandering Earth* (*Liulang diqiu*, 2019) have proven their capacity to surpass Hollywood blockbusters in domestic financial performance.

Thus, this chapter operates from a firmly domestic point of view and pays heightened attention to the developing trajectory of the Chinese commercial cinema and market, upon which *Hero* had the most lasting impact. In the pages that follow, an overview of the Hollywood blockbuster model will be presented, followed by an analysis of the Chinese film culture and market in the 1990s, which identifies the fantastic as a possible breakout area for Chinese blockbusters. Then, the fantastical nature of *Hero*'s narrative and visual strategies will be probed to demonstrate why I believe the fantastic, as mobilised by the martial arts film genre, played a crucial role in turning *Hero* into China's first successful blockbuster.

Hollywood Blockbusters and Chinese Commercial Cinema

Originally referring to the World War II bombs used to decimate entire blocks of streets, the term 'blockbuster' entered the lexicon of popular culture directly from insider Hollywood trade talks in the postwar years. Through some inevitable evolution, the term as we understand it today defines the kind of film that is characterised by one or all of the following traits: 'outsized production budgets, elaborate promotional campaigns, and significant box-office results'.[8] As Sheldon Hall chronicles, although similar kinds of expensive event films have historically been made in Hollywood since the start of the twentieth century, it was not until after the mid-1970s that Hollywood began to establish the regular production of blockbusters as its 'principal mode of operation'.[9] In particular, Steven Spielberg's *Jaws* (1975) is identified by many scholars as the prototype that set the precedent for many practices associated with contemporary blockbusters, such as prime-time television advertisement, summer release, wide opening, the use of presold book materials, sequel-spawning franchising, merchandising and the targeting of mainly young male audiences.[10] Since the release of *Jaws*, Hollywood has embraced the regularisation of blockbusters with increasing enthusiasm. Harvard business professor Anita Elberse's book *Blockbusters* begins with a case study of Alan Horn (b. 1943), who took the reins of Warner Bros in 1999.[11] While Elberse finds Horn instrumental in championing the blockbuster business model in Hollywood in the new millennium, Thomas Schatz links this continued reinforcement of Hollywood blockbusters to the forces of conglomeration, globalisation and digitalisation.[12] In particular, the multimedia entertainment giants, to which Hollywood's six major studios are now all subordinated, demand and, at the same time, enable expensive blockbuster films on a global scale. The expense involved renders the pursuit of blockbusters prohibitive for independent American studios and foreign film companies.

It is against the global dominance and monopoly of Hollywood blockbusters that the Chinese film industry has been attempting to succeed commercially since the mid-1990s. At the time, many scholars treated blockbusters as a business and cultural practice exclusive to Hollywood, hence evoking scepticism regarding China's efforts toward emulation. While China was certainly spurred by the influence of Hollywood practices, the production of Chinese blockbusters was motivated more by a desire to survive industrially than to challenge Hollywood's global share directly.

As Anita Elberse emphasises, the blockbuster was, first and foremost, a new business model. Under the socialist film system, every finished work was sold to the China Film Corporation first for a fixed wholesale price, meaning that the lower a movie's cost, the more profit it could generate. The practice of investing heavily in a handful of projects at the expense of other smaller films seems counterintuitive everywhere, and especially so in China, but it worked for Hollywood as well as for other American entertainment businesses. It is a risky strategy by any account, so much so that Elberse frequently uses the word 'bet' to describe the process of blockbuster making. She admits that 'only a mighty studio with significant scale and resources can aggressively pursue a blockbuster strategy', as the bet may end in colossal financial losses.[13]

For China, to make such a bet in the 1990s was arguably even riskier. In addition to the scarcity of capital investment, the weak production capacity of state-owned studios and a rudimentary national advertising apparatus, Chinese audiences largely abandoned film theatres for alternative outlets of entertainment. During the 1990s reforms, which pushed the film industry to transition from a solely ideological tool to a primarily commercial enterprise, productions were generally grouped into three categories: art films, main melody/propaganda films and entertainment/commercial films. Among the three types, main melody films[14] usually boasted the highest budgets and biggest productions, often with direct state subsidies, while art films enjoyed all the laurels lavished by international film festivals. Meanwhile, Chinese film scholar Ni Zhen estimates that, in 1994, entertainment films accounted for about 75 per cent of total output.[15] Although making entertainment-oriented films for profit had already become an unavoidable reality for debt-ridden state-owned film studios, these mostly cheaply made genre films generally lacked production values and cultural prestige and, thus, were disparaged by both authorities and audiences.[16]

How could a high-powered hit like *Hero* emerge out of such a weak commercial film culture? Writing prior to the release of *Hero*, Chris Berry ponders both the metaphysical and the financial challenges of such a quest.[17] Ambivalent towards Chinese emulation of an American practice, Berry cites Xie Jin's *The Opium War* as a cautionary tale.[18] Indeed, *The Opium War*, despite its record-setting budget, appeared more like a big production main melody film than a Hollywood entertainment juggernaut. Even after the success of *Hero*, Jenny Kwok Wah Lau rejects the blockbuster model to which *Hero* conformed. She states, 'At a time when globalization seems to drive global uniformity, what Chinese cinema needs is not world domination but ways to protect its diverse local expressivity.'[19] Both Berry and Lau pit Hollywood against China, drawing on the dichotomy of global commercial Hollywood versus local artistic cinema. What *Hero* achieved was breaking down this very dichotomy that perpetuates Hollywood's financial dominance in the real world. The actual dynamics were far more complex. Chinese cinema could not sustain its 'local expressivity' amidst continued financial crisis. Neither could it simply replicate Hollywood blockbusters, even if it desperately wanted to. The transplantation of the Hollywood blockbuster model to the Chinese industry required localised aesthetic strategies. All the failed attempts before *Hero* in the second half of the 1990s remain a testament to the difficulty of arriving at such a solution.

Budget, Story and Genre

In the making of any film, three questions need to be answered in preproduction: what is the budget? What is the story? And how or in what genre will the story be told? In terms of budget, it was no accident that *Hero*'s director, Zhang Yimou, could attract 250 million yuan ($31.25 million), the largest investment known to the Chinese film industry at the time, even though there was not a single prior success exceeding even one-fifth of such a budget. In retrospect, only a director of his domestic and international stature could attract the overseas investment necessary to overcome China's paucity of domestic capital. Zhang's film was financed by an international bank, and the budget was supplemented by additional investments from one mainland company (New Picture) and one Hong Kong company (Elite Group Enterprises). The film also gained financing by preselling North America distribution rights to Miramax.[20] Zhang's artistic filmmaking past was viewed by investors as an asset rather than a liability in this significant financial gamble. However, transitioning from making art films to blockbusters, and from managing a modest budget to handling an exorbitant one, was a process fraught with challenges for Zhang's personal career, as well as for Chinese cinema at large. While Zhang's skills as a trained cinematographer with a keen sense of colour and visuals translated smoothly to *Hero*, the rest depended on his artistic temperament and acumen, and maybe a little bit of luck, too.

The story Zhang chose for *Hero* is a familiar one. During the last years of the Warring States period (475–221 BCE), Yan Prince Dan hired Jing Ke to assassinate Ying Zheng, King of Qin, when the state of Qin was on the verge of conquering Yan. In 227 BCE, Jing Ke gained an audience with the King by presenting him with two gifts: a map of the Dukang area of Yan and the head of a fugitive general wanted by Qin. While unfolding the map, Jing Ke drew the dagger concealed at the end of the scroll and tried to attack the King. However, Jing Ke missed, and was subsequently killed by the palace guards.

The original text about the attempted assassination from *Strategies of the Warring States* (*Zhanguo ce*) is a required classical piece in Chinese high-school textbooks. Yet contemporary audiences' familiarity with the story goes well beyond this mandatory curriculum. In the 2,000 years since the recorded incident, the story has been revisited time and again in various forms. Yuri Pines traces many classical poems and essays commenting on this story throughout history, and concludes that many imperial intellectuals were able to 'sympathize with Jing Ke emotionally while negating his deed politically'.[21] In modern times, however, Pines observes a more absolute dichotomy in the assessment of the assassination attempt, which was invariably advanced to serve the commentator's own political agendas.[22] To many, Jing Ke has been glorified as the embodiment of courage and a symbol of resistance to hegemonic power, especially in light of the First Emperor's brutal repression of intellectuals and regional cultures. To others, Jing Ke's action lacked political and moral legitimacy, and his attempt to stop the wheel of history was futile. In recent years, the intellectual interpretation has become noticeably favourable to the First Emperor. Chinese film scholar Dai Jinhua argues that the rise of China as a new global power compels contemporary filmmakers to identify with the achievements of Ying Zheng, the person who unified China for the first time in history and laid the foundation for the Chinese empire and the modern Chinese nation.[23] Just as Pines describes, for contemporary audiences and critics, the story of Jing Ke tends to solicit a judgement call to support either Ying Zheng or Jing Ke. Anyone who chooses to reinterpret this age-old story has to manage this divide.

To a great extent, the story of Jing Ke can be considered 'presold', which for an American blockbuster means that the audience has pre-existing knowledge of the film material, usually through books, television, games or other films, hence effectively mitigating the financial risk of introducing original, untested material. It is thus understandable for Chinese directors to turn to this very historical period for their blockbuster tryouts, as if by prior agreement. Not long before Zhang, Zhou Xiaowen and Chen Kaige told similar stories in *The Emperor's Shadow* (1996) and *The Emperor and the Assassin* (1998; hereafter *Emperor*), respectively. Chen Kaige's *Emperor*, in particular, used exactly the same source material as *Hero*, and Chen had similar career trajectories and comparable status in the field to Zhang Yimou. However, *Emperor* is a daunting epic, running over two and a half hours. Despite added battle scenes to flaunt the bigger budget and some melodramatic plot twists for emotional appeal, *Emperor* remained firmly rooted in the dominant aesthetic traditions of Chinese cinema: the dramatic, the melodramatic and the realistic. Not surprisingly, *Emperor* was anything but a crowd-pleasing blockbuster.

With *Hero*, Zhang Yimou employed a different approach to storytelling by choosing the fantastic martial arts film as the generic vehicle. In Hollywood, as Sheldon Hall observes, the new blockbuster phase initiated by *Jaws* saw a transformation in generic patterns, along with the adoption of the wide release strategy. From the mid-1970s on, Hollywood blockbusters changed from 'historical epics, musicals, Westerns, war films and even comedy', to 'fantasy, science fiction and occasionally horror, but most often action-adventure films', the origins of which can be traced to the less respected generic territory of old Hollywood.[24] By the end of 2018, the ranking of all-time box-office champions in China revealed that the Chinese audiences' palate enjoys this generic development.[25] Action films, fantasies and comedies dominated the Chinese charts with films like *Wolf Warrior 2*, *Avengers: Infinity War* (Anthony Russo and Joe Russo, 2018) and *The Mermaid* (*Meirenyu*, Stephen Chow, 2016). Thus, the core generic ingredients of big-budget blockbuster culture in the current marketplace are indeed fantasy and action. The line between the two is increasingly blurred, as many action films are not entirely realistic and many fantasy films are action-driven. Both elements, however, are expected to be projected on screen in a spectacular fashion. Stephen Prince emphasises the importance of 'fantasy' to the appeal of blockbusters. He believes that the genre of fantasy easily lends itself to the special effect-aided 'novel and wondrous cinematic' sights and sounds that are 'more sensual, vivid, kinesthetic, and sonically enveloping than ever before'.[26]

Indeed, the fantastic is one promising area left open for the emergent Chinese commercial cinema to break through, even just in terms of product differentiation. In the second half of the 1990s, realism dominated Chinese cinema. The main melody films clung to the legacy of socialist realism that screened an idealised version of history, presenting milestones of the communist revolution and life stories of communist leaders as indisputable truth. *The Opium War* premiered in Hong Kong on the eve of its return to Chinese sovereignty and largely operated within the generic bounds of the main melody films. Exemplified by Jia Zhangke's *Xiao Wu* (1997), art films, too, were dominated by realism, albeit of a gripping, raw kind that directly countered the official realism.[27]

In Hollywood, fantasy films can be divided into three kinds: sci-fi, horror and other films with unrealistic premises.[28] Although American fantasy films were not immune to the criticism of intellectual frivolity, the fantastic genres are well established (especially in sci-fi and horror) and the fantastic mode is widespread. In the PRC, amidst the dearth of film fantasy due to atheist communist ideology and the past dominance of socialist realism, the most prominent fantastic element one could find in the 1990s lay within the martial arts film. In this well-established film genre, gravity-defying physical moves performed by larger-than-life heroic individuals perfectly blend action and fantasy, hence always possessing modern blockbuster potential. In many ways, these martial arts warriors are comparable to Hollywood superheroes. The cinematic fantasy is so codified in the genre that it can sail through atheist PRC film censorship, while other genres, such as horror, have a harder time. Better still, the martial arts film is a thoroughly native film genre, beloved by Chinese audiences. The chance of success is far greater than taking on a Hollywood-originated superhero film or science fiction movie. However, like the action adventure films that contemporary Hollywood blockbusters turned to in the mid-1970s, martial arts features are usually relegated to the bottom of the aesthetic hierarchy. Thus, even though there was no shortage of martial arts films produced in both Hong Kong and the PRC in the 1990s, few had been produced according to the high-investment and high-return blockbuster model. What the martial arts film needed was a spectacular makeover, which did not seem necessary or possible until Ang Lee's *Crouching Tiger, Hidden Dragon* (*Wohu canglong*) was released in 2000. Breaking both cultural boundaries and aesthetic hierarchies, *Crouching Tiger, Hidden Dragon* became a world-wide phenomenon and certainly was an inspiration for Chinese filmmakers.

With *Hero*, it was exactly this martial arts film genre that Zhang Yimou adopted and the mode of the fantastic he employed to reinterpret the age-old

Jing Ke story. Market analysis aside, tapping into the fantastic energy embedded in martial arts films presents the chance to create a brand-new audiovisual experience for the broadest possible audience. After all, cinema was born as what Tom Gunning calls an 'attraction', displaying an initial exhibitionist impulse that was distinct from the narrative one which dominated cinema later.[29] Gunning affirms that this exhibitionist legacy of early cinema is carried on by contemporary blockbusters among others, or what he dubs 'spectacle cinema' and 'the Spielberg–Lucas–Coppola cinema of effects'.[30] To a great extent, *Hero* actively engages with this 'exhibitionist' power and creates a sense of technological wonder and magical possibilities by reinventing the Jing Ke–Ying Zheng narrative and curating spectacles through cinematic fantasies.

Fantasy and Narrative in *Hero*

The martial arts style that Zhang Yimou pursues in *Hero* is a fantastic iteration of the brand, like what Ang Lee does with *Crouching Tiger, Hidden Dragon*. In this style, characters can fly and perform other unrealistic movements. Stephen Teo deems this tradition-entrenched school '*wuxia*', to be distinguished from a more realistically styled '*kung fu*', which focuses more on portraying convincing physical combat.[31] However, the fantastic energy unleashed in *Hero* does not just capacitate exaggerated action sequences. Within the narrative, the fantastic serves to build an internal logic and mythicise the characters and themes into 'high concept', hence alleviating historical truth-based judgement calls between the King of Qin and Jing Ke.

First, the original story underwent a drastic martial arts makeover. The film still retains the core aspect of the original tale: an assassin tries to kill the King of Qin by getting close to him in the court while presenting items to interest him, instead of, say, secretly poisoning him. Thus, the source tale is still instantly recognisable, although the main character is not named Jing Ke but Nameless, and the introductory intertitles defy the definitive historical truth by emphasising the existence of 'multiple legends' about the assassination attempts against the King of Qin.

Adopting the martial arts genre determines that the narrative will be built around individual combat rather than large-scale battle scenes, as Chen Kaige had done in *Emperor*. Thus, instead of following the linear, Jing Ke-centred narrative drive in the original text (that is, will Jing Ke succeed in his mission?), the bulk of the film adopts a circular structure, propelled by an interactive exchange between the assassin and the King. It is in the process of 'telling' – a narrative action – that the assassin eventually changes his mind and proceeds to (non-)action. In other words, the film ascribes the failure of the assassination to the assassin's voluntary disengagement, based on the mutual understanding reached between the assassin and the King on the spot. The process of spiritual consensus-building, instead of the physical assassination act itself, assumes the narrative gravity of the film, which is a sensible transformation given the audience's preknowledge of the final outcome.

Three stories are told by Nameless and the King to explain how the former captured the weapons of Qin's three most wanted assassins: Long Sky, Flying Snow and Broken Sword. In the first story, Nameless lies to the King, saying that he succeeded by stirring up jealousy between Snow and Sword and causing them to kill each other. Dismissing this right away as false, the King offers his own guess: Nameless's killer move ('kill-within-ten-steps') is so skilful that all three assassins volunteered their lives or careers to help him. Since the King's imagination does not resolve the puzzle, Nameless finally reveals the truth in the third story, which contains pieces of the first two stories as well. Snow and Sword are indeed in a strained relationship, not because of Snow's affair with Sky, but over the couple's divergent opinions on killing the King of Qin. Snow vows to avenge her dead family, while Sword insists on entrusting the King to bring lasting peace by military conquest and unification. By telling the truth and seeing the King's palpable spiritual connection to Sword in the palace, Nameless eventually gives up on his plan for revenge and sides with Sword, only faking a stab at the King. The two earlier stories pave the way for the third, which allows the film to return from flashbacks to the narrative's present time: the historically recorded portion of the assassination attempt and the death of the assassin. The motivation driving the action in these three stories progresses from concrete to transcendent: the self-centred romantic passion in the first story gives way to sacrifice for loved ones, and finally elevates to sacrifice for the greater good 'under heaven' (*tianxia*). Coloured by Confucianism, this narrative design excels not in its historical truthfulness, but in its efficient internal logic. As a matter of fact, many aspects of this tenuous narration disregard realism. The King is far too perfect, with his good looks, sharp intellect and martial arts prowess. And a true assassin would never have volunteered the truth (the third story), not to mention that his fatal secret move ('killing-within-ten steps') could not possibly exist, except in a fantastic martial arts world. Unlike Chen Kaige's preoccupation with historical accuracy, in particulars as minute as the 'wolf-like' voice of Ying Zheng, noted in historical records,[32] Zhang lets the martial arts film's generic conventions take precedence and allows the fantastic free play.

Through a martial arts makeover of the narrative, what Zhang Yimou achieved is essentially the phenomenon of world-building. 'World-building' is an important concept in critical discourses on fantasy literature and film. David Hartwell identifies two opposing modes in fantasy literature: 'Lovecraftian' and 'high fantasy'. Lovecraftian fantasy, named after the American horror fiction writer H. P. Lovecraft (1890–1937), features fantastic elements in the modern world, while high fantasy embraces self-contained realities, often in medieval settings. The beloved J. R. R. Tolkien's *The Lord of the Rings* is a classic example of high fantasy.[33] In terms of building a new reality, *Hero* can be compared to *The Lord of the Rings*, although its martial arts film designation naturally leads to an entirely different critical destination that is shaped by both formalist and cultural conventions. The fantastic world-building of *Hero* manifests not only in its invented interlocking narrative structure but also in its distilled and aestheticised screen space. The film features only a few sets that primarily serve as the backdrop for physical combat. Gorgeous natural landscapes from all over China are assembled without regard for any geographical explanation. The audiences see one next to the other: the Dunhuang desert of Gansu Province in the northwest, the golden *Populus euphratica* forest of Inner Mongolia in the north, the Jiuzhai Valley of Sichuan Province in the southwest and the limestone karst hills of Guangxi Autonomous Region in the south. In these pristine landscapes, the main characters fight or converse, unaccompanied by the presence of other human figures. In fact, the main characters are featured so prominently that the film is almost entirely bereft of extras. We see extras only as the Qin army, the Qin court officials and palace guards, and the Zhao calligraphy students. In all these instances, they are treated as massive visual spectacles instead of autonomous individuals that can add to the texture of lived history. *Hero* certainly does not contain any of the classic martial arts film mise-en-scène – traditionally filled with extras in settings such as a tavern, an inn or a market – which can be seen in fan favourite *New Dragon Inn* (*Xin longmen kezhan*, Raymond Lee, Siu-Tung Ching and Tsui Hark, 1992) and also *Crouching Tiger, Hidden Dragon*. It is ironic that a film premised on the lasting peace of the people does not feature their meaningful presence at all.

While all martial arts films engage in world-building to varying degrees, *Hero* goes further, entering the new territory of 'myth'. In its common usage, as defined by the *Oxford English Dictionary*, a myth refers to a genre of 'a traditional story, especially one concerning the early history of a people or explaining a natural or social phenomenon, and typically involving supernatural beings or events'. *Hero* labels the story as a 'legend' through intertitles at the very beginning of the film, not only to rationalise its employment of the fantastic but also to aspire to the timelessness of a myth. Seen from a critical lens, the 'mythification' of *Hero* manifests in the film's use of archetypal characters and motifs, which would agree with Hollywood screenwriting manuals inspired by Joseph Campbell's study of 'mythic heroes',[34] and also with Roland Barthes's ideologically charged semiotic system that 'transforms history to nature'.[35] In both of its critical capacities, the concept of 'myth' illuminates the characterisation and themes of *Hero*.

Hero constructs simple characters and offers crystal-clear themes. Here, a comparison with Chen Kaige's *Emperor* is especially apt. To make *Emperor*, Chen stated in a printed interview that his biggest question was, 'Do the ends justify the means?' In other words, did Ying Zheng's brutal killings justify his efforts toward unification that laid the authoritarian foundation for the Chinese empire? Chen's answer is 'no – never'.[36] In his eyes, *Emperor* is a film about 'humanism', which is used to 'negate and attack the phenomenon of hero worship'.[37] Accordingly, Chen's Ying Zheng is an exceedingly complex character, steeped in Shakespearian traditions of tragedy. Tormented by his obligations to unite China and his emotional ties to his family and lover, Ying Zheng transforms from a guileless and ambitious young man to a morbid, ruthless conqueror over the course of the film. While Chen wants to problematise hero worship, Zhang Yimou interestingly names his film precisely: *Hero*. In *Hero*, both male assassins (Nameless and Sword) and the King are celebrated as true heroes based on their shared understanding of '*tianxia*': that is, sacrificing paltry individual concerns for the greater good. This is a clever way to bypass the 'either/or' dichotomy between the assassin and the King, even though one can argue that this 'co-option' of the assassins is equal to an absolute siding with the King. Despite existing in three iterations, all the characters are as one-dimensional as mythical figures lacking in backstory: the determined Nameless, the loyal Moon, the wise Sword and the irrational Snow. All characters exist and interact only to propel the plot forward, eventually to a final reconciliation among the three male heroes, hence underscoring the main themes.

The themes of *Hero* are not in any way ambiguous: self-sacrifice for true friendship and for the greater good. Both themes are familiar to Chinese audiences as a persistent component of Chinese cultural tradition – a tradition easily discerned in the original text about Jing Ke. In the King's second story, both Sky and Snow want to volunteer their own lives to assist Nameless's assassination plan, echoing the self-sacrifice in the original text of General Fan Yuqi, who committed suicide at the request of Jing Ke to help him approach the King of Qin. The film's motif of self-sacrifice is derived from the original text but amplified as the sole focus (as opposed to Jing Ke's bravery against hegemonic power, for example). Through the interlocking three-story narrative structure that proceeds with an increasingly higher purpose and deliberate incorporation of core Chinese traditional values, *Hero*'s message acquires a distinctly mythical dimension. Like all myths, it is subject to ideological criticism. Unsurprisingly, *Hero* elicited some of its strongest condemnations from scholars, who equate Zhang's rationalisation for cosmic peace to an embrace of fascism.[38]

However, for general audiences in the context of a blockbuster, the mythification of the historical tale can be directly linked to Justin Wyatt's 'high concept films', which commonly possess 'the look of the images, the marketing hooks, and the reduced narratives'.[39] *Hero* fully embodies this integrated creative and marketing strategy from Hollywood with its neatly typified characters, conspicuous themes and strong emphasis on images. Whether seen from the critical lens of 'mythification' or 'high concept', *Hero*'s narrative aligns with Hollywood's mass commercial formulas in the postclassical era. Most important, the fantastically mythicised tale, which withdraws from historical details, ultimately facilitates the visual spectacles. Unencumbered by the conventional forward thrust of film plot, the circularly streamlined and fantastic narrative provides sufficient internal rationale and room for the display of its spectacular visuals.

Fantasy and Spectacle in *Hero*

Even to the harshest critics, *Hero*'s achievement in the realm of visual spectacles is undeniable. Through visuality, *Hero* delivers to the audience an ontological rupture, 'a break between what the audience agrees is "reality" and the fantastic phenomena that define the narrative world'.[40] To Zhang Yimou, this visual pursuit probably takes precedence over narrative in *Hero*. Dialogue in *Hero* is minimal and curt in a deliberately simplified manner, distinct from the verbose outbursts of Ying Zheng in *Emperor* and the lengthy political deliberations of the Qing officials over the British military challenges in *The Opium War*. The plot is also uncomplicated, thanks to the audience's preknowledge and the repetitive circular narrative structure. Eclipsing dialogues and plots, the imagery thus takes centre-stage in *Hero*, through aestheticisation, screen multitudes and the manipulation of cinematography. Each is aided by the fantastic premise and contributes to a viewing experience that is beautiful, awe-inspiring and unique.

The strategy of aestheticisation in *Hero* simply refers to the inclusion of screen images that exceed the level of beauty found in a regular martial arts film. The film's extravagant yet deliberate use of colour produces perhaps one of its biggest visual impacts on the audience. The three narrative segments and a flashback sequence are each costumed in a single colour, echoing the narrative theme and emotional tenets of each story. Specifically, the colour red evokes passion and jealousy, blue indicates melancholy and sacrifice, green represents youthfulness and optimism, and white symbolises truth and death. It should be noted that such eye-catching use of colour functions best in an imaginary environment. After all, it opposes realistic conventions for all characters to be

Figure 4.1 Moon fights Snow. Source: *Hero* (2002).

garbed in the same colour in one monochromatic setting. It also helps that the three stories are told from the subjective perspectives of two narrators (Nameless and the King), thus further rationalising the unrealistic colouring by creating distance from objective reality. One of the most memorable scenes of the film shows the two women (Snow and Moon) dressed in red, fighting amidst a backdrop of swirling golden leaves. Stunningly accented by the two women's lithe movements, the scene's intense crimson juxtaposed against bright gold offers as dazzling a spectacle as any cinema can (Fig. 4.1).

The featured landscape also helps to augment the visual impact of the film. As described in the previous section, the world-building of the narrative features immaculate landscapes that are undisturbed by other human beings or history, as with various fairylands. Be it the expansive vista of yellow dunes or the serene crystal-clear blue lake, the landscape on screen is breathtaking to behold. Correspondingly, the fight sequences, staged against such gorgeous natural backgrounds, are also highly aestheticised. While effectively utilising many martial arts film conventions to modify the ancient tale, *Hero* simultaneously deconstructs the notion of physical combat and violence as the ultimate means to achieve goals in the martial arts world. This displacement of convention aligns with the highlighted creed of swordsmanship that the King has grasped from Sword's calligraphy: 'not killing' and 'peace'. The King's explanation of three kinds of swordsmanship (instrument of killing, air of killing and not killing) may have been inspired by Zhuangzi's three kinds of swords (swords of the emperor, officials and civilians) in 'Delight in the Sword-Fight'.[41] Although the two schemes are not exactly the same, Zhang's reach for the Daoist doctrine of 'inaction' (*wuwei*) in *Hero* is apparent. In addition, Zhuangzi's passage contains the exact idea of 'killing-within-ten-steps', another piece of evidence of its influence on

Hero. Guided by this Daoist spirit, the fighting sequences in *Hero* are never truly violent. The gruesome finale of *New Dragon Inn*, in which the villain has his leg pared to the bone by a butcher, has no place in *Hero*. Throughout *Hero*, the martial arts are philosophically extolled as a psychological endeavour or an emotional expression, consistently compared to such cultured activities as music, chess and calligraphy. In the actual execution, the martial arts sequences are practically de-physicalised, while the usual emphasis of the bodily movements, impact, grit and kinetic energy are replaced by grace, beauty, culture and fantastic possibility.

The fight between Nameless and Sword in the second (blue) story, conceived entirely in the King's imagination, fully demonstrates this aestheticisation strategy. Like the fight between Snow and Moon in the golden forest, this scene appears after the narrative arc of its embedded story (Snow killing Sword in the red story, and Snow killed by Nameless in the blue story), which fulfils little narrative function but somehow becomes one of the film's signature scenes because of its aesthetic exhibitionism. This three-minute-long scene occurs in the characters' minds (*yinian*), to commemorate Sword's dead wife, Snow. The dialectic opposition between physical actions and metaphysical ideas is reconciled by the fantastic in this fight sequence. With an otherworldly lightness, the two sword-wielding warriors glide over the blue lake, their feet only occasionally skimming through the water or their swords lightly dipping into the lake for support. In one stunning long shot, framed by orange foliage in the foreground against the emerald lake, one small human figure chases the other, both skipping on the water's surface in slow motion. While superimposed with Nameless's contemplative visage to emphasise the imaginative nature of the sequence, the scene cuts to an extreme long shot, again featuring striking natural vistas (Fig. 4.2). The

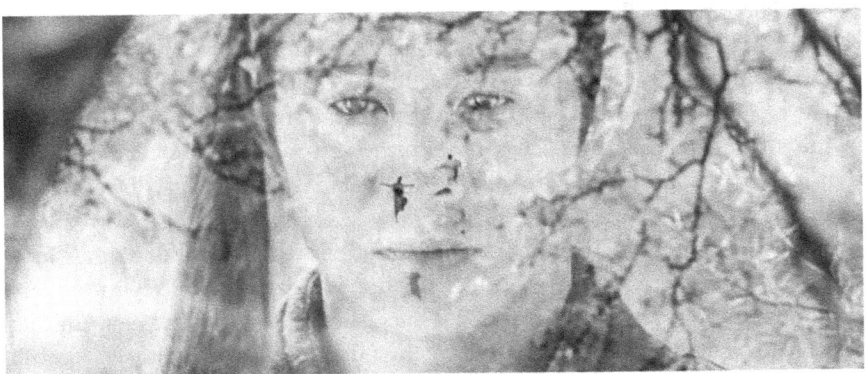

Figure 4.2 Nameless. Source: *Hero* (2002).

frame is filled in equal parts by the crystal-clear lake and by the looming green mountains, which are wreathed in low-hanging clouds of white lace. On the surface of the lake, two tiny figures execute consecutive barrel roll turns along an invisible circle, rippling the water under their feet. Instead of confrontational combat, the two swordsmen seem to partner up for a performance. Elsewhere in this fight scene, the two of them twirl in the air and dive straight toward the water in synchronicity, with a grace that could be taken for a dance. Perfectly illustrating the aestheticised visual strategy with its use of colour, landscape and dance-like choreography, this gravity-defying sequence sparks screen magic.

Second, *Hero*'s visual extravaganza not only presents beauty but also inspires awe. *Hero* astonishes the audience through its visualisation of multitudes. The multitudes are specifically used to render the Qin army, their arrows and Qin court officials as representative of Qin's superior military and political power. A comparison with earlier Chinese blockbuster attempts will again facilitate the appreciation of this unique visualisation strategy and its impact. The most spectacular scenes in both *The Opium War* and *Emperor* are battle scenes: the 1840 navy action between the British and the Chinese in the former, and the military conquest of Zhao by Qin in the latter, ostensibly the same warfare portrayed in *Hero*. Both *The Opium War* and *Emperor* follow the same spectacle-building approach established by many earlier military-themed main melody films: employing plenty of explosives and extras while staging the wars in a largely realistic way. *Hero* does not resort to this kind of conventional depiction of warfare at all. The film instead chooses to portray the arrow attack as an alternative, presenting an entirely different spectacle. Again, this synecdoche of warfare is predicated on the fantastic premise of the story, the deconstruction of violent physicality by the Daoist philosophy, and the overall pursuit of visual beauty.

It is thus highly relevant to examine the scene of the archery attack more closely. Forgoing the chaos that characterises conventional portrayals of war, this battle scene begins with the progression of the Qin army, cavalry and archery towards Zhao and the viewers, all dressed in black in perfect geometric formation. No dialogue is featured in the prewar preparation sequence but there is frequent cutting and repetition to emphasise the vast number of Qin soldiers and their fearsome uniformity. Progressing from initial positioning, lowering the bows, drawing the arrows, waiting and finally releasing the arrows, each step is shown with slightly different angles and depths, between five to nine times. That means that the audience sees the soldiers' actions repeatedly. This repetition mirrors and reinforces the multitudes of the imaginary displayed on screen. The idea of multitudes is then fully carried out by the numerous arrows released towards the defence tower of Zhao. Through CGI, the innumerable streaking black arrows almost resemble a dark cloud or a flock of attacking birds, acquiring a menacing

Figure 4.3 Nameless and Snow amidst arrows. Source: *Hero* (2002).

character of their own. Even more mesmerising is the sight of Nameless and Snow blocking the onslaught of arrows with their martial arts movements alone, a hyperbolic exaggeration enabled by the fantastic conventions of martial arts film. The scene ends with a still frontal shot of endless ranks of Qin solders occupying four-fifths of the screen, followed by a tracking shot from the arrow-covered Zhao tower wall to Nameless and Snow posing amidst an excessive number of arrows (Fig. 4.3). Although the direct damage caused by the arrows is downplayed, the presence of the arrows in large quantities alone demonstrates the military might of the Qin army rather emphatically and poetically.

Other examples of similar multitude spectacles can be observed in the shots involving the Qin palace. The film's opening sequence features Nameless walking into the palace to meet the King. A medium tracking shot follows Nameless heading toward the entrance in slow motion, flanked by two rows of court officials, all bowing their heads in deference. The symmetrically staged, ceremonious scene becomes even more formidable with a cut to a high-angle extreme long shot, revealing several hundred more rows of people behind the two front rows of court officials, occupying the entire open space, save for the main avenue in the middle. Again, generated by CGI, the total number of people presented here exceeds a reasonable bound, overwhelming the senses. The visual impact is even greater when the multitudes are contrasted with Nameless's lone figure. Towards the end of the film, Nameless is surrounded by the overwhelming mass of court guards when he walks out of the palace after aborting his assassination mission. The crowd moves in tandem with Nameless, gathering increasingly tighter but never physically touching him out of fear. Although this scene lacks any significant action or beautiful landscapes, the sharp visual contrast alone makes it one of the most striking images of the film.

Last, some deliberate decisions concerning cinematography also contribute to the audiences' unique viewing experiences. Though distinct from the previously examined systematic strategies like aestheticising and duplicating screen imageries, these smaller-scale visual manipulations add captivating sparks to long sequences, including the lake fight and the archery attack scene. Two main applications are examined here: the unique point-of-view (POV) shots and the control of film speed. The techniques themselves are nothing new, but they work effectively with all other elements in the film to curate an emphatic accumulative impact.

The unique POV shots provide the audience with unexpected perspectives. For example, in the lake fight sequence featuring Nameless and Sword, two underwater POV shots exemplify this impact. The audience is often situated at a distance to observe the two fighters in their chase across the lake and, hence, kinetically across the screen; sometimes, the audience is brought closer to a medium-shot range to be able to follow the characters' swords in action. Inserted between these two conventional viewpoints are two memorable shots from underneath the surface of the water, in which the audience is positioned in the water and looking upward. Through the crystal-clear water, the audience first sees how the two fighters lightly skip on the water's surface, and then how they dip their swords vertically into the lake to gain support. Accompanied by the noticeable sound effect of water splashing, the viewing experience is exceptional (Fig. 4.4). Another outstanding example is an unlikely POV shot of a single arrow in the scene of the archery attack. After a low-angle shot reveals the release of numerous arrows into the sky, the camera and viewers are then made airborne, closely following the trajectory of several flying arrows and accompanied by the exaggerated sound generated by their flight through the gusty wind. As the arrows

Figure 4.4 Underwater shot of Sword. Source: *Hero* (2002).

near the target area, the camera then identifies primarily with just one arrow. Along with this single arrow, the viewers (or their vision) fly above the city tower, through its walls and into the classroom of the calligraphy school, finally ending up inside a sandbox. The blunt impact of the landing sets the film screen shaking and it even goes partially black, enhancing the perception that the viewers have truly become this single arrow. The film may have drawn inspiration from *The Matrix* (The Wachowskis, 1999), which features some similar POV shots of bullets in motion, but *Hero* represents one of the first instances of a martial arts film incorporating such an unusual sci-fi perspective. Thanks to *Hero*'s fantastic milieu, this sequence integrates well with other shots in the archery attack, without calling too much attention to itself.

Slow motion is used extensively throughout the film. In various instances, slow motion conveys the high speed of an action or the briefness of the passage of time by paradoxically prolonging the corresponding occurrence on screen. With the potential to disrupt the flow of onscreen action, the hyperbolic and flamboyant tendencies of slow-motion shots are enabled by, and at the same time reinforce, the Daoist performative reinterpretation of martial arts in *Hero*. One notable example occurs in the duel between Sky and Nameless in the chess club, the first major fight scene of the film. The two men have been engaging in a fight purely within the realm of their own minds, before the breaking of the music accompaniment alerts them to reality: whoever acts first wins the battle. In that pivotal moment, in which Nameless deploys his lethally fast attack of 'killing-within-ten-steps', time is slowed down to the degree that the raindrops and the water from the turning tassel of Sky's spear are all suspended in the air and form a pattern. Then, Nameless's head and sword slowly arc through the raindrops and finally reach Sky. The *Matrix* influence can again be detected in this scene, with similar visual grandeur and emotional fulfilment. Shifting attention from physical action to the environmental element of rain, it is something rarely seen before in other martial arts films. Conversely, in certain instances, time is also sped up. The film's opening landscape shot features rapidly moving shadows of clouds, cast on to a vast vista of the blue mountain and a white plateau. A similar technique is utilised again when Nameless rides his horse to the state of Zhao. Nameless's slow-motion riding is layered against the speeded-up shadows of the clouds to produce an awe-inspiring visual. This simple manipulation of time creates an intensely stunning spectacle, breathing life into the landscape and inviting the audience to view the setting in a new light.

To end the discussion of the fantastic visual spectacle in *Hero*, the concept of 'the machinic eye' is pertinent. Inspired by Tom Gunning's 'cinema of attractions', Eric Jenkins distinguishes the audiences' initial 'astonishment' over the projection of life-like screen images from their 'amazement' over the fantastic propensity of cinema.⁴² Summarising the theorists of the early twentieth century, like Heinz Ewers, Adolph Slaby and Hugo Münsterberg, Jenkins defines the fantastical spark of cinema in relation to the new 'vision' created by camera – that is, 'of seeing with human eyes what only cameras can reveal'.⁴³ This vision manifests through the camera's ability to manipulate screen space and time, such as 'slowing movement down, stopping it or speeding it up, as well as moving closer to or through space in ways not possible with the human eye'.⁴⁴ These descriptions perfectly summarise *Hero*'s new visual strategies as described above and further reveal the depth of the connection between the fantastic and the blockbuster visual spectacles created by *Hero*. Whether utilising aestheticisation through colour and landscape, the presentation of excessive multitudes through CGI, or the manipulation of camera angles and film time, *Hero*'s cinematic techniques all give rise to marvellous and wondrous new visuals that enchant Chinese audiences.

Conclusion

Tom Gunning and Eric Jenkins remind us of the importance of the non-narrative amazement inherent in early cinema and contained by modern Hollywood blockbusters. In many ways, creating a Chinese blockbuster at the turn of the twenty-first century was also a brand-new beginning for Chinese cinema and Chinese audiences. It is fitting that *Hero*, as a ground-breaking Chinese blockbuster, consciously channels the fantastic and taps into the core attractions of cinema through its mythicised narrative and spectacular visuals. The film creates a fantastic 'ontological rupture' for its audiences, which defines as much the non-realistic cinematic experiences inside the theatre as a reconsideration of the power of cinema against other entertainment outlets outside the theatre. With *Hero*'s introduction of the fantastic new possibilities of the screen, the film's audiences were both charmed and enthralled.

The fact that the blockbuster film model was initiated and perfected by Hollywood does not render the production of a local one any less meaningful or any easier. On the contrary, subverting the Hollywood blockbuster monopoly remains a significant undertaking. Instead of imitating Hollywood in a more ostensible way, *Hero*'s breakthrough success mainly stems from the creative use of a native fantastic film genre that attracts the audience with its spectacles, and effective narratives and themes. Therefore, what *Hero* problematises is the tension between art and commerce, more than that between China and Hollywood. Of course, the Hollywood-dominated power imbalance itself, to a great extent, created the scenario of having a former international auteur pioneering the blockbuster model in China, thus exasperating the potential conflict between art and commerce. This chapter demonstrates how the fantastic helps to bridge these two poles in the creation of a stylistically unique, yet crowd-pleasing local blockbuster, although the fantastic is often taken for granted and critically neglected in martial arts film. In the end, *Hero* is a singular film. It distinguishes itself unequivocally from the existing corpus of martial arts films, as well as from contemporary Hollywood blockbusters. Like a shot in the arm, it was exactly what the Chinese film industry and market needed at the time. The rest is film history.

Acknowledgements

The author would like to thank Georgia Salvatore of Lafayette College for her research assistance.

Notes

1. Chen Xuguang, 'Lun "Chaoji dapian leixing" de zhongguo dianying dapian' (On Chinese mega-blockbusters), 4.
2. Xi Ling, 'Shi xi haishi you? guochan dapianfeng toushi' (Comedy or tragedy? clearly viewing the trend for domestic blockbusters), 4.
3. Yin Hong, 'Zhongguo dianying chanyebeiwanglu 2012' (A memo on the Chinese film industry in 2012), 6.
4. Jenny Kwok Wah Lau, '*Hero*: China's response to Hollywood globalization' (last accessed 3 November 2020).
5. See, for example, Evans Chan, 'Zhang Yimou's *Hero* and the temptations of fascism', and Kenneth Chan, *Remade in Hollywood*, 75–104.
6. See, for example, Yuezhi Zhao, 'Whose *Hero*? the "spirit" and "structure" of a made-in-China global blockbuster'.
7. Gary D. Rawnsley and Ming-Yeh T. Rawnsley, *Global Chinese Cinema*.
8. Charles R. Acland, 'Senses of success and the rise of the blockbuster', 11.
9. Sheldon Hall, 'Tall revenue features', 15.
10. Thomas Schatz, 'New Hollywood', 24.
11. Anita Elberse, *Blockbusters*, 1.
12. Thomas Schatz, 'The studio system and conglomerate Hollywood'.
13. Elberse, *Blockbusters*, 28.
14. The main melody film acquired its name from a film policy slogan of 1987: 'Highlighting the Main Melody and Insisting on Diversity'. It came to refer to films that carry official ideological messages. Compared to socialist propaganda films, main melody films aim to educate through entertainment and also make profits whenever possible.
15. Ni Zhen, *Gaige yu Zhongguo dianying* (Reform and Chinese Film), 17.
16. For a discussion of the three Chinese film types in the 1990s, see Li Yang, *The Formation of Chinese Art Cinema*, 66–9.
17. Chris Berry, '"What's big about the big film?"'
18. Ibid., 223.

19. Lau, 'Hero: China's response to Hollywood globalization'.
20. CCTV Jingji banxiaoshi, 'Yingxiong xiao'ao shichang' (*Hero* triumphs over the market) (last accessed 31 March 2019).
21. Yuri Pines, 'A hero terrorist', 33–4.
22. Ibid., 28.
23. Dai Jinhua, '"Ciqin" bianzouqu' (Variations on the assassination of the King of Qin).
24. Hall, 'Tall revenue features', 23.
25. 'Neidi zongpiaofang paiming' (Mainland China historical highest box office rankings) (last accessed 31 March 2019).
26. Stephen Prince, 'Introduction: world filmmaking and the Hollywood blockbuster', 5.
27. For a discussion of realism in Chinese art cinema, see Jason McGrath, *Postsocialist Modernity*, 129–65, and Yang, *The Formation of Chinese Art Cinema*, 157–89.
28. Katherine A. Fowkes, *The Fantasy Film*, 2.
29. Tom Gunning, 'The cinema of attraction[s]', 66.
30. Ibid., 70.
31. Stephen Teo, *Chinese Martial Arts Cinema*, 2.
32. Chen Kaige, 'Answers questions about *The Emperor and the Assassin*' (last accessed 31 March 2019).
33. David Hartwell, 'Introduction: the return of the fantasy', 2.
34. David Bordwell, *The Way Hollywood Tells It*, 33–4. Joseph Campbell, *The Hero with a Thousand Faces*.
35. Roland Barthes, 'Myth today', 240.
36. Michael Berry, *Speaking in Images*, 99.
37. Ibid., 99.
38. Chan, 'Zhang Yimou's *Hero* and the temptations of fascism'.
39. Justin Wyatt, *High Concept*, 22.
40. Fowkes, *The Fantasy Film*, 5.
41. Zhuangzi, 'Shuo jian – delight in the sword-fight' (last accessed 31 March 2019).
42. Eric S. Jenkins, *Special Affects*, 37–8.
43. Ibid., 37.
44. Ibid., 38.

PART II
GENRES OF SINO-ENCHANTMENT

Chapter 5

The Restrained Fantastic in Hou Hsiao-hsien's *The Assassin*

Andrew Stuckey

This chapter argues that Hou Hsiao-hsien's *The Assassin* (*Cike Nie Yinniang*, 2015), which won the Best Director award at Cannes in 2015, makes two related alterations to the contemporary trend for fantastical filmmaking in Chinese cinema. First, Hou dramatically reduces, but does not eliminate, fantastic elements in his movie. This is seen not only in the minimising of martial arts fight sequences or reliance on computer-generated special effects, but also in Hou's characteristically long takes of natural scenery and domestic spaces. Second, he alters the typical moral stance that traditionally has developed and that aficionados of martial arts films have come to expect from their heroines.

The method I will employ is one of comparing Hou's film to a variety of source material (I use this term quite loosely here), including the literary stories that provide much of the basic plot, as well as the generic conventions that have evolved in martial arts literature and film. These narrative and formal comparisons will account for matters of intertextuality as well as transformation. They will also lead, quite naturally, to the moral questions the film poses.

Before moving to the specific analyses I will present for *The Assassin*, I believe a certain clarification of terminology – and more important, the distinctions in meaning that terminology enables – will be beneficial. Intertextuality, at least since Julia Kristeva introduced the term,[1] and its more recent cousin, intermediality, have been important and useful concepts in cultural and textual studies. The ease with which they indicate the kinds of relationships between and among texts or media is a significant reason for this importance and usefulness. But that same ease also belies the complexities which arise as soon as specific examples are considered, since the methods, qualities, modes or extent (to name merely four possible factors) of any given intertextual relationship vary perhaps to an infinite degree.

This situation makes a precise and definitive taxonomy practically impossible, but at the same time the lack of such a taxonomy can lead to many confusions. The best attempt I have seen at constructing such a framework is surely Gérard Genette's *Palimpsests*. Genette categorises the sorts of relationships I will be concerned with here, with what I called source materials above and which have generally been the focus of intertextuality in scholarship, as instances of hypertextuality:

> any relationship uniting a text B (which I shall call the *hypertext*) to an earlier text A (I shall, of course, call it the *hypotext*) . . . To view things differently, let us posit the general notion of a text in the second degree.[2]

Of course, it is also possible, as in our case here, that there be more than one hypotext, but already we can see the benefit of this terminology. Genette argues that there are two basic procedures for producing the hypertextual relationship: that of transformation and that of imitation. Transformation is a matter of changing the story of the hypotext, whereas imitation reflects the style of the hypotext. Although, for Genette, transformation and imitation are mutually exclusive, we will see here that *The Assassin* employs both procedures in regard to its hypotexts. The distinction in this case (between Genette's claim that these do not mix and my contrary assertion in regard to *The Assassin*) is probably a function of the fact that Genette is concerned with literary hypertextuality (the relationship that obtains between two or more written texts) while *The Assassin* builds relationships with both literary and filmic hypotexts (this is the extra dimension implied by the term *intermediality*). On the one hand, it is in relationship to those literary hypotexts that we will see how *The Assassin*'s hypertextuality is based on transformation. On the other hand, in its hypertextual relationship with other films (here the genre of martial arts as a whole), *The Assassin* is imitative, to a degree.[3]

Here a word on the difference between a hypertextual relationship between specific texts and hypertextual relationships between a class of texts (a genre) may be in order. In the first case, Genette's book explores a huge variety of possibilities, including parody, translation, caricature and forgery. Pastiche is the term Genette uses to describe the imitation of a particular author's style. He has very little to say, however, about the imitation of collective styles, as one might characterise different qualities of a genre. The conventions that have evolved in a particular genre, moreover, such as the depiction of martial arts combat in martial arts film, involve not stylistics, but rather aspects of narrative that are repeated, or invoked, in particular instances of that genre. Thus, we will see that the imitation of such genre conventions involves both their iteration and their simultaneous modification (or transformation, in Genette's terms). Here again, the distinction between these two actions are shown to blur somewhat in practice.

It is precisely in this grey area, however, that Hou Hsiao-hsien applies his touch. He updates (that is, both repeats and alters) the martial arts film's moral value structure, as well as its reliance on the presentation of spectacular feats of martial ability. The examination of the hypertextual relations that *The Assassin* establishes with its various hypotexts allows us to see both the imitation and the transformation that leads to a fundamental revaluation of fantasy filmmaking, which in turn infuses it with moral significance.

Adaptation

Martial arts filmmaking is a practice which has come to be, and perhaps always has been, thoroughly intertextual (hypertextual, in Genette's terminology) and intermedial. Although I am doubtful that any such thing as a 'pure' genre exists,[4] it seems worth remarking how thoroughly mixed the martial arts form actually is, even beyond the inherent hybridity of other genres. Zhang Zhen says the early martial arts films from Shanghai were 'a hypergenre characterized by disorder, chaos, and cross-fertilization' and that it 'served the dual function of both experimental cinema and commercial entertainment in a form that may be called "avant-pop"'.[5] Stephen Teo, likewise noting its motley sources, calls the genre 'schizophrenic. An early association with the historical period-costume film (*guzhuang pian*) evolved into further associations with another genre, *shenguai*.'[6] Teo argues that this inherent adaptability is a major reason behind martial arts' perennial popularity. Weihong Bao, in contrast, emphasises the meshing of 'sentimentality and sensation', the affective range of melodrama mixed with the exhilaration of action sequences that audiences experience, which, she argues, marks the true resonance of martial arts films with Chinese audiences.[7] The inclusion and integration of these various strands into the martial arts genre, which, on first appraisal, may seem to have clear delineations – namely, the depiction of martial arts – instead shows the impurity and hybridity of the form.

More than simply a prolific borrower of contiguous genres, however, martial arts films have also long drawn on other narrative forms. It is no accident that the first 'craze' for martial arts film in China, 1928–32,[8] followed hard on the heels of a 'wave' in popularity of martial arts fiction in the burgeoning commercial press, beginning in 1923 but reaching its peak in 1927–30.[9] Indeed, not a few of the martial arts films were adaptations (of closer or looser formulations) – including the most successful of these films, *Burning of the Red Lotus Temple* (*Huoshao hongliansi*, Zhang Shichuan, 1928) – of precisely these popular novelistic accounts.[10] This trend of adapting popular literary texts into film has continued into the present, including texts written by twentieth-century authors such as Jin Yong and Wang Dulu, as well as premodern classics.[11] *Journey to the West* (*Xiyou ji*, sixteenth century) alone has provided material for countless films, not to mention television or video game adaptations. Of course, not all martial arts films are adaptations from literature (fictional, historical or dramatic); even so, a certain hybridity – repeating again, though on a different level, the hybridity of the genre itself – prevails and original scenarios remain the minority.[12] This may be illustrated for us in the subtle parody (though perhaps, in Genette's terms, burlesque travesty is more accurate) of the clichés of martial arts (both literature and film) in the tavern fight sequence from *Crouching Tiger, Hidden Dragon* (*Wohu canglong*, Ang Lee, 2000), when Yu Jiaolong (for some reason, this name is subtitled as Jen in English, played by Zhang Ziyi) narrates her own prowess and ridicules the ostentatious names of the other fighters as she proceeds to decimate them utterly, seemingly without breaking a sweat.

It will come as no surprise, then, that *The Assassin* is adapted from a classical-language tale (*chuanqi*), 'Nie Yinniang', with significant elements also drawn from another story, 'Hongxian' (Red Thread), both of which date to the late Tang Dynasty.[13] The process by which this story was developed for film has been extensively documented by Xie Haimeng, the niece of Hou's long-time collaborator, Chu T'ien-wen, and, along with Chu and Zhong Acheng, one of the three credited scriptwriters for the film. Later in this chapter, I will have more to say about some of the differences that exist between these Tang tale hypotexts and the finished film. But for now it is worth noting that the method of adaptation seems to have involved a long period of discussing, exploring and fleshing out the original Tang tale, followed by further rounds of elaborating an extensive script that fills in many gaps (especially in terms of motivations for Nie Yinniang's actions).[14] There are significant differences between this final script and the finished film, and so it seems the script was then whittled down to its barest bones – in terms of either simply not filming scenes or leaving them on the editing-room floor – by Hou and his team during production and postproduction. The sequential order of scenes in the finished film also deviates from the script.[15]

Gérard Genette, in *Palimpsests*, has categorised the relationship between a hypertext and hypotext(s) (as in this adaptation of 'Nie Yinniang' into Hou's film) as that of transtext.[16] Genette considers a huge variation of possible transtexts: from parody to translation to sequels, and so on. In his study, however, Genette is solely concerned with the transformations performed in a transtext when both hypotext and hypertext are literary (that is, they take the form of written language).[17] For film adaptations of literature, the complexities multiply since we are also dealing with transformations from one medium to another. Moreover, the method of literary adaptation into film, perhaps, proves unique in each case, as each individual literary text (or combination of texts) remains amenable in different ways to realisation in audiovisual form. Given this variety, systematic theorisations of the processes and effects of film adaptations of literary texts frequently remain limited in applicability to the analytic samples chosen to support those studies.[18] This, of course, is not to malign the insights offered in those studies; rather, it is merely to say that generalising those insights to other cases requires further adaptations of the theory to the specifics of the new sample, and in some instances may not even be possible at all. In certain cases, the wheel may need to be reinvented each time this particular question is considered.

Even so, one nearly inevitable concern for adaptation studies is fidelity. Some scholars argue for the importance of fidelity, while others, of course, contend that the two texts, while related, are nevertheless distinct and cannot be arranged hierarchically.[19] For myself, I am more inclined to the latter view, but in the current circumstances that is neither here nor there. In fact, what close attention to the debate over fidelity in film adaptation reveals is an abiding concern for canonicity. That is to say, certain people will always complain of a lack of fidelity when it is, for example, Shakespeare, Dickens, Forster or Austen whose literary text is being adapted to the screen, but when it comes to a Mickey Spillane novel, well, then critics are more generous in their assessment. The case of Peter Jackson's *The Lord of the Rings* adaptations (2001–3) is quite interesting in this regard, since Tolkien is not typically included in the standard canon as taught by university English departments but nevertheless commands a huge and devoted fan base of readers, who were a principal target audience for the films.[20]

The example of Jackson is not gratuitous in this context, since the underlying fan base for martial arts literature may impose stringent demands on, say, an adaptation from Jin Yong.[21] In the case of *The Assassin*, however, a somewhat different dynamic applies. On the one hand, as a literary text that has survived the vagaries of time and the vicissitudes of manuscript transmission for roughly 1,200 years, and as having been collected into an important anthology a century or so after its composition, 'Nie Yinniang' is automatically canonical. On the other hand, as *xiaoshuo* – small talk, hearsay, fiction – from the beginning 'Nie Yinniang' has always been considered an example of a low form relative to poetry, philosophy and history: in other words, outside the canon. To complicate matters, 'Nie Yinniang' holds a seminal position within the tradition of martial arts literature, among the lowest genres in contemporary Chinese literature, since it is one of the earliest stories to centre on a heroine: a thematic concern that has continued to fascinate and drive martial arts narratives, both literary and cinematic.[22] That is to say, in the largely Confucian social structure of traditional China where women are mostly, but not invariably, confined to the domestic inner quarters of the home, a vigorous and effective female martial artist begs questions of respectability, especially inasmuch as her actions outside the home imply sexual impropriety. At the same time, many of these heroines seek to avenge their fathers, and thus are examples of the highest Confucian virtue, filial piety. It is precisely this moral tension that makes the female martial artist a perennial fixture in the genre and why 'Nie Yinniang', as an early example, holds such an important position in the canon. And, on top of all this, Hou Hsiao-hsien himself is among the most canonical filmmakers in Chinese cinemas, certainly in Taiwanese cinema.

The dynamic interplay and oscillation between lowbrow and highbrow cultural discourses that I have described above marks (once again) the kinds of hybridity and boundary crossing that the martial arts genre habitually enacts.[23] What seems determinative, in this case, is Hou's status as canonical auteur within the Chinese (and indeed global) industry. Peter Lev offers an interesting counterpoint in his discussion of *Vertigo* (Alfred Hitchcock, 1958). In short, Lev argues that Hitchcock's canonical status obscures literary appreciation of the French mystery novel, *D'entre les morts* (1954), by Pierre Boileau and Thomas Narcejac, from which his film is adapted.[24] Again (and no surprise), Hou's case is somewhat different. Hou's sources, 'Nie Yinniang' and 'Hongxian', are already canonical, though perhaps only within the devalued tradition of martial arts literature,[25] so we cannot in good faith say that Hou's reputation has obscured the literary source for his film. At the same time (at least in the reviews I have seen), no one has complained about the alterations Hou has made to Nie's story in his adaptation or accused him of being unfaithful to his source.

Moreover, the jury panel at Cannes that awarded Hou the Best Director award presumably had little, if any, knowledge of the Tang tales on which Hou's film was based.[26] What this reaffirmation of Hou's status as a global auteur filmmaker obscures, then, is not the literary source for his film, but rather the dynamics of the interrelationship between these texts. And a remarkable thing about Hou's film is, despite the fact of the alterations (and indeed clarifications) he makes to Nie Yinniang's narrative, the experience of viewing the film is quite similar to the experience of reading the story. The famous obliqueness of Hou's storytelling style, the terseness of dialogue, the ellipses in character development and the opaque motives that viewers must confront and attempt to decode is, in truth, not unlike reading classical Chinese, which is notoriously difficult and immensely economical (and consequently open to multiple possible interpretations) in its linguistic structures. The difficulty stems from trying to understand Nie and her active choices in a context that works against the easy interpretive conventions that have developed in martial arts narratives, in a way not unlike how the defamiliarised grammar of classical Chinese appears to the unpractised contemporary reader.[27] It is precisely the ways in which Hou's film establishes such resistance to, and upsets, our familiar viewing habits that will be the focus of the rest of this chapter.

Restraint: The Anti-Blockbuster

While in the previous section I focused on the hypertextual relationship between *The Assassin* and the literary hypotexts that provide the basis for narrative character and actions in Hou's film, in this section I will consider a different kind of hypotext, that of the genre of martial arts film itself. The closest term Genette uses to refer to this relationship is pastiche: the imitation of a style, though, for him, this is usually the style of one acclaimed master (Homer, Cervantes, Flaubert). Even so, while Genette's use is much more technically precise, the typical notion of pastiche as cutting-and-pasting – of characteristic or identifying features, even direct quotation – is not far off the mark, for our purposes. A style to be imitated, then, is no less a matter of content, including flourishes of 'grammar and syntax' in so far as they may be representative.[28] When it comes to genres as a whole, Rick Altman suggests we see a function of discursive forces. This view requires a combination of attention to syntactic, semantic and pragmatic factors.[29] In other words, one must consider not only typical narrative elements and their usual arrangement in the genre in question (semantic and syntactic) but also the contexts of their creation and circulation, the purposes they serve and the meanings they generate (pragmatic). Accordingly, while I will also note some changes Hou makes to the original story of 'Nie Yinniang', my focus here will tend more to aspects of the typical kinds of characters, storylines or styles found in martial arts films as a whole, and then discern the shifts Hou has effected on these through the specifics of his film.

In order to see the idiosyncratic alterations Hou makes to our expectations for martial arts film, first we must recognise that, for better or for worse, the Chinese martial arts film is now fully enveloped in the transnational blockbuster form. Stephen Teo has succinctly summed up this state of affairs in the following manner:

> The *wuxia* film is now steeped in the era of the blockbuster production mode.... It attests to the near-total assimilation of the genre by the Chinese mainland film industry such that any *wuxia* film released over the last fourteen years or so would invariably be made in China, either partly

or completely, often as co-productions in partnership with Hong Kong and Taiwan but also Japan and South Korea. Such a production would just as invariably be undertaken as an expensive blockbuster, a term that is translated into Chinese as *dapian* (which literally means 'big film'). A concerted move by the Chinese government to drive film production along the line of Hollywood-style blockbusters has resulted in the rise of the *dapian*.[30]

The blockbuster form, as it is concerned with martial arts, incorporates a number of different strands – further reflecting the fundamental hybridity I discussed in the first section of this chapter – including the period film (*guzhuang pian*), folk religious beliefs in mystical powers deriving from a variety of different sources, and, of course, the long tradition of martial arts filmmaking going back to China's silent period. Thus, as an example, summer 2016 saw the release of *League of Gods* (*Fengshenbang*, Koan Hui), a film adapted from the traditional novel of the same name (c. sixteenth century; the novel's title in English is usually rendered differently, however, as *Investiture of the Gods*). In large degree, we see here a return to the cinematic form's origin as *wuxia shenguai*, or films depicting martial and mystical prowess, including that of supernatural creatures. These characteristics can then also be combined in different proportions with the horror film, the detective film, popular history or science fiction, as some of the other chapters in this collection show. Thus, as one more example, we see Zhang Yimou's film, *The Great Wall* (*Changcheng*, 2016), starring Matt Damon and performed largely in English, which combines the war epic, martial arts and monster film in the blockbuster format in an attempt to appeal to international audiences.

The Assassin shares some of the traits that Teo notes as characteristic of the current phase of the genre's development, but also works against these trends in significant ways. Financing was sourced from China, Taiwan and Hong Kong. Parts of *The Assassin* were filmed in China, but studio space was utilised in Taipei,[31] and location shooting also prominently included Taiwan and Japan. Moreover, the sets and locations can only be described as lavish. Dialogue is in Mandarin, with actors from China and Taiwan. Notably, however, the lead role of Nie Yinniang is played by the Taiwanese actress Shu Qi, while the role of Tian Ji'an is likewise taken by a Taiwanese actor, Chang Chen, and the mirror polisher is performed by the Japanese star Tsumabuki Satoshi. That is, none of the major roles are played by PRC actors. Thus, in terms of financing, location shooting and stars, the film is very much a transnational production. However, in its emphasis on Taiwanese and Japanese stars and locations, the film very much destabilises the significant gravitational pull that Teo has argued China exerts in the transnational blockbuster martial arts film. In James Udden's words, 'this is China from the margins, not from some elusive core'.[32]

The most important deviation that *The Assassin* makes from this transnational trend, however, is avoiding the very notion of the blockbuster in its production values. IMDB estimates that the film's budget was around $15 million. While not insignificant, this is, for sure, a fairly mediocre budget by Hollywood blockbuster standards, and only one-tenth of *The Great Wall*'s budget of $150 million. Still, it seems clear that most of the budget for *The Assassin* went into the sets, costumes, actors' salaries and so on, rather than into special effects, which have been a major engine behind the spectacular rise in fantastical films as well as their ballooning budgets.[33] Special effects, such as they exist in the film, mostly involve quite basic wirework, allowing the protagonist, Nie Yinniang, to leap lightly from rafters or rooftops. The one clearly computer-generated effect in the film is the voodoo homunculus's attack on Tian Ji'an's concubine, Hu Ji (played by Hsieh Hsin-ying), which Nie foils. This computer-generated effect, I think it is fair to say, notably lacks the bells and whistles incumbent on contemporary effects in blockbuster films.

Thus, though clearly not spurning entirely the resources presented for creating visual images by new computer technology, Hou is quite restrained in his employment of these resources. Likewise, instead of revelling in the spectacle of bodies in fight and flight that is, by definition, the *raison d'être* of martial arts film,[34] here too Hou restrains his depiction. James Udden notes that the seven combat sequences in *The Assassin* total a mere five minutes and twenty seconds combined (out of a 105-minute film).[35] In addition, fighting, as often as not, is captured in a long shot, occurring in the distance and obscured by trees or other impediments to our viewing pleasure. Furthermore, the speed of these fights – in terms both of the action itself and of the editing – is noticeably 'lethargic' in comparison to recent martial arts fare.[36] Likewise, the killing blow is left just out of the camera's frame. Indeed, for the most part, Nie does not kill her opponents (the two main exceptions are her first assassination on the orders of her mistress and teacher, which opens the film, as well as the death of the soldiers who have attacked her father and uncle on the road). Instead, typically, she merely defends herself from others' woefully inadequate attempts to attack her. As a result, depictions of blood and gore are minimised. In such situations, as with the limited use of special effects, we do see that Hou allows clear depictions of fighting (though, to be sure, not much flying). Thus, I would suggest that we see, in instances such as these, that the film is not a deconstruction of martial arts genre conventions, but rather an engagement with them that works counter to the recent trend of blockbusterisation.

These moments of the depiction of fighting, whether obscured or in detail, allow us to transition to a consideration of the second intervention that I see Hou making in this film: this time, in terms of the moral character of Nie Yinniang herself. We see in all of these cases that Nie, in her mistress's words, has 'mastered the sword, but [her] heart lacks resolve'.[37] However, her mistress has fundamentally misunderstood Nie; while she certainly has mastered the sword, rather than lacking resolve, like Hou in his visual depiction, she shows restraint again and again over the course of the film.

Here, we should go back and, briefly, look at the development of cultural representations of *xia*, martial artists, over the course of Chinese literature and film. The social role of *xia* developed in China during the Warring States period (c. fifth century BCE to 221 BCE). The primary ethic of *xia*, as is perhaps most easily seen in Sima Qian's 'Biography of Assassins' (Cike liezhuan),[38] is that of righteousness and loyalty (*yi*), which, as Christopher Lupke astutely notes, is based on a notion of reciprocity.[39] A patron recognises the talent of the *xia*, irrespective of the *xia*'s social position, and lavishes gifts, support and, most of all, respect on the *xia*, who then reciprocates by serving his or her patron in ways that are politically useful, including the assassination of rivals, without regard for his or her own safety. The discernment, on the patron's part, of the *xia*'s inherent talent or value is taken in this classical worldview to be *ipso facto* proof of the patron's moral quality and perspicacity. Thus, the *xia* does not question the moral validity of the political cause in which a patron employs his *xia*-retainer.

The Tang Dynasty tale on which Hou's film is roughly based, as Lupke observes, makes an important deviation from this basic ethical stance, in that Nie shifts her loyalty from one patron to another over the course of the story.[40] While it is true that such a move is unusual, my reading of the story suggests that she does so because her second patron displays a deeper understanding of her inherent talent than her first had, and as such she owes the second patron a deeper bond of loyalty. And thus, her switch of allegiance does not, I would argue, imply a moral shortcoming on Nie's part.

Be that as it may, an even more important aspect of the Tang tale is that it is one of the very first instances in Chinese literature to centre on a female *xia* (of course, and as Lupke also reports, the screenwriters also incorporated many elements from another Tang tale, 'Hongxian', which also features a woman *xia*).[41] As a mode of literature, and perhaps even more as a mode of film, the martial arts narrative, as Stephen Teo argues, has been centrally concerned with the sexual and moral quandaries that arise when women act as *xia* in a Confucian patriarchy.[42] Typically, this tension is resolved in one of two ways: celibacy on the one hand, or, on the other hand, the female *xia* splits her life into two distinct periods, one in which she acts as *xia* and one in which she is a wife and mother.

Nie Yinniang, in Hou's version of the story, twists these ethical conventions of the *xia* hero in new and quite interesting ways. First, although the predominant moral quality of *xia* in the classic configuration is, as I have said, *yi* or loyalty to one's patron, in modern martial arts, both literature and film, this moral value has been transferred, according to a certain resonant analogous character of various Confucian virtues, into *xiao* or filial obedience owed to one's master in the martial arts, who has taught the *xia* his or her skill and enabled the martial artist's identity to exist in the first place. Thus, although the Tang tale shows Nie serving two different patrons, this particular storyline is dropped by the filmmakers. Instead, Nie is instructed by her teacher, the Daoist nun (played by Sheu Fang-yi), to assassinate Tian Ji'an, her childhood friend and former betrothed. Thus, the moral quandary that Nie faces is, does she return her mistress's care and training with obedience by carrying out the assassination, or does she use the skills she has developed to protect her family and a man she (possibly) still cares for? And while Nie does obey the nun in the opening two minutes of the film (after the credits) by killing someone on her behalf, she ultimately rejects this obligation and refuses to engage in any further political assassinations. Even so, throughout the film, Nie remains respectful of the nun and appears a dutiful protégée. Even in their brief altercation at the end of the film, she holds back from a killing blow, demonstrating only her martial superiority and the fact that she has transcended her teacher's skill and philosophy, before she proceeds to walk away with a proud and self-sufficient bearing.

Second, Nie engages in a relationship with a man of her own choosing. That is to say, Nie neither submits to parental (patriarchal) control over her marriage prospects and sexuality, nor conforms to the typical demand of female *xia* celibacy. The choice itself is drawn from the Tang tale, though Hou's treatment twists this as well. In the Tang tale on which this film is based, as Lupke also points out, Nie chooses a mirror polisher (played by Tsumabuki Satoshi), seemingly at random, who is distinctly below her social standing, but out of fear for her extraordinary abilities her father raises no objection.[43] In the film, however, the internal and external politics of the Tang Dynasty Commandery Weibo play an increased role. Nie had been betrothed to Weibo's current Commander, Tian Ji'an, when they were children. This betrothal had been broken when Tian's father, the former Commander, wanted to cement an alliance with a neighbouring Commandery. When her mother (played by Mei Yong) discusses this history, Nie weeps inconsolably, but says nothing. Despite this betrayal, Nie refuses her mistress's orders to assassinate Tian and goes even further, saving his favourite concubine, Hu Ji, and her unborn child from a supernatural attack orchestrated by Tian's principal wife, Tian Yuanshi (played by Zhou Yun).

Likewise, Nie remains a dutiful daughter to her parents. Though, as in the Tang tale, they seem to express some apprehension upon Nie's return, in the film they also convey their regret at having allowed the nun to take her away in the first place.[44] Nevertheless, Nie rushes to the aid of her father (played by Ni Dahong) when he and her uncle (Lei Zhenyu) are attacked on the road. It is here, in the film, that she meets the mirror polisher, when he attempts to help her father and uncle fight off the ambushers before she arrives. Although Nie remains stoic and terse throughout the film, and so her motivations are difficult to parse precisely, it seems to me that she develops an affection for the mirror polisher in recognition of his aid in fighting off the attackers. Their relationship then builds on this foundation when he helps treat a wound she sustained in the fight, which, of necessity, involves physical contact between the two. This contact is chaste, to be sure, but intimate touching none the less.

At this point in the film, Nie still needs to wrap up some loose ends: she saves Hu Ji from the supernatural voodoo attack, she defeats – but does not kill – Jingjinger,[45] and she likewise defeats – but does not kill – her own mistress, the Daoist nun. The refusal to kill marks a clear moral stance that Nie takes, requiring no verbal articulation. This moral stance is echoed in Hou's refusal to allow the camera to capture the death blows when Nie does kill (the exception, the very first assassination at the beginning of the film, is nevertheless remarkably bloodless, not to mention presented in black and white). In combination with the decidedly low-key special effects and diminishment of martial arts encounters with which I began this section, this restrained camerawork marks Hou's de-emphasis of violent spectacle in the mode of recent blockbuster fare as a stance equally as moral (and likewise requiring no verbal elaboration) as Nie's refusal to kill.

Conclusion

It is noteworthy that Nie does commit one assassination at the very start of the film. Perhaps it is her emotional response to this experience (which, except for her weeping when her mother discusses her former betrothal, is never granted any external manifestation susceptible to capture by the camera) that enables Nie to hold the conviction that it is moral to use her martial arts skills only in order to protect others. Be that as it may, it is likewise notable that Hou's minimal use of special effects, as well as his de-emphasis of violent spectacle, does not constitute a deconstruction or negation of the martial arts generic form. Instead, it is an emotional, ethical and, above all, visual argument against the blockbusterisation and spectacularisation of martial arts films. Indeed, Hou, as I have been at pains to demonstrate, does not reject extraordinary martial ability – or even voodoo magic; nor does he revel in these fantastic aspects that have become so prominent in the recent blockbusterisation of martial arts cinema.

We might even go so far as to say that Hou's characteristic (and acclaimed) long-take and long-shot aesthetic serves to naturalise the fantastic and incorporate it into a staid and minimalist depiction of everyday life. In this context, it is worth considering several implications which stem from Hou's inclusion in *The Assassin* of non-narrative depictions of natural scenery (Fig. 5.1). First, this willingness on Hou's part to bring the narrative to a complete halt reinforces his inclination to work counter to the frenetic and ceaseless pace of contemporary blockbuster martial arts films (and mainstream film in general). Second, the beauty and balance in cinematographer Mark Lee Ping Bing's composition of these images reflect, on the one hand, a traditional Chinese aesthetic sensibility that has often been noted as a significant feature of Hou's style,[46] and accordingly recall other moments from Hou's film work, perhaps especially scenes from his so-called Taiwan Trilogy, *City of Sadness* (*Beiqing chengshi*, 1989), *The Puppetmaster* (*Ximeng rensheng*, 1993) and *Good Men, Good Women* (*Haonan haonü*, 1995). On the other hand, these natural landscapes also reflect concepts of humanity's position in the cosmos derived from the same sort of Daoist philosophy that underlies the nun and Nie's martial abilities.[47] The moral qualities I have argued that Nie displays in the film, and that Lee's camera reinforces in

Figure 5.1 Natural scenery. Source: *The Assassin* (2015).

its style, may also be buttressed by a religious or philosophical connection to traditional cosmology.

Third, and most important for my current concerns, these serene images of nature simply existing, juxtaposed to the (restrained) fantastic images of martial prowess throughout the course of *The Assassin*, actually (and perhaps counterintuitively) work to reveal the fantastic in mundane reality. One way of making this argument, as I have been doing throughout this chapter, is to show that Hou does not negate the role of the fantastic in martial arts narratives, but he does seem to reject the hyperbolic mode and the drive for the spectacular that leads to a vicious cycle in contemporary blockbusterised martial arts film for more and more fantasy, and that conversely makes it all seem so very fake. Instead, by restraining, but not denying, his depiction of amazing skill or even magical events, Hou seems to bring them back into a realistic register and include them in a category of unusual and dramatic, but certainly possible, incidents that might actually happen in our own lives. Another way of making this argument is to note the parallel formations of long shot and long take that characterise both the martial arts action of the film and the static images of natural landscapes. This, in turn, implies a certain equality between these images which are usually considered different, if not actually contradictory. If they are equivalent, however, a certain fantastic quality adheres to the mundane images of nature running its course (and the striking beauty of these images reinforces this aspect),[48] while by the same token, a certain naturalness comes to characterise the fantastic martial skills and spiritual refinement described in the film. This re-enchantment of our disenchanted modern lives works not by bludgeoning us with computer-enhanced images of impossible feats, but rather by showing us that the fantastic exists in the world and can be grasped in human hands.

Notes

1. Julia Kristeva, *Desire in Language*. There are any number of full-length academic studies of intertextuality. One of my favourites is Juvan, *History and Poetics of Intertextuality*.
2. Gérard Genette, *Palimpsests*, 5.
3. For other takes on the film, see Peng Hsiao-yen (ed.), *The Assassin*. Most of the chapters included in this collection also address such hypertextual relationships, either with the fictional stories adapted into the film or with the martial arts genre, though seldom, if at all, together.
4. See my discussion in G. Andrew Stuckey, *Metacinema in Contemporary Chinese Film*, 10–13.
5. Zhang Zhen, *An Amorous History of the Silver Screen*, 205. Liang Luo, in her study of Tian Han, has further elaborated on the connections between the avant-garde and the popular; see *The Avant-Garde and the Popular*.

6. Stephen Teo, *Chinese Martial Arts Cinema*, 11.
7. Weihong Bao, *Fiery Cinema*, 39–90. The terms 'sensation' and 'sentimentality' are combined in different orders and discussed in more detail, 82–90.
8. The dates and the term 'craze' both come from Zhang, *An Amorous History of the Silver Screen*, 199.
9. These dates, as well as the term 'wave', are drawn from E. Perry Link, Jr, *Mandarin Ducks and Butterflies*, 22. Teo, *Chinese Martial Arts Cinema*, 22, dates a slightly earlier example of this fiction to 1922.
10. An excellent historical and critical account of the ways that Chinese martial arts films developed in response to influences from both contemporary literature and foreign action films can be found in Teo, *Martial Arts Cinema*, 17–36.
11. Here are only a few examples from some more prominent directors: Wong Kar Wai's *Ashes of Time* (*Dongxie xidu*, 1994) is loosely based on Jin Yong's *Legend of the Condor Heroes* (*Shediao yingxiong zhuan*, 1957); Ang Lee's *Crouching Tiger, Hidden Dragon* (2000) is adapted from Wang Dulu's novel of the same name (*Wohu, canglong*, first serialised in 1941); King Hu's *A Touch of Zen* (*Xianü*, 1971) is drawn from a story by Pu Songling in *Strange Stories from a Chinese Studio* (*Liaozhai zhi yi*, eighteenth century); while Zhang Yimou's *The Great Wall* (2016) draws inspiration for its monsters from *The Classic of Mountains and Seas* (*Shanhai jing*, c. fourth century BCE).
12. Zhang Yimou's *Hero* (*Yingxiong*, 2002), while unprecedented in its details, does draw from historical accounts, perhaps especially Sima Qian's *Records of the Grand Historian* (*Shi ji*, first century BCE). Similarly, Peter Chan's *Dragon* (*Wuxia*, 2011) is a creative remake of Chang Che's classic martial arts film *The One-Armed Swordsman* (*Dubi dao*, 1967). The disabled martial arts hero, meanwhile, is itself a longstanding cliché of the genre, both literary and cinematic.
13. Both of these Tang tales are eponymously titled with their respective heroine's name and have been collected in the Song Dynasty compendium *Taiping guangji* (*The Taiping Anthology*), where they are classified in the group Extraordinary Heroes (Hao xia), *juan* 194 and 195, respectively. In the edition I have to hand, they can be found here: *Taiping guangji*, vol. 4, 1551–6; both stories are also collected in Yang Jialuo and Liu Yanong (eds), *Tangren chuanqi xiaoshuo* (*Tang Chuanqi Tales*), 260–3, 270–2. A translation of 'Nie Yinniang' can be found in Chi-Chen Wang (trans.), *Traditional Chinese Tales*, 98–103, and reprinted in Peng (ed.), *The Assassin*, 197–201, while a summary of relevant details of both stories can be found in James J. Y. Liu, *The Chinese Knight-Errant*, 89–91.
14. See Xie Haimeng, *Xingyun ji* (*Records of Flying with the Clouds*). Xie notes that Hou had the idea to film Nie Yinniang's story beginning in the 1980s, but that it was not until he discovered Shu Qi in *Millennium Mambo* (*Qianxi manbo*, 2001) that he believed any actress could effectively portray this character. Even then, the scriptwriting did not begin until 2009, filming did not start before 2012, and the film was not complete until 2015!
15. This discussion of the development of the story from script to finished film naturally indicates that the script is a further hypotext for *The Assassin*, and therefore the

relationship between the script and film is likewise subject to the sorts of analyses I am performing in this chapter.
16. Genette, *Palimpsests*.
17. It is true that Genette also considers a small number of examples drawn from music, as well as one Woody Allen film, but the relationships in each of these cases remain firmly intramedial.
18. Two examples of such valuable – but requiring careful handling in order to extend their insights – studies are Brian McFarlane, *Novel to Film*, and Robert Stam, *François Truffaut and Friends*. In the context of the Chinese film industries, see Hsiu-Chuang Deppman, *Adapted for the Screen*.
19. In addition to McFarlane, *Novel to Film*, and Stam, *François Truffaut and Friends*, nearly all the contributions to two recent edited volumes discuss the issue of fidelity to a greater or lesser extent. See James M. Welsh and Peter Lev (eds), *The Literature/Film Reader*, and Deborah Cartmell and Imelda Whelehan (eds), *The Cambridge Companion to Literature on Screen*.
20. See I. Q. Hunter, 'Post-classical fantasy cinema: *The Lord of the Rings*', in Cartmell and Whelehan (eds), *The Cambridge Companion to Literature on Screen*, 154–66.
21. To wit, the reception of Wong Kar-wai's *Ashes of Time* is as an auteurist production from a famous art house director, not as a central development of martial arts film, nor as a successful adaptation of Jin Yong's novel.
22. The question of the female martial artist is probably the central recurring theme that Teo develops in *Chinese Martial Arts Cinema*.
23. The recurrent focus on female *xia* in martial arts literature and film is, likewise, another way in which the genre mixes cultural forms and expectations. I will have more to say on this point in the following section.
24. Peter Lev, '*Vertigo*, novel and film', in Welsh and Lev (eds), *The Literature/Film Reader*, 175–85.
25. Anecdotally, neither story is collected in typical anthologies of translated Chinese literature that would be used in undergraduate courses, and as a graduate student, one would also be unlikely to encounter these stories, unless one's doctoral research focused on the Tang tale.
26. James Udden discusses the Cannes jury briefly; see his *No Man an Island*, 187–8.
27. Udden, *No Man an Island*, 187, notes that viewers both inside and outside China had tremendous difficulty understanding the film's narrative structure.
28. See Genette, *Palimpsests*, 98–120. The quotation is from page 111.
29. See Rick Altman, 'A semantic/syntactic approach to film genre', as well as his refinement and expansion of these ideas in *Film/Genre*, 207–15.
30. Teo, *Chinese Martial Arts Cinema*, 192.
31. Christopher Lupke notes that the backlot of the CMPC studio was rebuilt with structures constructed according to Tang Dynasty methods. See his *The Sinophone Cinema of Hou Hsiao-Hsien*, 222.
32. Udden, *No Man an Island*, 189.
33. For more on the rise of special effects, see Dan North's Chapter 3 in this volume.

34. See Teo's extended discussion of terminology in *Chinese Martial Arts Cinema*, 1–6.
35. Udden, *No Man an Island*, 202.
36. My thanks to my co-editor, Kenneth Chan, for making this point and for describing the scenes as lethargic.
37. According to the script published by Xie Haimeng, this line is delivered via flashback in scene 23. The finished film deviates dramatically from this script, however, and here the line is delivered in the black and white opening 'preface'. The first half of this line is a direct quotation of the original Tang tale, but the second half, added by the filmmakers, redirects the statement's import nearly 180 degrees. See Zhong Acheng, Zhu Tianwen and Xie Haimeng, '*Cike Nie Yinniang* juben' (Script for *The Assassin*), in Xie, *Xingyun ji*, 366.
38. Sima Qian, *Shiji* (*Records of the Grand Historian*), vol. 8, 2515–38.
39. Lupke, *The Sinophone Cinema of Hou Hsiao-Hsien*, 217.
40. Ibid., 217.
41. Ibid., 218–19.
42. Teo, *Chinese Martial Arts Cinema*.
43. Lupke, *The Sinophone Cinema of Hou Hsiao-Hsien*, 216.
44. Parts of the screenplay that did not make it into the finished film make the reasoning behind this regret clear. In the wake of the broken betrothal, Nie could have faced political danger from being perceived as a threat to the new alliance and her parents' choice was based on the need to protect her.
45. Jingjinger is played by the same actress, Zhou Yun, who plays Tian Yuanshi, Tian Ji'an's principal wife. It is unclear if they are meant to be the same person or are just played by the same actress. The script states that when Jingjinger's mask is cut it reveals Tian Yuanshi, but the finished film seems much more ambiguous. See Zhong, Zhu and Xie, '*Cike Nie Yinniang* juben', 389.
46. In addition to Lupke, *The Sinophone Cinema of Hou Hsiao-Hsien*, and Udden, *No Man an Island*, see also Emilie Yueh-yu Yeh, 'Poetics and politics of Hou Hsiao-hsien's films'.
47. Here I am not claiming some comprehensive conception of Daoist principles; rather, I see a reflection of popularised understandings of Daoism derived from classic texts such as *Laozi* and *Zhuangzi* but also embodied in many Wudang-influenced martial arts films, including *Crouching Tiger, Hidden Dragon*. It is possible that the reason that the nun in *The Assassin*, who is Buddhist in the Tang tale, becomes Daoist in the film lies in this connection.
48. Udden daringly states: 'The 200-plus shots that make up *The Assassin* are not only arguably among the most beautiful that Hou and his team have ever created, they are also among the most beautiful ever seen anywhere.' See *No Man an Island*, 188.

Chapter 6

An Auteurist Journey through the Fantastic Mode: A Case Study of Ho Meng-hua

Shi-Yan Chao

In her seminal book *Fantasy and Mimesis*, Kathryn Hume seeks the most inclusive definition of fantasy, settling on the term 'fantasy impulse' alongside a 'mimetic impulse' as equally important to Western literature. Mimesis, for Hume, is 'felt as the desire to imitate, to describe events, people, situations, and objects with such verisimilitude that others can share your experience', whilst fantasy indicates 'the desire to change givens and alter reality – out of boredom, play, vision, longing for something lacking, or need for metaphoric images that will bypass the audience's verbal defense'.[1] All literature, in Hume's formulation, is informed by these two impulses, to varying degrees. Fantasy in this sense establishes itself as a natural activity rather than a niche genre, and we – as Hume cautions – need not 'claim a work as a fantasy any more than we identify a work as a mimesis'.[2] This notion of two core impulses in literature – namely, fantasy and mimesis – is aligned with much of the writing on early film history, which conventionally identifies, as Siegfried Kracauer puts it, 'two main tendencies',[3] expressed in the contrasting approaches in the late nineteenth and early twentieth centuries, of the 'strict realist' Lumière brothers on one hand,[4] and on the other, Georges Méliès, who 'gave free reign to his artistic imagination'[5] in films such as *A Trip to the Moon* (*Le Voyage dans la lune*, 1902) and *Indian Rubber Head* (*L'Homme à la tête de caoutchouc*, 1902).[6]

From the perspective of film studies in particular, an elaboration on the term 'verisimilitude' (also mentioned in Hume's quotation above) is of crucial importance to further our discussion of fantasy. According to Steve Neale, film genres do not consist only of films; they also consist of 'specific systems of expectations and hypothesis'[7] that spectators bring with them to the cinema as a means of recognising and understanding what is happening on the screen.

These systems of expectations and hypothesis, critically, involve a knowledge of various 'regimes of verisimilitude', wherein verisimilitude (meaning that which is 'probable' or 'likely') entails 'notions of propriety, of what is appropriate and therefore probable (or probable therefore appropriate)'.[8] An actor bursting into song and dance, for instance, is deemed appropriate and probable in a musical, but less so in a thriller or a war film. Regimes of verisimilitude, therefore, vary from genre to genre. Following Tzvetan Todorov, Neale further makes a distinction between two types of verisimilitude pertinent to representation: 'generic verisimilitude' and 'a broader social or cultural verisimilitude'. Whilst the regimes of generic verisimilitude, to paraphrase Neale, can ignore, sidestep or transgress those of broader sociocultural verisimilitude, the extent to which this transgression of sociocultural verisimilitude 'has implications for conventional notions of realism' varies.[9] Certain genres appeal more directly and consistently to sociocultural verisimilitude, and are considered more realistic; 'other genres, such as science fiction, Gothic horror . . . make much less appeal to this kind of authenticity',[10] but instead, allow me to add, draw more from the fantastic in many cases. That is, different genres correspond to different regimes of generic verisimilitude, and certain genres have been premised upon, and indeed characterised by, their greater or marked susceptibility to the fantastic.

Vivian Sobchack, for instance, groups together three particular film genres – namely, fantasy adventure, horror and science fiction – under the overall heading of 'the fantastic'.[11] As Sobchack notes, each of these three genres 'imaginatively constructs alternative – "fantastic" – worlds and tells stories of impossible experiences that defy rational logic and currently known empirical laws'.[12] Citing Tom Hutchinson, Sobchack claims that horror is 'the appalling ideas given sudden flesh; science fiction is the improbable made possible within the confines of a technological age'. Fantasy adventure or fantasy romance, she adds, is 'the appealing and impossible personal wish concretely and objectively fulfilled'.[13]

Given the above accounts of fantasy that range from literature to film, taking fantasy as either an impulse or a tendency, in this chapter I consider fantasy or the fantastic as something characterised by its '[defiance of] the constraints of our current empirical knowledge and rational thought'[14] or simply its 'divergence from what is possible in our known world'.[15] As a 'trait or character which a number of distinct genres share',[16] fantasy or the fantastic, I propose, can also be properly approached as a mode, in much the same way as Christine Gledhill and Linda Williams assess melodrama as a transgeneric expression.[17] Amongst the transgeneric fantastic mode lie the particular film genres of my analysis: fantasy adventure, horror and martial arts, to be detailed below.

More importantly, my analysis challenges the confines of the textual and the internal, as privileged by certain accounts of fantasy. My approach seeks an understanding of the interaction between the textual and the contextual, the private and the public, so as to address the sociocultural in and through the (trans)generic. Here enters the Lacanian psychoanalytic concept of fantasy vis-à-vis the human subject. Following Laplanche and Pontalis, fantasy is not the object but the setting of desire. The cinematic term 'mise-en-scène' provides a compelling analogy between dreams and film. 'In fantasy the subject does not pursue the object or its sign: He appears caught up himself in the sequence of images.'[18] Crucially, the fantasiser has no fixed place or identification; he or she is 'de-subjectivized' and is 'in the very syntax of the sequence in question'.[19] As dreamers create and effectively represent all the characters in their dreams, so do film viewers not necessarily identify with just one character, but may find pleasures in the whole structure of the fantasy. Generic conventions or generic verisimilitude, in this formulation, can thus be understood as 'the means by which the structuring of desire is represented in public forms'.[20] Inasmuch as fantasy is the mise-en-scène of desire, 'What is necessary for any public forms of fantasy, for their collective consumption, is not universal objects of desire, but a setting of desiring in which we find our place(s).'[21] To paraphrase Žižek, it is in and through the staging of the fantasy that human subjects learn to desire and come into being,[22] wherein the realms of the personal and the collective, the private and the public, are mutually blended into one another.

Three key aspects of my subsequent enquiry are therefore: first, the articulations of the fantastic mode in different genres, and in fantasy adventure, martial arts and horror in particular; second, the kinds of setting or 'mise-en-scène of desire'[23] facilitated by the public forms of generic conventions, particularly those inflected by the fantastic through its double appeal: its focal defiance of rational or empirical principles, and its basic reliance on aural and visual attractions. The interplay between this double appeal – between what I shall term 'fantastic impossibility' and 'spectacular probability' – is to be addressed in the next section. And third, the sorts of 'desiring subjects' or preferred subject positions animated by the different kinds of mise-en-scène of desire in question. Taken together, the reconfiguring of the preferred subject positions aligned with different genres of the fantastic mode through an examination of Hong Kong commercial filmmaker Ho Meng-hua's (1929–2009) œuvre constitutes the core subject of my subsequent investigation.

My investigation notably takes an 'auteurist' approach in a sense that regards the film director not so much as a fully autonomous artist with total control of her/his work, but foremost as an agent embedded in the commercial system, engaging constant negotiation with her/his host studio that further represents specific agendas, be they economic or sociopolitical.²⁴ As the studio's agendas must evolve over time, so do the terms of negotiation faced by the filmmaker, be they monetary, creative or institutional. Here, regimes of generic verisimilitude, along with different uses of the fantastic across genres, as will become clear, can function as certain parameters indicative of the negotiations between the studio, the filmmaker and audiences, and in particular the changing 'structure of feeling' of audiences that reverberates through, as in Ho Meng-hua's case, a film auteur's longer career as a contract film director for the Shaw studios. This auteurist approach thus locates my proposed enquiry (the reconfiguring of the preferred subject positions aligned with the different genres of the fantastic mode through Ho's work) within the interplay between the mainstream studio, its contract filmmaker and their targeted general audiences.

Overall, this chapter contends that audiences' changing structure of feeling is perceivable through the trajectory of the evolving mise-en-scène of desire painted by the filmmaker and the studio, and that the evolving mise-en-scène of desire can be approached through the fantastic by means of its double appeal: its focal defiance of rational or empirical principles, and its basic reliance on aural and visual attractions. By examining the interplay between fantastic impossibility and spectacular probability through Ho's work, this chapter eventually argues that Ho's career at Shaws' during the 1960s and 1970s simultaneously reflected the way that Hong Kong people negotiated their distinct subjectivity in a transnational framework. That is also the sociopolitical significance of the fantastic mode in its Hong Kong articulation.

Ho Meng-Hua and Fantasy Adventure

Born in Shanghai in 1929, Ho Meng-hua studied drama with China's leading playwrights, including Tian Han and Cao Yu at Shanghai Municipal Experimental Theater School (today's Shanghai Theatre Academy), before he moved to Hong Kong in 1948.²⁵ He first worked for Yung Hwa Company as a scriptwriter and assistant director. Although his directorial debut, *The Wild Girl* (*Ye guniang*, 1957, released in 1960), was a Cathay production, that film paved the way for Ho's entrance to Shaw Brothers as a contract director. As a commercial filmmaker at Shaws', Ho made about thirty films in two decades in a wide range of genres. His early films were largely melodramas or of the *wenyi* genre,²⁶ including the Asian Film Festival Best Picture, *Shanshan* (1967). These melodramas, however, generally did not generate handsome revenues.²⁷ With the commercial success of *The Monkey Goes West* (*Xiyou ji*, 1966), he churned out three other fantasy films, all based on the Chinese classic *Journey to the West* (*Xiyou ji*): namely, *Princess Iron Fan* (*Tieshan gongzhu*, 1966), *Cave of the Silken*

Web (*Pansidong*, 1967) and *The Land of Many Perfumes* (*Nüerguo*, 1968). Amidst Shaws' tremendous success in the martial arts genre, Ho was then commissioned to direct martial arts pictures and became known for, among others, *Killer Darts* (*Zhuihunbiao*, 1968), *The Jade Raksha* (*Yuluocha*, 1968), *Lady of Steel* (*Huangjiang nüxia*, 1970), *The Lady Hermit* (*Zhong Kui niangzi*, 1971), *The Master of Kung Fu* (*Huang Feihong*, 1973) and *The Flying Guillotine* (*Xuedizi*, 1975). In the mid-1970s, Ho further gained a reputation for horror filmmaking, in particular with his *Black Magic* (*Jiangtou*) trilogy between 1975 and 1976, which was immediately followed by *The Mighty Peking Man* (also known as *Goliathon* [*Xingxingwang*], 1977), a horror/fantasy adventure loaded with special effects and a direct response to Hollywood's *King Kong* (John Guillermin, 1976; distributed in Hong Kong by Shaws' chief competitor, Golden Harvest). After 1977, Ho directed only a handful of other martial arts and 'exploitative' films before retiring from Shaws' in 1980.[28]

The particular way in which the fantastic mode plays out in Ho's filmmaking, along with its sociopolitical significance, deserves further examination. Here, we may take a closer look at five of his best-known films across three 'fantastic' genres: fantasy films, *The Monkey Goes West* and *Princess Iron Fan*; martial arts pictures, *Lady of Steel* and *The Master of Kung Fu*; and finally a horror movie, *Black Magic*.

The Monkey Goes West is based upon *Journey to the West*,[29] the mythological tale about Monk Tang and his three disciples' westbound journey to bring Buddhist scriptures back to the Central Plains (*Zhongyuan*), or simply inland China. As the official delegate for the mission, Monk Tang (played by Ho Fan) is separated from his human escorts early in the film. In the film's fantasy world, populated by gods, fairies and demons, however, Tang's flesh is believed by the demons to be capable of helping them achieve immortality. With various demons eager to capture him, Monk Tang, a human being without magical power, none the less receives the blessing of the gods, who grant him three fairy apprentices, Monkey King, Pigsy and Sandy, in place of human escorts. *The Monkey Goes West* thus revolves around Tang's encounter with Monkey King (Yueh Wah), whom Tang releases from Buddha's punitive captivity under Five Finger Mountain, followed by their meetings with Pigsy (Peng Peng) and Sandy (Tien Shun), with the latter two finally surrendering to Tang to make amends for their wrongdoings. The film ends with the formation of the team of four, laying the foundation for the westward journey, which abounds with whimsical episodes to be exploited by the film's sequels.

With the montage of an explosion, rocks falling, lava running and a conflagration destroying a village, *Princess Iron Fan* starts with the team of four approaching Flaming Mountain, where the rampant fire fanned up by Princess Iron Fan (Pat Ting Hung) blocks their journey. The only way to pass through is to borrow the Palm Leaf Fan from Princess Iron Fan to put out the flames. Due to some bygone friction, Princess Iron Fan refuses to lend the fan to the Monkey King, who in turn plays tricks to get access to the fan, including masquerading as Princess Iron Fan's lover, the Ox King (Ching Miao). This culminates in the appearance of the real Ox King before Princess Iron Fan. The Ox King likewise shapeshifts into Pigsy to get even with the Monkey King. The whole conflict and state of confusion are finally resolved by the intervention of the Jade Emperor. The fantastic play of magic and doubling via cinematic techniques is further exploited for the second part of *Princess*, wherein the team has passed Flaming Mountain and is approaching Skeleton Peak. There await White Skeleton (Cheng Pei-pei) and her sister (Lily Ho), who attempt to abduct Monk Tang from his disciples for the sake of his flesh and immortality. With various tricks involving shapeshifting, the two sisters succeed in seducing Pigsy, deceiving Sandy and, most importantly, alienating the invincible Monkey from Monk Tang (Fig. 6.1). This is epitomised during the final sequence where Tang, Pigsy and Sandy are in captivity, whilst the two sisters demonstrate to their mother – in the presence of Tang, Pigsy and Sandy – how they have managed to break the team: they have first disguised themselves as innocent country girls (only to be 'killed' by Monkey for the demons he sees underneath), and then as their grieving 'human' parents (again, to be 'killed' by Monkey for the same reason) and finally as a pair of male official deities delivering God's denouncement of Monkey's behaviour, which eventually forces Tang to expel Monkey, thus making the team vulnerable. After the two sisters' demonstration and clarification for those beguiled and captured, the sisters' mother then reveals herself to be the Monkey coming to rescue Tang, Pigsy and Sandy, whose success paves the way for the continuation of their pilgrimage.

Figure 6.1 Temptations of the flesh. Source: *Princess Iron Fan* (1966).

Here I would like to highlight two interrelated dimensions pertinent to these two instalments of the fantasy adventure: the aforementioned double appeal of fantastic impossibility and spectacular probability. By fantastic impossibility and spectacular probability, I primarily refer to fantasy and spectacle, respectively. But I use impossibility alongside the former to reiterate fantasy's essential ability to diverge from what is possible in our known world, while I employ probability alongside the latter to underline the far-reaching terrain of the spectacular that is not necessarily premised upon whimsical narratives to engage audiences, but is more foundational to cinema's capability to solicit audience attention, even by simply presenting what is perceived as audiovisually spectacular yet empirically probable in our known world. It resonates with what Tom Gunning has called 'the cinema of attractions', where the visual pleasure, curiosity, excitement and wonder that the viewers find in the cinematic imagery *per se* help solicit their attention.[30] With an additional emphasis on the aural alongside the visual impact, I propose a spectrum of fantastic experience in film that is characterised overall by audiovisual attractions, with fantastic impossibility and spectacular probability constitutive of two ends of this spectrum. A film's particular positioning on the spectrum, together with its interplay with the film's particular narrative focus and generic verisimilitude, as shall become clear, is key to an understanding of the mise-en-scène of desire or subject position privileged by the film's production team, whose ideas and agendas are mediated by particular economic and sociopolitical concerns that change and reformulate over time.

Regarding *The Monkey Goes West* and *Princess Iron Fan* vis-à-vis fantastic impossibility, the fantastic effect of numerous seemingly impossible shapeshifts is notably rendered through cinematic tricks (aided by props, set designs, characters' long sleeves and blocking in the scenes) and montage editing to gloss over the changes made between shots. The popping up of various nonhuman characters on screen, the conjuring up of their devices via magical power (such as Monkey King's Golden Cudgel and Ox King's Palm Leaf Fan) and the returning to their original forms (such as the charming White Skeleton sisters returning to dreadful white bones) rely heavily on editing as well. Other important techniques include, for instance, matte work, superimposition, animation and ratio change to help generate such seemingly impossible imagery that depicts some characters being enlarged (such as Monkey King exercising his body upon release from 500 years of captivity), some being attacked by gigantic monsters (such as the Dragon Demon in the first instalment) and some flying in the sky. Of course, the fascinating costumes and make-up (like Pigsy's vivid style; see Fig. 6.1) and the fanciful sound effects (such as the dubbing of the sounds from animals or beasts to signify the real identities behind the characters' human forms) also help enhance the audiovisual attractions and credibility of the seemingly impossible, fantastic imagery.

In the mean time, the audiovisual attractions of the fantastic imagery further intersect with other audiovisual attractions that are not so much impossible as simply spectacular. The latter are manifested particularly by the colourful and marvellous settings, costumes and make-up, as well as the delicate theatrical acting and operatic song and dance. Take, for example, the scene where the White Skeleton sisters attempt to seduce and deceive Pigsy (see Fig. 6.1). Here the two sisters have just conjured up a garden-like setting out of a barren area on the mountain (its magical effect realised by editing and by dubbing the birds' chirping), and have transformed their original martial-style clothing into feminine attire simply by passing behind the tree in the background (which helps gloss over the changes between shots). In tandem with such magic-inflected audiovisual designs are, notably, the very look of the beautiful garden and the ladies' gorgeous costumes, commonly seen in other period dramas of the time, and the three characters' flirtation with each other by performing humorous cross-talk (*shu lai bao*) and singing Chinese folk tunes in standard Mandarin, accompanied by Chinese-style musical instruments and theatrical body gestures.

Marked by spectacular probability, such attractive audiovisual designs are very much in line with the conventions of *huangmei* opera films[31] and, more broadly, the period dramas and historical sagas that comprised the main staple of the Shaw studio's output. The cinematic world animated by the Shaw studio, as veteran film critic Shek Kei notes, was first and foremost a 'China dream'.[32] According to Shek,

> When the Chinese in Hong Kong, Taiwan, and overseas were pining for a China from which they were banished, and when Communist China was increasingly 'alienated' from Chinese tradition, Hong Kong cinema's recreation of the 'China dream' became all the more appealing. And [Shaw Studios] was in the best position for the task.[33]

By way of 'simulations of the real [Chinese settings and landscapes]', Shaws' numerous movies that dealt with 'ancient history, tales, and legends'[34] (as best exemplified by the tremendously popular 'Beauties of Beauties' series, *The Love Eterne* (*Liang Shanbo yu Zhu Yingtai*, Li Han-hsiang, 1963) and the *Journey to the West* series, respectively) echoed overall a kind of Chinese sensibility. Involving a way of imagining China,[35] they helped build what film historian Edwin Chen calls 'an aesthetic environment that could bring the audience closer to "an impressionistic, dreamlike but near-realistic ideal of China"'.[36]

Given that the source material of *Journey to the West* is itself an immensely popular Chinese classic, its film adaptations from the mid- to late 1960s in effect helped perpetuate the cultural heritage and Chinese cultural lineage among their audiences in Hong Kong and beyond. Through the fantastic imagery and its interplay with other audiovisual attractions that are not so much impossible as simply spectacular, the series animated a kind of mise-en-scène or subject position privileged by the Shaw studio: the projected cinematic world of a China dream. Aided by both fantastic impossibility and spectacular probability, the verisimilitude of Ho's/the Shaws' fantasy adventure and its preferred staged subjectivity for its audiences are hence marked by a sense of Chineseness at their core. This sense of Chineseness and preferred staged subjectivity, however, was about to undergo certain reformulations that were aided by different proportions of fantastic impossibility and spectacular probability in the wake of the revitalised martial arts genre from the late 1960s and early 1970s, followed by a new cycle of horror pictures beginning in the mid-1970s.

The Role of Fantasy through Martial Arts and Horror Genres

After his final chapter of the *Journey to the West* series (namely, *The Land of Many Perfumes*), Ho Meng-hua brought out his first martial arts picture, *Killer Darts*, at a time when Shaws' martial arts film productions were gaining momentum. It should be noted that the martial arts genre largely comprises two subcategories: *kung fu* and *wuxia*.[37] Due to the history of its development, the *kung fu* picture, as Stephen Teo notes, was usually considered the domain of Cantonese cinema, whilst the *wuxia* genre was more closely associated with 'the northern style', influenced by Peking opera.[38] Further, the northern style was believed to be 'more ancient and historical' than the southern style, materialised in the *kung fu* film.[39] That is, *wuxia* films tend to be set further back in time than their *kung fu* counterparts, detailing the chivalrous exploits of 'knights-errant' and 'lady knights' in ancient dynasties, whilst the *kung fu* picture opts for more recent and comparatively realistic settings, frequently celebrating the Shaolin heroes of Guangdong Province. The most fundamental difference between *kung fu* and *wuxia*, none the less, lies in their fighting styles: *kung fu* highlights fist fighting and body combat, whilst *wuxia* emphasises swordplay and sword fighting. Whereas *kung fu* highlights the body, training and physicality, *wuxia* has a stronger reliance on fantasy and the supernatural than *kung fu* does.[40]

Here we may use two of Ho Meng-hua's martial arts pictures, *Lady of Steel* and *The Master of Kung Fu*, to address relevant issues better. *Lady of Steel* starts with a private security agency led by Chief Fang, whose team and family – while delivering flood relief to refugees along the Yellow River – have been ambushed by Han (Huang Chun-hsin) and Wei (Li Yunzhong). As the sole survivor of the attack, Fang's young daughter, Yingqi (Cheng Pei-pei), has been raised and taught martial arts by Daoist priest Xuanzhen. Now an outstanding martial artist, Yingqi is sent by Xuanzhen to join Lord Xia (Fang Mien) to help defend the country, which is under the threat of a Jin invasion. Her path crosses that of Han and Wei, now both traitors working for the Jins: Han has renamed himself Cai in order to infiltrate Xia's Fortress. Before Yingqi figures out Han's and Wei's real identities and their treason, she is fooled and framed by the two. With the aid of Qin (Yueh Wah) and the Gang of Beggars that he leads, Yingqi manages to clear her name, however, and get rid of Han and his company; she then saves Xia and the other righteous ones from Han's trap.

Whilst *Lady of Steel* features a lady-knight who sets out to fulfil her mission to defend her country while, at the same time, avenging the death of her parents, *The Master of Kung Fu* is based on the exploits of Wong Fei-hung, the turn-of-the-twentieth-century *kung fu* instructor, Chinese medical practitioner and Cantonese folk hero. Here a middle-aged Wong (Ku Feng) avenges the treacherous death of his fellow *kung fu* teachers and his own apprentices while interceding in some illegal activities involving an English businessman. The film starts with a public performance of a lion dance that materialises the tension between Master Wong's disciples and the members of another martial arts school led by Wong's cousin, Mai Gen (Chan Shen). At the same time, in Canton, English businessman Gordon (Shih Lu-chieh) teams up with local middle person Fox (Wong Hon), trading opium and tobacco for jade ornaments that fetch high prices in the West. Fox then tries to bring his accomplice, villainous *kung fu* master Li Tian-dao (Wang Hsieh), into the team as the security chief by means of a martial contest, wherein Mai, the only challenger to Li, is severely injured by Li with a hidden gadget, and later poisoned when Fox contaminates Wong's medicine. With Mai's murder planted on Wong, Wong's students become the targets of retaliation, either killed or captured by Fox and Li. Four of Wong's upright friends are subsequently framed and executed as well. Together with his surviving disciples, Liang Kuan (Lin Wei-tu) and Su Nan (Norman Chu), and their sympathisers, Master Wong finally confounds the treacherous deal involving Fox, Li and Gordon, defeating Li with his powerful 'Invisible Kick', and restoring his name, medical practice and martial arts school at Bao Zhi Lin.

In accordance with Stephen Teo's distinction between *wuxia* and *kung fu*, two aspects of *Lady of Steel* and *The Master of Kung Fu* deserve special attention. First, regarding fighting styles, *Lady* features the uses of swords, flying darts and daggers, alongside arrows and some built-in traps or gimmicks. During the fights, scouting and chases, the characters can easily jump on and off high walls, leaping around different floors, roofs and tall trees. For example, in an early sequence where Yingqi is about to face an ambush in her hotel room staged by Wei and Han, Qin tries to save Yingqi by getting her out through the window. Yingqi chases Qin into the street, where a misunderstanding leads to the breakout of a fight. We see the two engaging in swordplay around the buildings, and even on top of thin wooden poles. The fight is a tie and Qin, after revealing his good intentions, leaves the scene by leaping above and across a river. In another sequence where Yingqi, upon arriving at Xia's Fortress, is encouraged to showcase her martial arts skills, she leaps up in the front yard, while remaining balanced on top of a twig and catching things with ease. All the fantastic images in *Lady*, like those involving gravity-defying leaps, standing on a twig and stepping across water, are made possible by means of editing and other cinematic techniques such as the employment of wireworks, trampolines and reverse shooting. The appeal to the fantastic against the empirical principle in *Lady* is, so to speak, much in keeping with the *wuxia* convention.

The fighting style in *Master*, by contrast, features body combat, alongside occasional uses of simple weaponry like bamboo poles and nunchucks. No swords are employed in the entire film, whilst daggers are used only in one sequence, where Wong's students are under attack shortly after Mai's death. The use of daggers here (in a *kung fu* film) by those disguised as Mai's students implies something treacherous in nature, and unlike in *Lady*, daggers are only held in the hands of the villains and are never thrown. When chases occur, some characters manage to jump down from just one flight above (Wong achieves this only with the aid of a tree), and unlike in *Lady*, the characters do not perform fantastic gravity-defying leaps or moves. All the fight scenes between the major characters, including the contest between Mai and Li and those centring on Wong and Li, showcase fist fighting and powerful kicks (as best exemplified by Wong's 'Invisible Kick'). Underlining a tangible sense of probable physicality, the fascinating action in *Master*, in other words, appeals not so much to fantastic impossibility as to spectacular probability.

Second, from *Lady* to *Master*, in tandem with the downplaying of the fantastic in their fighting styles also come the different articulations of their story settings and narrative foci. In *Lady* in particular, the Jin invasion indicated as part of the story background plausibly positions the film's fictional world during the Song Dynasty (960–1279), whilst the title character of *Master*, by contrast, refers to the Cantonese folk hero Wong Fei-hung, who is first and foremost a historical figure (1847–1924), widely known in the south of the Five Ridges (*Lingnan*) region. It is worth noting that while *The Master of Kung Fu* was made in the wake of the international 'kung fu craze' initiated by Bruce Lee (1940–73) in the early 1970s,[41] *Lady of Steel* was produced as part of the *wuxia* trend revitalised by directors like Chang Cheh (1923–2002) and King Hu (1932–97) under the banner of 'Shaws Colour Wuxia New Century' in the second half of the 1960s.⁴² Echoing the 'emphasis on realism in action'⁴³ of the Shaws *wuxia* new century, *Lady* notably differs *already* from earlier *wuxia* pictures and resorts to the fantastic in a restrained manner, wherein the decades-old fantastic *wuxia* genre (or magic spirit–martial arts film, *shenguai wuxia pian*)⁴⁴ even showcased as part of its verisimilitude fantasy-inflected devices (like palm power and deadly sound waves) and fantasy-oriented characters (such as fairies, demons and strange beasts).⁴⁵ Such fantastic devices and characters resonate with the fantastic imagery and effects showcased by the fantasy genre in general, but they are nowhere to be found in *Lady*.

If we bring together the fantasy genre of the *Journey to the West* series, a pattern becomes evident running through Ho Meng-hua's career. From *The Monkey Goes West* and *Princess Iron Fan* to *Lady of Steel* and *The Master of Kung Fu*, these films not only marked a reformulation of the fantastic, with a decreasing stress on impossibility while retaining a certain appeal to the spectacular premised upon the probable. They also cast their stories against different backdrops, moving temporally from the Tang (618–907, in *Monkey* and *Princess*) and Song (*Lady*) Dynasties to the modern (the turn of the twentieth century in *Master*), and geopolitically from the connotations of the Central Kingdom to the denotations of Lingnan culture. Whilst the Shaw studio, as mentioned, had been known for its re-creation of a cultural China, the significance of this Shaw production telling the story of Cantonese folk hero Wong Fei-hung, as Hong Kong film critic Matthew Cheng points out, lies in the fact that the local Cantonese factor had become an undeniable concern when the Shaws tried to optimise its revenue, even though the ambiguous portrait of Wong as a Mandarin-speaking Cantonese personality poignantly embodies 'the tension between the local (Hong Kong) and the national (Mainland China)' in 1970s Hong Kong.⁴⁶

In comparison with *Lady of Steel*, *The Master of Kung Fu* further manifests a shift in narrative focus: from that of a female protagonist to that of male dominance. It is arguable that, concomitant with the gradual downplay of the fantastic in the widely popular martial arts genre, also came the transformation of Hong Kong's mainstream cinema of the time. In place of the female stars dominating local screens by the late 1960s, *kung fu* films started to celebrate staunch masculinity (*nanxing yanggang*) as a newly formed subjectivity for the local general public.⁴⁷ By way of conclusion, I would like to use Ho Meng-hua's horror classic *Black Magic* to address further the issue of fantasy and subject position vis-à-vis staunch masculinity in Hong Kong mainstream film culture in transformation.

Amongst the most celebrated masculine male bodies in 1970s Hong Kong was that of the actor Ti Lung. Born in 1946, Ti Lung's acting career began in 1969 and was continuously associated with director Chang Cheh. With his breakthrough parts in Chang's *Dead End* (*Sijiao*, 1969), *Vengeance* (*Baochou*, 1970), *The Duel* (*Dajuedou*, 1971) and *Duel of the Fists* (*Quanji*, 1971), Ti Lung soon established a screen persona characterised by candour, charisma and a young, virile, *kung fu* physique. It is worth noting that between Chang Cheh's *kung fu* classics *Five Shaolin Masters* (*Shaolin wuzu*, 1974) and *Shaolin Temple* (*Shaolinsi*, 1976), Ti Lung also starred in Ho Meng-hua's fantasy horror film *Black Magic*. In *Black Magic*, a young couple, Xu Luo (Ti Lung) and Wang Juying (Lily Li), become tormented by a rich, sexy widow, Luo Yin (Tammy Tien Ni), who appeals to a necromancer (Ku Feng) to cast a 'love spell' on Xu as the unwilling object of her affection, and a 'death spell' on Wang as her rival for love. The scheming sorcerer, though, has plans of his own, and the film culminates in a fantastic battle between two powerful magicians representing light and darkness, respectively.

Although in *Black Magic* Ti Lung does not practise *kung fu*, he is shown doing some indoor exercise, with his well-built torso and physique on display. In semantic terms, this masculine *kung fu* body is further aligned with a series of socially sanctioned practices: Xu Luo is a hard-working, promising construction engineer about to marry a high-school teacher in a Catholic church to form a middle-class nuclear family. This masculine body and socially sanctioned subject is, none the less, under threat from what Barbara Creed terms 'the monstrous-feminine'[48] on two levels. On one level, this threat is directly embodied by Luo Yin, the voluptuous woman who – thanks to her conspicuous inherited wealth – does not need to work, but – by paying the black magician – mesmerises Xu Luo, making him indulge in sex and an extravagant lifestyle while abandoning his original family and profession. Simply put, she turns the male protagonist into a good-for-nothing, a 'non-subject' outside the family-based social economy (Fig. 6.2). On another level, this scenario is staged against a backdrop that involves a particular geopolitical constellation. As Xu Luo's profession and social circle in the modern city and the sorcerer's base in the remote forest indicate, it involves an urban/rural divide. Importantly, this urban/rural divide is further aligned with a reimagination of Hong Kong's international status vis-à-vis Southeast Asia.

As this displaced Hong Kong story (alongside its Hong Kong cast and crew) unfolds in Malaysia,[49] it is also, metaphorically, the premodern 'black magic' in rural Malaysia that threatens the modern 'masculine subject' of cosmopolitan Hong Kong. If, for Creed, the kernel of horror film lies in the restoration of the social order through boundary drawing and redrawing, what comes with the staged rehabilitation of Xu Luo's subject within the family-based social economy is, then, simultaneously a self-affirmation of Hong Kong's rising international status in the region during the 1970s. The fantastic narrative and imagery in *Black Magic* significantly help facilitate, so to speak, a kind of mise-en-scène for

Figure 6.2 Luo Yin seducing Xu Luo. Source: *Black Magic* (1975).

the staging of a subject position that is far removed from ancient China but leans toward contemporary Hong Kong, imag(in)ing itself as a modern political economy gaining momentum in a transnational framework.

Whilst *The Monkey Goes West* and *Princess Iron Fan* portray an enclosed fantasy world with escapist overtones, and *The Master of Kung Fu* approaches a modern folk hero with a burgeoning awareness of Hong Kong indigenous culture, *Black Magic*, to a large extent, reflects the formation of 'Hongkonger' identity in the 1970s.[50] This Hongkonger identity not only departs from the 'China dream' characteristic of *Monkey*, *Princess* and *Lady*, but, by way of the remasculinisation of male bodies through *kung fu*, it appeals to and incarnates Hong Kong's growing significance on the contemporary international stage. In terms of the fantastic's double appeal, *Black Magic* notably also reversed the trend set by the recent *kung fu* craze, recuperating the stress of impossibility alongside the fantastic's general reliance on audiovisual attractions. This renewed stress on the impossible was to reverberate through the revival of the martial arts genre in the years to come (most particularly by way of New Wave director Tsui Hark's spectacular *wuxia* films from the 1980s onwards)[51] and the contemporary CGI-enhanced media cultures[52] that redefine constraints of time, space and the body, defying any 'rigid categorization – zoological, behavioral, social, spatial, and historical'[53] – through forms of mobilised fantasies.

In sum, this chapter uses Ho Meng-hua and his fantastic work to address the three main lines of enquiry proposed early on: namely, the articulations of the fantastic mode across different genres, and the kinds of mise-en-scène of desire facilitated by the public forms of generic conventions, as well as the sorts of preferred subject positions animated by different kinds of mise-en-scène of desire in question. Along with the particular manoeuvre of the fantastic mode through fantasy adventure, martial arts and horror genres, coupled with a changing formulation of the fantastic's double appeal to fantastic impossibility and spectacular probability, this chapter comes to the conclusion that Ho Meng-hua's career at Shaws' during the 1960s and 1970s simultaneously reflected the way Hong Kong people negotiated their distinct subjectivity in a transnational framework. That, I contend, is the sociopolitical significance of the fantastic mode in its Hong Kong articulation.

Notes

1. Kathryn Hume, *Fantasy and Mimesis*, 20.
2. Ibid.
3. Siegfried Kracauer, 'Basic concepts', 293.
4. For instance, *Workers Leaving the Lumière Factory* (*La Sortie de l'usine Lumière à Lyon*, 1895) and *Arrival of a Train at La Ciotat* (*L'Arrivée d'un train en gare de La Ciotat*, 1896).
5. Kracauer, 'Basic concepts', 293.
6. Richard Rickitt, *Special Effects*, 14–15.
7. Steve Neale, 'Questions of genre', 279.
8. Ibid., 279.
9. Ibid., 279–80.
10. Ibid., 280.
11. Vivian Sobchack, 'The fantastic', 312.
12. Ibid., 312.
13. Ibid., 312.
14. Ibid., 316.
15. David Butler, *Fantasy Cinema*, 20.
16. J. P. Telotte, 'Editor's note', 2.
17. Christine Gledhill, 'Prologue: the reach of melodrama', xiii; Linda Williams, 'Melodrama revised', 43.
18. Jean Laplanche and Jean-Bertrand Pontalis, 'Fantasy and the origins of sexuality', 26.
19. Ibid., 17, 26.
20. Elizabeth Cowie, 'Fantasia', 167.
21. Ibid., 168.
22. Slavoj Žižek, *Looking Awry*, 6.
23. Cowie, 'Fantasia', 159.
24. Thomas Schatz, *Hollywood Genres*, 7–10.
25. Chung Po-yin, 'Big studio, minor story', 106–7.
26. Stephen Teo, 'Chinese melodrama', 203–13.
27. Chung, 'Big studio, minor story', 115.

28. Wong Ain-ling, 'Ho Meng-hua', 316–17.
29. The novel of *Journey to the West* was written by Wu Cheng'en, and was first published in the late sixteenth century. Allegedly, various earlier writings had directly or indirectly influenced Wu's novel. For a recent, nuanced account of this, see Gao Quanzhi, *Journey to the West Reconsidered*.
30. Tom Gunning, 'The cinema of attraction[s]'. For an elaboration on Gunning's cinema of attractions vis-à-vis fantasy, see also this volume's introduction.
31. Edwin W. Chen, 'Musical China, classical impressions', 51–73.
32. Kei Shek, 'Shaw movie town's "China dream" and "Hong Kong sentiments"', 37.
33. Ibid., 40. For an account of the scale and operation of the Shaw Film Studio during the 1960s and 1970s, see Chung Po-yin, 'The industrial evolution of a fraternal enterprise', 7–11.
34. Shek, 'Shaw movie town's "China dream" and "Hong Kong sentiments"', 40, 41.
35. Poshek Fu, 'Imagining China: Shaws cinema', 16–19.
36. Chen, 'Musical China, classical impressions', 53.
37. Lau Shing-hon, *Dianying fubixing (Exposition, Comparison and Affective Imagery in Film)*, 206–19.
38. Teo, *Hong Kong Cinema*, 98.
39. Ibid., 98.
40. Ibid., 98.
41. David Desser, 'The kung fu craze', 19–43.
42. Kar Law, 'The origin and development of Shaws' colour *wuxia* century', 129–43.
43. Ibid., 134.
44. Zhang Zhen, *An Amorous History of the Silver Screen*, 199–243.
45. Law Kar, Ng Ho and Cheuk Pak Tong, *Xianggang dianying leixing lun (On Hong Kong Film Genres)*, 12–13.
46. Matthew Cheng, 'Destroy the old to establish the new', 80.
47. Chang Cheh, *Chang Cheh Remarks on Hong Kong Cinema*, 51–9; Teo, *Chinese Martial Arts Cinema*, 94–107.
48. Barbara Creed, 'Horror and the monstrous-feminine', 63–89.
49. Ng Ho, *The Alternate Cult Films*, 173, 192.
50. Kwong Kin-Ming, *The British Hong Kong Era*, 173.
51. Teo, *Chinese Martial Arts Cinema*, 159–66; Kenneth Chan, *Remade in Hollywood*, 75–103.
52. See for instance, Bob Rehak, *More Than Meets the Eye*, and Kristen Whissel, *Spectacular Digital Effects*.
53. Whissel, *Spectacular Digital Effects*, 17.

Chapter 7

Tracing the Science Fiction Genre in Hong Kong Cinema

Tom Cunliffe

Hong Kong cinema may be known as a cinema of genres, but one genre it has never fully developed is its own variant of science fiction. The genre is viewed as being a recipe for box-office disaster for locally produced films.[1] Given the dominance of Hollywood in the world-wide marketplace, the Hong Kong film industry has absorbed and reconfigured various genres from Hollywood to fit ideologically with Hong Kong's culture, but science fiction has never flourished in Hong Kong cinema.[2] This is because popular genres generally have strong economic and ideological roots in their respective mass cultures. The aim of this chapter is to trace the sporadic historical development of the science fiction genre in Hong Kong cinema and to analyse several films made in Hong Kong since 1979, which adopt science fiction elements to negotiate cultural and ideological anxieties related to modernity, coloniality and Chinese nationalism.

Wing-sang Law contends that colonial power in Hong Kong was never simply a top-down project of political power but was instead structured upon a complex web of relationships, or collaborative colonialism, which included a tacit collaborative contract between British colonisers and Chinese elites. Law argues that nationalism and colonialism were deeply interwoven in Hong Kong's historical context, and that to understand the creation of the 'mosaics of Hong Kong culture', it is essential to take on board how colonial power constantly disembedded and reintegrated Chinese identity.[3] In short, 'colonial power always functioned in establishing discursive and non-discursive possibilities and boundaries for different forms of Chinese subjectivity to be constituted and negotiated'.[4] Chinese cultural nationalism in Hong Kong, contained as it was by colonial power, became largely apolitical and abstract, and was promoted by the ruling class in forms that posed little threat to the status quo. The development of this abstract nationalist cause took place in conditions where social problems ran rife in Hong Kong due to colonial capitalist rule, and it motivated anti-colonial movements in the

1970s. From the mid- to late 1970s, young intellectuals in Hong Kong, working in cultural and artistic spheres including cinema, began to reject the binary frameworks of East versus West/nationalism versus colonialism, and instead attempted to 'establish a new local focus negotiating between these opposing poles'.[5] It is, however, partly the tensions and compromises between Chinese cultural nationalism and Western modernity, linked to capitalist institutions and oppressive uses of science and technology as embodied by science fiction, that account for the scarcity of Hong Kong science fiction films, since the way science fiction conceptualises reality and life does not sit well with local traditions in Hong Kong cinema.

Yet, science fiction, however unpopular in local cinematic iterations, was on the radar of the Hong Kong film industry. The films I analyse in this chapter blend science fiction motifs, iconography and narratives with other local genres such as *wuxia*, *kung fu*, comedy and the undercover cop/agent thriller. They are *The Butterfly Murders* (*Diebian*, Tsui Hark, 1979), *Health Warning* (also known as *Flash Future Kung Fu*) (*Da lei tai*, Kirk Wong, 1983), *Twinkle Twinkle Little Star* (*Xingji chuntai*, Alex Cheung, 1983) and *The Final Test* (*Zuihou yizhan*, Lo Kin, 1987). This mixing of genres foregrounds Hong Kong cinema's particular ideological perspective, which sometimes undermines, challenges or embraces the conventions of the science fiction genre. The different responses that each film articulates in the face of science fiction elements speak to the local culture in Hong Kong, being made up of constantly developing differences that resist being tied down to essentialist definitions of 'identity'. These varying responses are part of the complicated discursive enunciations of Chinese subjectivity conditioned by colonial power in Hong Kong, which refuse to be reduced to the strict East–West binary. In this experimental stage, from the late 1970s to the 1980s, Hong Kong science fiction films reveal the locus of Hong Kong cinema as one that shuttles between the local, national and global, both resisting and welcoming the modernity that the imagination of science fiction offers. This negotiation is a reaction to Hong Kong's position in between Chinese nationalism and British colonialism.

The Instability of Science Fiction in Hong Kong Cinema

Compared to many other film genres, science fiction took a long time to garner critical or theoretical attention in film studies. This was partly due to the difficulty of defining what exactly science fiction cinema as a genre is, especially as it overlaps with other genres like fantasy and horror.[6] The overlap with fantasy especially will be elucidated in this chapter since Hong Kong cinema appears to favour the imagination of fantasy in *wuxia* films over the 'scientific' outlook of science fiction. Although the conventions of both genres are similar, fantasy presents various impossibilities within the real world, while science fiction, however improbable, presents various possibilities that may come to be in the future. It is partly Hong Kong's contested history of never having political autonomy of its own due to residing in between two undemocratic sovereign powers that leads to the difficulties of representing or constructing a future, since Hong Kong's future has historically been, and still is, racked with uncertainty. This, perhaps, is why the impossible in fantasy is usually favoured over the possible. The immediately recognisable iconography of science fiction films – rockets, robots/cyborgs, futuristic cities, alien encounters and invasions, fantastic technology[7] – is rarely seen in Hong Kong cinema. The three most dominant narrative types of science fiction – encounters with alien beings and planets; projections of science and technology altering societies, cultures and the future; and technological advancements that have the potential to replace, or alter, human life[8] – are also uncommon in Hong Kong cinema. The films I analyse below do contain some of these elements but are also blended with numerous narrative or visual elements from locally popular genres to fit the ideological orientation of Hong Kong society during the 1970s and 1980s better.

Rick Altman proposes that genres are built up of repetitions but also variety and differences, so a genre should be studied by examining its syntactic structure (the narrational paradigms that are shared by individual films), semantic relationships (by seeing the genre as a system of differences) and pragmatics (those industrial and market conditions that reshape spectatorial expectations).[9] In short, the semantic elements of a film are its content and the syntactic is the narrative structure within which this content is entered and arranged. As for the pragmatics, Moine states that if this organisation of the semantics into a stable syntax allows a genre to exist fully, 'it only exists socially . . . when a community agrees to recognize its semantics and syntax'.[10] Throughout this chapter I will be assessing how science fiction is blended with other genres. The semantic–syntactic model can help explain the phenomenon of genre mixing since a typical narrative structure (the syntax) could be used from one popular genre while the semantic elements could come from another or numerous others. Certain genres are identified by very recognisable semantic traits, and various genres can be represented in a film simply by including a few suggestive semantic elements.[11] The way science fiction elements are blended into other genres spotlights how filmmakers negotiate the East–West dichotomy that is in constant flux under Hong Kong's colonial conditions.

Before the mid-1970s, there were almost no science fiction movies produced in Hong Kong. In other media, however, science fiction found a larger audience. From 1963, the Hong Kong newspaper *Ming Pao* began publishing Ni Kuang's long-running *Wisely* series, a collection of over 150 science fiction adventure stories that ended only in 2004. This success did not translate into film adaptations. While the 'new school' *wuxia* literature that emerged in the mid-1950s as newspaper serials by authors like Jin Yong were already being adapted into Cantonese films by the end of the 1950s,[12] the first *Wisely* film appeared only in 1986. Ni Kuang himself wrote over one hundred scripts for *wuxia* and *kung fu* films in the 1960s and 1970s but wrote only a single script for a science fiction film – the *Ultraman* rip-off, *The Super Inframan* (*Zhongguo chaoren*, Hua Shan, 1975). This suggests that the imagination, themes and topics of science fiction somehow did not fit well with the ideological perceptions of what Hong Kong cinema should be.

More concrete reasons for the box office failures of locally produced science fiction cinema link to audience expectations. Huen Ching Kwok observes that Hong Kong audiences find it difficult to get used to Hong Kong actors they are familiar with appearing in films related to science fiction themes of space and the future, but readily accept Hollywood science fiction films since they are connected to America's advances in space travel and technological development.[13] In audience reception studies, constraints of genres are often discussed as being social rather than textual since they are defined by the expectations viewers bring to a film in a particular genre operating in a specific sociopolitical context.[14] Kwok's point elucidates how audiences in Hong Kong were unwilling to accept a direct transplant of a Hollywood variant of science fiction to Hong Kong cinema.

Roger Garcia's discussion of the Hong Kong film industry's lack of daring producers also explains the dearth of science fiction films. Garcia states that it is unusual to see such a strong sense of wanting to do an old thing (the *kung fu* film) differently, as evident in *Health Warning*'s melding of *kung fu* with science fiction, since producers were only willing to follow trends and 'the system doesn't allow for experimentation or development in the [film] medium'.[15] The poor box office performance of Hong Kong science fiction films caused producers to avoid the genre.

This situation leads us to how the hugely popular genres of *wuxia* and *kung fu* have long negotiated anxieties over how colonial modernity could impact traditional Chinese culture, a juncture that further helps explain the lack of Hong Kong science fiction cinema. To jump forward a moment, Takashi Miike's *Dead or Alive: Final* (2002) is set in a dystopian futuristic world and is partly filmed on Hong Kong streets as a stand-in for the future, clearly inspired by the aesthetic of *Ghost in the Shell* (*Kokaku kidotai*, Oshii Mamoru, 1995). Curiously, *Dead or Alive: Final* opens with a montage of shots from different episodes of the 1960s Hong Kong Cantonese *wuxia* film series *Buddha's Palm* (*Rulai shenzhang*, Ling Yun, 1964). These images include fights between mythical beasts and swordfighters, light rays emitting from swordfighters' hands that shimmer in beautiful animated light, and a character flying on a mythical bird in the clouds, before this image dissolves into a shot of somebody waking up in the film's 2346 setting. This montage pays homage to the history of Hong Kong action cinema that has influenced Miike; it also projects the dreamlike nature of cinema and of a fantastical imagination imbued with optimism which, as the voiceover heard over these images suggests, has been eradicated in *Dead or Alive: Final*'s grim future setting. These images stand in for a future world that has lost its light and life to technology and is a direct illustration of the way that the fantastic rebels against the modernist disenchantment of the world, as this volume's introduction argues.

One of the images in this montage is that of a swordfighter using the 'Buddha's Palm' to strike open a metallic door, only to be confronted by two robots he must fight. Siu Leung Li argues that this sequence from the second episode of *Buddha's Palm* negotiates head-on the anxieties caused by the clash between traditional Chinese culture and Western modernity in colonial Hong Kong.[16] Li points out that, prior to this scene, the palm-power fighter cannot blast open a steel door with his palm power and mutters: 'Why? . . . I think this must be a steel door! That's why it can't be cracked open.' First, the anachronism of this steel door in an ancient *wuxia* world sets up a contrast between modern technology and the presently inferior nature of martial arts. However, immediately after this moment, the hero blasts open a different steel door by using a more advanced strike from the Buddha's Palm set. Li points out that if the martial arts level is advanced enough, it can defeat modern technology. This is when the hero meets the 1950s Hollywood science fiction-style robots that eventually injure him, causing him to flee. Curiously, he fights the two robots with his sword. It is as if using magic against the 'modern technology' that the robots represent would be contradictory. Yet, he loses to them because he opts to use his sword rather than magic. Li posits that this oscillation between conquering or being subdued by modern technology and the strange sight of this blending of a mythical Chinese past with symbols of the modern West perhaps materialise from a 'hidden cultural anxiety at large derived from the confrontation between the native and traditional on the one hand, and the foreign and technological on the other'.[17] This tension explains Kwok's assertion above about Hong Kong audiences accepting Hollywood science fiction but rejecting a Hong Kong variant. Hong Kong is, in some ways, a contradictory embodiment of a kind of Asian modernity that challenges the tradition-versus-modernity discourse imposed on Chinese cultures, particularly by the West. By blending science fiction with other popular genres, the science fiction elements of the films I analyse below generate critical discomfort by forcing into view the problematic aspects of the tradition-versus-modernity discourse.

The cinematic *wuxia* genre often expressed similar anxieties in Hong Kong cinema that science fiction films did in Hollywood and elsewhere. For instance, many 1950s Hollywood science fiction films expressed anxieties over the 'communist threat' or nuclear war. Alien invasions were commonly associated with the former and some of the science fiction *Wisely* stories written by Ni Kuang at the height of 1960s Cold War paranoia took up similar themes in the very different sociopolitical conditions of Hong Kong. Several *Wisely* stories allegorise communist China as a threat to modern life in their plots about chlorine-breathing antagonists, scientists from Neptune, jellyfish, egg-like parasites or even disembodied brainwaves, all of which invade Earth and attempt to shape it into what they desire.[18] In Hong Kong cinema, however, it was the *wuxia* genre that engaged in negotiating such anxieties, from the setting/safety of the distant past. Raymond Tsang notes how the Cantonese *wuxia* film series *The Six Fingered Lord of the Lute* (*Liuzhi qinmo*, Chen Liping, 1965) allegorises the fear of ideological infiltration via communist brainwashing in the way that the sound of the evil lord's lute can take over people's minds and make slaves of them by controlling their wills.[19] Many *wuxia* films also feature a narrative of heroes and villains searching for a destructive secret weapon that can either destroy or maintain the martial world,[20] which draws parallels with numerous Hollywood and Japanese science fiction films that similarly express fears over the potential of nuclear war destroying the world. In terms of superhuman robots or androids that feature in many science fiction films, including *Robocop* (Paul Verhoeven, 1987) and *The Terminator* (James Cameron, 1984), *wuxia* films can also deal in similar concepts by means of a more localised formula. For instance, in the *wuxia* film *The Deadly Breaking Sword* (*Fengliu duanjian xiaoxiaodao*, Sun Chung, 1979), a professional assassin is badly injured. After an alchemist doctor treats him using acupuncture and magic potions, he is completely transformed. As Siu-fung Koo puts it, 'with his strength quadrupled, he functions like an invincible fighting robot'.[21] The two genres can share narrative patterns, but the *wuxia* iterations replace futuristic imaginings that relate to technology or other worlds with more locally recognisable ideas.

The Hong Kong critic Noong-kong Leung's bemusement at the intense focus on the spiritual world over the scientific world in Hong Kong cinema also helps explain the lack of Hong Kong science fiction cinema. Writing in 1982, Leung compares the American film *Tron* (Steven Lisberger, 1982) and the Hong Kong film *The Dead and the Deadly* (*Ren xia ren*, Ma Wu, 1982) to highlight the way that the former's visual language reveals the 'scientific reality of the microchip world' while the latter showcases the 'excessive extent to which Hong Kong films capitalise on the Dead'.[22] Leung outlines Hong Kong cinema's inclination towards the spiritual world over the scientific one by describing how the realm of ghosts and spirits is an essential component of Hong Kong's cultural imagination. Leung considers Hong Kong cinema's intense fascination with the spiritual world over the scientific one surprising, as illustrated by Hong Kong's filmic imagination frequently focusing on the mythological world of the past rather than filmic depictions of the future.[23] Leung's point indicates other reasons why the science fiction genre struggled to gain a foothold in the industry, where horror and the fantastic, appealing more to 'impossibilities' rather than 'possibilities', align more precisely with the cultural imagination of Hong Kong.

Although not a science fiction film, Kirk Wong's horror–comedy *Lifeline Express* (*Hongyun dangtou*, 1984) negotiates these tensions between spirituality and science, the former ultimately prevailing over the latter. Tiger's (Teddy Robin) brother (Kent Cheung) becomes neurotic due to a fortune-teller informing him he will soon die. Throughout the film, Tiger constantly protests against superstition and fortune-telling, and desires a scientific solution to his brother's problems. His incredulity at the 'pseudo science' of superstition, as he describes it, is tempered by the fact that he still brings along his brother's birth date and time to a professor after he is advised to do so. Tiger and the professor engage in a long debate about science and spirituality. When the professor states that the study of times of birth is also a science, Tiger asks: 'Can a professor be so superstitious?' The professor replies: 'Sceptical? Why bring your brother's birth details then?' This interaction suggests that superstition related to spirituality is something that science cannot explain and is somehow ingrained in local Hong Kong culture, as illustrated by the highly sceptical Tiger's inability to detach himself completely from superstition. The professor's challenge to Tiger's scepticism could be read as an attempt at bringing together spirituality and science into cultural confluence. The film ends with a special Daoist rite guided by the professor, which, as long as they can keep a number of candle flames burning until after 11 p.m. while a typhoon blasts strong winds, will cause Tiger's brother to survive. They succeed and celebrate, and so the film appears, finally, to advocate for superstition. The movie's questioning of the cultural imagination of Hong Kong (cinema) is, in some ways, an attempt to come to cultural terms with both spirituality and science as parts of Hong Kong's reconfigured modernity. The film's ultimate choice of spirituality and superstition over science, however, offers clues as to why the science fiction genre has never integrated well into Hong Kong cinema.

Science Fiction Enters Hong Kong Cinema

From the start, science fiction films in Hong Kong were blended with other popular genres of the time and usually took a more fantasy approach. An early example is *Riots in Outer Space* (*Liangsha danao taikong*, Wong Tin-lam, 1959). This film utilises the popular two-fools comedy genre, where the two protagonists dream of visiting other planets and encountering aliens, thereby turning the science fiction elements into a fantasy since they are part of a dream. In 1976, Hong Kong film critic Sek Kei mentions that many Chinese translations of books from the West about UFOs and mysterious traces of aliens appeared in Hong Kong bookshops. But, in the realm of Mandarin cinema, *Laugh In* (*Haha xiao*, Lung Kong, 1976) was extremely fresh material, since the only other Hong Kong film that resembled *Laugh In*'s blending of special effects and farce, up to that point, was the Cathay production *Monkey in Hong Kong* (*Sun Wukong danao Xianggang*, Tang Huang, 1969).[24] This latter film features the *Journey to the West* (*Xiyou ji*) characters, magically transported to contemporary Hong Kong, and while to some extent it shares the narrative structure of *Laugh In*, and many other science fiction movies that feature people/aliens/creatures from another realm arriving on Earth and observing human society, it resides firmly in the fantasy realm. At around the same time, the Shaw Brothers released *The Brain Stealers* (*Diehaihua*, Inoue Umetsugu, 1968), which utilises science fiction imagery and ideas as window dressing for a spy thriller, fitting into the popular series of Hong Kong Bond-esque spy films released in the mid- to late 1960s. Aside from the aforementioned *Ultraman* rip-off, *The Super Inframan*, which was released in 1975, there seems not to have been any other science fiction films produced in Hong Kong until *Laugh In*. In this film, Lung Kong deploys the science fiction genre to spread his favoured message of universal love through the auspices of an extraterrestrial being, a message that humankind, it seems, is no longer in a position to promote. The film blends didactic melodrama into this mix along with comedy, which localises the film and strengthens its satirical look at Hong Kong society through an extraterrestrial's eyes. It was only from the late 1970s that Hong Kong cinema began tentatively engaging more with science fiction.

Now, turning to analyse several of these films, I will showcase a spectrum of different approaches to science fiction that reveal the tense and ambiguous relationship that Hong Kong cinema has in the period under discussion with science fiction. At times, there is a clash between the Western modernity and technology that the science fiction genre represents and locally developed genres and Chinese culture, while at other times, this seeming opposition is either embraced or articulated in an ambiguous way.

Science Versus Magic in the *Jianghu*: *Butterfly Murders*

Tsui Hark injected new life and innovation into the *wuxia* genre with *Butterfly Murders* and *Zu: Warriors from the Magic Mountain* (*Xin Shushan jianxia*, 1983).

Both are tangentially connected to science fiction in inverse ways: the former looks to explain the normally unexplained fantastic feats of flying and magic through scientific reasoning, whereas the latter uses hitherto unseen modern special effects imported from Hollywood to update the fantastic imagination of *wuxia*. They both mix traditional traits of the *wuxia* film with modern technology and science, but to different ends; *Butterfly Murders* undermines myth through technology, while *Zu* celebrates myth with an explosion of light and colour rendered by technology. Although neither succeeded at the box office, *Butterfly*'s science fiction-inspired tampering with the conventions of the *wuxia* genre rarely happened again, while *Zu*'s fairy-tale world is more emblematic of the genre. This section will focus on the science fiction aspects of *Butterfly Murders* and the ways that it attempts to blend tradition and modernity rather than setting up an opposition between the two.

Butterfly Murders opens with a series of mysterious killings at a castle, ostensibly perpetrated by killer butterflies. The master of the castle calls in a number of martial artists to investigate, which precipitates many twists and turns, and the arrival of more martial artists from different clans, who proceed to kill each other off. The scholar Fang Hongye, who records the happenings in the martial arts world, also investigates. It is eventually revealed that the master of the castle has orchestrated this gathering and the butterfly killings to eliminate other martial artists in order to become king of the martial world. The film is set in a desolate desert wasteland bleached in a dusty yellow haze, resembling a post-apocalyptic world. Annette Michelson notes that many science fiction films, from *Metropolis* (Fritz Lang, 1927) through to *Barbarella* (Roger Vadim, 1968), seem to regress from a sustained, coherent visual design to a 'fatigue of the imagination', a type of gothic past, and 'a style of medievalism . . . [that contains] billowing capes and gothic arches'.[25] This gothic look, including black capes, a black suit of armour and a dark castle, is precisely the design that Tsui opts for in his futuristic *wuxia* world set in the distant past, which fits well with the anachronistic technology used to explain otherworldly feats (Fig. 7.1).

Methods to modernise the *wuxia* genre include attempts to explain the flight of characters by showing them using a complex grapple hook and cable/rope system that can also turn into a type of zip-line. This zip-line leads to one character's death, a seeming commentary on the illusion of flight. In another sequence, two fighters glide across the screen on their respective ropes, with one catching the other with her rope and tying him up, the implication being that flight on these ropes is slower than the speed of otherworldly flight usually seen in *wuxia* films. Rather than magical palm power, homemade bombs containing gunpowder are used to explain smoke-filled explosive attacks by the martial fighters. The scholar even explains the ingredients used to make gunpowder, which are held

The Science Fiction Genre in Hong Kong   137

Figure 7.1   Flying with grapple hook and rope. Source: *Butterfly Murders* (1979).

in an underground cave in the castle. A metallic coat of armour is also used for defence. Critic and New Wave filmmaker Pak Tong Cheuk considers this attempt to blend the divisions between tradition and modernity, myth and science, and 'East' and 'West' to be a kind of creatively experimental failure. This is because he finds that the scientific explanations neglect the boundless potential of the imagination, especially when 'the metaphysical arts and extraordinary powers of the Orient contain their own spectacular attributes, which are well suited to the exercising of the imagination'.[26] Cheuk's discontent here links back to how fantasy rebels against a modernist disenchantment of the world, and is a direct illustration of the way that fantasy and science fiction operate in different registers: the impossible that gives free rein to the imagination versus the improbable that reins in and limits what can be depicted. *Butterfly Murders* operates in a sombre, modernist vein that does not accord with the transcendent qualities of fantasy.

Perhaps Tsui Hark chose butterflies as the ostensible killers due to the way they appear at times almost like an alien species in several prolonged close-ups, and also because they create a striking visual effect, including their appearance in several extraordinary butterfly-attack sequences that resemble onslaughts by science fiction aliens. However, the explanation of how the butterflies are controlled plays into more local traditions. Rather than being an alien attack, or even making the butterflies robotic, it turns out that a type of 'butterfly controlling medicine' controls the butterflies. When one character discovers this, he states: 'the art of controlling butterflies has reappeared'. On one level, it is treated like a traditional art with a long history in the *jianghu*; yet, on another level, one could argue that this medicine is chemical, which brings the notion back into the realm of science fiction. There is an ambiguity and overlap between tradition and modernity here, as there is throughout the entire film. Ultimately, the film lays out a new vision of the *wuxia* genre in which martial artists' skills and powers are boosted by their ability to harness technology and other science-based weaponry, which tempers the flights of fantasy familiar to many *wuxia* stories with scepticism and rational enquiry. This amalgamation of a venerable old Chinese genre with a modern vision is a sign of a distinctly local approach bound up with Hong Kong's colonial history.

Undermining Science Fiction through Comedy: *Twinkle Twinkle Little Star*

Twinkle Twinkle Little Star appears to be Shaw Brothers' response to *Zu*, an outward show of muscle-flexing to boast that they could also do big-budget special effects films. Shaw Brothers marketed the film as 'an amazing science fiction film'[27] and were clearly trying to cash in on the success of *Star Wars* (George Lucas, 1977). Yet, the comically inflected opening sets the tone for the entire film: over images of space and stars in a dark sky, similar to the openings of the *Star Wars* films, the 'Twinkle, Twinkle Little Star' nursery rhyme plays on the film's soundtrack. What follows is a series of comic sketches roughly bound together to form the thread of a narrative, in which jokes are constantly made about the conventions of science fiction and technology. This complete rejection and parodying of these conventions betray an anxiety about cultural values at risk in the face of technology. It is a sign of the process that Stephen Teo outlines, in which many Hong Kong filmmakers, from the New Wave period (1976–84) onward (of which Alex Cheung, the director of *Twinkle*, is a part), navigated their conflicted and ambivalent relationship with Chinese culture and politics and their own local identity in their cinema. They strove to create a postcolonial identity while preserving Hong Kong's distinct history. Yet, the fact that this history is constituted by the colonial experience complicated their efforts in constructing a Hong Kong identity disconnected from both colonial and national identification.[28] *Twinkle*'s approach to science fiction embodies these anxieties.

The film riffs on *Close Encounters of the Third Kind* (Steven Spielberg, 1977) in part of its plot about a UFO that lands on Earth. Meanwhile, a wholly unrelated story of two private detectives seems almost to belong to another film. The articulation of the two bumbling private detectives, who represent everyday Hong Kong citizens struggling to make ends meet, fits into the ideological orientation of the majority of Hong Kong comedies made during this period, which often focused on ordinary people fighting to survive in a cut-throat world. This plotline links to the science fiction plot only at the film's halfway point, through the character Li (Cherie Cheung). Li is set to marry a rich heir, but after she is 'abducted' and raped by aliens from the UFO, the heir's father rejects the marriage and a despondent Li goes off to commit suicide. The private detectives coincidentally bump into Li and they decide to help her by investigating the alien mystery. The science fiction plot, up to this point, is barely featured in the film, and when it is, it functions as a gimmick to show off special effects, including the effects-heavy UFO landing, and as a way of achieving comedic purposes.

Once the private detective, Eden (James Yi Lui), enters the UFO, designed like a *Star Wars*-style spaceship, he ends up fighting a Darth Vader clone with lightsabres. As he tries to escape from 'Darth Vader', he yells out various passwords to try to open the high-tech doors in the futuristic UFO. This scene replicates a similar comedic interlude in *Security Unlimited* (*Modeng baobiao*, Michael Hui, 1981), showing the film's debt to the Hui Brothers' comedies. Eden then calls out the name of a popular comedian who had a long career in Cantonese cinema from the 1930s to the 1950s, Yee Chau-sui, who is the real-life father of James Yi Lui.[29] This oscillation between high-tech modernity and tradition resembles the scenario in the *Buddha's Palm* second episode, discussed above. Here, Eden faces a hi-tech door as the lightsabre-wielding Darth Vader clone chases him. James Yi Lui, playing Eden, desperately calls out the name of his real-life father, who evokes the traditional Cantonese cinema of the 1950s and traditional patriarchal society. In the face of this threatening technological onslaught, tradition linked to 1950s Cantonese cinema is sought through a joke. Technology is then mocked when 'Darth Vader's' lightsabre runs out of batteries just as he is about to kill Eden. Eden then proceeds to beat 'Darth Vader' before a flying kick sends him smashing through a UFO window, vanquishing this technological threat through a display of physical prowess.

The ending reveals that the UFO/spaceship and everything associated with it is a fake, constructed by the doctor character. The film, finally, finds it impossible to accept the convention of UFOs/spaceships from outer space and the technology associated with them, which is why it spends its entire running time undermining and cracking jokes at the conventions of the science fiction genre. Perhaps engaging with these conventions would be a tacit acknowledgement that local Hong Kong culture was at risk in the negotiations between tradition and modernity, or national and colonial identifications. *Twinkle* was not prepared to confront this and so it parodied the conventions that it refused or was unable to use.

Imaginings of the Future: *Health Warning* and *The Final Test*

There are very few Hong Kong films set in the future.[30] This seems strange, given that many science fiction films from other countries have been inspired by the aesthetic clash between the bright, gleaming and commercial and the dense, urban and run-down that marks Hong Kong's cityscapes. *Ghost in the Shell* is the most famous example that depicts a futuristic city inspired by the excessive urban modernisation of Hong Kong. Neither of the two Hong Kong films set in the future analysed below utilises the city's iconic neon lights and outpouring of information flowing through the bustling streets. Instead, desolate, decaying streets and high-tech factories dominate, rejecting the image of a postmodern city on which much other science fiction cinema trades. Science fiction films depicting the future typically imagine bleak/apocalyptic/dark futures that are caused solely by human behaviour or human inventions.[31] This pessimistic imagining of bleak futures, often under the control of an authoritarian power, seems to embody a deep discontent in society at the time that they were made. *Health Warning* takes the future setting as an opportunity to negotiate anxieties about cultural tradition against technology, while *The Final Test* articulates the future as being threatened by a combination of ruthless capitalism and authoritarianism. In these ways, both films address anxieties related to Hong Kong's peculiar position in between China and Britain.

Health Warning is a *kung fu* film set in an imagined dystopian future. Its director, Kirk Wong, explained his disappointment at its box-office failure since, if it had been more successful, other filmmakers would probably have tried making more futuristic science fiction films, adding that he is 'sure a lot of people are quite frustrated in trying to find new ways of shooting kung fu films'.[32] So, Kirk Wong saw the movie primarily as a *kung fu* film, fused into a science fiction world. Yet, the oscillation between tradition and technology rendered by the merging of *kung fu* and science fiction is apparent from the film's opening.

Due to the low budget, onscreen text describes the film's future world as being one where huge advances in science and technology have caused people to become idle and decadent, leading to the crumbling of social order and the destruction of civilisation. Survivors roam the rubble-strewn, desolate, dark streets, affiliating themselves with martial arts schools. It is suggested that training in *kung fu* is a method to combat the social decay wrought by modern technology. The Straight Path school bases itself on traditional values, enforcing a strict training regime on its disciples and carrying forward martial arts virtues from the past. This tradition is articulated visually in the opening, with the master of the school (Eddie Ko) wearing a simple white T-shirt, and shots of his disciples carrying dragon and lion dancing equipment, playing the lion dancing drum and practising martial arts moves in a dilapidated old building. In comparison, the X school has recently appeared and its leader uses drugs and medicine–technology cocktails on his members to train and control them. He also lobotomises them to create an army of obedient warriors. Nazi symbols emblazon the X school while the modern-dressed leader punches some white-coated scientists after a failed lobotomy experiment. This contrast immediately pits tradition, here embodied by *kung fu*, a legacy of southern Chinese culture, against a sinister modernity. This set-up also takes the classic *kung fu* genre staple of clashing martial arts schools, usually one upstanding institution and one corrupted, and transports it to a fascist dystopia.

The dialectic between tradition as good and pure and technological advancements as corrupt and a threat to tradition runs throughout the film. Killer (Wang Lung-Wei) is the leading disciple of the Straight Path school and tests his martial skills in underground fights. An injured woman, whose child he saved, asks him why he believes only in 'ancient herbal stuff' when there are now all sorts of neo-medical treatments. Killer brushes this off, linking the 'neo-medicine' to the neo-Nazis that now roam this world. Later, the Straight Path school master cooks medicine using traditional Chinese ingredients to heal the wounds of a disciple. When Killer is attacked with chemicals, his master refuses the advice of a doctor to cure him with this 'neo-medicine' since it is 'against our principles to use such twisted treatments'. The doctor then proceeds to rub the blood of a chicken on to Killer's wounds and gives him other traditional forms of medicine to revive him. Killer's traditional school rejects the medicine associated with technology, which, by extension, is a rejection of the capitalist modernity that has brought about this film's dystopian world.

Classic elements of the *kung fu* genre are also utilised in a rapidly cut montage of Killer chopping down trees after his master orders him to gather firewood, which resembles a *kung fu* movie training sequence. It also highlights the traditional way of life that the school still encourages. These strict conditions are sharply contrasted with the exotic and decadent lifestyle of the X school, whose members revel in a drug-fuelled existence in their disco-arcade headquarters. The members imbibe drugs through gas masks, a transvestite strips and howls with drug-induced laughter, and women stand around naked among the flickering arcade machines as dancers slowly move to the pulsating electronic synth score. Killer's friend becomes involved with a female member of the X gang, and she murders him. In a transfixing scene, Killer goes to confront the female assassin. He wanders through this den of futuristic sin to the sounds of a remixed and slowed-down cover of the Eurythmics' 'Sweet Dreams (Are Made of This)'. The camera slowly tracks his progress as he throws or hits members of the neo-Nazi gang out of his way, cascades of bright artificial light illuminating his path. The combination of cuts between close-ups and the fluid motion of the camera, slowly moving between the dancers to the slow synth score, represents the drug-fuelled hazy atmosphere. Killer is attacked by one of the female assassins with multicoloured chemical syringes and returns to be healed by his master. After the X gang destroy the Straight Path school, Killer and his master enter the X gang leader's base to exact revenge.

Further opposition between tradition and technology is evident as they enter the X gang's base. The film chooses to ignore guns altogether, to replicate the patterns of *kung fu* cinema. For instance, in *Once Upon a Time in China* (*Huang Feihong*, 1991), Tsui Hark shows how martial arts were ineffective in the face of the guns of Western imperialism in nineteenth-century China. It would have been unrealistic and disconcerting to equip the high-tech X gang with sophisticated weaponry and allow the gun-less Killer to defeat them, which speaks to the tension between what science fiction and *kung fu* represent. The *kung fu* genre places boundaries in the science fiction world of the film and limits its technological fantasy. Pak Tong Cheuk considers the X gang's lack of weapons absurd in the film's futuristic setting, the gang representing high-end technology as it does,[33] while Kwai-Cheung Lo argues that the emphasis on the human body over advanced technology 'can be understood as a self-realising mode of responding to modernity and a rejection of the blind replication of imported sci-fi films'.[34] The film complicates this idea of the empowerment of the body to combat sinister technology/modernity in the sequence where Killer advances toward the leader of the X gang and faces a group of black-masked fighters, seemingly products of lobotomy and under the complete control of the leader (Fig. 7.2). They appear superhuman in strength and barely seem to notice Killer's attacks. They beat Killer and he has no apparent way of overcoming them. But Killer's master, in a computer control room, gains access to a computer program and manages to shut it down, which causes the black-masked assassins to malfunction and become harmless. Killer quickly dispatches them. Despite it not being explained how the master, a symbol of tradition, understands how to operate the computers, this sequence again brings into focus the battle between tradition and technology/modernity, as Killer initially cannot defeat the black-masked figures using his martial arts, but it is a technological flaw that ensures their downfall and allows tradition to overcome technology. The fact that the master must use computers to help Killer, however, suggests that modern technology is not unconditionally rejected. This sequence, in fact, simultaneously demonstrates both the failure of tradition (*kung fu* cannot overcome the technologically modified fighters) and the failure of modern technology (those modified fighters malfunction).

The film ends on an ambiguous note, with Killer driving off into the smoke in a futuristic-looking car, complicating the message of tradition overcoming technology/modernity. With almost everybody dead and his school wiped out, where is he driving to? This thrilling and experimental take on the *kung fu* genre forges another step in the struggle between tradition and technology in Hong

Figure 7.2 *Kung fu* fight involving technology and technological flaws.
Source: *Health Warning* (1984).

Kong science fiction cinema and is an attempt to recover a past at risk of being destroyed by the future.

After *Health Warning*, the next Hong Kong film to depict a futuristic, dystopian environment is *The Final Test*, made in 1987. It is set almost entirely inside a factory, where workers are treated as dispensable slaves and controlled by deadly performance-enhancing drugs. It blends elements of the *kung fu* and crime thriller genres into its science fiction iconography of sparse grey corridors, neon tube lighting, flashing lights, metal fences and a generally grungy aesthetic. The story is heavily influenced by *Outland* (Peter Hyams, 1981), with some significant variations that reveal its reorientation to reflect the preoccupations of Hong Kong cinema.

Outland tells the story of a grizzled Marshal (Sean Connery), who is assigned to a post in a mining colony on one of Jupiter's moons. The Marshal desires to eradicate the ills of the world, in this case the barbaric manager of the labour colony, who oversees part of an intergalactic drug ring that feeds workers braindestroying amphetamines. The Marshal, accordingly, wages a one-man war against this vicious system. In *The Final Test*, Ying Mo (Austin Wai) is introduced in a brutal fight sequence in which he defeats an opponent to gain the right to be assigned the role of security chief. *The Final Test* then diverges further from its source by making Ying Mo an undercover agent, sent to investigate how the factory is using drugs to boost worker productivity, fitting it into a long line of Hong Kong undercover crime thrillers. Ying Mo is given his mission, funded by the 'International Labour Organisation' high up on the peak with the Hong Kong cityscape sprawling out below, linking the story to Hong Kong and departing from *Outland*'s outer space setting. Although not much more is made of Ying Mo's undercover status, Wing-sang Law argues that the repeated motif of undercover cops being dragged down by their confusion over their identity in Hong Kong thrillers (from at least 1981) reveals a series of identity crises of the Hong Kong people.[35] In *The Final Test*, this typical Hong Kong crime thriller convention is used in a science fiction setting to investigate a sinister organisation that kills its workers for 'spreading rumours that damage the company'. The film opens with a security officer confronting the factory manager (Yuen Wah) over the stimulant used to exploit the workers by increasing their energy levels, which makes them mental slaves to the company. He is hunted down and killed in the factory as a loudspeaker announcement blares out that he has been exposed as an enemy: 'He spreads rumours harmful to our interests. You must raise your vigilance.' This heightens *Outland*'s depiction of the ideal of capitalism: disposable workers who obediently accept their fate, while articulating the future factory as an authoritarian system that brainwashes its workers and destroys those who attempt to change it. The plot tweak to make Ying Mo an undercover agent, sent to investigate an authoritarian system that wipes out any form of protest, reveals anxieties both about the extraordinarily exploitative system of capitalism, as science fiction tends to do, and also perhaps about the looming date of 1997. The undercover element also subtly shifts *Outland*'s futile one-man crusade into an organised resistance against corruption and exploitative working conditions.

Ying Mo arrives by boat at the mining factory. There are several shots scattered throughout the film of boats moving across the horizon and little islands dotted around that signal the setting as Hong Kong, which further links the plot to Hong Kong's sociopolitical context. Perhaps it was for budgetary reasons that the action was relocated to Earth, but it also situates the film in a local context. Both works focus on the dire conditions of the labourers, who inhabit this prison-like environment and put up no resistance. The workers sleep in cages in both films, but if futuristic science fiction usually rewrites a known city, then this bleak future projection was already a reality in Hong Kong, where some of the poorest do sleep in 'cage homes', a brutal example of stark economic inequalities resulting from the government's laissez-faire policies (Fig. 7.3).

The Science Fiction Genre in Hong Kong 145

Figure 7.3 Workers sleeping in cages. Source: *The Final Test* (1987).

Once Ying Mo discovers that the manager is manufacturing the drug in the factory, the message 'He spreads rumours harmful to our interests. You must raise your vigilance' is again blared out on loudspeakers across the building. A doctor has been coerced into producing these drugs and ends up helping Ying Mo fight against the assassins sent to kill him. When Ying Mo and the doctor finally confront the factory manager, the latter pragmatically states that 'we're not enslaving these workers, if man makes machines work incessantly, machines can do the same to man. This will increase productivity and lower productions costs. Human life is cheaper than machines.' The manager, who is revealed to be a cyborg when his ripped shirt uncovers a metallic body, is in charge of a conspiracy to make humans work for robots. He cannot be killed by bullets and is eventually taken down when a metallic door crushes him. This variation on *Outland*'s human-only plot articulates the way that science and technology are used, not to end domination and alienated labour, but to reinforce both. Ying Mo and the doctor attempt to leave but several more assassins appear and gun down Ying Mo in a hail of bullets, sparks and blood. The doctor rushes towards him as he slumps down dead, before picking up his machine gun and firing wildly, creating a shower of sparks around her. The film concludes with this freeze frame, an incredibly abrupt and bleak ending.

Outland ends with the Marshal successfully dispatching the corrupt manager and the hired assassins sent to kill him before returning to Earth to reconcile with his wife and son, satisfied that he has done his bit, while the system he rebelled against remains exactly the same. This depiction of a man rebelling against the system and achieving personal victory consolidates the individualistic ideology of Hollywood, while nothing fundamentally changes. *The Final Test*'s bleak ending suggests that the system destroys those that attack it and business resumes as normal. These similar points are oriented to the democratic ideals of America in the former, and to the lack of democratic rights in Hong Kong in the latter. The altered plotline in *The Final Test*, which highlights people's lack of power when they face an authoritarian system, here embodied as an extreme form of capitalism, seems to reflect again on how films responded to the lived reality of Hong Kong: a reality structured by mercenary capitalism and designed to serve a small elite, combined with a lack of democratic rights and institutions under British colonialism and also under the future rule of the PRC from 1997, making it difficult for people to control their own lives, free from the dictates of state and capital.

As a coda, it is worthwhile highlighting a couple of recent examples of the meeting of science fiction and Hong Kong cinema to show how the genre still negotiates various anxieties in relation to Hong Kong's (political) subjectivity. In Wong Kar-wai's *2046* (2004), Tony Leung's character writes science fiction stories about a time-travelling express train that takes passengers to reclaim lost memories from the future in 2046 – the date when the one-country, two-systems formula is set to expire. Kwai-cheung Lo suggests that the way that the characters in *2046* 'are transfixed by a "future" that resists any ultimate signification' could open up interesting political readings.[36] This again links to the way that Hong Kong cinema seems to struggle to imagine or construct a concrete future due to Hong Kong's own political subjugation. Louis Koo's long-cherished, $56 million science fiction film *Warriors of Future* (*Mingri zhanji*) is forthcoming. Koo himself, who stars, produces and was heavily involved in creating the universe of the film, recently said that the movie shows how the 'Hong Kong people can also make world class special effects'.[37] Koo's focus on 'Hong Kong people' here is revealing. Kwai-Cheung Lo describes how Chinese-language criticism often argues that Chinese filmmakers should not give up on the science fiction genre, since science fiction films

> symbolise the way the future can be conquered and imagined, and how advanced technology is mastered (as proven in the ability to produce such a genre), that would easily be translated into an index of national strength and cultural (soft) power.[38]

This is now happening in mainland Chinese cinema; witness, for instance, the recent mainland box-office smash hit *The Wandering Earth* (*Liulang diqiu*, Frant Gwo, 2019), which has been acquired by Netflix with world-wide streaming rights. That Louis Koo, long a supporter of local Hong Kong cinema, wants *Warriors of Future* and its special effects to show the world that Hong Kong cinema can compete with the films of other nations world-wide is a sign that science fiction is a genre that continues to navigate Hong Kong's predicament over its place in the world, now, most especially, in relation to China.

Conclusion

These films that engage the science fiction genre all negotiate various contemporary social problems and contradictions in colonial Hong Kong. *Butterfly Murders* attempts to temper the fantastic with scientific reasoning and an affirmation of (admittedly ancient) technology, while *Twinkle Twinkle Little Star* takes a polar opposite approach and completely undermines and mocks the technology associated with the science fiction genre, betraying anxieties about technology's potential impact on local culture in Hong Kong. *Health Warning* also lays out a wide range of views on and reactions to an encroaching modernity entwined with technology, working through the oppositions, and finding convergences, between technology and traditional Chinese culture, finally ending on an ambiguous note. Through its bleak imagining of a future that was almost a reality in some aspects, *The Final Test* erases the liberating potentialities of science and technology by showing how they are used in a totalitarian way to enslave and dominate human beings.

Every film analysed in this chapter performed poorly at the Hong Kong box office. This fact, compounded with a lack of daring producers, ensured that barely any science fiction films were produced in Hong Kong during the period under discussion. A sense of wonder related to fantasy and the impossible, rather than technology and the 'possible', was favoured, a phenomenon that has arguably continued up to the present day. The sporadic development of the genre in Hong Kong, combined with the way that it was usually mixed with other popular local genres, meant that there was no set pattern for films to follow. Each film here utilises science fiction to comment on dissatisfactions or anxieties at the time they were made, which specifically embody the contradictions that Hong Kong historically faced in its struggles between Chinese culture and nationalism on the one hand, and coloniality on the other. Yet the fact that the science fiction genre continued, and still continues, to be reconfigured and mixed with other staple Hong Kong generic forms also marks the ongoing relevance of this cultural and sociopolitical struggle between the local, the national and the global.

Notes

1. Keeto Lam, 'Film workshop', 12.
2. Yingchi Chu, *Hong Kong Cinema*, 67.
3. Wing-sang Law, *Collaborative Colonial Power*, 5.

4. Ibid., 5.
5. Wing-sang Law, 'Hong Kong undercover: an approach to "collaborative colonialism"', 528.
6. Annette Kuhn, 'Introduction', 1.
7. J. P. Telotte, *Science Fiction Film*, 4.
8. Ibid., 12.
9. Rick Altman, *Film/Genre*.
10. Raphaelle Moine, *Cinema Genre*, 62.
11. Altman, *Film/Genre*, 132.
12. Stephen Teo, *Chinese Martial Arts Cinema*, 84–5.
13. Huen Ching Kwok, 'Hong Kong produced sci-fi movies and series are difficult to succeed'.
14. Sarah Berry-Flint, 'Genre', 27.
15. Roger Garcia, 'Dialogue 3: Evans Chan–Roger Garcia', 12.
16. Siu Leung Li, 'The myth continues', 51–2.
17. Ibid., 52–3.
18. 'Ni Kuang', *The Encyclopaedia of Science Fiction* (last accessed 4 August 2020).
19. Raymond Tsang, 'Wuxia fantasy'.
20. I thank Raymond Tsang for this point.
21. Siu-fung Koo, 'Philosophy and tradition in the swordplay film', 29.
22. Noong-kong Leung, 'Golden years', 12.
23. Ibid., 12.
24. Sek Kei, 'Haha xiao: ticai xinxian, shihe ertong' (*Laugh In*: fresh theme suitable for children), 141.
25. Annette Michelson, 'Bodies in space', 61.
26. Pak Tong Cheuk, *Hong Kong New Wave Cinema (1978–2000)*, 86.
27. *Twinkle Twinkle Little Star*, DVD Extras (Hong Kong: IVL, 2002), DVD.
28. Stephen Teo, *Hong Kong Cinema*, 250.
29. Kwai-cheung Lo, 'Tech-noir', 146.
30. *Life Is a Moment* (*Zhaohua xishi*, Teresa Woo, 1987) and *I Love Maria* (*Tiejia wudi*, David Chung and Tsui Hark, 1988) are also relevant in this section. However, the majority of the former is a romantic drama set in 1987 and only a small section is set in the future, while the latter implicitly criticises present-day institutions and social structures as being the cause of a bleak future that humanity attempts to take a stand against.
31. Bruce H. Franklin, 'Visions of the future in science fiction films from 1970 to 1982', 21–2.
32. Roger Garcia, 'Dialogue 1: Kirk Wong–Roger Garcia', 3.
33. Cheuk, *Hong Kong New Wave Cinema (1978–2000)*, 191–2.
34. Lo, 'Tech-noir', 148.
35. Wing-sang Law, 'The violence of time and memory undercover', 388.
36. Lo, 'Tech-noir', 153.
37. 'Chi 4.5 yi paozhi gangchan kehuanpian "Mingri zhanji"' (Splashing 450 million on Hong Kong produced science fiction film *Warriors of Future*).
38. Lo, 'Tech-noir', 142.

Chapter 8

Chick Flick Fantasy and Postfeminism in Chinese Cinema: *20 Once Again* as a Transnational Remake

Elaine Chung

Fantasy film, which was once prohibited for its incompatibility with socialist realism, has rapidly developed in mainland Chinese cinema in the past two decades. Although CGI-filled fantasy epics like *Monster Hunt* (*Zhuoyao ji*, Raman Hui, 2015) and *Journey to the West* (*Xiyou xiangmopian*, Stephen Chow, 2013)[1] have dominated the box office as well as the media spotlight, they account for only part of the booming fantasy cinema in the country. Defined broadly by a set of 'volatile elements' that provide a feeling of 'ontological rupture from reality',[2] fantasy is highly flexible in hybridising with other genres.[3] While most Chinese fantasy epics are adventure movies set in virtual worlds created by computer graphics with reference to Chinese mythologies, 'contemporary fantasy film',[4] which relies less on special effects and more closely engages the real world inhabited by the audience, is on the rise in China too. *Ultra Reinforcement* (*Chaoshikong jiubing*, Lam Tze Chung, 2012), *If I Were You* (*Bianshen nannü*, Li Qi, 2012) and *How Long Will I Love U* (*Chaoshikong tongju*, Su Lun, 2018), for example, integrate romantic stories with fantastical tropes, such as time travel and body swap, that are visualised primarily by acting performances and the changing of film locations. To shed further light on the growth of the contemporary fantasy film in Chinese cinema, this chapter specifically focuses on the chick flick fantasy, a subgenre that centres around the fantastical trajectory and romantic life of the female protagonist. I will analyse *20 Once Again* (*Chongfan ershisui*, Leste Chen, 2015), a remake of the Korean film *Miss Granny* (*Susanghan Geunyeon*, Hwang Dong-hyuk, 2014), which tells the story of a seventy-year-old woman transformed into her twenty-year-old self. Borrowing the Hollywood-derived framework to read this hybridised genre in relation to postfeminism, I explore how the Chinese remake rewrites gender representations in the original

Korean text and, by extension, reveals the sociocultural meanings of chick flick fantasy within the context of Chinese cinema.

The Postfeminist Encounter Between Chick Flicks and Fantasy Movies

Critiques of the filmic representations of women have been an integral part of Euro-American feminism. Most representatively, influenced by second-wave feminism, a group of film scholars initiated a psychoanalytical framework in the 1970s, critiquing Hollywood cinema for objectifying women to cater to male visual pleasure.[5] But this argument has been vigorously challenged by third-wave feminism, which denies the assumption that all women face the same patriarchal oppression and emphasises the diversity of female subjectivities across different races, classes and age groups.[6] In the 1980s, when third-wave feminism produced a poststructuralist turn in feminist media studies, scholarly attention shifted to the question of how individual female audience members interpret and potentially subvert the dominant gender discourses encoded in media texts.[7] To complicate the dynamics of feminism further, the 1990s witnessed the rise of postfeminism. Described by Rosalind Gill and Christina Scharff as a 'sensibility' instead of a theoretical orientation,[8] existing definitions of postfeminism in film studies are multifold and incoherent, mainly derived from a cluster of female characters represented in American films and TV series.[9] An American postfeminist film, archetypically, features a young career woman and traces the 'makeover' of her appearance. More importantly, in the process of pursuing feminine beauty ideals by consuming luxury garments, accessories and cosmetic products, she also experiences an internal moral change and realises her need for heterosexual romance, marriage or companionship.[10] This explains why a postfeminist film always ends by rewarding a (re)femininised woman with the prizes of social mobility, popularity and new or rekindled heterosexual romance.[11] Although the representations of women's obsession with beauty and romance are labelled by feminist critics as patriarchal and regressive, they are legitimised in postfeminist films as signs of female empowerment as long as the heroine enjoys the process, voluntarily chooses her own lifestyle and achieves that lifestyle through her own endeavour and financial ability. In other words, laying stress on women's free will, postfeminism has posed a challenge to feminism by celebrating its completion and announcing its redundancy.[12] Although postfeminism itself does not have an explicit political mission to undo feminism or to advocate a particular form of femininity, combined with consumer culture, it is often manipulated to reinstall normative gendered stereotypes and numbs resistance against them.[13]

While postfeminist female characters can be spotted in many different genres of films, the chick flick, a subgenre that appeals to female audiences by highlighting the pleasures women can obtain from being girly and from engaging in intimate relationships, is an essential component of postfeminist cinema.[14] To amplify and dramatise the makeover process, fantastical elements are widely utilised in chick flicks. While ordinary chick flicks can, at most, transform a woman by changing her hairstyle, taking off her glasses or helping her lose weight, the fantastical devices of time travel, time slip and body swap justify more unrecognisable and scientifically impossible conversions, such as a mother exchanging bodies with her daughter (*Freaky Friday*, Mark Waters, 2003), a teen girl transforming into her thirties overnight (*13 Going on 30*, Gary Winick, 2004) and a single mother returning to the time when she was in high school (*Peggy Sue Got Married*, Francis Coppola, 1986). However, at the end of the narratives, the status quo is invariably restored. For example, after gaining a miraculous chance to escape from their mundane lives and reigniting a vivacious sense of femininity by dating younger men, most middle-aged and older female protagonists in chick flick fantasy films, upon realising the importance of motherhood and family love, prefer returning to their older selves with refreshed perspectives.[15]

Whereas existing literature on chick flick fantasy and its postfeminist implications, as summarised above, centre on the representations of white Western women,[16] one should not overlook the fact that postfeminist media, including chick flick fantasy, has been gaining mainstream recognition in other cultures too.[17] Jinhua Li observes that, beginning in the new century, Chinese cinema has been producing more 'postfeminist female characters', who are financially independent and emotionally mature, yet conscious of being feminine.[18] Chick flicks and their hybridisation with fantasy have been popular in China as well. However, not limited to the big screen, the cycle of chick flick fantasy in China is a cross-media phenomenon originating in internet literature, valorised by television and later expanded to cinema. *Love Through Different Times* (*Chuanyue shikong de ailian*, Feng Li, 2002), a story about two women who accidentally travel back to the Ming Empire (1368–1644) and fall in love with princes, is one of the earliest and prototypical chick flick fantasy dramas in Chinese television. Though it might have appeared innovative in the early 2000s as a TV drama, such a plotline has been ubiquitous enough to form a cliché in the realm of internet novels, especially among those published on a leading site, Jinjiang Literature City (www.jjwxc.net).[19] *Starling by Each Step* (*Bubu jingxin*, 2005–6), which begins with the heroine's soul being exchanged with that of another woman from the Qing Dynasty and traces her subsequent love polygon with several sons of Emperor Kangxi (1654–1722), is a classic example. The story has become even more sensational after being adapted into a trendy TV drama

Scarlet Heart (*Bubu jingxin*, Lee Kwok-lap, 2011). Interestingly, *Palace* (*Gong*, Yu Zheng, 2011), another drama that sketches a strikingly similar story about the romantic entanglement between a time-travelling contemporary woman and the same group of Qing princes, was aired in the same year and was equally welcomed by domestic audiences. Since the two dramas came in ninth and first, respectively, in the annual viewership rate ranking across the country, we can conclude that what is widely known in China as time-slip drama (*chuanyue ju*) has become a distinctive genre and has already formed a sustainable cycle in Chinese television.

But in comparison to the popular term time-slip drama, chick flick fantasy may better grasp their postfeminist nature. Being a highly educated career woman in the present-day world, immediately after the trip back in time, a typical female lead in Chinese time-slip dramas strongly resists the patriarchal society of imperial China, either by rejecting arranged marriages or building equal friendships with underprivileged handmaids. While her knowledge of history and modern science makes her an eccentric yet exceptionally bright woman in the eyes of powerful men, she often falls in love with one of them, usually a prince, gives up on finding her way home and willingly observes the conventional gender roles in that society. Her intelligence and agency, though retained, are then no longer used for her own sake but to help her lovers survive and triumph in political struggles.[20] Echoing their Western counterparts in terms of the emphases on women's personal growth and reorientation to traditional femininity, this cycle of time-slip dramas can be seen as a Chinese variation of chick flick fantasy, a subgenre first classified in Euro-American cinemas.

Though proven trendy and lucrative as a literary and a TV genre, chick flick fantasy has been comparatively less successful as a film genre in China. Maintaining a close relationship with Hong Kong filmmakers since the 1980s, mainland Chinese directors certainly are not new to the convergence of romantic and fantasy films.[21] However, concentrating on the growth of the male heroes who have exclusive access to fantastical experience and powers, most romantic fantasy or family fantasy films made in China, especially those that have topped the box office, can hardly be categorised as chick flick fantasies.[22] Although Chinese cinema has been producing more postfeminist female characters and some chick flicks like *Go Lala Go!* (*Du Lala shengzhiji*, Xu Jinglei, 2010) that were warmly received,[23] chick flick fantasy has been less capable of mobilising Chinese moviegoers to the theatres. The big-screen adaptation, *Time to Love* (*Xin bubu jingxin*, Song Di), in 2015, for example, failed to replicate the novel and the TV drama's popularity. None the less, *20 Once Again* is an exceptional case that attained both commercial and critical acclaim. The film earned $59.25 million at the box office, and ranked twenty-fourth among all domestic productions of the year. If, as discussed, chick flick fantasy is a subgenre that contrasts different feminine ideals and reflects the postfeminist thoughts of a society, the commercially successful *20 Once Again* provides us with a case study to explore not only the latest trends in Chinese cinema of blending fantastical motifs in chick flicks, but also the hybridised genre's sociocultural meanings to Chinese society, especially in relation to gender and sexuality.

A Comparative Analysis of a Transnational Film Remake

My analysis of *20 Once Again* involves an additional layer of complexity, as the film is remade from the Korean movie *Miss Granny*. Since CJ E&M, the Korean media conglomerate that launched the project, planned a Chinese version from the outset, when *Miss Granny* was still being filmed in Korea, the script had already been translated and handed to the Chinese producers. Although the original idea was to release both of them at the same time in Korea and China, respectively, the Chinese version was delayed for a year due to the complicated but opaque censorship procedures in China. As Higbee and Lim rightly argue that transnational cinema should not mean a negation and dissolution of national boundaries,[24] the notion of national identity is inseparable from the dynamics of transnational film remaking too, since the remade version often struggles to distance itself from the source text to invoke the construction of its own national culture.[25] The remaking of foreign films in China is no exception. While talents from Hollywood and Hong Kong have been heavily drawn to mainland China for the making of fantasy epics, Korean partners are equally important to the expansion of China's fantasy cinema, contributing to the development of more light-hearted, romantic and women-oriented content. This mainly results from the widespread reputation of Korean Wave (*Hallyu*) TV dramas in China, which sophisticatedly repeat the overarching theme of tear-jerking romance while constantly refreshing themselves with unexpected fantastical elements like time travel, spiritual possession, superpowers and aliens.[26] But the process of imitating or remaking Korean media products is accompanied by a sense of national anxiety that 'Chinese' cultural identity and, by extension, China's soft power will be weakened.[27] It is therefore not surprising to see that, despite its nearly sequence-to-sequence identity with *Miss Granny*, *20 Once Again* was publicised and later celebrated in China as an exemplary 'national film' because it was 'perfectly localised' to tackle Chinese cultural specificities.[28] The evidence for this claim, however, is limited to the addition of Chinese cultural artefacts on screen – Audrey Hepburn is replaced by Taiwanese pop singer Teresa Teng as the female protagonist's idol, and her favourite leisure activity is altered from working part-time in a café to playing mahjong at a recreation centre.[29] However, given that nearly every film remake relocates the original story's geographical or cultural background to one closer to the targeted audience, we should further identify the in-depth changes that the Chinese remake implemented to adjust the underlying sociocultural discourses of *Miss Granny*.

Juxtaposition of the source texts and their remakes is a common approach to identify the impact of cultural differences on transnational filmmaking. Under the premise that some of the most overt changes relate to the representations of gender and family,[30] a number of research works explore how the female characters of some American films were recharacterised in their Chinese remakes to suit the social reality of China, aiming to explore the conflicting gender discourses in the two countries.[31] However, there is a paucity of similar case studies on Chinese remakes of non-Hollywood films, largely due to a widespread assumption that the shared East Asian identity will minimise the need for cultural translation in film-remaking activities between China, Japan and South Korea,[32] though this has been proven to be an overly simplistic view.[33] To shed light on the realm of inter-Asian film remaking, since chick flick fantasy is itself a gendered genre, this chapter pays special attention to the question of how the postfeminist discourse of *Miss Granny* is translated and reconstructed to address the context of China. More specifically, the analysis below discusses how the two versions use the same fantastical device of body transfiguration to characterise their female protagonists differently – Malsoon in *Miss Granny* and Mengjun in *20 Once Again*.

Miss Granny and *20 Once Again* as Postfeminist Chick Flick Fantasies

At the beginning of *20 Once Again*, Mengjun, a seventy-year-old widow, is a nasty and foul-mouthed troublemaker in the community. Harbouring a deep-rooted mentality of privileging male offspring, she habitually treats her daughter-in-law and granddaughter harshly while being caring and tender to her only son and grandson. One day, when the exhausted family decides to send her to a nursing home, a disappointed Mengjun wanders the streets and serendipitously enters a photo studio for a portrait. At the moment when the camera light flashes, an unknown force transforms her into her twenty-year-old self. Although she has berated her daughter-in-law about the familial responsibilities of women, now that she is a young woman once again, she decides not to tell her family but to pursue her unfulfilled youthful dream of being a popular singer. Without revealing her true identity, she joins the band of her grandson, Qianjin, and participates in a TV singing contest, where she develops a crush on the charming music director, Ziming. After the transformation, she thoroughly enjoys her life as a young single woman. But, at the end of the film, in realising that her 'magical' blood can heal Qianjin, who is in critical condition after a car accident, Mengjun voluntarily donates her blood to him and returns to her seventy-year-old self. Because of her struggles during the fantastical experience, she is now a more easygoing grandmother and mother-in-law than before. Since *20 Once Again* is a close remake of the script of *Miss Granny*, except for their respective Chinese and Korean background setting and language, the two films share an identical plotline.

In many respects, the story of *Miss Granny* and *20 Once Again* closely follows the American formula developed in Hollywood chick flick fantasy films, characterised by their use of fairy tale-like makeovers to contrast and reconcile the past and present concepts of womanhood.[34] While postfeminist cinema is defined by its celebration of women's pursuit of traditional beauty ideals, in *Miss Granny* and *20 Once Again*, the first things Malsoon and Mengjun do after the transfiguration are to improve their looks by withdrawing cash from the ATM, going on a shopping spree and visiting a beauty salon. Since postfeminist discourse, as discussed above, views female beauty as a form of feminist empowerment, Malsoon's and Mengjun's makeovers are also represented as their independent choices, enabled by their financial independence and performed for their own pleasure. The satisfaction of putting on the clothes they once considered not suitable for an old woman and dared not buy is an example. Although their 'seventy-year-old fashion sense', in fact, made them appear bizarre in the eyes of pedestrians, Malsoon and Mengjun do not seem to be bothered by them and still confidently walk like fashion models on the street.

Michele Schreiber argues that time travel in postfeminist cinema is a 'matchmaker' since the past is depicted nostalgically as slower in pace but full of romantic potential, a place where an independent and strong-willed woman can relax and admit her need for love.[35] To reach this final destination, a woman's beauty makeover has to be followed by an internal 'makeunder',[36] by which she learns to be less aggressive and more elegant, charming and thus more desirable to men. Although Malsoon and Mengjun do not time-travel to the past, as their bodies have been restored to a more youthful version, both of them are granted more romantic possibilities with other male characters in different age groups. However, given the mismatch between a seventy-year-old soul and a twenty-year-old appearance, before attracting male attention and engaging in romantic relationships, both Malsoon and Mengjun must hide their real identities, suppress their 'old' minds and behave in ways that befit their age. This makeunder is particularly necessary when they encounter and try to impress their love interests, the music directors Seungwoo in *Miss Granny* and Ziming in *20 Once Again*. But it is also at this point that the dissimilar degrees of makeunder steer the films towards divergent characterisations of Malsoon and Mengjun.

Malsoon and Mengjun: How Feminine Can a Grandmother Be?

The seed of disparity between Malsoon and Mengjun is sown as early as in the first morning after the fantastical transfiguration. In *Miss Granny*, sleeping in a sauna for a night and fascinated by her now young and flexible body, Malsoon excitedly turns multiple cartwheels across the room. Framed with a static camera from a low angle, the scene highlights how weird she is in the eyes of the other sauna customers sitting on the floor. As the Korean title of *Miss Granny – A Strange Lady* – exemplifies, throughout the film Malsoon is never fully successful in assimilating the 'old lady' in her mind with her newly gained young body. She retains her unabashed personality, continues to swear in public, always inadvertently reveals her identity by slip of tongue and refuses to give up her fondness for excessively colourful vintage dresses. Despite a good-looking face, Malsoon's femininity is undermined by her reluctance to make-under and detach herself from her grandmother identity. This feature is underscored in the scene at a water park that takes place in the second half of the film: Malsoon's conservative and strange choice of costume – a yellow-life jacket and a yellow swimming cap decorated with colourful, stereoscopic flowers – makes her sexual attractiveness pale in comparison to the bikini-wearing women in the background (Fig. 8.1). Her unwillingness and inability to conform to the normative femininity that people expect from a twenty-year-old woman then become the

Figure 8.1 A rejuvenated Malsoon banters with Park at the waterpark.
Source: *Miss Granny* (2014).

obstacles in her romantic life. Most remarkable is the scene when she is drinking with her crush, Seungwoo, in his flat at night, in which he suggestively asks her if she has a boyfriend. In this critical moment, Malsoon, mildly tipsy, mutters that it is impossible since she has a late husband, son and grandson. A prospective romantic night is then abruptly and comedically wrapped up by Seungwoo, who is taken aback by her statement, spurting his wine on her face. On their next date at a park, Seungwoo asks Malsoon how she perceives him. Being sober this time, she is terrified, as the idea of dating him reminds her of her 'old' identity. Seeing her looking at the ground and telling herself that 'the age gap is no joke', Seungwoo seems to give up his pursuit of her, as he misunderstands that she has rejected him because he is older than she is. The romantic possibility between this pair thus comes to an end when Seungwoo, at last, looking at the full table of food she has prepared, says she reminds him of his late mother. The same pattern of interaction between the pair, from their first encounter until the end, demonstrates that Malsoon, though in a new body, never forgets her fantastical origin and consequently restrains herself from totally enjoying life as an ordinary young woman.

The supernatural transfiguration in the films, without any CGI to engineer the process, is simply visualised by changing the actress who plays the role – from an older actress (Grace Gua in *20 Once Again* and Na Moon-hee in *Miss Granny*) to a younger one (Yang Zishan in *20 Once Again* and Shim Eun-kyung in *Miss Granny*). The 'strangeness' of Malsoon in *Miss Granny* is therefore expressed solely by Shim's exaggerated facial expressions, comedic reactions and gestures, highly accented dialect and rude tone of voice. Unlike the unrealistic strangeness performed by Shim to remind both Malsoon herself and the audience of the miraculous experience she has undergone, Yang Zishan interprets her character Mengjun more naturally and in a relaxed manner (Fig. 8.2). As going to the sauna is a less popular leisure activity for elderly people in China, *20 Once Again* shifts the location to a plaza, packed with middle-aged women doing morning exercises, in which Mengjun finds herself waking up after the magical night. In this scene, the camera focuses deeply on Mengjun, seeing her moving happily through the crowd and joining the dance workout synchronically, without raising the attention of anyone in the crowd.

This early scene paves the way for the later parts of the story that depict Mengjun as more capable than Malsoon of adjusting and controlling her behaviour to suit the new identity, which enables the Chinese version to position her in more serious romantic scenes. When she and Ziming stay in the same flat overnight, the romantic potential between the pair is maximised and free from any unintentional comic interruption. After showing the two staring into each other's eyes deeply and sincerely, through the perspective of Ziming, Mengjun is captured in soft lighting and with a glowing effect no different from how a

Figure 8.2 Mengjun transformed into an attractive young woman. Source: *20 Once Again* (2015).

charming female protagonist in a romantic drama would be. The subsequent date between the two is similarly intensified from a picnic in *Miss Granny* to a candle-lit dinner in a dreamy Western restaurant. Unlike Malsoon, who made a big frowny face because of the bitter taste of red wine, Mengjun sips hers elegantly and takes the initiative to ask Ziming seriously if he likes her and whether he will love her, no matter what happens. Besides the treatment of this relationship with Ziming, *20 Once Again* is also ambitious in romanticising Mengjun's relationships with other men around her, including her longtime friend Daihai (Park in the Korean version) and her grandson, Qianjin (Jiha in the Korean version). In *Miss Granny*, interactions between Malsoon and Park are predominantly hilarious, as they always banter with each other. Although he did like Malsoon when they were both young, at the moment when she tells him of her affection for the music director, Park composedly accepts the fact and ends the conversation. But in the equivalent scene in *20 Once Again*, against the wistful, non-diegetic piano music in the background, Daihai more explicitly expresses his disappointment with the bitter statements: 'I have missed you twice in a life' and 'a young woman should not always stick with an old man, do not find me again'. The interaction between the female protagonist and her grandson is rewritten by *20 Once Again* in a similar manner. Whereas, in *Miss Granny*, the possible romantic moments between Malsoon and Jiha are laughed off by Malsoon's comedic lines and actions when she pampers him as if he is a little child or yells at him in public that he is not her type, more earnest conversations are inserted in *20 Once Again* between this pair. The addition of a rooftop scene, in which Mengjun softly and formally tells him in the rain that he will meet a better girl in the future, is an example. From the recharacterisation of Malsoon of *Miss Granny* into Mengjun of *20 Once Again*, the Chinese remake consciously distinguishes itself from the Korean original version by maximising the makeover effect, or more specifically, further feminising the heroine.

As Ferriss and Young suggest, in the name of postfeminism, chick flicks tend to destigmatise traditional feminine ideals by reconciling their conflict with the notion of female agency. Hence, after a series of makeover and makeunder plot events, at the end of the story, a chick flick heroine can freely indulge in personal grooming, lifestyle and romance without feeling that her independence is compromised.[37] Collapsing a seventy-year-old grandmother and a young single woman into the same body, the plot of *Miss Granny* and *20 Once Again* indicates the same intention to reconcile the sexual identities harboured by different generations of Korean and Chinese women. But the results of negotiation provided by the two films are divergent. While Malsoon's eccentricity demonstrates the unresolvable conflicts between the old and new femininities since her 'real age' restrains her from completely returning to and appreciating her girlhood, Mengjun, who is more sophisticated in managing her dual identities, on the contrary, symbolises a model postfeminist character – a woman who perfectly integrates (grand)motherly wisdom and youthful pleasures. From this, we can conclude that the postfeminist message of the source text has been strengthened during the process of transnational remaking.

The primary goal of feminist activism in Europe and North America, despite multiple 'waves', is to promote gender equality and condemn the marginalisation of women as 'non-men', an inferior social group. The women's movement in South Korea, similarly, is framed by a demand for the state's institutionalised efforts to protect women's equal rights within the family and workplace.[38] Western theories of feminism, however, are 'untranslatable' to Chinese conditions, by and large,[39] thanks to the radical gender policies enforced during the rule of Mao Zedong from 1949 to 1976. Under the slogan 'the times have changed, men and women are the same', gender equality was hyped by Mao as a hallmark of the Chinese Communist Revolution. But rather than encouraging free choice and the expression of sexualities, the so-called equality was achieved by masculinising women. Not only were they supposed to do heavy manual work like men, women at that time were also required to perform a 'socialist androgyny' by cutting their hair and wearing plain-coloured, loose-fitting clothes.[40] Although the 'gender equality' promoted in Mao's China may appear to be a feminist utopia from the Western perspective, it was paradoxically remembered by many Chinese women as an age of state violence.[41] As one can expect, in a relatively liberal society in postsocialist China, many women support the revival of gender essentialism, in a bid to counteract the 'equality' imposed by the state and to search for their own subjectivities. This phenomenon, together with the country's rapid capitalistic development, consequently generates a postfeminist, or in Tani Barlow's terms, a 'market feminist' discourse,[42] by which young women, especially those dwelling in cosmopolitan cities, believe that their hopes, passion, capability and success should be realised and articulated by conspicuous consumption and beauty enhancement.[43] Due to this happy marriage between traditional femininity, consumerism and female emancipation, women's culture in China has finally found a long-awaited common language: namely, postfeminism, with its European and American counterparts. In fact, while Western postfeminists constantly have to defend themselves from feminist critiques, given the history of the state-led gender erasure, postfeminism is more conveniently perceived by the mainstream of Chinese society to be a progressive concept that liberates Chinese women from mandatory mass movements. The postfeminist discourses presented by Chinese chick flicks, therefore, can be more vocal in romanticising the full embrace of femininity but less explicit in verbalising any radical political or feminist stance.[44] In *20 Once Again*, Mengjun's stronger commitment to make use of her second youth and be a feminine young woman is also a way for the remade version to address the experience of the Chinese female audience and the gender politics specific to China better. While Chinese cinema has been constructing this distinctive postfeminist discourse through different film genres,[45] the case study in this chapter not only finds that *20 Once Again* sits perfectly with the cycle, but also demonstrates how fantasy film is joining, enriching and vitalising it by contributing the unique devices of time slip, body swap and body transfiguration.

Closing the Open Ending: The Uncertain Future of Chinese Chick Flick Fantasies

Although it has been increasingly common to see the integration of chick flick and fantasy to renew the cinematic representation of Chinese postfeminism, whether this subgenre can continue its flexibility and vibrancy in Chinese cinema is still uncertain due to the all-encompassing film censorship system. The divergent endings of *20 Once Again* and *Miss Granny* provide some hints on this question. Since postfeminist films tend to reinstate traditional femininity and fantasy films favour a happy ending and redemption,[46] the chick flick fantasy film has little choice but to wrap up its narrative often by terminating the heroine's fantastical experience and reshaping her into the good wife or mother after restoring her to her actual age.[47] Adhering to this genre convention, both Mengjun in *20 Once Again* and Malsoon in *Miss Granny*, after the narrative climaxes, voluntarily sacrifice their newly gained freedoms and young bodies in exchange for the lives of their grandsons. Upon returning home, they are now more pleasant and lovable grandmothers. However, this 'happy ending' is not identically delineated by the two films. In *Miss Granny*, after the hospital scene in which Malsoon donates her blood, she returns to her seventies and the character is played once again by Na Moonhee, the older actress. Right after that, Malsoon is found at a TV broadcasting station along with her family, who have come along to watch Jiha's music performance. When she comes out from the building amid a large group of young female fans, she sees Seungwoo in the distance. After some cross-cutting shots between her and Seungwoo's faces, Malsoon turns around and the camera offers a close-up of her shiny hairpin, which is a present from Seungwoo. He, then, stares at her for a few seconds with a confused facial expression. The scene arguably indicates that he will be able to recognise her some day. In the next and final scene, Malsoon reappears at a bus station when Park is coming into sight on his motorbike. When he takes off the helmet, surprisingly he is now a young and handsome man, played by Korean Wave heartthrob Kim Su-hyun. He explains that he has just accidentally visited the photo studio that transfigured Malsoon. Closing the film by placing the seventy-year-old Malsoon behind a twenty-year-old man on a dashing motorbike under the gaze of some stunned passersby, *Miss Granny* ends on an ambiguous note that her fantastical voyage is never-ending, as it is still possible for another rejuvenation of herself, a reunion between Malsoon and Seungwoo, and beyond. Much of this room for imagination, however, was axed by the Chinese remake. Once she is sent back to her aged body, Mengjun, who is played by Grace Gua again, is, from then on, confined in the domestic space. In a living room rather than the broadcasting station, she watches her grandson's performance on television and reminisces about her time spent with Ziming, which is presented through flashbacks of their encounters and dates. The youthful Mengjun and the older Mengjun in this way are strictly divided, and her love interest, Ziming, can appear only in memories after the fantastical part of the story is concluded. Like a dream, no one in the film, including Mengjun herself, can stumble across such an inexplicable experience again. But the Chinese version is not unaware of the open ending of *Miss Granny*, as, in the middle of the closing credit sequence, Qianjin reappears and speaks directly to the audience: 'Bye! There are no bloopers.' Reminding the audience of the fact that they have just watched a narrative film, it discourages any fantastical imaginations beyond the film's running time.

One can only speculate on the factors leading to this alteration of the narrative. But it is not unreasonable to attribute it to the censorship of fantastical media contents imposed by the Chinese party state. While, on paper, media products that promote 'superstition' are prohibited, in practice, many domestic and foreign fantasy films that deal with monsters and ghosts have been granted access to the market.[48] But without any official guidelines to define the censor's bottom line clearly, fantasy films are still highly subject to unpredictable regulations. For example, although chick flick fantasy TV dramas could be readily found in the 2000s, the sudden boom of the genre through *Scarlet Heart* and *Palace* in 2011 alarmed the Chinese government, causing it to blame time-slip dramas for distorting national history and to issue a ban on them in the same year.[49] One senses that linking fantasy to reality, either in history or contemporary society, is regarded as sensitive, if not dangerous, by the Chinese government, as opposed to stories that take place in a virtual vacuum built by CGI. The government's suppression has immediately led to a decline in chick flick fantasy shows on Chinese television, as producers nowadays tend to avoid the iconic time-travel tropes, even when they adapt popular internet novels that invoke them. The female protagonist of *Legend of Fuyao* (*Fuyao*, Yang Wenjun, Xie Ze and Li Cai, 2018), who originally is a time-travelling woman in the book, for example, is modified to be merely a historical figure. Meanwhile, although the ban was not directly imposed in the realm of cinema, parallel to their disappearance from television, there have not been any other chick flick fantasy films that are comparable in terms of either popularity or profit earned to *20 Once Again*. None the less, since this hybridised genre has proven lucrative in the market, Chinese producers have been manœuvring through the loopholes of censorship to meet the high demand. The recent revival of chick flick fantasy dramas spearheaded by *The Eternal Love* series (*Shuangshi chongfei*, Yuen Tak and Wu Qiang, 2017–20) and *Cinderella Chef* (*Mengqi shishen*, Zhao Jindao and Zhang Jinxing, 2017), internet dramas that follow the recipe to pair up an unorthodox contemporary woman and a prince-like man in (virtual) history via time travel, demonstrates the potential capacity of over-the-top media service providers in rebooting and perpetuating the cycle. Nevertheless, as long as the Chinese government still maintains a strong grip on the production and distribution of media content, its tug-of-war with commercial players will continue to influence the development of chick flick fantasy, as well as China's postfeminist entertainment media as a whole.

Analysing the case of *20 Once Again*, this chapter investigates the interwoven dynamics of genre, gender and the transnational remake in contemporary mainland Chinese cinema. Although the film was a close remake of *Miss Granny* from South Korea, its modification of the story and recharacterisation of the female protagonist reconfirm the importance of the 'notion of the national' in transnational, inter-Asian film remakes.[50] That is, aside from language, background and film aesthetics, translation of sociocultural discourses is also a key strategy for a remade film to cater to its targeted culture. This chapter pays special attention to the changes of gender representation, since the subgenre chick flick fantasy, in accordance with corresponding studies in the Euro-American context, is closely related to the zeitgeist of postfeminism. The accentuated feminine qualities and heterosexual attractiveness of Mengjun in *20 Once Again*, in conclusion, show the film's attempt to bridge an imported script with the distinctive postfeminist discourse in China, which prescribes women's fuller embrace of traditional feminine ideals. But the analysis provided above also demonstrates how fantasy film can contribute its idiosyncratic tropes, like time travel and body exchange, to heighten and renew the postfeminist cycle in Chinese cinema. While this chapter focuses on the Chinese version, it is notable that the lucrative play of *Miss Granny* has also been remade in Vietnam (*Sweet 20, Em là bà nội của anh*, Phan Gia Nhat Linh, 2015), Japan (*Sing My Life, Ayashii Kanojo*, Nobuo Mizuta, 2016), and the Philippines (*Miss Granny*, Joyce Bernal, 2018). From this case study, one can see the significance of national specificity in transnational film remaking, how the same story is rewritten in other Asian countries, and how fantasy and the chick flick are combined in various national cinemas to build genre conventions and to produce specific (post)feminist discourses, all issues that deserve further analysis and research.

Notes

1. For more on these two fantastic films, see Mei Yang's Chapter 11 and Kenneth Chan's Chapter 12, respectively, both in this volume.
2. Katherine A. Fowkes, *The Fantasy Film*, 5.
3. Ibid., 2.
4. Holly Hassel, 'Fantasy film: nineteenth and twentieth centuries', 101.
5. Laura Mulvey, 'Visual pleasure and narrative cinema'.
6. Kimberle Crenshaw, 'Demarginalizing the intersection of race and sex'.
7. Liesbet van Zoonen, *Feminist Media Studies*, 107.
8. Rosalind Gill and Christina Scharff, *New Femininities*, 4.
9. Gill and Scharff, *New Femininities*; Joel Gwynne and Nadine Muller, *Postfeminism and Contemporary Hollywood Cinema*; Hilary Radner, *Neo-Feminist Cinema*; Michele Schreiber, *American Postfeminist Cinema*.
10. Suzanne Ferris, 'Fashioning femininity in the makeover flick'.
11. Gwynne and Muller, *Postfeminism and Contemporary Hollywood Cinema*, 60.
12. Angela McRobbie, 'Post-feminism and popular culture'.

13. Michelle M. Lazar, 'Entitled to consume'.
14. Suzanne Ferriss and Mallory Young, 'Introduction: chick flick and chick culture', 3.
15. Margaret Tally, '"She doesn't let age define her"', 1.
16. Ana Moya, 'Neo-feminism in-between'.
17. Ferriss and Young, 'Introduction: chick flick and chick culture', 9.
18. Jinhua Li, 'Consumerism and Chinese postfeminism', 567.
19. Jin Feng, 'Jinjiang' (last accessed 12 August 2020).
20. These motifs are deduced mainly from the plotlines of *Scarlet Heart* (2011) and *Palace* (2011), though they can also be found in other recent Chinese chick flick fantasy TV dramas like *Rule the World* (*Dubu tianxia*, Zhao Jinghui, 2017), *The Eternal Love* (*Shuangshi Chongfei*, Yuen Tak, 2017) and *The Eternal Love II* (*Shuangshi Chongfei 2*, Wu Qiang, 2018), *Cinderella Chef* (*Mengqi shishen*, Zhao Jindao and Zhang Jinxing, 2017) and *Lust for Gold* (*Jueshi qianjin*, Yuen Tak, 2019).
21. Hong Kong cinema, in its golden age in the 1980s and the 1990s, has been famous for innovative attempts to mix different film genres. Star-studded titles like *God of Gamblers III: Back to Shanghai* (*Duxia 2 zhi Shanghaitan dusheng*, Wong Jing, 1991), *He Ain't Heavy, He's My Father* (*Xin nanxiong nandi*, Peter Chan, 1994) and *Demoness from Thousand Years* (*Qiannian nüyao*, Cheng Wing-Chiu and Patrick Leung, 1990) are family dramas, comedies and romantic dramas framed by time-travel narratives. These practices have been extensively imitated by mainland Chinese filmmakers to develop the newly liberalised Chinese film market. For instance, Zhang Yimou's first co-production project with Hong Kong producers, *A Terra-Cotta Warrior* (*Gujin dazhan qinyong qing*, Ching Siu-Ting, 1989), is about a couple reincarnated from the Qin Dynasty (221–206 BCE).
22. *Goodbye Mr. Loser* (*Xialuo Tefannao*, Peng Da-mo and Yan Fei, 2015) and *Duckweed* (*Chengfeng Polang*, Han Han, 2017) are examples of male-oriented contemporary fantasy films in Chinese cinema. In such fare, the heroes reboot their troubled lives by travelling back in time.
23. Li, 'Consumerism and Chinese postfeminism'.
24. Will Higbee and Song Hwee Lim, 'Concepts of transnational cinema'.
25. Lucy Mazdon, *Encore Hollywood*, 26.
26. Jeongmee Kim, 'Say Hallyu, wave goodbye'.
27. Elaine W. Chung, 'Post-2014 Chinese–Korean film co-production'.
28. Niu Mengdi, '*Chongfan 20 sui* Zhong Han *hepai xin changshi dianying juben huhuan bentu yuanchuang* (*20 Once Again*: China–Korea new co-production format, calling for made-in-China script)' (last accessed 12 August 2020); Zhou Nanyan, '*Chongfan 20 Sui* zhanhuo 3.5yi Zhong Han hepaipian mishang "yiji liangchi" (*20 Once Again* gained 350 million, China–Korea co-production obsessed with "one script two versions")' (last accessed 12 August 2020).
29. Kai Soh and Brian Yecies, 'Korean–Chinese film remakes in a new age of cultural globalisation'.
30. Sarah Woodland, *Remaking Gender and the Family*, 13.

31. Jinhua Li, 'National cuisine and international sexuality'; Jinhua Li, 'You won't believe her eyes'; Jinhua Li, '*Mulan* (1998) and *Hua Mulan* (2009)'; Woodland, *Remaking Gender and the Family*.
32. Gary Xu, 'Remaking East Asia, outsourcing Hollywood', 201.
33. Basil Glynn and Jeongmee Kim, 'International circulation and local retaliation'.
34. Schreiber, *American Postfeminist Cinema*, 19.
35. Ibid., 88.
36. Joel Gwynne, 'The girls of Zeta', 61.
37. Ferriss and Young, 'Introduction: chick flick and chick culture'.
38. Seung-kyung Kim and Kyounghee Kim, *The Korean Women's Movement and the State*.
39. Shu-mei Shih, 'Toward an ethics of transnational encounters, or, "when" does a "Chinese" woman become a feminist?'.
40. Bret Hinsch, *Masculinities in Chinese History*, 154.
41. Emily Honig, 'Maoist mappings of gender'; Yang and Yan, 'The annihilation of femininity in Mao's China'.
42. Tani Barlow, *The Question of Women in Chinese Feminism*, 253.
43. Jiaran Zheng, *New Feminism in China*.
44. Li, 'Consumerism and Chinese postfeminism', 567.
45. Li, '*Mulan* (1998) and *Hua Mulan* (2009)'; Li, 'Consumerism and Chinese postfeminism'.
46. Fowkes, *The Fantasy Film*, 6.
47. Tally, '"She doesn't let age define her"'.
48. Rob Cain, '"Coco" got all of its ghosts past China's superstition-hating censors' (last accessed 5 November 2020).
49. 'China bans time-travel' (last accessed 5 November 2020).
50. Mazdon, *Encore Hollywood*, 26.

Chapter 9

The Sacred Spectacle: Subverting Scepticism in Tsui Hark's Detective Dee Films

Ian Pettigrew

Mainland China possesses one of the richest and most diverse religious histories of any nation. Yet, major events in the country during the twentieth century (such as the nationalist and communist governments' desires to modernise the nation and the latter's push during the Cultural Revolution to eradicate 'the Four Olds',[1] including all traditional ideas and beliefs about the extramundane) fundamentally altered how major segments of the Chinese population have since interacted with religion and traditional beliefs. Though the current Chinese government no longer regards compliant religions solely in a negative light, or (as was once the presumption immediately following the Chinese Civil War) as something that will fade away as its population becomes more secularised, religions in general are still viewed suspiciously as possible tools of enemies, foreign or domestic, seeking to undermine the Chinese Communist Party (CCP) and the country's status as a major world power. If religions refuse to submit completely to the state, they are in danger of being persecuted and viewed as enemies. Yet, in spite of the continued threats to their existence, Chinese religions have continually persevered, occasionally underground, as hundreds of millions of mainlanders currently practise the rituals and traditions of their ancestors, foreign faiths and newer belief systems.

Over the past century, mainland Chinese cinema has reflected these developments in its representation, or lack thereof, of traditional Chinese beliefs and religions. Since around 2010, the tremendous growth and success of China's film industry have led to a return to Chinese fantasy films, which often freely employ figures and elements from Daoist, Buddhist and other Chinese folk religions. Among the directors behind these films, Tsui Hark has perhaps the deepest roots in the genre. A leading filmmaker of the Hong Kong New Wave, and referred to regularly as the 'Spielberg of Asia', Tsui brings decades of experience depicting Chinese religious traditions in Hong Kong films such as *Zu: Warriors from the Magic Mountain* (*Xin Shushan jianxia*, 1983) and *Green Snake* (*Qingshe*, 1993) to the new fantasy-friendly market.[2] Three of Tsui's recent contributions to the genre centre around Detective Dee, a rational, Sherlock Holmes-like inspector, investigating crimes and mysteries of supposed supernatural origin. However, Dee and the narratives' scepticism are undermined by Tsui's choice to make this trilogy into *wuxia* films, with the resulting sense of awe they present to audiences through their spectacular visual effects. Building upon Tan See-Kam's assertion that Tsui utilises 'collage practice' in his films to 'render the familiar, the known, into fragments of distortions, or parodies of [their] former [selves]',[3] in this chapter I will look at the director's three Detective Dee (2010–18) films to demonstrate how, through collage, the films subvert their own negative narrative framing of the supernatural and religion, laying bare longstanding and new tensions between official lines on religion and the actual quotidian practice of belief by mainland Chinese citizens.

Stomping Out Superstition on the Screen

The relationship between religion and Chinese film has received little scholarly attention. Though this is likely to change as a growing number of Chinese fantasy films continue to adapt Chinese myths and tap into religions to justify their characters' superhuman abilities, the current lack of scholarship is probably due to the dearth of films containing religious subject matter because of the policies that prevented them from being made for most of the twentieth century. As Vincent Goossaert and David A. Palmer report, China's move from empire to republic at the beginning of the twentieth century was the moment that governments in China began to make concentrated efforts to mould followers of the Three Teachings (Buddhism, Confucianism and Daoism), practitioners of Chinese folk religions and Chinese Christians and Muslims to fit into their vision of a more modern China. The Guomindang government initially wanted Chinese religions to function as institutions, as Christianity did in post-Enlightenment Western nations.[4] 'Destroying the religion of the old regime and inventing a new place for religion in the nation-state were important components of all the modernizing projects that reshaped China.'[5] These efforts continued unabated when the communists took control of the government in 1949.

However, during the country's tumultuous and tragic Cultural Revolution, all religious practice was forbidden, though many continued to follow their beliefs and faiths in private and in underground associations. Zealous pillagers, eager to prove their loyalty to Chairman Mao and his new vision of the country, destroyed places of worship. In an effort to abolish old traditions that were viewed as prohibiting China from becoming a modernised country, the Red Guards were specifically ordered to destroy anything related to Confucianism. In Qufu, Confucius's hometown, they demolished everything associated with him that they could, including the world's largest Confucian temple and Confucius's family mansion and its cemetery.[6] Following Mao's death and the end of the Cultural Revolution, the government adopted a more tolerant view of China's past traditions and of religious belief in general. The complex in Qufu has since been rebuilt and the government now uses the philosopher's name to promote China in the Confucius Institutes it builds at universities around the world. However, the CCP remains wary of any kind of religious institution over which it does not have complete control, as clearly evident in its continuing incendiary relationships with Falun Gong practitioners, the Dalai Lama and Tibetan Buddhists, the Islamic Uighur minority group in Xinjiang province and the Catholic church (though a recent thawing in tensions between the latter and the CCP has led to new accords between Beijing and the Vatican).[7]

Without an intimate knowledge of China, many outside of its borders assume that through its policies (and because the nation is officially 'communist'), the country has succeeded in ridding itself of religious beliefs beyond its minorities and the uneducated. Frequent newspaper articles bemoaning 'China's moral crisis' often comment on the lack of religion in China, supporting these assumptions.[8] However, as Fenggang Yang writes, these are mistaken views 'of the armchair philosophers and theologians who read texts instead of observing human beings'.[9] Although official numbers have previously been difficult to gather due to a lack of independent studies measuring modern China's religious life, a thorough survey of face-to-face interviews, excluding the populations of the Tibet and Xinjiang provinces, conducted in 2007 by an international team of scholars, has revealed that '85 percent of the Chinese either hold some religious beliefs or practice some kind of religion', and that even among the CCP and the Communist Youth League of China, which require their members to be officially atheist, '17 percent ... self-identified with a religion and 65 percent indicated they had engaged in religious practices in the last year'.[10]

But the Republican government did succeed in the 1930s, through policies that the communist government largely held to and augmented, in effectively eradicating anything from movie screens that they supposed could promote belief in Western religions and indigenous folk traditions.[11] Foreign films endorsing Christianity were banned, as was the *wuxia* genre (martial arts films with knights that often feature fantastic supernatural elements, such as floating through the air by means of the *qinggong* technique), 'for spreading superstition and unscientific thinking'.¹² As Stephen Teo writes, the *wuxia* genre 'was . . . seen as backward, running contrary to the principles of the May Fourth Movement that was driving China since 1919 to refashion itself as a modern nation conforming to the precepts of science and democracy'.¹³

For most of the twentieth century, these bans stood in place, and some still do. For example, nearly all films featuring ghosts (with the exception of opera films and movies where the ghosts are revealed to be humans or the products of a deranged mind) are still banned in China, including Hollywood imports like *Crimson Peak* (Guillermo del Toro, 2015) and the 2016 reboot of *Ghostbusters* (Paul Feig).¹⁴ As Laikwan Pang accurately states, even with the potential economic gain of opening up other genres for the Chinese film industry to thrive in, China's censorship board, SARFT (State Administration of Radio, Film and Television), is not likely to lift these restrictions any time soon:

> Contrary to the assumption that current film policy in China merely pays lip service to the cultural imperative of local film and instead focuses on cinema's economic rewards, anti-superstition is still a prominent film policy and the state has not stopped using cinema as a propaganda tool.¹⁵

The censorship on superstition and supernatural themes has also had long-standing effects on China's art cinema. S. Brent Plate argues that even though the government's stance toward religion has changed, 'the linkage between the vibrant, creative and even subversive potentials of "art" and "religion" has been severed'.¹⁶ SARFT's goal for all of mainland Chinese cinema is for it to reflect the secular society that the CCP wishes to create in the country's national imagination and to promote throughout the rest of the world.

However, Hong Kong and Taiwan, which have both taken Western-style approaches to the principle of freedom of religious belief in the recent past and had their own film industries with separate censorship regulations from mainland China, have been under no restrictions on making films with supernatural elements or religious content, nor on genre films featuring ghosts or monsters. In both territories, films have played a part in larger cultural dialogues about various aspects of the Three Teachings and Chinese traditional beliefs and folk religions. For instance, in Taiwan, the traditional belief in foetus ghosts has been represented in films such as *Yingling* (Ding Shanxi, n.d.), a work that Marc L. Moskowitz describes as not only discouraging abortion, but also creating a space 'to reflect, and possibly to form, popular belief about the spirit[s]'.¹⁷ Both Taiwan and Hong Kong were instrumental in keeping alive and developing *wuxia* films following the mainland ban. King Hu's *A Touch of Zen* (*Xianü*, 1971), a Hong Kong–Taiwan co-production, is perhaps the most influential *wuxia* film in the history of the genre and contains overt Buddhist symbolism, even attempting to represent the concept of Buddhist enlightenment in its conclusion.

In Hong Kong, elements of Chinese traditional beliefs not only have made clear contributions to *wuxia* and horror films, but have also seeped into otherwise non-supernatural movies. These films even occasionally reflect upon the complex ideas of faith and belief in relation to Chinese traditions. For instance, in Dante Lam's *Jiang Hu: The Triad Zone* (*Jianghu gaoji*, 2000), a comedy gangster film, Guan Yu (Anthony Chau-Sang Wong), a general during the Eastern Han Dynasty who has been worshipped in China since at least the sixth century CE, comes to life and interacts with a dishonourable group of gangsters who have given offerings and bowed in front of his statue. At one point, Guan Yu holds a discussion with the boss's wife about whether they actually believe in him or even abide by the principles he represents, indirectly accusing them of hypocrisy and mindless worship. Such reflections on belief and overt discussions of the purpose of Chinese traditions would never have occurred in mainland Chinese cinema until recently.

Although these films were not being made in mainland China, they were eventually seen there and they had a tremendous effect. Following the Cultural Revolution and Mao's death, when China opened its doors again to the rest of the world's cultural output in the 1980s, martial arts and *wuxia* media became immensely popular and informed the country's popular religious imagination. Goossaert and Palmer write that

> all these novels, films, and TV shows were populated with Buddhist monks, Taoist magicians, and invincible heroes who could fly, disappear and reappear at will, read people's minds, and neutralize adversaries with their miraculous inner powers or secret magical potions. Indeed, for the younger generations, these stories were the main, if not the only, source of knowledge on Taoism and perhaps to a lesser degree on Buddhism as well; they inspired many vocations to enter the clergy.[18]

Though the Three Teachings and traditional beliefs were still followed and were being practised underground by some when these media were first distributed in mainland China, for the majority of younger Chinese the works played a major role in rekindling interest in religious ideas that were illegal to participate in only a decade before. It is easy to imagine how the many Hong Kong films set in the Shaolin Buddhist temple, such as *The 36th Chamber of Shaolin* (*Shaolin sanshiliufang*, Liu Chia-Liang, 1978) and *Tai Chi Master* (*Taiji Zhang Sanfeng*, Yuen Woo-Ping, 1993), would have made the prospects of a religious life not only exciting but also capable of giving life meaning for individuals grasping for identity within their ethnicity but beyond the nation and the party. This is a clear example of the kind of re-enchantment discussed by the editors in this collection's introduction. Religious beliefs in China have indeed survived, and former traditions have not completely given way to new forms of belief or Western religious systems.

Late twentieth-century China not only was a period of a literal re-enchantment with religion but was also the beginning of a national reclamation of Chinese cultural heritage on the mainland that culminated in the astonishing growth of the country's film industry. As the Chinese blockbuster proved key to the success of the increasingly thriving film industry and became an important tool of soft power, at the beginning of the twenty-first century, government officials began to reconsider and loosen many, though not all, of the regulations concerning the supernatural and the fantastic that had ruled the market since the 1930s. Chinese fantasy films have now taken full advantage of this relaxation of censorship.

As Hong Kong's film industry began to decline in the 1990s and merged increasingly with that of the mainland, its filmmakers brought with them both their experience making fantasy-oriented films based on Chinese culture and traditions and the required know-how to create the stunts, as well as visual and special effects. For example, filmmakers like Ching "Tony" Siu-Tung, director and action coordinator behind Hong Kong fantasy films such as *A Chinese Ghost Story* (*Qiannü youhun*, 1987), *A Terra-Cotta Warrior* (*Gujin dazhan qinyong qing*, 1989) and *The Mad Monk* (*Ji Gong*, 1993), brought his fantasy background to China, with a much larger budget at his disposal, to make an adaptation of the legend *The Sorcerer and the White Snake* (*Baishe chuanshuo zhi fahai*) in 2011. Many other Hong Kong filmmakers have followed the same path. The most prolific of these is Tsui Hark, whose representations of Chinese culture stimulate a sense of wonder in China and its civilisation.

Tsui Hark: Irreverent Nationalist

A captivation with China's history and traditions runs through all of Tsui's cinema. His films cover key moments in Chinese history, Chinese folklore and contemporary Chinese identity. Teo maintains that these perpetual preoccupations of the director display 'a Chinese nationalism which runs through [his] films like a red thread'.[19] Elsewhere, Teo contends that Tsui's 'nationalism must be seen in the context of selling Hong Kong cinema to outsiders', an argument suggesting that the Chinese aspects of the director's films are meant to diversify Chinese and Hong Kong movies away from other film products on the market.[20] But Tsui's nationalism extends beyond mere commercialism. Like so much of the Hong Kong cinema that Tsui helped characterise during its defining period in the 1980s and early 1990s, many of his films treat Chinese heritage with a fond irreverence, constantly seeking, as Tan See-Kam puts it, to 'foster new ways of seeing the familiar and the known'.[21]

Taking a cue from Hamid Naficy's concept of 'accented cinema',[22] Tan argues that Tsui's style accentuates difference when he adapts Chinese history and traditions because of the director's diasporic Chinese identity.[23] Tsui, who is ethnically Chinese, was born in Vietnam, moved to Hong Kong as a teenager and completed his university studies at Southern Methodist University and the University of Texas at Austin in America. When he returned to Hong Kong, Tsui became a leading figure of the Hong Kong New Wave, beginning his career with decidedly non-mainstream fare. He made films experimenting with form (*The Butterfly Murders* [*Diebian*, 1979]) and a controversial, violent work featuring three young terrorists threatening Hong Kong (*Dangerous Encounters of the First Kind* [*Diyi leixing weixian*, 1980]). All of these were commercial failures. And after this, as David Bordwell reports, many see Tsui as effectively betraying the New Wave by overtly seeking wide commercial success. Because of his involvement in so many Hong Kong productions through his company, Film Workshop, some even condemn him for leading the New Wave away from blossoming into a more artistically determined cinema: 'In this version of history, Tsui pulled the New Wave into the mainstream, dumbing down local cinema and leaving no niche for personal filmmaking. Ambitious directors stifled their own inclinations and obediently stamped out Tsui Hark product.'[24]

However, though often less startling and provocative than *Dangerous Encounters*, many of Tsui's later films retain much of the same visual style (for example, quick cutting, grotesque imagery, a heavy use of special and visual effects and Dutch-tilt camera angles), thematic interests (strong female characters, cross-dressing or identity disguises and the aforementioned obsession with Chinese culture) and the tendency to turn on their heads the genres in which he began his career. As a producer, Tsui had a hand in developing nearly every genre in Hong Kong cinema during the 1980s and 1990s. As a director, alongside his *wuxia* and fantasy works, he also tried his hand at many of these genres, including comedies (*All the Wrong Clues* [*Guimazhi duoxing*, 1981]), action films (*A Better Tomorrow III: Love and Death in Saigon* [*Yingxiong bense 3: xiyang zhi ge*, 1989]), period films (*Peking Opera Blues* [*Daomadan*, 1986]), kung fu (*Once Upon a Time in China* [*Huang Feihong*, 1991]), film noir (*Time and Tide* [*Shunliu niliu*, 2000]) and even a couple of American-style action films featuring Jean-Claude Van Damme (*Double Team* [1997]). The majority of these films, including the Van Damme film *Knock-Off* (1998), contemplate Chinese identity in one way or another. Beginning with *Zu: Warriors from the Magic Mountain*, Tsui devoted himself to meeting audience entertainment expectations, exceeding them and adapting the zeitgeist in his works. He states, 'We're going to reflect the general feeling of the public, that's the thing I have in mind.'[25] It is this desire to reflect popular sentiment in mainstream works, and Tsui's continued reflections on Chinese culture that make an analysis of his three Detective Dee films worthwhile. Tsui's Dee films succeed in bringing forward certain contradictory aspects of contemporary religious life in mainland China, where believers and practitioners of most creeds face new challenges under the current regime. Managing to express this gap, between the government's desire to render religions into controlled apparatuses in the service of the state and the religions' pull toward unchecked practice of their beliefs, is a feat that no other filmmaker could accomplish on mainstream Chinese screens.

Detective Dee in History and Literature: Ancient Chinese Sceptic?

Di Renjie was an actual statesman during the Tang Dynasty (618–907 CE). J. K. Van Dover notes that under Empress Wu Zetian, Di (hereafter, I will refer to him as 'Dee' as he is commonly known in the West) served as deputy minister of public works, deputy minister of finance, an official and governor in many provinces and districts, a military commander and twice as chancellor.[26] He was also a Confucian judge, who, according to legend, solved over 17,000 criminal cases.[27] In accordance with his status as a Confucian scholar and official, he was also suspicious of the supernatural. Though Confucius is never recorded as directly confirming his non-belief, many scholars feel that he and his followers expressed doubt regarding the supernatural claims of Chinese folk religions. Hu Shih writes that Confucianism's agnosticism was 'probably . . . meant to be an intellectual veil or shield for a denial of human intelligence after death, and a denial of the existence or reality of all gods, spirits, and ghosts'.[28] In this regard, Confucianism prefigured the attitudes to religion that are officially held by the current Chinese government. Additionally, the historical Dee reflected a desire to limit the influence of unregulated religions in his recorded actions. He is reported to have burned between 700 and 1,700 shrines to local deities of folk religions in southern China in order to control those that threatened authority.[29]

However, the most famous literary adaptations of the character of Judge Dee did not carry forward this Confucian scepticism in his reaction to supernatural explanations for crimes and mysteries.[30] This fictional character first appeared in an anonymously authored eighteenth-century Chinese novel, *Dee Goong An* (pinyin: *Di gong an*), and then in a series of stories and over a dozen novels written by the Dutch diplomat, East Asian scholar and novelist Robert van Gulik (who also translated part of *Dee Goong An* as *Celebrated Cases of Judge Dee*).[31] In *Dee Goong An*, the judge accepts the existence of ghosts and guidance provided through dreams. Van Gulik's Dee, still a Confucian official, occasionally debunks the supernatural but the stories often counter his conclusions. For example, at the end of *The Chinese Gold Murders*, the ghost of a murdered magistrate appears, indicating that he had guided Dee in his investigation, even though sightings of the spirit had previously been explained by the judge through his discovery that the official's twin posed as his brother's ghost.[32]

For the English title of his films, Tsui decided to abandon the confusing, archaic label of judge (used by justice officials who served in numerous capacities, including investigating crimes) and call Dee a detective. The marketing of the films is clearly one reason for the title change (an adventure film with a 'judge' hero promised in the title might conjure images of older, black-robed men and women swinging mallets at their foes) but, as Kenneth Chan suggests, there is another purpose for this adjustment. The films (through their mirroring of the visual effects used when Sherlock Holmes [Benedict Cumberbatch] pieces together evidence in the recent BBC series) link Dee to the recent popularity of Sherlock Holmes, specifically the Cumberbatch BBC drama, and the sceptical, scientific rationality he uses to solve his cases. Discussing Charlie Chan and Holmes's utilisation of this method together, Chan argues that, when following the two detectives' line of thinking, audiences 'find the vicarious intellectual pleasure of logical, scientific rationality as a route towards explaining the inexplicable'.[33] Holmes's determination to eliminate the 'impossible' when piecing together the causes of crimes he investigates points toward a rejection of the supernatural.[34] With Tsui's Dee, this rationalism contributes to a paradox in the three films (*Detective Dee: The Mystery of the Phantom Flame* [*Di Renjie zhi tongtian diguo*, 2010] and its two prequels, *Young Detective Dee: Rise of the Sea Dragon* [*Di Renjie zhi shendu longwang*, 2013] and *Detective Dee: The Four Heavenly Kings* [*Di Renjie zhi sida tianwang*, 2018]) that I will examine below.

Countering Scepticism and Suspicion of Religion with Spectacle

In the Dee films, foreign entities and corrupt Chinese powers utilise religion and traditional beliefs to deceive the populace, murder political rivals and threaten the Chinese state. The three films take place as Empress Wu Zetian (Carina Lau) ascends to power from her role as a concubine, with seemingly paranormal forces constantly challenging her rise and the strength of the empire. *Phantom Flame* welcomes us into this world by having us accompany a foreign dignitary as he visits Luoyang, then the capital of China. Officials direct him through a giant

Buddha that the empire is building in honour of the future Empress's imminent coronation. But once they reach the top of the statue and stand outside, one of the guides combusts into flames. When pressed by inspectors, the site's building supervisor, Zhong Shatuo (Tony Leung Kafai), suggests that the death was divine retribution because the deceased officer moved protective amulets placed around the statue's base. And from here, Tsui spreads figures and imagery from Chinese traditional beliefs and religions throughout the film as Dee uncovers a plot by the Empress to murder her political rivals through her chaplain, Shangguan Jing'er (Li Bingbing), and an additional plot by Zhong Shatuo to assassinate Empress Wu by collapsing the Buddha on top of her during her coronation.

In the two prequels, Mark Chao replaces Andy Lau as a younger version of the detective. As *Rise of the Sea Dragon* starts, Dee arrives in Luoyang for the first time, twenty-four years prior to the events of *Phantom Flame*, and immediately following the destruction of a fleet of military ships by an apparent sea dragon.[35] Because of their religious beliefs, the city's people feel that they need to appease the dragon by offering it a woman, the much-desired courtesan, Yin Ruiji (Angelababy). As she is preparing to be given to the dragon at a temple, Dee, Yuchi Zhenjin (Feng Shaofeng), the head of the imperial justice department and other detectives fend off a group of men that seem to want to kidnap Yin, but are actually there to find Yuan Zhen (Kim Bum). Yuan has come to the temple to rescue Yin but flees because of the battle. He has been transformed into a green-skinned sea creature by a minority people, the Dondo. This group resides on a small island between China and Japan. They have bred and trained the 'dragon', actually a giant squid, that demolished the navy's ships. They scheme to overthrow the Chinese empire and take revenge for being displaced from their home by China's wars. With the assistance of Zhong Shatuo (Kenny Lin), who serves as Dee's sidekick in the two prequels, and Yuchi, Dee defeats the Dondo and the kraken. The film concludes with Emperor Gaozong (Sheng Jian) awarding Dee the mace used in *Phantom Flame*.

The Four Heavenly Kings begins with a scene from the previous film, prompting Wu, who is afraid of losing her power, to retrieve the mace from the detective. She enlists the assistance of Yuchi, now a close friend of Dee's, and Daoist priests who claim to have supernatural powers (but actually perform naturally explainable illusions). While inspecting a crime, Dee uncovers the conspiracy against him and goes into hiding. As tension continues to brew between Wu and Dee, the Wind Warriors, a bitter Indian mercenary group that feel betrayed by the empire after they assisted a former emperor in claiming power, plot to overthrow the dynasty with their own religion-inflected illusions and Dee's mace. They have even hypnotised Wu and are influencing her tyrannical behaviour. Xuanzang (Gao Xian), the Buddhist monk whose actual pilgrimage to India inspired *Journey to the West*, advises Dee but when he dies, his apprentice, Yuan Ce (Ruan Jingtian), joins the detective in defeating the Wind Warriors. Yuan Ce projects a huge white gorilla avatar that he rides into battle to defeat the clandestine group's demon.

In the three Dee films, icons of religion and folk beliefs (a Christian church, the giant Buddha and the sea dragon from the legend of Nezha), prominent figures claiming spiritual authority (the imperial chaplain, the Daoist priests, the leaders of the Dondo people and the Wind Warriors) and a fear of divine punishment (the deaths caused by touching the Buddha's protective amulets, and the intended sacrifice of Yin Ruiji to appease the sea dragon) all promote the ideological position that religion is manipulative, fraudulent and dangerous to the health of the nation.[36] These claims are all similar to those the contemporary Chinese government makes as it replaces religious leaders with those it appoints itself, continually denounces the Dalai Lama, bans and denigrates the Falun Gong movement, tears down crosses from atop Christian churches, and places over a million of Xinjiang's Islamic Uighurs in internment camps to force them to denounce many of their religious practices and beliefs. Indeed, it would not be unwarranted to suspect that the films' narratives, along with the inclusion of the Holmesian reluctance to accept events of paranormal origin, were developed with the aim of pleasing SARFT.

In the stories, and their mise-en-scène and production design, Tsui implants significant details or scenes that counter these negative portrayals of religion and belief. In the first film, underneath the surface of contemporary Luoyang, Dee seeks out a mysterious doctor, Donkey Wang (Richard Ng), to establish what has caused various people seemingly to combust into flames when they have apparently committed sacrilege. Wang hides in a black market, known as the Phantom Bazaar, disguising his identity as the former imperial physician, Wang Bo (Teddy Robin Kwan). Spread across mysterious caves, the location itself of the old city of Luoyang (where mysterious, pale cave dwellers reside in mist alongside the bazaar where Donkey Wang peddles magical items) suggests that, underneath the officially sanctioned capital, where the supernatural has no place, there is a home in the city's subconscious for the preternatural creatures and magical items that have been forced out. The design of the underground city has a completely different look from the above-ground capital. Hard lighting creates heavy, long shadows of the abject inhabitants over the mysterious writing on the walls. Everything here appears taboo. Like the subconscious and unconscious parts of the mind, old Luoyang houses forbidden and repressed memories and beliefs that can and will resurface over time, as they do in these films and just as Chinese religious traditions have disappeared and reappeared in contemporary mainland China.

Rise of the Sea Dragon also has a doctor, Wang Pu (Chen Kun), who carries out strange, mystical experiments (which have led to his use of an ape's arm on his left side from a shoddy transplant) in an ancient Chinese laboratory. This is not a place where rational, science-based medicine is practised but more akin to the kitschy, underground magical Chinese store where Gizmo is bought in the American film *The Gremlins* (Joe Dante, 1984) or the Hong Kong black market shop selling dead *Kaiju* (monster) parts in *Pacific Rim* (Guillermo del Toro, 2013). In other words, the Phantom Bazaar and Wang Pu's lab are designed to evoke, in foreign and Chinese audiences, the associations with magic and the supernatural that traditional Chinese culture frequently conjures in mainstream films. One of Wang's experiments, and an example of Tsui's continuing anti-authoritarian streak, demonstrates this connotation. To rid the empire of the parasites with which the Dondos have poisoned the imperial court, Wang concocts a remedy made of eunuchs' urine that the Emperor commands all of his servants to drink to force the bugs to crawl out of their bodies. Additionally, in *The Four Heavenly Kings*, the Wind Warriors exploit the people's religious beliefs and fears of the otherworldly to hypnotise them, leading them astray from reality, and yet the film's final ideological battle is won when a Buddhist priest uses supernatural powers that stem from his faith to counter the illusions summoned by the invaders.

These examples complicate the films' apparent anti-religious plots and Dee's rejection of the supernatural. However, what truly offsets the films' scepticism is Tsui's choice to make them part of the *wuxia* genre, its direct connections to religious belief and the creation of spectacle through visual effects that bring the films into the new era of the cinema of attractions. As characters in all three films levitate freely through the air using *qinggong*, their flights problematise attempts to take Dee's dismissal of the supernatural seriously, as *qinggong* is rooted in traditional folk beliefs about how *qi* (the life force in all living things, according to Chinese medicine and tradition) can grant practitioners special spiritual powers. In contemporary China, the concept of *qinggong* possesses significant religious implications. *Qinggong* is a form of *qigong* (the exercise of *qi*), and in the late 1970s to the 1990s thousands of groups formed, modifying Buddhist and Daoist cosmologies to offer a form of what Fenggang Yang calls 'implicit religion', or largely informal spiritual practice.[37] One of these groups was the Falun Gong movement, whose protests outside of CCP headquarters in Zhongnanhai in April 1999 led to the overall banning of *qigong* societies.

Some leaders and followers of the Falun Gong and other *qigong* groups insisted that they could heal the sick, practise clairvoyance or make themselves so light they could willingly float. The representation of these kind of powers in the Chinese cinema of the 1920s, including *qinggong*, caused great religious excitement among Chinese filmgoers. Stephen Teo cites historical accounts of mainland Chinese audiences being awed by an early *wuxia* film, *Burning of the Red Lotus Temple* (*Huoshao Hongliansi*, Zhang Shichuan, 1928) (made before censorship restrictions were put into place), that prompted them to worship at the cinema:

> Audiences reputedly put up incense altars before the cinema to pray to the gods before watching the film, and young people were reported to be so affected that they 'left their homes and took to the hills, heading to Mount Emei in Sichuan Province in search of immortals to teach them the supernatural arts'.[38]

With the use of *qinggong* and other supernatural elements, *wuxia* films tap into longstanding beliefs that are part of China's religious and folk beliefs. Early *wuxia* films adapted stories and novels (known as *shenguai* [spirits and devils] fiction) that borrowed heavily from Chinese traditions about supernatural beings, such as demons, ghosts and Daoist gods. One of the directors behind an early *wuxia* film stated that

> we believe that films based on *shenguai* sources are much better in expressing art than all other forms of drama because they are strange as well as fantastical; possessing new things, new lives, new ideas which we cannot imagine even in our dreams.[39]

As Hong Kong and Taiwanese films would do later in mainland China, these movies operated as loci of spiritual encounter. In this earlier director's insistence that these films' treatment of ancient religious ideas and figures exposed audiences to 'new' things, he suggests that these films operate as a bridge between the traditional and the modern, enabling viewers to reconceive their beliefs and adjust them to contemporary life. The materialisation of the heroes' powers through visual effects may have prompted some devotees to desire to obtain the heroes' abilities for themselves, but the fact that believers were motivated to erect altars in front of cinema houses indicates that they also provoked spiritual introspection.

In Tsui's choice to hybridise the Detective Dee films by blending the detective genre with the fantasy *wuxia* tradition, these recent works carry with them deep-rooted cultural associations. I will now illustrate this with a specific example from *Rise of the Sea Dragon*. After they deliver the remedy to relieve the imperial court of parasites, Dee and Yuchi reason that a mole has penetrated the capital's justice department and has leaked important information to the Dondos. They set up a trap by having Yuchi issue an order that they know will force the spy to attempt an escape and alert his allies. In the courtyard, the department has gathered all of its officers who await the command to seek out the Dondos. Dee, as if he is performing a religious rite to ascertain divine will, lights a joss stick in front of the men and informs them that when the incense burns out, they will know when they need to attack. Zhong asks Dee if he actually believes in 'that stuff'. The detective briefs his sidekick about the plan, to provide just enough time for the spy to leave the courtyard and be apprehended by Yuchi.

After the mole exits, Yuchi rams his horse into the traitor's mount and hurls them both into the air. Using *qinggong*, the combatants float over buildings before making controlled landings. Following the spy's revelation that he betrayed the justice department to receive a noble title from the Dondos when they control the government, the two begin a lengthy battle. They flip off walls and launch themselves in the air as they attempt to pierce one another with their weapons. In one particular moment of interest during their fight, the spy flings a set of daggers at Yuchi in slow motion. To deflect the blades, Yuchi splits into three versions of himself to parry them aside. The battle soon ends when the spy escapes to the sea.

This scene is exemplary of Tsui's distortion of the detective genre in this trilogy for several reasons. First, Tsui follows Dee's outright rejection of the possibility of receiving divine will through the joss sticks with an extended *qinggong* fight sequence, juxtaposing the sceptic's position with the supernatural. This is the kind of collage practice in Tsui's films that Tan argues 'yield bizarre forms, preposterous situations, mind-boggling distortions, and surreal(ist) mishmashes'.[40] Here, this surreal consolidation reflects some of the inconsistencies of religious life in contemporary China, of the tension between official and encouraged atheism and the general population's very visible, widespread, quotidian displays of their extramundane beliefs (the wearing of Buddhist prayer beads, ancestor worship, *qi gong*, visiting fortune tellers and mediums and the burning of spirit money). By infusing the *wuxia* tradition into these films, Tsui rebuffs the idea of a thoroughly secularised country, opening Chinese mainstream cinema back up to China's religions. The division suggested in these moments underscores the fact that China is, and has always been, a poly-religious country and the push to bring all of its religions' adherents into theological and ideological alignment is doomed to fail.

By rendering detective movies into *wuxia* fantasy films through special and visual effects, Tsui also contributes to a new Chinese cinema of attractions capable of invoking a type of spiritual wonder in the context of films with religious subject matter, as was the case with early *wuxia* films. In the scene described above, when Yuchi multiplies himself, Tsui references a key influence for all films in the new cinema of attractions, *The Matrix* (The Wachowskis, 1999).[41] *The Matrix* utilises the links between religion, martial arts and *wuxia* to justify its hero's singular abilities to challenge his previous vision of reality. Citing the earlier film's scene when Neo (Keanu Reeves) shoots at one of the Matrix's agents (Robert Taylor), who dodges the bullets by appearing to reproduce shadows of himself, in 'bullet time', Tsui brings *The Matrix*'s appropriations back to their origins. Within the framework of films that materialise, through special and visual effects, abilities supposedly gained through spiritual mastery, the spectacle of the attractions disrupts the narrative and asks viewers to examine their beliefs, to contemplate what is possible in their belief system or the understanding of existence that they hold. As Scott Bukatman writes in his discussion of spectacle and special effects, 'Extending the boundaries of the known reminds us of all that remains unknowable.'[42] Resurrecting powers linked with ancient traditions and giving them new form through advanced technology generates a fresh space to contemplate how one's beliefs answer questions about the ineffable.

Conclusion

In the case of the Dee films, Tsui uses the attractions' reminders of the 'unknowable' as a redoubled dispute of the narratives' repudiation and defamation of religion. They open a fissure outside of the films' diegesis as we come to terms with spectacles that challenge and enlighten our sense of the possible. For adherents of Chinese belief systems, these moments may even be faith-expanding as the films' heroes use of *qinggong* cannot be divorced from its past and current cultural implications. These three films celebrate the survival of Chinese faith traditions in spite of repression by authoritative governments, as represented by Empress Wu. Indeed, *The Four Heavenly Kings* has been released at a time when the CCP has increased pressure on religions to hand over to the government more control over leadership and day-to-day religious practice.[43] The Detective Dee trilogy reiterates that believers in Chinese religions and folk beliefs may superficially defer to regulations on their faith but these belief systems will survive all efforts to control and quell them.[44]

Notes

1. As part of his plan to rid the Chinese Communist Party of opposing views during the Cultural Revolution, Chairman Mao and his allies encouraged the Red Guards to destroy 'the Four Olds', specifically referring to old ideas, old customs, old habits and old culture. This led to the closure and destruction of traditional sites of belief, as well as churches, schools and universities. Citizens accused of practising 'the Four Olds' were punished with beatings, occasionally to death.

2. Tsui Hark, interview by Stephen Short, 'Tsui Hark: "you have to touch people with film"' (last accessed 13 April 2019).
3. Tan See-Kam, 'Surfing with the surreal in Tsui Hark's wave', 35.
4. Vincent Goossaert and David A. Palmer, *The Religious Question in Modern China*, 41.
5. Ibid., 43.
6. Daniel K. Gardner, *Confucianism*, 117.
7. These stories appear almost on a weekly basis, if not more frequently, in news about China.
8. For example, see Lijia Zhang, 'How can I be proud of my China if we are a nation of 1.4bn cold hearts?' (last accessed 13 April 2019).
9. Fenggang Yang, *Religion in China*, xi.
10. David Briggs, 'Study: rising religious tide in China overwhelms atheist doctrine' (last accessed 13 April 2019).
11. Laikwan Pang gives a much more detailed account of the evolution of the CCP's censorship from the Guomindang's in her article, 'The state against ghosts'.
12. Stephen Teo, *Chinese Martial Arts Cinema*, 40.
13. Ibid., 37.
14. Pang, 'The state against ghosts', 470.
15. Ibid., 470.
16. S. Brent Plate, 'Religion and world cinema', 92.
17. Marc L. Moskowitz, *The Haunting Fetus*, 83.
18. Goossaert and Palmer, *The Religious Question in Modern China*, 277.
19. Stephen Teo, *Hong Kong Cinema*, 163.
20. Stephen Teo, 'Tsui Hark', 148.
21. Tan, 'Surfing with the surreal in Tsui Hark's wave', 34.
22. See Hamid Naficy, *An Accented Cinema*.
23. Tan, 'Surfing with the surreal in Tsui Hark's wave', 34–5.
24. David Bordwell, *Planet Hong Kong*, 85.
25. Tsui Hark, interview by Beth Accomando, 'Army of Harkness: Hong Kong director Tsui Hark takes on the west', in *Giant Robot* 8, 1997, quoted in Lisa Morton, *The Cinema of Tsui Hark*, 5.
26. J. K. Van Dover, *The Judge Dee Novels of R. H. van Gulik*, 10.
27. In Chinese detective literature, judges also play the role of detectives. Ibid., 9.
28. Hu Shih, 'The right to doubt in ancient Chinese thought', 296.
29. David McMullen, 'The real Judge Dee', 8–11.
30. Many other writers, from the West and the East, have given Judge Dee new mysteries to solve, including Liu Qianyu, on whose novel Tsui based his first Dee film.
31. The book was also known by the title *Wu Zetian sida qi'an* (*Four Great Strange Cases of Empress Wu's Reign*). Dee Goong An is a non-standard romanisation of Di gong an (Dee's cases).
32. Robert van Gulik, *The Chinese Gold Murders*, 196. Van Gulik apparently did not identify with any specific religion but was fascinated by Chinese religions, weaving details about them into the Dee novels and even writing an academic article exploring a Daoist ritual.

See Janwillem van de Wetering, *Robert van Gulik: His Life His Work*, chapters 4, 5, 10 and 12.
33. Kenneth Chan, 'Tsui Hark's *Detective Dee* films', 139.
34. Arthur Conan Doyle, *Sherlock Holmes*, vol. 1, 159–60.
35. Some of the geography of the second Dee film is confusing. When the film begins, we presume the action takes place somewhere along the East China Sea. But Luoyang, the location of the rest of the film, is a landlocked city. There are some rivers near it but most of the scenes with the dragon appear to take place in an ocean.
36. Though the appearance of the Christian church in *Phantom Flame* may appear anachronistic to some, Christianity was indeed present in China during the period when the three films are set. There is some evidence, chiefly based on bas-relief sculptures found in Lianyungang (previously thought to have depicted Buddhist figures), that Christianity could have entered China as early as the first century of the common era. However, most scholars agree that the religion was never firmly established in the country until 635 CE, during the early Tang Dynasty, when a group of Nestorian Christians arrived in Chang'an (now Xian), met Emperor Taizong, built a church and developed a significant following. The religion mostly disappeared from the country by the end of the Tang Dynasty and reappeared during the Mongol conquest of China. See Daniel H. Bays, *A New History of Christianity in China*, 7–11.
37. Yang, *Religion in China*, 113.
38. Teo, *Chinese Martial Arts Cinema*, 32.
39. Ying, Dou, 'Shenguaiju zhi wojian' ('My View on Shenguai Drama'), *Yinxing* (SilverStar) 8, 1927, reprinted in *Zhongguo wusheng dianying* ('The Chinese Silent Cinema') (Beijing: China Film Press, 1996), 662, quoted in Teo, *Chinese Martial Arts Cinema*, 28.
40. Tan, 'Surfing with the surreal in Tsui Hark's wave', 36.
41. I have previously discussed *The Matrix* and its ties with the new Chinese cinema of attractions in my article on Yuen Woo-ping. See Ian Pettigrew, 'Entering the cinema of attractions' Matrix'.
42. Scott Bukatman, *Matters of Gravity*, 115.
43. See Samirah Majumdar, 'Recent Chinese dealings with faith groups reflect a pattern of government restrictions on religion' (last accessed 13 April 2019).
44. An earlier version of this chapter was delivered at the 12th Asian Cinema Studies Society International Conference, July 2017, at Lancaster University.

PART III
ETHICS

Chapter 10

Almost Wild, But Not Quite: The Indexical and the Fantastic Animal Other in China-Co-Produced (Eco)Cinema

Yiman Wang

Ecocinema has emerged as a new direction in Chinese cinema studies since the publication of *Chinese Ecocinema: In the Age of Environmental Challenge* (2009), co-edited by Sheldon Lu and Jiayan Mi.[1] In practice, ecocinematic consciousness has given rise to ethnographic documentaries made by ethnic minorities with digital video, as part of the visual anthropology project named the Yunnan Qinghai Rural Moving Image Project (Yunnan Qinghai xiangchun yingxiang jihua). Sponsored by the EU–China biodiversity programme, this project was launched by the Baima Mountain Cultural Research Centre of Yunnan Academy of Social Sciences, in collaboration with Beijing's Shanshui Conservation Centre and three environmental protection associations in Qinghai. Importantly, the ecocinematic consciousness also seeps increasingly into China-co-produced commercial cinema and becomes conjoined with the fantastic and the spectacular.

In this chapter, I study the technological production and cinematic treatment of China's trademark exotic animal species in two co-produced films, *Wolf Totem* (*Lang tuteng*, Jean-Jacques Annaud, 2015) and *Born in China* (*Women dansheng zai Zhongguo*, Lu Chuan, 2016). I examine the ways in which these films leverage local and global human, other-than-human, environmental and technological resources to manufacture cinematic spectacles for the gaze of Chinese and global audiences. I ask how the border-crossing commercial logic of co-production and resource-pooling mirrors, instigates and is also challenged and reshaped by the tension-ridden shuttling at multiple levels, between humans and wildlife, the indexical and the fantastic, the natural and the technological, the Han and non-Han ethnic groups, the local and the planetary, and, finally, the Chinese and the global.

Wolf Totem, based on Jiang Rong's semi-autobiographical novel, centres on the re-education of two young Han men in inner Mongolia, sent down during the Cultural Revolution. Co-produced with China Film Co. Ltd (Zhongguo dianying gufen youxian gongsi) and directed by Jean-Jacques Annaud, who, ironically, is known for being banned by the Chinese government after making *Seven Years in Tibet* (1997), the film adaptation differs significantly from the mainstream 'scar literature' (shanghen wenxue).[2] Departing from the well-rehearsed narrative of the sent-down youths' edifying and/or traumatic experiences in rural China, Annaud's *Wolf Totem* privileges one young man's *Bildungsroman* through learning from the Mongolian people's interaction with the wolves and with the broader prairie ecosystem.

Due to Annaud's insistence on casting real wolves (instead of CGI ones, or large dogs passing for wolves), the film sparks intense public interest in the process of preparing for and making it, including acquiring wolf cubs, training them to act with other animals (such as horses) and human actors, filming the wolves acting and, finally, the postfilming settlement of the semi-wild wolves. All these concerns pivot on the ostensible incompatibility between indexicality (the wild wolves that resist human and technological manipulation) and theatricality (the wolves that lend themselves to training and even acting in alignment with the filmmaking purpose). This incompatibility, as I argue below, is precisely the root of the fantastic.

Born in China, financed by the Paris-based Disneynature, is a part of the Disneynature wildlife series filmed around the world. *Born in China* features exotic rare animal species inhabiting remote Chinese regions. China's Lu Chuan was selected to direct on the basis of his directorial credit for *Kekexili: The Mountain Patrol (Keke xili,* 2004) – a film that exposes the poaching of Tibetan antelopes and catalysed China's legislation of anti-poaching and antelope conservation. The documentary footage of *Born in China* was captured by five wildlife cameramen and their teams recruited internationally, and they filmed simultaneously in different parts of China for eighteen months. The production results from multinational collaboration – Chinese (for local coordination), American (for budget and structural management), British (for postproduction) and German (for 3D camera equipment). Two of the three producers, Brian Leith and Phil Chapman, who are affiliated with the BBC, also served as screenwriters for this film. They had previously collaborated on the Emmy award-winning six-part TV documentary series *Wild China* (2008).[3]

Geared toward international audiences of all ages (including children), the film features wild animals with human names to facilitate characterisation and audience identification. Furthermore, the wildlife footage is edited in analogy with human family drama, depicting the mother–daughter relationship in the panda family, the sibling rivalry in the golden monkey family and the snow leopard family's impending demise due to the mother's fatal injury following a failed hunting attempt. To make the animal version of family drama even more legible to the audience, the film features a voiceover narrative (respectively delivered by John Krasinski, Zhou Xun and Claire Keim for the American, Chinese and French versions) that vocally performs the dramatic twists and turns.

If *Wolf Totem* risks distracting from the human protagonists' *Bildungsroman* narrative by featuring real wolves in breathtaking sequences, then *Born in China* seems to undermine the power of wildlife documentary footage by containing it in the structure of anthropocentric family drama. Shuttling between the indexical truth claim for the wild animals' presence and the anthropocentric fictional drama, the two films struggle to conjoin two contradictory audience appeals – the rarely seen zooetic attractions that push beyond anthropocentrism on the one hand, and the human-oriented drama that reinstates the power of the human gaze on the other. This struggle creates the fantastic, or the zooetic and ecocinematic consciousness that opens up a pathway of globalising Chinese cinema different from the dominant commercial logic.

Defining the Fantastic

First, I identify two modes of the fantastic, based on its etymological root. The word 'fantastic' is derived from the Greek *phantastikos* and *phantázein* (φαντάζειν), meaning 'making visible'. Thus, the fantastic has to do with conjuring something and making it visualisable or figurable. Relatedly, phantasmagoria refers to a succession of elusive and ghostly visual illusions projected on smoke or other translucent surfaces with a magic lantern. It emphasises the illusory yet impactful (nearly convincing) quality of briefly visible images. Thus, the fantastic suggests two potentially contradictory methods for the human subject to relate to its environment. One is to make visible the previously inaccessible, which can disturb and expand the viewer's comfort zone. The other is for the viewer to maintain their habitual orientation and for the newly visible phenomena to be subsumed to the viewer's a priori subject position.

The second relationality oriented around the human subject is further developed in Freud's psychoanalytic approach to fantasy. According to Freud, fantasies, like dreams, work as wish fulfilments through which imaginary scenarios arise from childhood memories, with the subject as the protagonist.[4] Teresa de Lauretis interprets Freud's theory of fantasy in terms of subject formation through psychic reality. Psychic reality

> takes on the force of reality, has all the consistency of the real, and on the basis of which we live our lives, understand the world, and act in it. Fantasy is the psychic mechanism that *structures subjectivity* by reworking or translating social representations into subjective representations and self-representations.[5]

Similarly interpreting Freud, Elizabeth Cowie sees fantasy as 'the arranging of, a setting out of, desire; a veritable mise-en-scene of desire'.[6] Defining fantasy as a mise-en-scène for enacting a desire, Cowie prioritises the process of structuring and articulating a desire over its fulfilment. Cowie and de Lauretis share the understanding of fantasy (both private and public) as conducive to psychic reality that is intrinsic to the human subject formation. In other words, the fantasy makes visible, image-able and actionable a wish or a desire in such a way that it helps to construct and consolidate the human subject position.

As stated earlier, this human-oriented fantasy or fantastic goes hand in hand with the other mode of the fantastic: namely, visibilisation with the result of defamiliarising and disturbing human subjectivity. This mode of the fantastic challenges the anthropocentric perspective. The structuralist Tzvetan Todorov describes this mode of fantastic as the 'supernatural' – the power that exceeds the human-nature domain. As he puts it, the fantastic results in 'that hesitation experienced by a person who knows only the laws of nature, confronting an apparently supernatural event'.[7] For Bliss Cua Lim, the fantastic has the ability to 'insinuate the *failure* of modern disenchantment to completely supplant nonmodern worlds'.[8] The persistence of the fantastic, therefore, holds up the possibility of re-enchantment that undermines the teleological project of disenchanting modernisation. It not only renders time recursive, but also pushes human consciousness to encounter what is previously unexperienced. My study shows that the fantastic that defamiliarises and disturbs the conventional human-nature domain is not limited to the supernatural; nor is it antithetical to modernisation (especially cutting-edge filming technologies). In fact, nature (as illustrated by wildlife and ecosystems in the films under study) is equally capable of impinging upon the taken-for-granted structures, be it the human subject position or a social system. And the fantastic, de-anthropocentric nature, understood in terms of nature made visible, depends on modern filming technologies. Yet, nature per se does not yield to such technologies and remains in a tension-ridden relationship with the latter.

In *Wolf Totem* and *Born in China*, the two modes of fantastic find expression in the previously invisible but now hyper-indexical wildlife and the human-oriented drama. In the human-oriented drama, the fantastic serves to consolidate the human subject position by orchestrating wildlife to align with human purposes. Techniques of orchestration include making wolves perform in and for the film narrative and using editing and the voiceover narrative to fit elusive animal species into human cognitive and emotional parameters. Meanwhile, by making a truth claim of presenting wildlife with minimal interference (the wolves were said to be kept as wild as possible, and the wild species in *Born in China* were simply observed and filmed from a distance, with powerful filming equipment), the films mobilise hyper-indexicality with the potential result of challenging anthropocentrism, thus conducing to the mode of fantastic by 'making visible' what is disturbing and disorienting. This de-anthropocentric fantastic bespeaks a consciousness of ecocinema and ecomedia – that is, the criticism and practice of film and media that address ecological issues – and, furthermore, reflect upon the ecological impact of the practice of film- and media-making. Scott MacDonald describes the fundamental task of ecocinema as

> a retraining of perception, . . . a way of offering an alternative to conventional media spectatorship, or . . . a way of providing something like a *garden* – an 'Edenic'" respite from conventional consumerism – within the machine of modern life, as modern life is embodied by the apparatus of media.[9]

He identifies long takes and other experimental techniques as conducive to producing ecocinema.

In the context of commercial co-productions like *Wolf Totem* and *Born in China*, MacDonald's 'Edenic' ecocinema must be reconsidered. I undertake this task by linking the ecocinematic consciousness with the de-anthropocentric fantastic, which crops up in commercial cinema as much as it governs non-commercial ecocinema. I ask how these two films evince an ecocinematic consciousness, what they help to make visible, what kinds of fantastic and alternative perceptions they enable in tandem with transnational commercial logic, and how technology and techniques facilitate the de-anthropocentric fantastic. In addressing these questions, I challenge the dichotomy of commercial and avant-garde, nature and technology, fantasy and modernity. I argue that the films display a fantastic ecocinematic consciousness that is neither supernatural (as Todorov would argue) nor countermodern (as Lim suggests) but is rather predicated upon the mediation of natureculture through modern filming technologies. As Sean Cubitt argues, techne (the technological) plays a key role in mediating polis (the human world) and physis (the green world).[10] Similarly, I point out in a different context, 'technology not only enables, but also shapes and conditions filmic renditions of non-human animals'.[11] In the following pages, I use *Wolf Totem* and *Born in China* to delineate their fantastic ecocinematic consciousness and the ways that this unfolds in contention with the transnational commercial logic, as articulated in Sino-Western film co-production.

Sensing the Fantastic Ecocinematic Consciousness in *Wolf Totem* and *Born in China*

In *Wolf Totem*, the fantastic ecocinema and transnational commercial cinema intersect, giving rise to feel-good middle-class environmentalism, which became a selling point for the film. Upon its release in 2015 on Valentine's Day, also the Lunar New Year Festival, *Wolf Totem* was celebrated by Chinese media practitioners and critics as a major milestone in Sino-Western co-production, in that it combines 'universal value' (*pushi jiazhi*) with commercial appeal. The said 'universal value' refers to environmentalism, which is also paradoxically characterised as a quintessential Eastern value that is effectively exported to the world via this film. One reviewer claimed that the film was so popular with white-collar viewers that it appeared to be requisite viewing for them. The film reportedly appealed to the same group of middle-class viewers that also applauded the journalist Chai Jing's *Under the Dome* (*Qiongding zhi xia*, 2015), an environmental reportage documentary that exposes the causes and damage of China's smog pollution. In other words, as a trendy global topic, environmentalism is susceptible to neoliberal consumption that confers on Chinese audiences a middle-class and quasi-intellectual status while reinforcing essentialism in the oxymoronic 'universal Eastern values'. What is elided in such consumption is real engagement with the de-anthropocentric perspective and the correlated ecocinematic concerns as a transformative sociopolitical intervention. Similarly, *Born in China* packages the wildlife footage in the genre of family drama that is then orientalised with the so-called Eastern philosophy of the life cycle. While succeeding in celebrating the splendour of rare animal species in remote Chinese regions, it risks forestalling a deeper understanding of the urgent global crisis concerning the precarious and declining ecosystems sustaining those species. As such, Disneynature's gesture of donating the revenue from its North American opening day screenings to wildlife conservation amounted to no more than a feel-good self-patting on the back.

Despite such commercial hijacking of environmental concerns (whether by the production team or the audience), I argue that the films do have the potential of offering a fantastic ecocinematic consciousness, one that prompts us to ponder the value of de-anthropocentrism and the ways of practising it. I start with the opposite endings of the two films. *Wolf Totem* concludes with optimism – a major departure from the tragic ending of Jiang Rong's novel. As director Annaud explains, contrary to the novel, which ends with the death of the adopted wolf, and hence the extinction of Mongolian wolves, he chose to conclude on a hopeful note by showing a white cloud that evokes a running wolf, indicating the survival of the adopted wolf and its species. Such optimism is consistent with the happy ending in his earlier wild animal films, *The Bear* (*L'Ours*, 1988) and *Two Brothers* (*Deux frères*, 2004), the latter being about two tigers in colonial Indochina. Yet, the very fact that he cast real wolves battling gazelles, horses and sheep prompted a reviewer to describe the film as 'probably too brutal for younger children and more sensitive animal lovers'.[12] The concern with challenging human (especially children's) sensitivity escalated for Chinese audiences of *Born in China*.

Given the overpowering effect of the hyper-indexical documentary footage that not only makes visible the wild and elusive animals, but also brings them into extreme close-up, *Born in China* has been commonly received as a documentary that tracks and films wild species in their native habitats. In comparison, the well-trodden family drama is taken for granted, and therefore hardly questioned as a sentimental structure inappropriately imposed upon wild animal species. The unquestioning belief in the film's verisimilar indexicality caused great audience distress when the film's concluding tragedy is taken literally: that is, the audience believed that the snow leopard mother named Dava really did die of a fatal wound sustained in a failed hunting attempt captured on camera, leaving her young cubs to face certain death from starvation. The enraged viewers questioned Lu Chuan as to why he allowed this to happen instead of helping the near-extinct species to survive by feeding Dava and/or rescuing her cubs.

Lu's response is twofold. First, he states that, as wildlife filmmakers, he and the cinematographers uphold the non-interference principle: that is, observing from a distance without attempting to change the course of nature, the goal being to preserve the pristine order in the ecosystem. Second, he points out that the audience's emotional reaction to Dava's death is misplaced because the film is *not* a documentary, but a wildlife film that, by definition, hinges upon dramatisation. He explains that Dava's story grows from footage of multiple adult snow leopards that he edited together, and that the shot of a dead leopard that is narratively identified as Dava is not necessarily the mother of two cubs who are shown as facing impending starvation. Lu's twofold response, while sensible, offers no solace, as it unleashes two contradictory viewer expectations and leaves them unreconciled. These two viewer expectations are: the voyeuristic desire to see actual wild animals in pristine habitats (that is, scopophilia for rarely accessible indexicality, or the fantastic in the etymological sense of what is made visible); and the desire for stories that are legible and self-reassuring. Lu's insistence on non-interference seems to ensure documentary verity and satisfy the voyeuristic desire, but it fails to deliver a feel-good narrative. On the other hand, the narrative he delivers – the snow leopard family's demise – cannot be easily brushed off as harmless fiction, even when recognised as resulting from Lu's editorial sleight of hand. For after all, the indexical footage leaves no room for doubt that a leopard was wounded during hunting and a leopard died. Whether they were the same leopard named Dava is beside the point. The death of an adult leopard always suggests the possible death of her cubs. So, the recognition of the composite and fictional nature of one family tragedy only alerts us to the certainty of more than one family's demise. The filming of one example left many more demises unfilmed.

It is precisely in encountering the distressing reality of wildlife that these films reference, dramatise, commercialise and yet inadequately address, that we might discern the potential fantastic ecocinematic consciousness. In other words, while the films' animal footage is contained by the anthropocentric drama, its impactful hyper-indexicality, as testified in its ability to challenge audience sensitivity, suggests a de-anthropocentric impulse. This impulse is first indicated in the two directors' approach to these films. Annaud explains that he views film as a dream about and a passion for a different world, what he calls 'divertissement', which allows him to drop the work routine and go to another place. In making *Wolf Totem*, the other place that offers him divertissement is not only a foreign country like China, but, more importantly, a non-Han region, specifically Inner Mongolia, characterised by a nomadic and sheep-farming culture. Furthermore, Annaud took the opportunity to work with real wolves as co-stars with the leading human actors. Similar to Annaud's desire to detach from routine work to enjoy divertissement, Lu Chuan accepted Disneynature's invitation to direct *Born in China*, seeing it as an opportunity to flee the criticism by Chinese audiences and critics of two of his previous films. Thus, he treated the opportunity of directing a wildlife film for Disneynature as self-exile into the wild with no need to worry about the box office. Despite Disneynature's focus on family audiences, which reduces this film to what Lu calls the 'elementary school' level, he claims that he uses this opportunity to pitch Chinese wildlife and natural landscape internationally, countering the Western stereotypical perception of China's dense population and rampant animal consumption.

For both directors, making these films signals freedom from the beaten path. This discourse could suggest their romanticisation of the unfamiliar and the faraway, but also indicates a desire to develop a film aesthetics centred on the other-than-human, even when the narrative structure is still anthropocentric.

Their de-anthropocentric impulse informs the technological mediation of wildlife, which I describe as almost wild, but not quite. More specifically, I argue that *Wolf Totem* features 'cultivated wildness', while *Born in China* depends on 'intercepted wildness'. Both bespeak fantastic ecocinematic consciousness without carrying it to full fruition.

Cultivated Wildness in *Wolf Totem*

As mentioned earlier, a major attraction of *Wolf Totem* is the real wolves who feature as actors performing with sheep, horses and humans. Boasting a crew of 480, including a team dedicated to ensuring good filming practice that avoids environmental damage, *Wolf Totem* at the time was the biggest animal movie ever made in China, with a budget of $41 million, and predominantly financed by China Film Co. Ltd (Zhongguo dianying gufen youxian gongsi). At the beginning of production in August 2009, producer Wang Weiyi, an ethnic Mongolian, obtained seventeen wolf cubs from the Harbin Zoo in northeastern China, and spent three years raising them for filming purposes. This led to his book, *Cloudy the Star Wolf* (*Mingxing lang*, 2015), which features the wolf lead in the film and is endorsed by Jiang Rong, who penned the preface for the book. Filming started in July 2012 and continued through four seasons in chronological order. The decision as to which wolves would make good actors is of particular interest. Andrew Simpson, a world-class Canadian trainer, was recruited to train the wolves. Simpson believes that there is 'no point' in forcing animals to act. 'We had a couple that were nice wolves, they were sweet, but they didn't want the attention. They just wanted to be wolves; they didn't want to be movie wolves.' So the 'movie wolves' reportedly selected themselves by 'readily jump[ing] in the truck each morning, and show[ing] enjoyment on set'.[13] Simpson further emphasises the necessity for capturing the 'glinting eyes of a *real* wolf' in order to carry a story about the 'interplay of animal and human intelligence as wolves and herders battle to live off the same flocks'.[14]

While Simpson sees no point in making apes and chimpanzees into movie actors, he considers wolves (especially wolves raised by humans in a semi-wild environment)[15] potential actors – contingent upon their self-nomination, so to speak. This reference to the wolves' 'self-nomination' or voluntary participation suggests a delicate balance between tameness and wildness, between human–wolf alignment and divergence, and between the wild animals' body language and human interpretation. In fact, the balance is so speculative that the two states of behaviour constitute not so much opposites as the two sides of a Möbius strip, one term coexisting with and constitutive of the other, at least for the movie-making purpose. This unstable balance underscores the ambivalence and the inherent paradox in the cultivated wildness, which is summarised in Simpson's qualified truth claim that '98% of everything [the gore] the audience sees is real', but 'done safely'.[16]

'Real' wildness with guaranteed safety (for both human and nonhuman actors) is enabled by specific technologies that capture, simulate and mediate the almost-wild, but-not-quite indexicality. To produce the life-like effect, 3D cameras were procured from Germany; extra lighting was used to generate and capture the glint in the wolves' eyes; close-up and animals' perspectival shots are heavily employed to insinuate their psychic states through anthropomorphic associations; multiple cameras filmed simultaneously to capture different angles, despite the wolves' discomfort with the heavy crew and technological presence; and animatronic dummies were used in dramatic scenes featuring the horse and Mongolian gazelle carnage resulting from the wolf attack and the wolf–sheep battle.[17] All of these techniques and technologies are deployed to achieve naturalistic aesthetics. Not only presenting cultivated wildness within the film, the film crew also took special care to make sure that the filmmaking activity would not adversely affect the local prairie ecosystem. A designated Environmental Preservation Department, as part of the crew, made sure that no fake snow was used (instead, real snow was shipped in long distance, with the ironic consequence of an increased carbon footprint), and that wooden planks paved over the grassland when vehicles had to be used for transporting heavy filming equipment. After the filming was completed, the wolves, not wild enough to be released, were transferred to the trainer, Simpson, and now live on his ranch in Canada.

The wildness of wolves and of the prairie ecosystem, therefore, paradoxically exists within the circumference of a contained, human-dependent/managed environment, while retaining a degree of its unique materiality. It is also subjected to biotechnological mediation and biogovernance (as illustrated in the entire filmmaking process, from prefilming wolf raising and training, through rehearsing and retakes during the filming, to postfilming wolf settlement in Canada). Such filmic wildness is neither wild nor tame, neither nomadic nor completely converted into an agrarian economy. It shuttles between anthropocentrism and the potential for its decentring.

The use of close-up shots of the other-than-human animals is a case in point. A fundamental idiom in film language that has been experimented with since the inception of film, close-up shots initially caused much heated discussion, even anxiety. While some early critics and practitioners saw close-up as being capable of revealing the interior psyche of the character, others argued that it distorted the human appearance and perturbed the audience. Since the close-up became codified in the grammar of film, especially in the Classic Hollywood style, it almost automatically cues the audience's projection of their emotions on to the character in close-up. If this automatic projection (with results ranging from empathy to repulsion) goes unquestioned in human-centred films, it becomes problematic when the character in close-up is an other-than-human animal. On the one hand, as Derek Bousé criticises, facial close-ups in wildlife films serve 'to ascribe to animals almost whatever feelings and emotions the filmmaker wishes to assign them according to the requirements of the storyline at that moment'.[18] In other words, an other-than-human animal rendered through close-up shots and other anthropomorphising techniques is made epistemologically and emotionally available to human cognition. Reframed in the anthropocentric paradigm and stripped of its animality, the other-than-human is reduced to a fascinatingly different Self. On the other hand, however, the close-up shot, understood apart from the codified film language, is still capable of distorting and defamiliarising what is taken for granted. As such, the close-up shot could be decoupled from the audience's anthropomorphic projection to highlight the other-than-human animal's opaque visage, making visible and foregrounding a de-anthropocentric consciousness. The extra lighting used to capture the 'glint' in the wolves' eyes indicates precisely the film's efforts to accentuate the wolfly materiality – different not only from that of humans, but also from that of large dogs and CGI wolves.

This wild animal difference, whether indexical or imaginary, results in the paradox that wildness can be recognised only when it is cultivated enough to be filmable by human agents with specific filming technologies and techniques. The tension between wild materiality (that resists symbolism) and cinematisation (that adheres to certain conventions of representation even when reinventing them) makes possible a fantastic divertissement – a potentially de-anthropocentric engagement with the wolves' almost-wildness that leads to an ecocinematic consciousness in *Wolf Totem*. It strives for zooesis: that is, taking wild animals seriously on their own terms, to the extent allowed by the commercial film format.[19] In this light, the film's hopeful ending, showing a white cloud evoking a free-running wolf, suggesting that the human-raised cub is rehabilitated in nature and promising to keep the Mongolian wolf lineage alive, can be read in two registers. The overly easy hope risks glossing over the irreversible species-environmental damage and reabsorbing the wolf into a feel-good anthropocentric wish fulfilment that is one mode of fantasy. Or, it could offer a different mode of fantasy, one that cultivates the audience's consciousness of de-anthropocentric ecoconservation, even if it has to be vehicled through cultivated wildness.

Intercepted Wildness in *Born in China*

If *Wolf Totem* acquires a potentially de-anthropocentric focus on the wolves (as opposed to the more symbolic binary of wolf culture versus sheep culture in the novel), it is because Annaud insisted on casting real wolves and therefore ineluctably introduced indexical wildness (cultivated as it was) that threatened to upstage the human drama. Different from such cultivated wildness, *Born in China* relies on wildlife footage (with the exception of some panda footage taken at a panda conservation site), but intercepts and refashions it into family dramas in human terms.

To obtain the vérité wildlife footage, the camera operators spent most of their time waiting in camouflage or the 'photo blind' for the targeted species to appear.[20] Lu Chuan likens the camera operators to hunters who crouch all day ready to pounce or shoot (pun intended), once the prey appears. He describes the principle of filming in these terms:

> The filming of the wildlife strictly adhered to the observational documentary convention with the associated documentary ethics that prohibits feeding, interfering, altering the natural habitat, or inducing the animals to do anything incongruent with their natural behavior. Following the jungle law in nature, death is another form of life continuation.[21]

The prolonged waiting meant contingency and other out-of-control shooting results. The question, then, is how to edit the footage that came from the long duration of waiting and filming, which, according to Lu, did not contain enough drama; and yet the filming had to wrap at the end of the designated filming period. The tension between observational documentary and Lu's emphasis on drama led to two edited versions. The first cut, done by the British production team, privileged the footage as the basis for a wildlife-centred scientific discourse. This version contradicted Lu's 'family drama' and 'life cycle' focus, edited in Beijing, resulting in a fierce struggle. Both parties appealed to Disneynature, and Lu's version was adopted due to its alignment with Disney's story-oriented tradition. The one challenge that Lu posed to Disneynature was the tragic ending for the snow leopard family, which Lu edited from footage already rejected (due to its goriness) and successfully persuaded Disneynature to keep, despite its disruption of Disney's family-friendly, happy-ending tradition. Lu did have to sanitise the image by digitally removing the blood from the snow leopard's body.[22]

Disney producer Roy Conli confirms the film's inevitable shuttling between documentary and dramatisation, between de-anthropocentrism and anthropomorphism. Commenting on Disneynature's wildlife films, he observes,

> in one way we think of these not as documentaries, but as true life adventures. So these are more narrative than a documentary in a sense. At the

same time, we kind of film within the rules of documentary, so we make sure that we don't interfere in any way, in terms of what we're seeing. . . . One of the things that we really try hard to do, because these are narrative in large part, we really try to be careful not to get too anthropomorphic. But it's often hard because you see behaviors in the animals that are very logically anthropomorphized.[23]

Intercepting observational wildlife footage for dramatisation is unsurprising, given the film's global commercial appeal. It is not only part of Disneynature's 'ongoing quest to bring the natural world to the big screen as never before', but also 'its most ambitious project to date, taking moviegoers on a grand journey into the wilds of China'.[24] As the first Disneynature film whose title contains a country name (China), this film commercialises the 'mystery of unexplored inland China' and the three native animal species for the external gaze. As Roy Conli proudly announces, 'we were the first westerners, actually, to get into the reserve and be able to film [them – that is, snow leopards and golden monkeys]'[25] and to 'showcase remarkably intimate family moments captured on film for the first time ever'.[26] Such promotion encourages Western voyeurism, reinforcing the entrenched West–China binary, as if the wildlife could be treated as yet more Chinese icons for Western consumption.[27]

Commenting on the mechanism of such commercial Otherisation (of other-than-human animals, as well as races/ethnicities and foreign countries), Derek Bousé describes wildlife film and television as depicting nature 'close-up, speeded-up, and set to music, with reality's most exciting moments highlighted, and its "boring" bits cut out'.[28] Furthermore, the vérité claim of capturing wildlife's natural spontaneous behaviour 'implies the willing participation of subjects', which, as Bousé argues, raises issues concerning 'animal subjectivity, consent, and what exactly "authentic" behaviour is'.[29] Bousé's critique powerfully underscores the difficulty with the vérité claim in wildlife films. That is, it may simply mask an anthropocentric desire to align wildlife with the human understanding of subjectivity and mode of living (with emphasis on drama and plot progression).

The question, then, is whether, despite the directorial interception and orchestration of the wildlife footage, the footage could still open up a de-anthropocentric and fantastic ecocinematic consciousness. In *Born in China*, a fundamental irony is that while the producer, the director and the publicity team all seek to Sinicise wildlife by associating it with China (as highlighted in the title), wildlife and their habitats do not recognise cut and dried geopolitical boundaries. Furthermore, the elusiveness of the wild species means that their imaging and visibilisation alone are fantastic enough to marginalise the family drama convention. Like the rare species, the harsh habitats, coupled with extreme weather conditions, also captivate audiences without the 'China' affiliation or dramatisation. In this sense, the truth claim regarding animal activities in remote regions is not simply a viewer teaser that is flaunted only to be contained by the ultimate dramatisation. Instead, to appropriate Elizabeth Cowie's theorisation of the paradox of documentary, the two aspects of vérité and fiction coexist, entailing and constituting each other. *Born in China*, being a wildlife film, does not purport to be a documentary. As such, it allows more room for fictionalisation and dramatisation that involve 'plot construction and character evolution', even while building upon 'the "vérité" of "actual", "found" material'.[30] To the extent that Dava's failed hunting and tragic death are edited from footage of nine different adult snow leopards, the film's dramatisation shuttles from 'fiction' to 'deception'. As Cowie explains, fiction originally refers to 'the act of fashioning or forming, notably in imitation of nature'. This could be an act that acknowledges its own fabrication and presents it as such. Deception, however, passes off such imitation as the original, eliding its own artificiality.[31] The illusion of the real is fully manifested in the audience's outcry against the tragic demise of Dava's family, as outlined previously.

Yet, the audience's (over-)reaction arguably also derives from the very stunning imaging of the wildlife itself that is filtered through, but also exceeds, the anthropocentric family drama. What makes *Born in China* appealing is not so much Lu Chuan's narration of his struggle with Disneynature to keep the snow leopard's tragic death scene, but more importantly, the crew's encounter with the intransigent difficulty of tracking and mediating the complex, vulnerable yet agential material beings of other-than-human species and their environments. Becoming aware of the extreme difficulty of obtaining hyper-indexical wildlife footage potentially raises the public consciousness of the precarity not only of these species but also of the broader ecosystem. This ecological consciousness, transmitted from the crew to the audience, was capitalised on by Disneynature's marketing strategy of donating portions of the film's revenues to the World Wildlife Fund. The emphasis on the distinctive wildlife forms, their uncooptable living styles and remote habitats encourages a de-anthropocentric, fantastic ecocinematic consciousness. As in *Wolf Totem*, despite the structural anthropocentric drama, what becomes transformative are the animal beings and the efforts of filmic mediation that make them visible, or fantastic. This means that the stages of prefilming (wolf-raising and training in *Wolf Totem*, travelling to remote regions and waiting in harsh climates in *Born in China*), the process of filming (rehearsing, waiting and leveraging state-of-the-art filming equipment) and postfilming (the wolf settlement in Canada in *Wolf Totem* and the lasting concern with the future of wildlife and of the ecosystem) figure more importantly than the anthropocentric fictional drama.

Conclusion

The fantastic wildlife (even when cultivated and intercepted) not only marginalises the anthropocentric drama and its commercial appeal, but also provides a perspective for understanding the mutually constitutive relationship between the border regions featured in the films on the one hand, and the mechanism of Sino-Western co-production on the other. As I mentioned earlier, the wildlife and their habitats refuse to recognise cut and dried geopolitical boundaries. They tend to occupy rarely mediated border zones, whether it is the prairie land in Mongolia in *Wolf Totem* or other remote regions, as revealed in *Born in China*. The filming of these areas, especially in Sino-Western co-productions, tends to cater to the exoticising Western gaze, as I discussed earlier with regard to the publicity of *Born in China*.

Yet, the imaging of these border zones also constitutes the fantastic that becomes visible without necessarily or completely being subsumed to the Western gaze or the Chinese nationalist interpellation. In fact, an unexpected spatial connection becomes possible with co-production; but it also exceeds the latter. This is illustrated in the wolf actors' relocation to trainer Simpson's ranch sanctuary in Canada. The wolves' trajectory of being taken from a zoo in northeastern China to being raised and trained in Inner Mongolia, to then being transported to and homed in a Canadian sanctuary may not apparently allow much room for the wolves' self-determination or agency. But it does produce a polylocal linkage that otherwise would not exist without the film. While every move is orchestrated by human agents, the polylocal linkage could not be accomplished without considering and working with the wolves' (semi-)wild agency. If this polylocal linkage started with a strictly human purpose of making a film, it evolved to encompass the other-than-human animals' interests and well-being. In this process, conservation of wolves and other wildlife emerges as an interconnected global issue that involves an assemblage of agencies beyond the human.

This de-anthropocentric consciousness is also articulated in *Born in China*. On the one hand, the audience scopophilia (or the desire to see what is normally invisible), compounded by the Western exoticising gaze, leads to the dramatic mash-up of vastly separate areas without sufficient contextualisation of each area. The locational shots could therefore be seen as a series of postcards on which to feast the eyes. On the other hand, the lack of contextualisation also relaxes the purported 'China' affiliation suggested in the title, thereby foregrounding the continuity of natural resources and the ecosystem, regardless of national and geopolitical borders. This locational concatenation was further expanded when the film premiered in the US on 22 April, Earth Day, which literally sutures the wildlife and ecosystems from specific parts of the world into the planetary scale.

Developing polylocal connectivities, these films participate in the processes of worlding, or collective world-making that is ethically responsive to and responsible for the world's holistic sustainability. Such worlding unfolds through the films' entanglement with the material profilmic and postfilmic worlds, making them visible and fantastic, acknowledging their agency, and promoting conservation and restoration of a biodiverse ecology. As Sino-Western co-productions geared for international marketing, these films also participate in worlding by featuring the assemblage of a multinational/multiethnic cast and crew, border-crossing technological and commercial deployment that evokes Arjun Appadurai's analysis of mediascape, technoscape and ethnoscape under globalisation.[32] Thus, the films bring together agential material ecology, human resources, film technology, commerce and geopolitics. Their interactions – sometimes converging, sometimes conflicting – open up multiple channels of world-making. But they all become possible by navigating the tension between the local, the native, the national and the global, between the ethnic/racial/cultural Other and the species Other, between material beings and technological mediation, between ecological consciousness and commercial aspirations, and finally between the de-anthropocentric fantastic (based on wildlife made visible) and the anthropocentric drama.

Importantly, these terms do not undermine each other, but rather come into dynamic, mutually constitutive interactions that redefine and reposition each other. These interactions invite us to engage with the varied terms as an assemblage of distributed, albeit unevenly, positioned sites of agency. To understand the complex interplay amongst these sites of agency, we must go beyond simple criticism of Sino-Western co-production as a mere commercial ploy that combines Chinese and Western capital to produce a palatable iconic China for global consumption. Instead, we must recognise that, aside from capital investment, these Sino-Western co-productions are predicated upon a range of interactive agencies encompassing wildlife, the ecosystem, human resources and technologies that are all simultaneously local and global. The fantastic, understood as technological mediation and visibilisation of the agential wildlife and ecosystem, is facilitated by co-production. Yet, the very difficulty of technological mediation amply manifests the clash among human intention, unwieldy and disruptive technological intervention, and material agency of wildlife and the ecosystem. Not only, therefore, is the fantastic hyper-indexical and de-anthropocentric, but its zooetic materiality also constantly eludes and frustrates the human and capitalist mechanism of making visible and representation.

My study of *Wolf Totem* and *Born in China* begins with delineating two understandings of the fantastic, one being the anthropocentric dramatisation that guides the narrative of the two films, the other being the de-anthropocentric visibilisation of the indexical wildlife and its habitats. I emphasise the second understanding, associating it with an ecocinematic consciousness that contradicts and ultimately problematises the anthropocentric dramatisation. I draw on the etymological meaning of the fantastic (namely, making visible) and the psychoanalytic reinterpretation of the fantastic (as a scenario for enacting one's desire), arguing that the impact of the fantastic resides in acknowledging and registering other-than-human agencies. I argue that this de-anthropocentric, fantastic perspective enables us to critique and recontextualise the overarching capitalist logic of Sino-West co-production, a logic that tends to reinscribe the Self–Other, human–nonhuman, West–China dichotomy, with the result of reducing the species, lingual–cultural and racial/ethnic Other into a mystified object of consumption. Leveraging the de-anthropocentric fantastic, my study goes beyond the profit-driven imaginary dichotomy in the Sino-Western co-produced films to underscore their navigation of the co-producing partners' capital, human, technological and natural resources. Thus, I foreground these films' potential role in worlding, or ethical world-making, through mobilising an assemblage of sites of agency that include yet also exceed the human and commercial pursuits. It is in this sense that contemporary co-produced Chinese cinema posits the hope of becoming global – with an ecocinematic consciousness.

Notes

1. Sheldon Lu and Jiayan Mi (eds), *Chinese Ecocinema*.
2. For a recent study of 'scar literature', see Sabina Knight, 'Scar literature and the memory of trauma'.
3. Cameraman Justin Maguire also worked on both *Wild China* and *Born in China*.
4. See Sigmund Freud, 'The interpretation of dreams', as quoted and explicated in Teresa de Lauretis, 'Culture, public and private fantasies', 306.
5. de Lauretis, 'Culture, public and private fantasies', 307. Emphasis added.
6. Elizabeth Cowie, 'Fantasia', in Cowie, *Representing the Woman*, 133.
7. Tzetan Todorov, *The Fantastic*, 25.
8. Bliss Cua Lim, *Translating Time*, 110. Original emphasis.
9. Scott MacDonald, 'Toward an eco-cinema', 109. Original emphasis.
10. Sean Cubitt, *EcoMedia*.
11. Yiman Wang, 'Of animals and men', note 10.
12. 'Trained wolves steal the show in "Wolf Totem" film adaptation' (last accessed 3 September 2019).
13. Mary Hennock, 'Wolf Totem animal trainer sees risks for Hollywood in China' (last accessed 3 September 2019).
14. Ibid. Original emphasis.
15. The wolf cubs selected from the Harbin Zoo were taken from mother wolves that were considered relaxed around humans. The cubs were taken from their mothers before they opened their eyes, raised in a controlled, fenced environment that

allowed some room for hunting, and taught to follow the trainer's hand gestures and buzzers.
16. Hennock, 'Wolf Totem animal trainer sees risks for Hollywood in China'.
17. Xiao Jin, a Chinese special effects artist, was responsible for making animatronic wolves, horses and Mongolian gazelles.
18. Derek Bousé, 'False intimacy: close-ups and viewer involvement in wildlife films', 128.
19. Una Chaudhuri, *The Stage Lives of Animals*.
20. Regarding the function of the photo blind in wildlife photography, see Jim Braswell, 'How to use a photographic blind' (last accessed 3 September 2019): 'If you are not seen by the subject, you have a good chance to see and capture behaviors that you wouldn't otherwise see. And one of the biggest advantages of using a photo blind is being able to capture closeup images.'
21. Quoted in Feng Yingxin, 'Observation and inaction offer the best attention' (last accessed 3 September 2019).
22. Wildlife film, according to Cynthia Chris, mobilises 'the strategy of minimizing human presence' and 'seems to invite viewers to forget that their view of nature is mediated'. Implicit in this genre is the fundamental split between human and wildlife; hence the irresolvable tension between the attempt to conceal human mediation on the one hand, and the persistent anthropocentrism and anthropomorphism on the other. See Chris, *Watching Wildlife*, 71. Chris's description of wildlife film succinctly summarises the tension inherent in *Born in China*. My study, however, seeks to understand how the inevitable human and technological mediation might still potentially give rise to a zooetic consciousness.
23. Mike Celestino, 'Interview' (last accessed 3 September 2019).
24. http://nature.disney.com/born-in-china (last accessed 3 September 2019).
25. Celestino, 'Interview'.
26. http://nature.disney.com/born-in-china.
27. This rhetoric is to be expected, especially following the panda's iconification in *Kungfu Panda* I and II (Mark Osborne and John Stevenson, 2008; Jennifer Yuh Nelson, 2011).
28. Derek Bousé, *Wildlife Films*, 2–3.
29. Ibid., 23, 27.
30. Elizabeth Cowie, 'Documenting fictions'.
31. Ibid., 55.
32. Arjun Appadurai, 'Disjuncture and difference in the global cultural economy'.

Chapter 11

Domesticity, Sentimentality and Otherness: The Boundary of the Human in *Monster Hunt*

Mei Yang

In retrospect, the phenomenal theatrical performance of *Monster Hunt* (*Zhuoyao ji*, Raman Hui) in 2015 encapsulated the then widespread anticipation that China's film market would imminently overtake the North American box office.[1] From a film critic's point of view, *Monster Hunt*'s success also denoted the normalisation of an overly heated industry hitherto characterised by the mismatch between a film's artistic calibre and its ticket sales.[2] To celebrate the film's multiple accomplishments, including becoming the highest-grossing Chinese movie,[3] China Film Association and China Film Press held a joint symposium entitled '*Monster Hunt*: A New Benchmark and New Era for Chinese Blockbusters' in August 2015. The symposium enlisted the film's production team, representatives of governmental bureaus and renowned film critics to applaud the fusion of technology and Chinese culture that *Monster Hunt* allegedly achieved.[4] The consensus reached at the symposium was shared by the general audience: the seamless integration of live action and animation, juxtaposed with imagery derived from classical Chinese tales, contributed to the film's astounding success. *Monster Hunt 2* (*Zhuoyao ji 2*, Raman Hui), the sequel made in 2018 with a stronger cast, having Tony Leung play the lead rather than relying on a relatively novice actor, touted even more spectacular visual effects, readily responding to the audiences' fondness for technological wonders.

Indeed, *Monster Hunt* marks the culmination of a group of Chinese fantasy films made in the 2010s that draw on historical images, legends and stories to showcase technological breakthrough. An incomplete list of these films includes *The Sorcerer and the White Snake* (*Baishe chuanshuo zhi fahai*, Ching Siu-tung, 2011), *Journey to the West: Conquering the Demons* (*Xiyou xiangmopian*, Stephen Chow, 2013), *Legend of the Demon Cat* (*Yaomao zhuan*, Chen Kaige, 2017) and *Detective Dee: The Four Heavenly Kings* (*Di Renjie zhi sida tianwang*, Tsui Hark, 2018). These films re-employ well-known traditional folk, fairy and other mythological tales to visualise the otherworldly (immortals, demons, monsters and ghosts). Adaptations of classical tales, it is said, reflect a global emphasis on cultural boundaries that looks to icons of tradition to differentiate one community from others.[5] Simultaneously, one may argue that fantastic narratives are well suited for displaying the marvels of technological advancement. In a time of increasing simulation and spectacle in world cinema, the integration of live action and CGI effects creates awe in the audience and technology itself becomes an admirable and fearsome other.[6]

The purported Chinese cultural elements in *Monster Hunt* come from one of the film's sources of inspiration: *The Classic of Mountains and Seas* (*Shanhai jing*), a compilation of geographical accounts and mythologies that dates to the fourth century BCE. Compared with other tales in the *zhiguai* (records of anomalies) literary tradition, *The Classic of Mountains and Seas* (henceforth *The Classic*) allows for only sporadic imagery loans in film adaptations due to its abstruseness and laconism. While critics unanimously praise the film's tribute to classical Chinese literature, few of them probe into whether or not the film is a mere spectacle, an unmistaken product of the film industry's frantic hunt for even more archaic cultural relics in an increasingly crowded market. After all, what has propelled a CGI-driven transnational production such as *Monster Hunt* to appropriate premodern images for the amusement of modern audiences, if seeking exotica is not the only mechanism at work?[7] Popular culture is indisputably fluid and incongruent, but the question remains as to how it can also be cathartic, performative or even prognostic of and prescriptive to contemporary concerns.[8] For that reason, the aspects of tradition that are selectively reused, both to follow the imperatives innate to a Hollywood-style summer blockbuster and to capture social realities particular to contemporary China, merit critical enquiry.

Beneath a spectacular façade, *Monster Hunt* mixes the epistemology manifest in classical tales with postmodern discussions on otherness to present an alternate type of monster film, one that positions monsters as the non-threatening other to human existence. The film shows not only that the real threat comes from within, but also that a remedy for such interior problems relies on the other species. The ubiquity of monsters is exactly what *The Classic* is about: we fear and embrace them at the same time. Centring on the question of how the human and its opposite side – the strange and the other – are understood, this chapter will examine three sets of issues. First, as a film deriving its primary monster images from *The Classic*, *Monster Hunt* proffers a perfect opportunity to explore the ways in which a contemporary monster narrative deviates from or reconnects with the imaginative world of early China. Second, issues related to love, romance and domestic sentimentality arguably continue to be some of the most important topics in studies of Chinese cinema.[9] By placing *Monster Hunt* in the context of Chinese film studies, I analyse to what extent scholars' claims about the significance of family relationships and personal feelings are applicable to 2010s fantasy films. Finally, the film's assemblage of the strange and miraculous, as captured in traditional tales and the abnormal and unexpected identified in popular culture, while boosting its allure among audiences, also points to the haunting monstrosity of contemporary life in which apparitions from the past forebode an unknown and uncertain future.

The Origin: The Hybrid Monsters

The film begins with the narrator's recollection of an ancient time when the human race lived peacefully alongside other creatures before humans drove the monsters into the mountains. Later, the established boundary must be crossed after a civil war breaks out in the monster realm – a minister has killed the King and is attempting to slaughter all of his relatives and supporters. While the pregnant monster Queen is instructed to flee to the human realm, as the film discloses, monsters have disguised themselves as humans to live among them for decades. Meanwhile, Song Tianyin, the mayor of a small village called Yongning (which literarily means 'peaceful forever'), is chosen by the monster Queen to carry the foetus in his belly before she is killed. With the help of a monster-huntress named Huo Xiaolan, Song delivers the monster baby and must decide how to deal with him.

Whereas the film's homage to *The Classic of Mountains and Seas* is highly publicised and well noticed, its plotline and imagery also come from Qing novelist Pu Songling's *Strange Stories from a Chinese Studio* (*Liaozhai zhiyi*), a collection of marvellous tales that has inspired many film adaptations. By referring to both *The Classic* and *Strange Stories*, the film reflects a type of hybridity, or a tension between two classical sources regarding how to understand the different, the anomalous and the wonderous, categories that Confucius chose not to dwell on.[10] Among the hundreds of monster characters in *The Classic*, the monsters in the film resemble mostly Dijiang (Thearch Long River),[11] sometimes referred to as Dihong (Fig. 11.1). As described in *The Classic*,

> There is a god here whose form resembles a yellow sack with a red aura like cinnabar. He has six legs and four wings and exists in a state of confusion with no face or eyes. He knows how to sing and dance for he is, in fact, *Dijiang*.[12]

Many commentators in Chinese history have interpreted Dijiang's body as *hundun* (chaos) – 'the undifferentiated cosmos in a primordial state of chaos'.[13] To be aligned with these descriptions, the monsters in the film appear befuddled, jovial and mischievous, using their knack for singing and dancing to trick a human, as shown in the first musical sequence in the film.

206   Mei Yang

Figure 11.1   Illustration of *Dijiang*. Source: Hu Wenhuan, *Xin ke Shanhai jing* ([1593] 2013).

The monster baby, Wuba, with his miniature size and amicable demeanour, also bears a close affinity to the anomalous creature depicted in a story from Pu Songling's *Strange Stories*. In 'The Haunted House', Pu Songling describes a family of monster people, whose apparition at night surprises a visitor to a minister's house. These mini-sized monsters live inside and are imbued with the ability to vanish suddenly and to merge with household structures, all characteristics Wuba shares.[14] In Pu Songling's time, the question of how to construe the strange remained crucial to the literati's discussion of Confucian classics. Whereas Guo Pu (276–324), in his preface to *The Classic*, has argued for the veracity of the creatures recounted in the collection and for 'its practical use as an omen book and as an encyclopedia of knowledge',[15] Pu Songling's contemporaries were not concerned about the factuality of marvellous descriptions any more. Instead, they considered empirical experience limited and deemed records of the strange valuable in widening mainstream literary and philosophical traditions.[16] Furthermore, different from *The Classic* that describes faraway lands, Pu Songling's stories repeatedly show the otherworldly residing among humans, a disposition on which *Monster Hunt* bears.

The film's depiction of the monsters as parallel to the human race but non-menacing reflects the evolution of a longstanding tradition of looking at the distinction between strangeness and normality. In an ancient Chinese view of cosmology, a tradition lasting from the time *The Classic* was compiled to the late Ming and early Qing periods, anomaly and irregularity are considered integral and natural existence that does not pose any real harm to the harmony of the universe.[17] For that reason, strangeness is a subjective and relative concept that lies in the eyes of the beholder rather than in the natural world. Guo Pu states that 'things are not strange in and of themselves' – they are considered strange by certain perceptions. 'Thus the strange lies within me – it is not that things are strange.'[18] What emerges later in place of such early thinking about anomaly is a deepened sense of moral judgement that shifts the focus from strangeness and otherness to evilness. And by that metric, strangeness in the natural world is nothing compared with what can happen in the human realm. In the tale 'Guo An' from *Strange Stories*, for example, the court case is amazing not because a servant saw a ghost but because of the stupidity of the presiding magistrate and his miscarriage of justice.[19]

In the spirit of these earlier Chinese thoughts, *Monster Hunt* does not draw an impervious line between species or portray the monsters as a monolithic group of enemies of the human world, as a typical (Hollywood) monster film tends to do. It adopts a moral and cognitive framework that allows for a multilayered distinction not just for humankind but also for monsters. The human characters in the film can be separated into the following groups: first, the mainstream/dominant, represented by the Emperor (a supreme political power), who mandates boundaries between species to keep a certain social order, and his supporters, including monster-hunters and businessmen who profit from monster transactions. The second, the challenger to this social system is represented by Song Tianyin and his family members, who hold the belief that the divergence between evilness and kindness is a more worthwhile measure than physical qualities. The third group can be designated as situational or in-between characters employed by the dominant group who, upon closer contact with the challenger and the monsters, change their stance because of their shared belief in such a moral code.

Rather than presenting the monster groups as purely evil or virtuous from an anthropocentric viewpoint – that is, whether or not the monsters present harm or threat to human existence, the monsters seemingly also abide by a moral code: the ministers who help the pregnant former Queen are shown as loyal, and the Queen who cuts herself to save her foetus is heroic and worthy of sympathy. The monster villagers in Yongning are good residents who desire nothing but a peaceful and simple life. Instead, the monsters who live as wealthy or powerful 'human beings' are evil because of their indifference to the suffering of others, their unrestrained pursuit of power and their unhesitant recourse to slaughter. In the film the real threat (or, for that reason, the otherness) to (human) existence comes from the dominant human group and the evil monsters alike. That is, strangeness arises not from the group to which one belongs but from one's deviation from these moral principles that are held as universal. One is individually responsible for one's choice based on these principles – this is traditionalism at heart by resorting to a Confucian moral structure about human agency, or self-cultivation, that transcends one's group identity.[20] Using a Classical Hollywood narrative mode, the proclaimed Chinese elements in the film do not simply come from traditional-style landscapes, architecture, cuisines and other quotidian details,[21] but from a reliance on such a moral structure being affirmative and affective, a point to be developed further.

The Storyline: Revisiting the Sentimental

Despite its fantastic visual effects, *Monster Hunt* tells a sentimental story about orphans, family relations and personal feelings. The young monster, Wuba, lost his mother prior to birth, while both the protagonist and the heroine lost their parents when they were young. Underneath the CGI monster images is a multifaceted relationship between children and fathers and the underpinning sentiment of family/biological ties.[22] In many of its maudlin moments, the film approximates the core of melodrama – extreme suffering and emotional duress.[23] The sentimental as shown in the film, as a concept, presents several questions: first of all, by comparing it to what is featured in Republic era romantic stories (Mandarin Ducks and Butterflies fiction), the film downplays romantic love and sexual desire in preference for the emotive bond provided by the structure of family life and family roles. Furthermore, the shared experience of suffering among monsters and humans, and the imminent destiny of life and death tear down the separation between them. Eventually, the engulfing magnitude of kinship in determining these character motifs points to the seclusion and exclusiveness of an interior/domestic space. If monsters in the film are successfully divested of their species identity by resorting instead to a moral standard that also holds humanity responsible, is it the case that their moral standing is determined solely by their role as an insider or outsider of a family?

In Haiyan Lee's investigation, *qing* (feeling) is not natural or even purely sensual, but instead is socially constructed. In the late Qing, the idea that selfhood is autonomous (a relatively modern and Western idea by some anthropological accounts) was employed to challenge Confucian family ties. And precisely due to its autonomy, *qing* was broken free from the feudalistic hierarchy, and reoriented one's subjectivity to nation-building. The different stages of the structure of feelings – the Confucian as portrayed in Mandarin Ducks and Butterflies novels, the Enlightenment idea of free love in May Fourth literature, or revolutionary devotion in the communist era that renders personal feelings supplementary to a collective enterprise – attest to the discursive evolution of *qing* over time.[24] Placed against the emancipatory and anti-traditional idea during the Cultural Revolution – that is, dissociating oneself from not only personal feelings but also family ties – the ascendance of family (home) in contemporary Chinese films is thought-provoking. Under conditions of postsocialism and transnational production, familial feelings become a Janus-faced mechanism that both questions authoritarianism (and its decree of modernisation in many cases) and serves as a microcosm of the nation. Now, family stands in as the legacy of tradition that both challenges the brutality committed in the name of the nation and simultaneously brings people together to serve the nation.

The irony of familial feelings thus shows a compounded facet of contemporary Chinese culture. Comparing the audiences' response to two fantasy films produced a decade apart, Chen Kaige's *The Promise* (*Wuji*, 2005) and *Monster Hunt*, I discern a persisting distrust for the elevated motif of romantic love, and a favourable reception of conjugal relationships determined by assigned family roles, especially when Chinese productions are concerned. In *The Promise* the heroine's pursuit of true love was ridiculed as fake,[25] as if audiences were not susceptible to a mawkish Eros tale packaged with special effects; yet they readily accepted a family narrative similarly achieved by CGI in *Monster Hunt*. The differences in tone, thematic aspirations and technical level aside,[26] *Monster Hunt*'s box-office miracle seems to confirm the superiority of familial affection – much to the chagrin of those who would like to assume the independence of selfhood over kinship.

The romantic relationship between Song Tianyin and Huo Xiaolan is almost exclusively germinated by their incidental roles as the father and mother of the newborn monster. The moment their romantic feelings towards each other begin, or how Huo Xiaolan changes from despising Song to admiring him, centres around their shared experience as orphans turning into parents. With a meek and mellow demeanour, Song asserts his understanding of masculinity as care and the fulfilment of family duties and chastises men who abandon their children as cowardly and impotent. In the second musical sequence of the film, Song and Huo share their childhood memory of losing their parents, and the scene shifts to Song meticulously taking care of Wuba while Huo quietly watches. With sound and visual cues, this sequence becomes the transition point of their romance as the film converts their reminiscence of suffering, particularly the experience of being an orphan, into an occasion of bonding (Fig. 11.2).

Figure 11.2 Song dances with Wuba. Source: *Monster Hunt* (2015).

The transformative role of human suffering in initiating and sustaining interpersonal relationships is not limited to romantic couples. The monster-hunter Luo Gang loses his virility and vigilance altogether when hearing the monsters singing around him about the toils and ephemerality of life for all creatures. After winning a bitter victory against a monster, Luo Gang is found lying in the road, begging for food in front of a wealthy businessman's sedan. He is then enlisted as a bodyguard. As the story discloses, the monster-hunters, once entrusted as superheroes who defeated monsters and guaranteed peace for humans, are dismissed by the current government as useless since monsters have disappeared from the human world. Monster-hunters in the current epoch have to serve wealthy businessmen to make a living.

Through this scenario, the film makes subtle innuendos about the arbitrary and seemingly unfair social divisions marked by the possession of wealth. When Ge Qianhu, owner of the superlative restaurant that prepares and cooks monsters, captures the villagers from Yongning, he comments that these monsters were foolish to disguise themselves as poor people instead of rich ones. At the end of the film, it is revealed that Ge is a monster who is disguised as a wealthy human, a strategy that places him on much higher ground in the human world than the villagers have achieved. The inept human couple in the inn might be taken as an easy reminder about China's *nouveaux riches*, with their luxurious clothing, their peculiar attention to nutrition and nourishment, and their assured manners. The film's exposé of their lifestyle reaches its climax at the restaurant, where various types of monsters are prepared exquisitely by top chefs to feed wealthy humans who are eager for the health benefits of these rare delicacies.

The film's apparent display of the extravaganza of wealth in the human world, without disclosure of its opposite – the downtrodden and impoverished – provides more of a spectacle than a critique, however. The suffering of the monster-hunters is mostly anecdotal and hastily glossed over rather than visually dwelled on, not intense enough to mount a social criticism or even a reflection on contemporary reality. One of the most grotesque moments of the film occurs when two human-like children (monsters in disguise) refuse to take off their human skin before being cooked. The inference that they will be consumed in human form by the diners transforms the nature of the entire monster-eating feast – the line between eating monsters/animals and eating humans becomes blurred. None the less, such an atrocity of eating human children (in its literary and metaphorical sense) is downplayed by the beguilement of the two monsters – a fatal display of their cunning cuteness. The mechanism that suffering achieves, if not pointing externally to a detrimental social environment, is a humane warmness and kindness that transcends various types of divisions, including those caused by social classes and species distinctions.

In a sense, the film's representation of orphanhood, family roles and prevalent suffering repeats the *wenqing* (warm sentimentality) tradition shared by many Chinese-language films, in which sentimentalism is understood as moderation, endurance, making peace, reaching harmony or accepting the status quo, instead of the overflow of emotions defined in Freudian terms.[27] Disparate spectacles that vaguely allude to social reality, one may argue, substantiate what Bill Nichols has called a revolt against master narratives – a shift away from universalism towards a particularism that defines equality in relation to attributive differences.[28] In light of Nichols's observation, Rey Chow identifies an alternative type of sentimentalism: rather than being emotional excess, or an individual consciousness's longing for an ideal 'whose attainment is always deferred, or affirmatively, in the form of (collective identity empowerment and the fight for social justice)', the weak and the marginal become visible and luminous. Such a transition from being affective to being discursive denotes that sentimentalism is not associated with 'the passing of time or the melancholy sensitivity of a lone lyric consciousness', but an instrument in the reinterpretation of power structures.[29] The visibility of suffering, or how *Monster Hunt* makes suffering more luminous than lamentable, might be a more appropriate perspective to understand the film's effervescent depiction of knotty social issues.

Structuring the storyline based on family roles and kinship ties and setting one's domestic position as a determinative factor in moral choices do more than reaffirm the importance of family and home in contemporary Chinese cinema.[30] A more ensnaring implication is how this type of domesticity might overshadow individuality or even degenerate into the practice of xenophobia by drawing an unbreakable distinction between insiders and outsiders. It is at this point that Rey Chow offers her critique of the centrality of kinship in Chinese-language cinema – that is, kinship, 'defined as an inviolable interiority of familial/familiar relations', risks becoming 'the last vestige of morality (and of humanity) left in an utterly amoral world – in the sense that, except for the protection and preservation of one's kin, nothing else matters'.[31] Drawing on Heidegger's critique of the status of humanism in the West, which tends to bypass the question of 'being', the 'irreducible surplus presence that sustains every human undertaking but forever exceeds rational human consciousness',[32] or what it means to be human, Rey Chow touches on the corollary of otherness: by a certain logic, some human beings can lack legitimacy in a particular group. So, the issue at stake is, with its emphasis on the predominance of family roles, does *Monster Hunt* offer yet another cinematic account of the intransigent demarcation between insiders and outsiders, identifying the outsider as the other (the illegitimate and the nonhuman) while letting the protection of one's own kind be the sole determinant of morality?

The Core: Otherness and Contemporaneity

The moral and affective ramifications of domesticity will be better understood with a closer look at the composition of the only viable family monad in the film, the one composed of Song Tianyin, Huo Xiaolan and Wuba. As discussed earlier, Wuba is, on the surface, an orphan adopted by Song and Huo, thanks to their own fatherless status. But more accurately, Wuba is an alien species transplanted into Song's body against his will. It is astonishing and comical enough that a man is chosen by the monster Queen to carry her baby, but it is more so when the man chooses not to exterminate this creature, especially in comparison with Hollywood narratives in which violation of one's body is almost always a metaphor for an impingement on one's selfhood. In *Alien* (Ridley Scott, 1979) and its later instalments, for example, bodily contact with unknown creatures is the start of physical invasion for the human race that usually ends in destruction and death.[33] To some extent, the *Shrek* series (2001–7) that Raman Hui worked on is not simply antithetical to Disney's princess stories.[34] It is also one of the fantasy narratives that rethink otherness within the Hollywood studio system.[35] As Raman Hui's major production in China, *Monster Hunt* appears to deviate from such anxiety about sameness and to connect with the epistemology manifest in classical Chinese tales that accepts anomaly, a point I briefly described earlier and will expound below.

By borrowing the image of Dijiang, *Monster Hunt* employs an early way of visually depicting a monster in Chinese mythology in which the line between humans and monsters is permeable. According to Strassberg, *The Classic* uses composite forms of construction to depict hybrid creatures that mostly belong to a certain species, with familiar features, but have added unexpected/strange elements. *Dijiang* resembles a round animal that has six legs and no eyes. He believes that the proliferation of the hybrid during its compilation – the latter part of the Zhou Dynasty – reflects its time: the strange creature, being nothing more than a core identity plus additional features, 'mirror[s] the pluralistic nature of the feudal state'. The hybrid thus visualises a concept about 'a superior power through an aggregation of elements rather than through synthesis or evolution'.[36] The monsters might have odd appearances, but they are not primitive powers that need to be overcome by human civilisation for the sake of progress; instead, by showing that their key features already exist in the natural or human worlds, they represent another overlapping order that is legitimate and has its own principles.

As observed by Emmanuel Levinas about (post)modern realities, if a relation between self and other is viable at all, the other tends to be reduced to the ego's horizon of consciousness, a model of appropriation or domestication that seems to deny 'the unmediatable and ultimately sublime nature of alterity'.[37] None the less, even though reducing the other to the logics of the self is lamentable, refusing a relation between the two is also a form of violence. The difficulty lies in how to 'acknowledge a difference between self and other without separating them so schismatically that no relation at all is possible'.[38] Thus, one should decentre the ego, opening the self to the incongruous and the unexpected – or, accept oneself as a stranger. Proposing an alternative to the Hegelian synthesis or the deconstructionist alterity, Richard Kearney argues for 'multiple traversals between seeming incompatibles', or 'affinities', 'interlacing alterities'.[39]

In many ways, *Monster Hunt* enquires into the possible coexistence of the incompatibles: self and other, humankind and monsters, classical tales and contemporary time. The types of relations between these distinct categories – synthesis or aggregation, separation or trespassing, homogeneity or incongruity – bridge the worldview evident in its source of inspiration and the film's rendering of contemporary realities. By amalgamating contrasting views about otherness from different cultural traditions, *Monster Hunt* embodies the idea of ourselves-as-others as the ground for the coexistence and relation between self and other. First of all, the unexpected self is shown in the film as a monstrous human reality: not only that monsters have disguised themselves as humans and lived among them for decades, but also that human society needs the intervention of the monsters. The traversal between incompatibles comes from the primacy of the monster species in shaping the functionalities of human society – the latter is otherwise transitory, incomplete or fundamentally flawed. Human characters in the film are far from fully developed, many appearing and disappearing as fleeting icons to offer a glimpse of contemporary concerns that Chinese audiences can easily identify with (or laugh about), such as the misbehaving child in the inn or the complacent upper class in the restaurant. Even the more fully-fledged characters act as isolated beings whose motifs and actions rely on their involvement in the monster world. As monster-hunters, Luo Gang and Huo, are caught up in the schemes of the formidable monster villain, Song's journey begins with his chance encounter with the two monster ministers. The only identifiable human societal unit, Yongning village, as it turns out, is fully composed of monsters (except for the Song household).

Even though the film is promoted as kid-friendly and suitable for the entire family, the innate value of monsters does not come solely from Wuba's cuteness, but it does arise from how he effectuates human relations that were formerly lacking. As it stands, coexistence does not take the form of separation or even domestication: that is, the monsters abiding by human laws. Rather, it begins with the crossing of boundaries and ends with the reconfiguration of human values with the help of monsters. The ostensible ability of monsters to transform their appearance into the human form, eventually, corresponds to their ability to transform the mores of humans. A threat presented to the human world from the inception, that the monsters are trespassing beyond the boundary, is alleviated by Wuba, the baby monster who, according to the film's prophecy, will cause cataclysm to the world, and turns out to be ameliorating. And through his presence, it is discovered that the human world requires remedy no less than the tumultuous monsters' realm.

As much as one might fault the film's facile representation of suffering and social division, critics may also have issues with how elements from popular culture, such as the cult of cuteness and inverted gender roles, serve as comic relief.[40] However, it is exactly due to the flexibility and fluidity of gender attributes between Song and Huo that they are able to form the only complete nuclear family in the film. Rather than dispelling the monster foetus as an alien parasite, Song carries it as a 'mother', indulging in his pregnancy and protecting the foetus at all cost. Against the motive of selling the sought-after monster baby for profit, the film lingers on Song preparing for his impending motherhood, such as caressing his bulging belly, speaking to the growing foetus and thinking of naming the baby.[41] Both Song and Huo struggle to explain, with the mercenary motive they openly admit, the painstaking care and the *de facto* parenthood they offer to the baby. Handicapped and effeminate, Song seems not only to accept but also to take pride in his pregnancy, demonstrating an unusual ability to welcome the unexpected, and accept the abnormal as normal. The jokes the film makes about the two leading human characters – one a feminised man, the other a masculinised woman – are therefore outweighed by its projection of these two individuals' unfailing ability to adapt to (inconvenient) situations and to chart a moral path against social confines. More importantly, through these two (laughable) characters, *Monster Hunt* corroborates the versatile, transformative and empowering roles of 'the unexpected', and by doing so, proves its relevance to Chinese audiences.

The film plays with the conversion between flexible gender attributes and the assignment of family roles to rejuvenate the validity of the domestic space under uncertain circumstances. After taking care of the sick monster baby, the young couple discuss who should breastfeed him. When Song instinctively looks towards Huo, the latter claims that Song, as Wuba's mother, should assume that task. After Song disputes his quasi-female identity, Huo reticently accepts her female and thus motherly status, and to consolidate this assignment, she instructs Song, being the father of the household, to discipline the unruly blood-imbibing baby. A highly flexible gender assignment that takes into account both physical attributes and social functionalities breaks the rigid patriarchal gender structure and restructures the family unit so that it stays as a strong moral compass in a society in constant flux, confusion and disintegration. The imperial order of killing monsters needs to be repealed to uphold a lost moral stance of coexistence. The mega-villains could have been the humans who drove the monsters out; pervasive suffering was, and still is, experienced by different forms of living beings, in the past and at present; and engulfing social divisions turn a feast of meat consumption into a metaphor for the consumption of humans, as analysed earlier, each of which, to be read as a political allegory, is far from an eulogy of contemporary China that the film bureaus would like to endorse.

Besides rewriting parenting roles so that family remains a bulwark against (possibly) detrimental external forces, gender fluidity in the film is also portrayed as a pathway to the co-inhabitance of different species. The inverted and mixed family unit formed by these two 'queer' individuals is conducive to them both accepting the monster baby as their own child and accepting Song's monster villagers (again) as their own kind. At that point, the film turns into a story about redemption: that is, Song accepting Wuba as his own, rather than abandoning him, constitutes a redemption of the wrongdoing conducted by Song's parents – and, notably, such redemption extends across and to different species. It is not mere coincidence that Song begins to carry the monster foetus on the same day that he discovers that his best friend Xiaowu is a green-skinned monster – his own distorted physicality coincides with the 'deformity' his friend involuntarily displays. When Xiaowu pleads for Song to save the villagers from the intruders, claiming, 'I look different, but I am the same Xiaowu . . . your best friend,' Song only runs away in shock. While Xiaowu is crushed to the ground by a monster-hunter, he turns his head to look at Song, who is hiding behind a fence and refuses to offer help. It is only through fostering and rescuing Wuba that Song realises the betrayals he has committed against his best friend, even though the latter belongs to a different species.

Despite an overall tendency to domesticate the monsters with human moral standards (Wuba is told not to drink human blood, for example), the film describes interspecies coexistence as a lost (golden) past that conscientious individuals strive to recuperate, an unequivocal reference to *The Classic*. A catalogue of strange phenomena on earth, *The Classic* keeps exhaustive accounts of the celestial/nonhuman realm, in which a few special mountains are identified as ladders to heaven (reserved for thearchs, shamans, heroes, those with special spiritual powers or by a chariot powered by dragons). Yet the primordial connection between heaven and earth is severed with the order from the thearch Zhuanxu.[42] The opening sequence of the film, displaying bronze relief sculptures to retell the diegetic past, retrieves both the peaceful coexistence and the eventual separation between the human race and the monster world, two discrete eras chronologised in the original tales.

The lessened mobility between different creatures, ordered by an imperial authority, has been mourned as a loss in the book, and is also challenged in the film by individuals of different camps (humans who choose to save the monsters and monsters who befriend humans). The ultimate monstrosity of the human world, the film unravels, in addition to excessive suffering endured by fatherless children and probably caused by the debauched (and literally monstrous) upper class, comes from the conflict between an individual's lonely moral stance and an amorphous authority that mandates the erasure of monsters from human civilisation. An individual is left alone to decide his or her actions, as moral guidelines that are usually provided by a social structure have collapsed.[43] As suggested in the film and confirmed in the sequel, Ge Qianhu, the supervillain who intends to cook the monsters as a culinary delicacy for the super-rich, is but one member of the haunting and ubiquitous authority.

Monster Hunt reveals a paradoxical state in the relationship between human and other species: while affection and empathy are established between them, such feelings are not legitimate. In order to be himself, the monster baby has to leave his human father and live only with his kind. Whether or not the film, by reusing the character of *Dijiang* from *The Classic*, intends for *Dijiang*'s more debated connotation – that is, a symbol for a chaotic cosmos – the narrative none the less displays a social order in crisis. It is up to a few courageous social outcasts to question the existent order and to seek a reconstruction, as the ending of the film evokes. When Song sees Wuba off, the scene merges with him reminiscing about his father, who said exactly the same words years ago, 'I don't want you anymore.' As Song bids farewell to Wuba, his own 'son' that he is not allowed to live with, he comes to the realisation that he needs to find his father so that his questions about the current world can be answered. Thus, the film embarks on its story with the formula of domesticating the otherworldly but ends with an anticipation for reunion, both between the human father and son, and between the human race and the monsters/others.

In that sense, the film's narrative, about the return of the monsters that were formerly dispelled from the human world, a past coming back to haunt the present life, or a repressed past that needs to be uncovered to solve present issues, denotes the temporal dimension of otherness. The return of the monsters is also a trope for the anachronistic display of disparate imagery references. The incompatible timeframes, the setting of premodern China where monsters abound, juxtaposed with the human characters' demeanours that are indicative of twenty-first-century China, bring classical images, tales and a bygone time to contemporaneity. Because of this incompatibility, the present time, both within and beyond the profilmic world, becomes uncanny and monstrous. I find Bliss Cua Lim's discussion of immiscible temporality particularly relevant to our understanding of the reuse of traditional fantastic tales and their combination with contemporary reality. In her view, one might be suspicious that translating the supernatural world into the current world in the end is obedient to 'the law of the strongest' – standard time. Indeed, supernatural elements from the past may simply become a consumable and dispensable spectacle to adorn and appease the current time. However, as Lim expatiates, this process of 'translation' still preserves some hint of untranslatability and retains a world outside of what is familiar: that is, some form of excess.[44]

The coeval existence of the past and contemporary time does not come from their seamless integration but is made possible exactly because of the presence of fissures – a hint about the otherworldly in the contemporary world (both in the film's diegesis and in the modern world in which audiences reside). What was once suppressed has reappeared and will return in new forms – this is relevant not only to the meaning of the uncanny, the unfamiliar familiar, but also to one's understanding of the future. After all, in the sense that the future is, or ought to be, unfamiliar, it is also monstrous. As Derrida argues, the future is 'necessarily monstrous: the figure of the future, that is, that which can only be surprising, that for which we are not prepared, . . . is heralded by species of monsters'. One needs to 'welcome the monstrous arrivant', 'to accord hospitality to that which is absolutely foreign or strange'.[45] *Monster Hunt* begins with monsters that were once ousted from but are now intruding on the human world and ends with anticipation of the return of the new generation of monsters. The solution provided by Song Tianyin's father, that the monsters are disguised as human to avoid being exterminated, does not work for Song any more. As Wuba's father, Song intends Wuba to have an undisguised life, and for that, the film suggests at the end, Song will have to ask his own kind to accept the monsters as equals, or accept the other as other. If monstrosity as an imaginary space heralds the opening-up of the future, Chinese fantasy movies such as *Monster Hunt* can be said to offer pathways to what is unknown and unappropriated by existing discourses of power/social structure.

In conclusion, *Monster Hunt* portrays the rediscovery of humane feelings as the main factor that saves the life of the monster baby, in which sense it reiterates, rather than challenges, the predominance of domesticity and sentimentality in Chinese films. None the less, at a time when the traditional patriarch fails to face the challenges imposed by a world in flux, the film projects a new type of family and, through its logic, a new type of relationship between monsters (the other) and humans. *Monster Hunt*'s ontological question about self and other, and its momentary revelation of realistic social concerns, are simultaneously earnest and farcical. All the moments that allude to irksome and ailing social environments are short-lived. The disappeared father and the left-behind children (by parents who prioritise their societal undertakings), the dissolution of social mores and conventional gender roles, and eventually a social order that needs restructuring, are hidden behind the film's comical display of archetypes/stereotypes in stunning visual effects. However, as much as premodern imaginings of the otherworldly infiltrate contemporary life as an esoteric other that is appropriated but is still unknown, the future is a monster that is not fully domesticated – the uncertainty indicates the possibility of change. The film, above all, presents a heterogenous and anachronistic contemporaneity where otherness can relate to us in the future, at a time when misdoings in the past are redeemed.

Notes

1. Ben Child, 'Will China's growing box office dominance change Hollywood for ever?' (last accessed 28 March 2019).
2. Zhou Xing, 'Zai wenhua hongguan yu yishu weiguan shang kandai Zhuoyao ji de shidai yiyi' (Contemporary significance of *Monster Hunt* from the perspectives of culture and art), 37.
3. *Monster Hunt* held this record until it was surpassed by *The Mermaid* (*Meirenyu*, Stephen Chow, 2016) the following year. See 'Patriotic movie *Monster Hunt* passes *Furious 7*, becomes first Chinese film to take domestic box office crown in two decades' (last accessed 15 March 2019). Despite being accused of inflating ticket sales, *Monster Hunt*'s success was still unprecedented.
4. See 'Zhuoyao ji: guochan dapian de xin biaogan yu xin shidai zhutiyantaohui' (*Monster Hunt*: a new benchmark and new era for Chinese blockbusters) (last accessed 15 March 2019).
5. Simon Harrison, 'Cultural boundaries', 10.

6. Marina Levina and Diem-My T Bui, *Monster Culture in the 21st Century*, 9.
7. For a relevant discussion of the transnational quality of Chinese blockbusters, see Michael Berry, 'Chinese cinema with Hollywood characteristics, or how *The Karate Kid* became a Chinese film'.
8. Discussions of the ambivalent functions of popular culture abound, such as the concept of 'kitsch' as developed by theorists such as Matei Calinescu and Clement Greenberg. Fiona Law, in her reading of *Monster Hunt* in the light of ecocinema, argues for the role of popular cinema in exerting 'ideological critiques'. See Law, 'Fabulating animals–human affinity'.
9. Zhang Zhen analyses the immense power of film as a vehicle for social change, and enquires how domesticity and personal and family issues were tied to the grand purpose of nation-building. See *An Amorous History of the Silver Screen*. Rey Chow argues that the sentimental is a discursive construct traversing affect and time, identity and history, varying across different genres and under different historical situations but persistent as a type of accommodation between clashing social forces. See *Sentimental Fabulations, Contemporary Chinese Films*.
10. None the less, despite the canonisation of Confucianism since the Western Han dynasty, stories about ghosts and monsters survived historical vicissitudes no less than authoritative (Confucian) classics. From *In Search of the Supernatural (Shoushen ji*, 350 CE) to *Strange Stories from a Chinese Studio*, the overall tendency is for monsters to become more like humans, endowed with human values and feelings, and able to be converted by human morals.
11. Thearchs are mythological rulers of prehistoric China who combine religious and political power in their authority.
12. Richard E. Strassberg, *A Chinese Bestiary*, 112.
13. Ibid., 48.
14. A. Herbert Giles and Sung-ling P'u, *Strange Stories from a Chinese Studio*. The description here is based on Pu Songling, *Quanben xinshu Liaozhaizhiyi*, 27–8.
15. Judith Zeitlin, *Historian of the Strange*, 18. For a description about an early usage of *Shanhai jing*, see Hung Wu, *Wu Liang Shrine*, 83.
16. Zeitlin, *Historian of the Strange*, 18.
17. For a historical introduction, see John Henderson, *The Development and Decline of Chinese Cosmology*.
18. Yuan Ke, *Shanhai jing jiaozhu* (*Annotated* Shanhai jing), 478. Pu Songling's *Strange Stories* articulates this subjective quality of strangeness in the tale 'The Rakshas and the Sea Market' (Luosha haishi): a young merchant travels to a foreign country and finds the residents there deformed and hideous while, at the same time, those residents are appalled by this merchant's monstrosity.
19. Zeitlin, *Historian of the Strange*, 22.
20. Even with a hierarchical vision of society, one must also realise that Confucianism does not stress blind obedience to the elders. To quote *The Analects* as an example, 'Showing no deference or respect when young, accomplishing nothing worth handing down when grown, and refusing to die when old – such people are nothing but pests.' See David Hinton, *The Four Chinese Classics*, 330.

21. Liu Chengyu, 'You *Zhuoyao ji* kan guochan qihuan dianying' (Viewing domestic fantasy films from the perspective of *Monster Hunt*), 93–5.
22. One may argue that films about monsters are particularly suitable for describing family relations. In the case of Hollywood, 'monstrous texts of the 1970s and 1980s often took place in enclosed, family-occupied spaces to reflect the unintended consequences of the dissolution of a traditional patriarchal family structure'. See Levina and Bui, *Monster Culture in the 21st Century*, 10.
23. Ben Singer, *Melodrama and Modernity*, 39.
24. Haiyan Lee, *Revolution of the Heart*.
25. Based on an interview with the film producers conducted by *sohu.com*, both *House of Flying Daggers* (*Shimian maifu*, Zhang Yimou, 2004) and *The Promise* are films about an individual's search for true love. See *Wu ji*: Chen Kaige dianying' (last accessed 28 March 2019).
26. Olivia Khoo attributes *The Promise*'s unfavourable reception to its technical shortfalls. See 'Remaking the past, interrupting the present', 250. *The Promise*'s downfall was that its CGI failed to deliver the epic romance it aimed for. In contrast, *Monster Hunt* was promoted to be a lighthearted monster film suitable for children.
27. Chow, *Sentimental Fabulations, Contemporary Chinese Films*, 18.
28. Bill Nichols, 'Film theory and the revolt against master narratives', 40.
29. Chow, *Sentimental Fabulations, Contemporary Chinese Films*, 17.
30. For an analysis of this topic, see Haiping Yan, 'Inhabiting the city', 93–135.
31. Chow, *Sentimental Fabulations, Contemporary Chinese Films*, 178.
32. Ibid., 168.
33. Such treatment can be said to reflect a predisposition identified as the ontology of sameness or 'logocentrism'. See Richard Kearney, *Strangers, Gods and Monsters*, 72. In psychoanalysis, the other is connected to the Freudian concept of 'the uncanny': what used to be seen (and should stay unseen) appears, or what has been repressed reappears. See Sigmund Freud et al., *The Uncanny*, 141–3; Julia Kristeva, *Strangers to Ourselves*.
34. Raman Hui was character designer/supervising animator for *Shrek* (Andrew Adamson and Vicky Jenson, 2001), and additional storyboard artist and supervising animator for *Shrek 2* (Andrew Adamson, Kelly Asbury and Conrad Vernon, 2004). He then co-directed *Shrek the Third* (2007) with Chris Miller.
35. A. Márquez Pérez, '*Shrek*: the animated fairy-tale princess reinvented', 281–6.
36. Strassberg, *A Chinese Bestiary*, 45.
37. Levinas maintains that the other does not exist in relation to one's ego or subjectivity but expresses itself, criticising Western philosophy's tendency to exclude the possibility of relating to the other as other. See Emmanuel Levinas, *Totality and Infinity*, 65. See also Jeffrey Bloechl, *The Face of the Other and the Trace of God*, 66–7. The quotation here comes from Kearney, *Strangers, Gods and Monsters*, 17.
38. Kearney, *Strangers, Gods and Monsters*, 9.
39. Ibid., 12.

40. *Monster Hunt* draws on cultural phenomena familiar to Chinese audiences, some shared with Japanese popular culture and Hollywood movies (such as the idolisation of cuteness) while some others, arguably, are indigenous. For instance, the monster-huntress Huo is easily identifiable as a 'nü hanzi' (a slightly derogatory neologism for a manly woman), and the protagonist, Song, takes on the gender trope of being effeminate. Admittedly, these queer gender roles both rewrite parenting roles and are executed to maximise the film's comedic potential. See Chen Yanjiao, '*Zhuoyao ji*' (Monster Hunt).
41. The notion of pregnant men is present in an episode of *Journey to the West* (*Xiyou ji*), by Ming novelist Wu Cheng'en (1500–82), and in films such as *A Slightly Pregnant Man* (*L'Événement le plus important depuis que l'homme a marché sur la Lune*, Jacques Demy, 1973), *Rabbit Test* (Joan Rivers, 1978) and *Junior* (Ivan Reitman,1994).
42. Strassberg, *A Chinese Bestiary*, 30.
43. In the words of Zygmunt Bauman, strangehood is a prerequisite of modern life, and for that condition, '[the] art of morality . . . may be only the art of living with ambivalence – and taking upon oneself the responsibility for that life and its consequences'. See *Postmodern Ethics*, 159–64, 182.
44. Bliss Cua Lim, *Translating Time*, 32. Also, see Spivak, *Outside in the Teaching Machine*, 181–3.
45. Jacques Derrida and Elisabeth Weber, *Points*, 386–7.

Chapter 12

Transforming Tripitaka: Toward a (Buddhist) Planetary Ethics in Stephen Chow's Adaptation of *Journey to the West*

Kenneth Chan

Introduction: Global Buddhism, Sino-Enchantment and *Journey to the West*

Buddhism, like most global religions, is neither homogenous nor static in its doctrines, philosophies, interpretations and practices. Its history is defined by multiple traditions and an ever-evolving contemporary relevance. In fact, it is precisely this cultural adaptability and openness to hybridisation that drive and power Buddhism's effective transmigration globally. Take China's reception of the religion as a historical example. The Indian aspects of Buddhist ideas and practices needed to be reinterpreted and reconfigured for a heterogenous Chinese audience, as historian Arthur Wright is careful to note – with local religions, Confucianism and Daoism serving as syncretic vehicles for Buddhism's transmission.[1] What Wright is observing about Buddhism's entry into and spread throughout China is not just the religion's ability to translate and insinuate itself into a country or a culture's linguistic, discursive and philosophical structures, but also its dexterity in adapting to the political and ideological conditions on the ground. The Tang Dynasty witnessed the zenith of Chinese Buddhism when its emperors embraced the religion as a means of consolidating their political hold on the nation.[2] Buddhism's impact on Chinese thought and culture is so deep that it spawned four different schools of Chinese Buddhism, including Chan Buddhism (also known as Zen Buddhism).[3] This last point is particularly helpful in understanding the modernisation of Buddhism and its transplantation to the West, particularly through Zen Buddhism.[4]

While I am unable to flesh out in great detail here the very complicated and multifaceted reconfiguration of Buddhist philosophy and practice within the Euro-American context, it is necessary to observe that Buddhism's nimble adaptability is what generated its global spread, especially through the networks of Western ideological, political and cultural hegemony. In the context of the Cold War, for instance, Tibetan Buddhism has gained significant ground, particularly with the Chinese annexation of Tibet, which led to the seemingly permanent exile of the 14th Dalai Lama to India in 1959. The American embrace of Tibetan Buddhism is, hence, inextricably tied to the politics of anti-communism and of human rights. These connections one finds reinforced in American popular culture with films like *Little Buddha* (Bernardo Bertolucci, 1993), *Kundun* (Martin Scorsese, 1997) and *Seven Years in Tibet* (Jean-Jacques Annaud, 1997). Cold War geopolitics, liberal ideals of civil liberties, and the neoliberal capitalist rise have conditioned the cultural ground for Buddhism to take root in the United States. But, more importantly, through America's hold on globalisation and transnational cultures, Buddhism is being reinterpreted and reframed for a new global following: a global Buddhism, so to speak. During the last couple of decades, Buddhist forms of meditative practice in North America, Europe and other cosmopolitan centres around the world (including Asia) have burgeoned and gained immense popularity. Some have described this enthusiastic embrace of mindfulness meditation[5] as the Mindfulness Movement[6] or, as one journalist from *Time* magazine calls it, a 'mindful revolution'.[7] In a stress-ridden and chaotic world, many are turning to mindfulness meditation to diminish anxiety, to find personal peace and to attain equanimity and balance in their lives. The digital realm has also helped proliferate the dissemination of various approaches to mindfulness, through a cornucopia of apps, podcasts, videos and websites, bringing gurus and teachers into virtual contact with many online users.

Global Buddhism's engagement with modernity in the new millennium, especially in and through the West, is a complex and nuanced affair, in that it is not a homogenous one. Some practitioners have immersed themselves fully in the more traditional forms of religious Buddhism as practised in Asian countries, replete with spiritualism, mysticism, supernaturalism and pantheism in all their fantastical glory. (I strategically use the term 'fantastical' here in a non-derogatory way in order to make, later, the connection between Buddhism and Sino-enchantment, as envisioned in the film adaptations of *Journey to the West*.) Others are more guarded and careful in the manner that they interpret and represent the teachings of Buddha to a modern global audience, usually by foregrounding the more relatable aspects of Buddhist philosophy and practice, such as mindful awareness and compassion towards others, while still retaining a cognitive openness to supernatural phenomena and concepts like reincarnation.[8] Many have now also adopted what Stephen Batchelor describes as 'a secular approach to Buddhism', which shows

> how the dharma can enable humans and other living beings to flourish in this biosphere, not in a hypothetical afterlife. Rather than emphasizing personal enlightenment and liberation, it is grounded in a deeply felt concern and compassion for the suffering of all those with whom we share this earth.[9]

While I find much of Batchelor's reinterpretation of Buddhist teachings appealing and useful, it is hard to deny that this secularisation of Buddhism has contributed, however unintended it may be on Batchelor's part, to the eventual and complete decoupling of mindfulness meditation from its religious source and intent, thereby leading to the cooptation and commodification of meditative practices into 'a capitalist spirituality'.[10] In his book *McMindfulness*, Ronald Purser insightfully points out that we are asked by this 'spirituality', implicitly, to shoulder the blame for our struggles and inaptitude in the neoliberal capitalist economy because 'the causes of suffering are disproportionately inside us, not in the political and economic frameworks that shape how we live'. The practice of mindfulness, now stripped of its Buddhist religiosity, then teaches us 'that [by] paying closer attention to the present moment without passing judgment', we attain 'the revolutionary power to transform the whole world', which, to Purser, is basically 'magical thinking on steroids'.[11]

The truncated transcription of the emerging story of global Buddhism above is designed to set the stage for my discussion of the film versions of *Xiyou ji* (*Journey to the West*) and, more specifically, a close analysis of Stephen Chow's *Journey to the West: Conquering the Demons* (*Xiyou xiangmopian*, 2013). The interpretive argument that I wish to make about Chow's film and the planetary ethics it articulates involves an intersection of global Buddhism, Sino-enchantment (of the fantastic in Chinese cinema) and the filmic institution of *Xiyou ji* adaptations.

The most obvious rationale for embedding my reading of the film within the context of global Buddhism is the fact that Chinese Buddhism, in its integration with Daoism and Confucianism, has defined the Ming Dynasty literary classic, upon which the film is based, as evident in its narrative structures, character choices, thematic content and historical allusions. But the cinematic and televisual iterations of *Xiyou ji*, including Chow's film, have additionally attained a global appeal that transcends its niche ethnic-Chinese market, hence serving to familiarise and popularise Buddhist imagery and concepts further, even if only in superficial ways. One might go so far as to suggest that the transnational confluence of global Buddhism and multimedia reworkings of *Xiyou ji* constitutes a kind of cultural feedback loop, where the reinforcement of audience appeal shuttles back and forth between the two.

To complicate this paradigm even further, I want to envision an interlocking structure of three discursive tracks, as a theoretical trope for thinking deeper about the relationships between, first, global Buddhism; second, pop cultural *Xiyou ji*; and third, the fantastic, all mediated through the theoretical lens of Sino-enchantment as the connecting mechanism. As Andrew Stuckey and I have laid out in the introductory chapter of this book, the concepts of enchantment, disenchantment and re-enchantment can work in problematic, contradictory and/or productive ways, thus generating a more nuanced and critical understanding of modernity and how it functions. Sino-enchantment grants us an expansive theoretical latitude to confront Chinese modernities in all their cultural richness, complexity and messiness – global Buddhism and *Xiyou ji* included.

First, Sino-enchantment as magical *enchantment*: Buddhism, in some of its more traditional forms, enchants believers through the religious fantastic, which those who advocate for a modern approach would dismiss as an 'unenlightened atavism yet to be swept clean' by modernity's rationalism.[12] The Buddha makes his way into *Xiyou ji* as a spectacular and supreme deity of the Chinese pantheon. He functions as the divine catalyst that sets into motion the journey that the monk Tripitaka takes, together with his magical disciples Monkey King (Sun Wukong), Pig (Zhu Wuneng or Zhu Bajie) and Sandy (Sha Wujing), from Tang China to the land of India to obtain the Buddhist scriptures. The cast of characters that includes gods, demigods, spirits and demons provides rich visual fodder for the production of spectacular cinematic attractions (to play off Tom Gunning's term), characterised by stunning action sequences featuring martial arts display and supernatural phenomena that are generated by stunt work, creature make-up, traditional special effects and, more recently, digital visual effects. The fantastic in the supernatural martial arts film (*wuxia shenguai pian*), the subgenre to which adaptations of *Xiyou ji* belong, hence enchants and enraptures its viewers through its commodification of the monstrous, the demonic, the spiritual and the divine.

Second, Sino-enchantment as modern *disenchantment*: modernity is usually defined by scientific rationalism, an 'enlightened' state of disenchantment from a premodern worldview governed by religious superstition and mysticism. Secular strains of global Buddhism have often reconfigured Buddhist practices and philosophies in positivistic epistemological terms. (It is no coincidence that Robert Wright, for example, provides his book *Why Buddhism Is True* with the subtitle 'The Science and Philosophy of Meditation and Enlightenment'.[13])

While Stephen Batchelor claims that his conception of secular Buddhism does not 'discard all trace of religiosity',[14] his approach ultimately still marginalises the religious in order to make its argument, just as the Mindfulness Movement often deploys meditation practices while simultaneously delinking them from traditional Buddhist spirituality and beliefs. As modern technology, the cinematic medium is perfectly suited to instrumentalising elements of the religious and the fantastic,[15] the way that global Buddhism does, in its secular rewriting of *Xiyou ji* for a modern audience. Hongmei Sun offers a surprising and illuminating example of how the Maoist regime in communist China – instead of rejecting, tout court, *Xiyou ji* and its pop cultural manifestations as propagating religious superstitions and bourgeois ideologies – retooled the classic as a revolutionary text and recast Sun Wukong as a heroic figure against the establishment. *Havoc in Heaven* (*Danao tiangong*, Wan Laiming, 1961–4), a mainland Chinese work of animation, is one such instance of cinematic political allegory.[16] *The Forbidden Kingdom* (Rob Minkoff, 2008) is Hollywood's method of reinventing *Xiyou ji* as a cinematic strategy to grapple with American cultural concerns, like questions of self-reliance and racial identity. Director Minkoff embeds Sun Wukong's adventures within a fantasy dream sequence, thus deploying the religious and fantastic imagery without straining the verisimilitude of the film's modern-day Boston setting that bookends the main protagonist's dream state.[17] Hong Kong films and recent transnational Chinese (co-)productions, while drawing from the fantastical plotlines within the literary *Xiyou ji*, also appeal to Chinese and global audiences by foregrounding the quotidian aspects of modern human experience, such as romantic love, sexuality, sensitivity to nonhuman life, and ecological and environmental awareness.

Third, and finally, worldly *re-enchantment*: in abandoning the binary and the dialectical models of modernity, Landy and Saler conclude that 'modernity is defined . . . by contradictions, oppositions, and antinomies', meaning that 'modernity is messy'.[18] This antinomial mode envisions, as the title of their book signals, a re-enchantment of the world, a 'modern enchantment . . . which simultaneously enchants and disenchants, which delights and does not delude'.[19] Our world 'must be enchanted with *dignity*, which is to say in concord with secular rationality, in full awareness of pluralism and contingency. And it must be *multiply* enchanted, so as to satisfy again all the pressing demands formerly satisfied by religion.'[20] It is hence fascinating to find, in this context, Stephen Batchelor using the same kind of language in his articulation of a secular Buddhism for the modern age. He advances the notion that this revised Buddhism 'works toward a reenchantment of the world', propagating 'a sensibility to what might be called the "everyday sublime"'.[21] This sensibility, I will argue later, is what an aesthetically sophisticated and culturally astute filmmaker such as Stephen Chow brings to his version of *Xiyou ji. Journey to the West: Conquering the Demons*, therefore, moves its audience to become enamoured with this world and its inhabitants in ways that are both personally affective and planetarily connective.

But these three individual parts of Sino-enchantment do not the whole make, as Stuckey and I have pointed out in our introduction. Their intersection and integration within Sino-enchantment can generate critical valences and energies that are additionally productive and efficacious. One key instance of special relevance to this chapter is this idea that religions in their traditional forms, and with all their magical enchantments, should not be simply ignored or, worse, suppressed. In her final book *Touching Feeling* (before her untimely passing in 2009), queer theorist Eve Kosofsky Sedgwick, a practising Buddhist herself, criticises Stephen Batchelor's secular approach as an 'agnosticism [that] is marked by its unresting disdain for *consolation*. He deprecates belief in rebirth, for example, as "the luxury of consolation".'[22] What Sedgwick is ultimately getting at and pointing us to is the possible comfort that magical enchantment can bring, or the immersive spaces of comforting possibilities it can open up, to a person facing the inevitability of their own impending death. Sedgwick latches on to the material tactility, the sense of touching and feeling, which the fantastic, the spiritual and the supernatural, in their own paradoxical way, can conjure. Or, as Sedgwick so eloquently puts it in her own words:

> I don't know that multiple samsaric rebirths sound all that consoling anyway. What is more palpable to me is the skillfulness of the Tibetan teachings as a presence in the world of people dealing with mortality. Being and learning to unbe a self are both less smothering in a space that already holds amnesia, metamorphosis, and ever-shifting relationality – indeed, that holds them as the crucible of all phenomena.[23]

It is in the context of this multifaceted and fluid conception of Sino-enchantment that I situate Stephen Chow's *Journey to the West: Conquering the Demons*. Chow's enterprising skill may be his ability to manufacture a film that draws on the many resources of Sino-enchantment to expand its box-office appeal to global audiences – hence, the film as transnational Chinese cinema – but Chow's real genius is his, often underappreciated, sensitive connection to the zeitgeist of the moment, which enables his creation of a cinema of global moral consciousness. His adaptation of *Xiyou ji* enchants us (fantastically) and re-enchants us (secularly) into the hope of living according to a (Buddhist) planetary ethics.[24] The expansiveness and generosity of this ethics may potentially strain against the commercial exploitation that is inherent in the cinematic commodification of *Journey to the West*; but this ethics also signals, to global audiences, the contemporary relevance of the Chinese Buddhist classic, as reconfigured for the screen today. Chow's entry, I contend, leads the way.

'Change!': Surveying the Transformations of *Xiyou ji* Film Adaptations

Before I begin my case study of Chow's film, it is necessary to trace, briefly, the rich history of *Xiyou ji* adaptations in Chinese cinemas and the discursive parameters that director Chow had to work with. In the hundred-chapter Ming Dynasty epic novel, reputedly written by Wu Cheng'en, 'the stone monkey',[25] as the Monkey King is initially called, is born out of 'an immortal stone' in 'the Flower-Fruit Mountain'.[26] After being celebrated by his fellow monkeys for his leadership, the 'Handsome Monkey King' becomes his new moniker.[27] Under the later tutelage of the immortal Patriarch Subodhi, the Monkey King is again rechristened with the religious name Sun Wukong and is taught the magical power of 'seventy-two transformations'.[28] By crying 'Change!' as part of a spell, Wukong has the ability to transmogrify himself into any being or object, while also often using strands of his own hair to replicate himself. These superhero powers to transform and multiply in order to meet the various crises and exigencies of the moment function as perfect metaphors for the manifold ways in which filmmakers and studios throughout Chinese film history have adapted and readapted, ad nauseum, this classic epic for audiences of different generations.

As I have observed earlier in my introduction, one cannot underestimate the fantastical appeal of the Monkey King's magical powers to readers and audiences. The extensive global archive featuring Sun Wukong and the other figures in *Xiyou ji* demonstrates the cultural and religious hold these characters have on us. As a multimedia catalogue, the archive includes literature, literary adaptations, parodies, theatrical productions, Chinese opera, paintings, comic strips, internet stories, animation, television series and, of course, cinema.[29] The contemporary appeal of *Xiyou ji* as classic epic fantasy is further encouraged by the success of Hollywood's adaptations of the literary fantasy genre, such as J. R. R. Tolkien's *The Lord of the Rings* and J. K. Rowling's Harry Potter series. The narrative richness of *Xiyou ji* as the classic Chinese iteration of the fantasy genre lends itself conveniently to filmmakers looking for a go-to text to produce another *wuxia shenguai pian*, ready for release during the Chinese New Year box-office season in many Asian countries.

More importantly, *Xiyou ji*, as classic religious literature, also conveys a kind of cultural gravitas, anchoring its readers (and audiences of the film adaptations) with a deep sense of tradition and religious resonance. The translator and editor of the authoritative English version, Anthony Yu, observes that the 'novel is steeped in a cultural milieu that affirms the Three Religions [Buddhism, Daoism and Confucianism] as belonging to the same fold in practice and belief'.[30] Hence, the films that this classic text has generated keep its audiences enthralled not only with its fantastical spectacularity but also through its religious themes and iconicity. The *Xiyou ji* adaptations, as examples of the *wuxia shenguai pian*, constituted an extremely popular subgenre of the martial arts film in the Shanghai industry of the 1920s and 1930s. Zhang Zhen foregrounds this connectivity between early Chinese cinema and its magical ability to project, into being, the luminous and ethereal forms of the gods for audiences to pray to, some even 'burning incense inside a theater', an instance that popular movie periodicals during the era often recounted.[31] In other words, the studios were eager to draw on the appeal of religious magical enchantments that these films offer, and they looked to Chinese folklore and classic literature as rich source material.

A specific example from Shanghai cinema, which Zhang has identified, is *The Cave of the Spider Spirit* (*Pansidong*, Dan Duyu, 1927), a Shanghai Film Company production.[32] This particular narrative of the seven spider spirits is drawn from Chapters 72 and 73 of the original literary text. While the role of the seven spirits is not particularly remarkable in the context of how they are just another instance of the many monsters and fiends in *Xiyou ji* that are out to capture and eat Tripitaka, filmmakers seem especially attracted to these arachnid characters – Hong Kong films that similarly draw on this plot scenario include the Shaw production *The Cave of the Silken Web* (*Pansidong*, Ho Meng-hua, 1967) and *A Chinese Odyssey: Part One – Pandora's Box* (*Xiyou ji zhi yueguang baohe*, Jeffrey Lau, 1995).[33] In fact, in the literary original, the seven spider demons suffer a demise that is rather anti-climactic, where Sun Wukong, in the middle of Chapter 73, unceremoniously 'raised with both hands [his magic rod] to smash to pulp those seven spider spirits',[34] which very much differs from the narrative flourishes and visual spectacles that attend the film versions. Zhang Zhen presents us with a theoretical reading of the Shanghai iteration that unpacks, in part, the cinematic fascination with and rewriting of this episode. In describing 'the martial arts–magic spirit film' (*wuxia shenguai pian*) as 'a promiscuous genre', or 'a hypergenre characterized by disorder, chaos, and cross-fertilization', she contends that these films embody a set of contradictions. 'The valiant fortitude and physical prowess in martial arts–magic spirit films were regarded as particularly empowering by a people who had internalized the image of the "sick man of the orient" . . . since China's defeat in the Opium Wars,' while, at the same time, these films were savaged for their 'outlandish use of "superstitious" motifs, cinematic tricks, sexual promiscuity, and gender ambiguity'.[35] This contradiction Zhang also sees in *The Cave of the Spider Spirit*, which offers visually stunning instances of traditional 'costume dramas' that 'appear ultramodern, replete with contemporary fashion, expressionist sets, and even seminude scenes'.³⁶ In other words, the filmmaker was drawing on the cultural energies of the religious iconicity and values – the instrumentality I discussed in the section on modern disenchantment – while presenting an aestheticism that conveys, in contradistinction, a sense of Chinese modernity to the film's twentieth-century audiences. This modernity is further articulated metadiegetically by the technological innovations of cinema at the time, in this case the first known instance in Chinese film of underwater cinematography capturing the sensual aquatic frolicking of the actresses who play these spider demons.³⁷

For me, the main takeaway from Zhang's analysis is that *Xiyou ji*'s central appeal as source material is in its potential malleability, through which filmmakers can concatenate Chinese religion, cultural traditionalism, and globalised and technological modernity, a synergism unveiled to us through Sino-enchantment. The recent spate of Chinese co-produced adaptations is illustrative of this phenomenon: Chow's *Journey to the West: Conquering the Demons*, Tsui Hark's sequel (to Chow's 2013 film) *Journey to the West: The Demons Strike Back* (*Xiyou fuyaopian*, 2017), Derek Kwok's *The Tales of Wu Kong* (*Wukong zhuan*, 2017)³⁸ and Pou-Soi Cheang's trilogy – *The Monkey King: Havoc in Heaven's Palace* (*Xiyou ji zhi danao tiangong*, 2014), *The Monkey King 2* (*Xiyou ji zhi Sun Wukong sanda Baigu jing*, 2016) and *The Monkey King 3* (*Xiyou ji nüer guo*, 2018).³⁹ Produced in an era of 3D revivalism and the emergence of 4K Ultra HD technology, each of these films progressively offers more and more stunning visual imagery through digital visual effects, while revisiting the traditional Monkey King–Tripitaka story with a modern emphasis on contemporary cultural themes and concerns. My analysis of Chow's film, in the next section of this chapter, illustrates this specific turn to a contemporary discursive appeal.

Finally, it is also relevant to underscore, even briefly, the questions of gender and sexuality in order to understand their presence in many of these *Xiyou ji* films. Regarding 'the supple and cunning female figures in *The Cave of the Spider Spirit*', Zhang Zhen theorises that

> the provocative, and often erotic, appeal of costume drama created a phantasmagoria of overlapping temporality; the alternative versions of 'history,' when rendered cinematic, became the place where magic and technology, archaic fantasy and modern desire fused into a feast of visual display.⁴⁰

I want to layer and complicate this reading further by noting that the Ming Dynasty novel is not itself innocent of the saucy and sensual narrative exploits, on to which the adaptations seem to latch. For example, in the novel, Zhu Bajie's insatiable appetite for food and erotic pleasures, and the multiple female monster spirits and the all-female community that attempt to entice Tripitaka with sexual desire, help define the narrative contours, a literary sensuality that is akin to, but not to the same extent of, Chaucer's *Canterbury Tales*. But the presence of 'rogue' female sexuality in the novel usually functions as foil to the Buddhist ideals of abstinence and self-control.

This conception of female sexuality as modes of entrapment and moral weakness assumes a spectacular form when filtered through the cinematic male gaze. It is no wonder that Shaw director Ho Meng-hua[41] dedicated much screen time particularly to female characters in his prestigious[42] quartet of *Xiyou ji* adaptations: the character Miss Gao in *The Monkey Goes West* (*Xiyou ji*, 1966), White Skeleton in *Princess Iron Fan* (*Tieshan gongzhu*, 1966), the seven spider spirits in *The Cave of the Silken Web* and the all-female kingdom in *The Land of Many Perfumes* (*Nüer guo*, 1968). Not unlike its Shanghai predecessor, *The Cave of the Silken Web* reruns the beauty-contest stylisation of these gorgeous women posing in skimpy attire and singing like sirens to lure the ever so vulnerable Zhu Bajie into their webs of deceit. The exploitative quality of this visual eroticism is consistent with the films that were emerging out of the Shaw studios at the time. While the gender and sexual politics of the last five decades have obviously, and fortunately, shifted from the sexist model of Ho's films, the erotic appeal of the female characters continues to permeate the contemporary *Xiyou ji* females, hence returning audiences to familiar characters: Princess Iron Fan in *The Monkey King: Havoc in Heaven's Palace*, White Bone Demon in *The Monkey King 2* and *Journey to the West: The Demons Strike Back*, and Womanland in Western Liang in *The Monkey King 3*. Furthermore, working in concert with erotic love is, of course, the ubiquitous presence of heterosexual romantic love. Romance as a plot device is evident in all of these films, including Chow's *Journey to the West: Conquering the Demons*. My highlighting of this element is intended to contextualise and underscore, later, a specific moment in Chow's film where romantic and erotic aspects of love are reconnected to a more universal ideal of love, which then serves as the foundation (of worldly re-enchantment) for a planetary ethics.

Stephen Chow's *Journey to the West: Conquering the Demons*

As a director of mainstream Chinese–Hong Kong cinema, Stephen Chow has proven to be a cut above the rest, mainly because he challenges aesthetic and narrative conventions, while always having his finger on the pulse of contemporary cultural issues and concerns. His 2013 film *Journey to the West: Conquering the*

Demons has helped revive cinematic attention to the *Xiyou ji* epic in this decade,[43] by providing a fresh perspective on the oft-told tale of Tripitaka and his long trek to India for the holy scriptures. I further conjecture that this film may have had a crucial role in generating, in its wake, a series of other film adaptations and sequels. In the remainder of this chapter, I analyse the nature of the film's appeal to contemporary audiences, specifically in its articulation of a cultural politics of alterity and relationality, a cinematic envisioning of a (Buddhist) planetary ethics.

In her book *Death of a Discipline*, Gayatri Chakravorty Spivak deploys the word 'planetarity' as a theoretical device to shift the direction of comparative literature as an academic field. She 'propose[s] the planet to overwrite the globe' because the latter term reifies the hegemonic force of globalisation as a signifier for global capitalism. 'The planet', in contrast, 'is in the species of alterity, belonging to another system; and yet we inhabit it, on loan.'[44] It is in this spatial conception of relationality that Spivak meditates on the ethics that it invokes:

> To be human is to be intended toward the other . . . If we imagine ourselves as planetary subjects rather than global agents . . . alterity remains underived from us; it is not our dialectical negation, it contains us as much as it flings us away.

Dwelling on the planetary 'is already to transgress, for, in spite of our forays into what we metaphorize, differently, as outer and inner space, what is above and beyond our own reach is not continuous with us as it is not, indeed, specifically discontinuous'.[45] The peculiar power of the planetarity rests on the seeming contradictions of its logical turns and folds, movements that are not dissimilar to the transgressive potentiality that the fantastic as an aesthetic modality can sometimes offer, which Chow's *Journey to the West* delivers in spades. But, more specifically, the film embodies the spatial expanse and density that a planetary ethics demands in its spiralling turns, both inwards and outwards. To unpack this understanding of the film, I examine, first, the setting that opens the film and the characters that inhabit it; second, the conical spatiality – from small to large, from personal to cosmic – of the reconfigured narrative that inverts the more conventional *Xiyou ji* adaptation's notion of living realms; and third, the final sequences that fling us into Earth's planetary expanse and into alternate realms of spiritual consciousness, particularly through the outsize image of the Buddha.

Like most epic religious literature (such as the Holy Bible, the *Epic of Gilgamesh*, the *Divine Comedy* and Milton's *Paradise Lost*), the novel *Xiyou ji*

Transforming Tripitaka 233

begins its origin story in the immortal and divine realm. The text devotes the first eight chapters to a recounting of Sun Wukong's birth, his rebellion against the Jade Emperor, his imprisonment by the Buddha for 500 years and his eventual release by the Bodhisattva Guanyin. These opening chapters set the stage for the second part of the story: the quasi-earthly affairs of the Tang Emperor Taizong and his commissioning of Chen Xuanzang as Tripitaka, to embark on a journey westward to obtain the religious scriptures from the Buddha himself. Many of the film adaptations also tend to adhere rather closely to this gods-and-kings plot structure, placing particular emphasis on the immortal Sun Wukong as their chief protagonist.

The epic scope of this initial narrative framework, one could argue, works in consonance with the planetary, as the ending sequence of Stephen Chow's film demonstrates. But Chow chose, instead, to start his version of the *Xiyou ji* tale by focusing, rather counterintuitively, on the humble beginnings of Xuanzang (played by Zhang Wen) as a novice demon hunter and devoted practitioner of Buddhist principles. In fact, to be even more precise, Chow zeroes in further, beyond Xuanzang, on to the quotidian and pedestrian aspects of human life by painting a brief but materially significant portrait of a sleepy fishing village, a picture of idyllic existence involving work, play and familial relations. This visual strategy not only situates Xuanzang as a part of the human microcosm that is this village community, but it also grounds the portrait in the textural and gritty feel of everyday life, and death – a picture of the 'everyday sublime',[46] of a worldly re-enchantment. After the opening title-credit sequence, the camera immediately transports viewers, through an aerial bird's-eye-view shot, to an emerald green estuary that connects the river to the sea. Embedded in this estuary is a quiet and seemingly peaceful fishing village. This extreme long shot then zooms in on to a little girl playing in a fishing boat by the dock and singing a children's song about sea creatures. After some playful banter with his daughter, the girl's fisherman father lifts her off the boat and tells her that 'Father is going into the water now. Play on the shore and don't get too near the water. If you fall in, the Big Lobster will grab you.'[47] This tactic, which parents are wont to use as a disciplinary device, such as the bogeyman, to frighten their children into good behaviour, soon morphs into an unintentionally ominous signal of a real threat about demons: 'If you eat the Big Lobster, then the demon will eat you,' the father forewarns her in jest. The disbelieving girl laughs off his tall tale, only to be scared into tears when her father quietly sneaks off into the water in order to leap out from its surface, mimicking a demon from the emerald depths. To appease and soothe his now distraught daughter, the fisherman begins to perform tricks, such as doing a handstand in the water with his legs sticking out in the air. The convivial atmosphere of familial love and parent–child relationality is suddenly ruptured by a menacing presence beneath. A giant fish demon, not visible at this point, violently drags the fisherman back and forth across the water, a scene reminiscent of the terrifying midnight-swim sequence that opens Steven Spielberg's *Jaws* (1975), replete with a similarly frightening accompanying music score. As the unsuspecting daughter continues to marvel at her father's skilled attempts at entertaining her, death arrives in a convulsive and visually material way: the fisherman, with his back to the camera, spurts forth a fountain of blood, colouring the emerald waters red. The camera provides another aerial shot of that growing spot of red, as the girl's mother and fellow villagers rush forth to witness the unfolding tragedy.

I detail both the granular visuality of the scene and the emotional trauma that this family tragedy produces so as to evince the spatial coordinates of the film's planetary ethics. To follow Spivak's 'planet-thought'[48] is to reflect upon the relational dynamics of alterity as a means of thinking beyond the expansiveness of the universal, to think beyond the lofty terms of the planet in the abstract, the intellectual, the political and the philosophical. It is to grapple closely, and even in an inward manner, with the affects of a material reality, grounded in the messy contiguities of the subjective body, the bodies of our near relations and the bodies of the communal. A useful theoretical gloss on this spatial ethics is Eve Kosofsky Sedgwick's reflections on the word 'beside':

> *Beside* is an interesting preposition . . . because there's nothing very dualistic about it . . . *Beside* permits a spacious agnosticism about several of the linear logics that enforce dualistic thinking: noncontradiction or the law of the excluded middle, cause versus effect, subject versus object.

Sedgwick unpacks a complex of interweaving relationalities that beside brings – 'desiring, identifying, representing, repelling, paralleling, differentiating, rivaling, leaning, twisting, mimicking, withdrawing, attracting, aggressing, warping, and other relations'. By 'invoking a Deleuzian interest in planar relations, the irreducibly spatial positionality of *beside* also seems to offer some useful resistance to the ease with which *beneath* and *beyond* turn from spatial descriptors into implicit narratives of, respectively, origin and telos'.[49]

Chow's opening sequence presses us up against and beside our relational other, forcing us not only to connect with those who are near and dear, but also to grapple and engage with an alterity that is alien and that which we have alienated. The giant fish demon, which turns out to be Sha Wujing, or Sha Monk, the third disciple of Tripitaka, is also revealed by Xuanzang's master as someone who used to be kind. One day he saved a child by the river. The villagers mistook him for a kidnapper. They killed him and tossed his body into the river, feeding his body to the fish and creatures. He was filled with such hatred and resentment that his spirit transformed into the Water Demon. He returned to seek revenge on the villagers.

The villagers' disconnection from and discrimination against the kind stranger leads to the tragic consequence of the Water Demon returning to kill the fisherman, his daughter and, finally, his wife. The wife jumps in to confront the demon face to face after it has dragged her daughter into the water, only to have the monstrous fish lunge at her with ferocity, thus making this Buddhist karmic turn even more poignant in terms of the individual tragic loss experienced by the family as payment for the corporate sins of the village (Fig. 12.1).

The moral quagmire that is this seemingly simple village, at least on the surface, is the very humanly flawed space in which Xuanzang, as an equally flawed human being, finds himself. His attempt at demon-wrangling by singing from his book of *300 Nursery Rhymes*[50] not only fails to convince the Water Demon to seek a righteous path, but instead irritates the creature so badly that it begins to pound at him violently. Coming to his rescue is Miss Duan (Shu Qi), who uses her magical gold bracelet, the Infinite Flying Ring, to subdue and capture the fiend. Xuanzang's supposed failure functions as the narrative inciting moment to lead him toward the goal of 'destroy[ing] the demons like the other demon hunters, using the easiest method'. In the rather comically absurdist scene

Figure 12.1 Bereaved mother battles giant fish demon. Source: *Journey to the West: Conquering the Demons* (2013).

where a hysterical Xuanzang is crying his eyes out and lamenting his failures, he and his master have this illuminating exchange:

> *Master*: Killing is not the best way. [He grabs a poisonous snake from a tree.] Never forget our principles and beliefs. A good man turns into a demon when his heart is overcome by evil. [He plucks out the snake's fangs and lets it go.] We must remove the evil and keep only the goodness. The *300 Nursery Rhymes* wakes up our inner goodness, conquering the evilness in our hearts. Are you doubting our beliefs?
> *Xuanzang*: No, just my own powers.
> *Master*: But you did your best. You saved a baby, didn't you?
> *Xuanzang*: I could have saved more people. [He starts to cry.] But I wasn't able to. Master, you didn't see that girl. She was only four or five. And I just couldn't save her. They're dead because of me. So many deaths. Master, I'm so useless. Maybe you chose the wrong disciple?
> *Master* (hugs Xuanzang): I did not choose the wrong disciple. Absolutely not. You're just missing that little 'something'.
> *Xuanzang*: What's that little 'something'?
> *Master*: Just that little 'something'. [He mysteriously gestures with his finger and thumb.] When you attain your enlightenment, you will fully understand and by that time, you will know the boundless powers of the *300 Nursery Rhymes*.

The absurdist comedy here appears out of sync with the tragic consequences of failing to relate ethically with the other, a cognitive dissonance that one could also find in the film's deployment of the fantastic to propound the philosophical weightiness of the planetary. But it is precisely this dissonance, much to Chow's credit, that creates a Brechtian estrangement effect and that, as a result, brings into deep relief the serious implications of a planetary ethics.

Mirroring this counterintuitive approach is the structural inversion of the plot, vis-à-vis *Xiyou ji* narrative norms. Instead of starting big and universal as one would expect, the film goes small and microcosmic. Replacing the immortal and powerful Monkey King as the main protagonist is the very human and frail Xuanzang, who drives the dramatic action in his quest to find enlightenment through a search for what his teacher describes as 'that little "something"', the minuteness of which is not incidental. The consequence of this dramatic conflict in Xuanzang's life, hence, moves the film's narrative spatially and psychically from the smallness of the fishing village to the vastness of the universe, from the materiality of the human quotidian to the transcendence of the spiritual universal. I reconstruct below this conical plot structure, in its linear temporality:

- The Water Demon (Sha Wujing) attacks the fishing village.
- Xuanzang fails to capture the demon but meets Miss Duan, who comes to his rescue and succeeds in the mission.
- The master points the emotionally distraught Xuanzang to the path of enlightenment through the search for 'that little "something"'.
- Xuanzang encounters the demon K. L. Hog, who will eventually become Tripitaka's second disciple, Zhu Bajie. Duan tries to capture this more powerful demon but fails, leading to Hog's escape.
- Romance blossoms between Duan and Xuanzang, though the latter seems resistant.
- In order to subdue Hog, the master directs Xuanzang to 'Sun Wukong, who has been imprisoned by Buddha under Five Fingers Mountain for 500 years'.
- On his journey, Xuanzang has a falling out with Duan, who has set out to trap him romantically and erotically.
- Arriving at Five Fingers Mountain, Xuanzang discovers that Sun Wukong has been imprisoned in a cave surrounded by lotus flowers. With the aid of Duan, Xuanzang and Wukong succeed in capturing the demon Hog. But Xuanzang succumbs to Wukong's trickery and accidentally frees him.
- Wukong rails against the Buddha, tortures Xuanzang by pulling out all his hair, and cruelly kills Duan when she attempts to protect Xuanzang.
- Xuanzang attains partial enlightenment when he realises and accepts that he loves Duan.
- Xuanzang is suddenly enveloped in a luminous aura. Wukong turns his wrath on the Buddha and tries to battle him.
- The Buddha conquers Wukong by transporting both Xuanzang and his new simian disciple to an alternate reality.
- The film closes with Xuanzang's master anointing his disciple as Tripitaka and commissioning him and his three demon disciples to begin their journey to the west. (This plot detail is obviously a departure from the original text, which has Emperor Taizong granting Tripitaka the royal imprimatur for his trip.)

The spatial expansiveness of the film's penultimate sequences (before the final shots of Tripitaka and his disciples starting on their journey) provides an asymmetrical counterpoint to the geographically localised intimacy of the fishing village. This asymmetry contributes to the conical spatiality of the plot structure that I discussed earlier. To accentuate the planetary, these final scenes depict the Monkey King take on the Buddha on an epic scale. In his fury, Wukong rushes to attack the mountain that is shaped like the Buddha, which rises to crush the rebellious creature. Wukong manages to destroy the mountain Buddha easily, but he could not overcome the real spiritual Buddha, who

Figure 12.2 Luminous Buddha looms over Planet Earth. Source: *Journey to the West: Conquering the Demons* (2013).

continues to loom over him. A low-angle shot of the chanting Xuanzang also features a translucent image of the Buddha serving as a panoramic backdrop in the night sky. To denote a sense of immense scale, this initial shot is cut to an aerial view of the Earth, with the enormous, translucent Buddha floating over the planet (Fig. 12.2). He lifts his right palm to press into the spot where Wukong is located. The space below the Buddha's palm resembles an aerial view of a hurricane. At that moment, Wukong transforms himself into a King Kong-sized gorilla to hold up, in vain, the Buddha's palm. The camera zooms outwards at great speed, as if it is also trying to flee from the Buddha's influence and grip. Suddenly, in a flash, Wukong finds himself in an alternate dimension where the hellish landscape of the previous scene is replaced by a paradisiacal space of bright sunshine, blue skies, verdant fields, fluttering butterflies and a beautiful tree in the centre. Wukong has returned to his previous human form. Dazed but humbled by his experience, he hugs Xuanzang's legs as his new master places on his head Duan's Infinite Flying Ring, which now becomes the Monkey King's iconic gold ring cap.[51]

Of course, the planetary magnitude of these final sequences signals the universal reach of religious enlightenment that Buddhism presents to the world. But this reading of religious Buddhism's salvific message should not eclipse or replace the broader emphasis of secular Buddhism, which is one of posthuman sensitivity to the preciousness and precarity of life, all life, on this planet (a lesson that religious Buddhism also teaches). In this era of rapacious capitalism and political corruption, where environmental catastrophes loom, where the gap between the rich and the poor widens, where authoritarianism is on the rise, where right-wing xenophobia is resurgent and where the suffering of the oppressed proliferates, a planetary ethics that demands a robust sense of connection and responsibility to alterity becomes a critical imperative. Chow's film cinematically envisions this imperative by creating a conical plot structure so that it may collapse, like an accordion, thereby compressing together the tiny and the enormous, the subatomic particle and the infinite universe, the material and the spiritual, the self and the other, into a singularity. This is the planetary ethics that Spivak gestures to, where 'alterity remains underived from us; ... it contains us as much as it flings us away'.[52]

Conclusion: Of Love and Life

As a conclusion to this chapter, I make one final turn inwards to two theoretical dimensions of unlikely intimacy that the film's planetary ethics fosters. As I have noted earlier, heterosexual romance is a staple in popular cinema as a default mode of ensuring audience appeal. Like many of the other *Xiyou ji* adaptations, Stephen Chow's film unexceptionally exploits this element in ways that are conventional in mainstream Chinese cinema. The love affair between Xuanzang and Duan melodramatically comes to fruition at the end when the former admits to the dying Duan that 'I've loved you from the moment I saw you.' However, what is distinctive about Chow's approach is that he has Duan, in many of the earlier parts of the film, come on to Xuanzang both romantically and erotically, thus granting the woman sexual agency and identity, without ultimately exploiting that sexuality in the way that earlier films, such as Ho Meng-hua's, have done. But in addition to this more modern take on female sexuality, the eroticism of the body in romance is not simply erased when relocated into the broader conceptions of love, where an abstract transcendent notion of universal love, in all its imagined ideological, moral and ethical purity (based on the dualistic hierarchy of mind or spirit over body), subsumes the messiness and dirtiness of erotic desires. Not only does the Duan–Xuanzang relationship take up much of the film's screen time, but other modes of eroticism, particularly queer ones, also find their way, though not unproblematically, into the narrative as part of its contemporary character. As Tripitaka reflects at the end,

> Love between a man and a woman is all part of the greater love. Love is neither greater nor lesser. Having experienced pain, I can truly understand life's suffering. Knowing stubbornness, one can let it go. Knowing what one wants, one can release it.

Clearly, Buddhist philosophy asserts its presence here, as evident in Tripitaka's statement and in the demise of Duan – her death is the only means by which Xuanzang is released from the clutches of worldly attachment, as a step toward the path of enlightenment. Her lingering presence as an image in Tripitaka's mind's eye in the film's epilogue suggests that the erotic body is still safely neutered and contained in the idealisation of universal love. But, in spite of this negotiated misstep, the film is correct in acknowledging the complexities of love in all its heterogeneity and multiplicity, thereby integrating the 'troublesome' body into its planetary ethics of relating to the other.

Finally, to stay with the trouble, as Donna Haraway would put it, of loving in a posthuman age, we need to rethink our ethical relations to all life, especially beyond the human. *Xiyou ji*, both the classic novel and its film adaptations, has always held the potentiality for such planetary thinking, which is very Buddhist in its inflection. It blurs the lines between humanity and animality. Xuanzang is taught to care for nonhuman life when he admonishes the villagers not to kill a stingray they have just caught, which they first believe to be the Water Demon: 'You're all mistaken. That's not the killer. It's just a stingray. He's gentle, kindhearted and cheerful. A fish of good character, just a bit too big.' Anthony Yu also makes the following observation about *Xiyou ji*:

> [T]he novel has provided its human protagonist, for all his reputed learning in Buddhism and habitual rehearsal of Confucian pieties, a monkey-tutor who . . . is the true hero of the novel. Although Tripitaka might be able to declare in chapter 85 that 'the lesson of all scriptures [presumably including those he was still seeking] concerns only the cultivation of the mind,' it is the novel's author who gave him a disciple and companion that incarnates mind itself. The figure of Sun Wukong, as conceived and developed throughout the book, brilliantly embodies the venerable idiom, 'the monkey of the mind'.[53]

Sun Wukong is deeply cognisant of this fact, which he points out to Zhu Bajie and Sha Wujing, when he explains that the purpose of the journey is about allowing his

> Master to go through all these strange territories before he finds deliverance from the sea of sorrows; hence even one step turns out to be difficult . . . [W]e cannot exempt him from these woes . . . Remember the adage: What's easily gotten / Is soon forgotten.[54]

In recentring Xuanzang within the narrative, Chow's film is not simplistically reasserting an anthropocentric perspective. Rather, it is exposing the weaknesses and inadequacies of that mindset. Xuanzang is taught to love by the Buddha only when that love also encompasses an expansive love, a love that includes the unlovable – the rebellious monkey, the greedy pig and the ugly sand creature. Conversely, we must also learn, as Tripitaka does in his philosophical transformation, from our fellow nonhuman travellers on this Earth, to be re-enchanted by them. We need 'to make kin in lines of inventive connection as a practice of learning to live and die well with each other in a thick present', as Donna Haraway suggests. She adds,

> In fact, staying with the trouble requires learning to be truly present, not as a vanishing pivot between awful or edenic pasts and apocalyptic or salvific futures, but as mortal critters entwined in myriad unfinished configurations of places, times, matters, meanings.[55]

In other words, we are in this for the journey, the journey of life on a planet that we, all creatures great and small, call home. For it is the journey that ultimately matters.

Notes

1. Arthur F. Wright, *Buddhism in Chinese History*, 36.
2. Ibid., 70.
3. The four schools of Chinese Buddhism are the Consciousness-Only School, the Hua-yan School, the Tian-tai School and the Chan School. For a detailed discussion of these schools, see JeeLoo Liu, *An Introduction to Chinese Philosophy*, 209–331.
4. According to Liu, during the twentieth century, the Japanese strain of Chan Buddhism is the route through which the religion finally arrived in the West. Liu, *An Introduction to Chinese Philosophy*, 304.
5. Interpreted in different ways and offering various practical inflections, the Pali concept of *sati* has been conceptualised by scholars and practitioners as 'mindfulness' in English. Joseph Goldstein, *Mindfulness*, 13.
6. See the documentary *The Mindfulness Movement* (Rob Beemer, 2020), executive-produced by Deepak Chopra: <https://themindfulnessmovement.com> (last accessed 8 March 2020).
7. Kate Pickert, 'The mindful revolution' (last accessed 10 November 2020).
8. I am thinking here of renowned teachers like Jack Kornfield and Joseph Goldstein. A lot of Goldstein's work is accessible in a podcast featuring lectures he gives at meditation retreats: *Insight Hour with Joseph Goldstein*, Be Here Now Network, Episodes 1–84, 2015–20, <https://beherenownetwork.com/category/joseph-goldstein/> (last accessed 9 March 2020). See also Goldstein, *Mindfulness*.
9. Stephen Batchelor, *After Buddhism*, 15.

10. Ronald E. Purser, *McMindfulness*, 18.
11. Ibid., 8.
12. Joshua Landy and Michael Saler, 'Introduction', 3.
13. Robert Wright, *Why Buddhism Is True*.
14. Batchelor, *After Buddhism*, 16.
15. Landy and Saler problematise the binary and the dialectical approaches to modernity, in favour of the antinomial, by offering the following argument: 'Whereas the binary approach depicts contemporary turns to the irrational and spiritual as atavistic and marginal reactions to the secular rationality of the modern world, the *dialectical* approach posits modernity itself as inherently irrational, a mythic construct no less enchanted than the myths it sought to overcome.' One of the examples of the dialectical they find in Karl Marx's analysis of modernity, which 'abound[s] with metaphors and similes of enchantment – specters, ghosts, fetishes, and so forth – linking the modern world with the religious world it had supposedly surmounted' ('Introduction', 4–5). I credit Landy and Saler for this notion of instrumentality.
16. Hongmei Sun, *Transforming Monkey*, 63–90.
17. See my essay: Kenneth Chan, 'The contemporary wuxia revival'.
18. Landy and Saler, 'Introduction', 6–7.
19. Ibid., 3.
20. Ibid., 14. Original emphasis.
21. Batchelor, *After Buddhism*, 17. For a detailed explanation of the everyday sublime, see page 232.
22. Eve Kosofsky Sedgwick, *Touching Feeling*, 178–9. Original emphasis. Sedgwick is citing an earlier book by Stephen Batchelor: *Buddhism without Beliefs*, 43.
23. Sedgwick, *Touching Feeling*, 179.
24. My intentional use of the parentheses around the word 'Buddhist' is not only to signify the religious–secular porousness of global Buddhism, but also to offer audiences a choice of retaining the film's planetary ethics in its Buddhist roots, or deterritorialising it from its religiosity for personal inspiration and edification.
25. Wu Cheng'en, *The Journey to the West*, vol. 1, 104.
26. Ibid., 102.
27. Ibid., 106.
28. Ibid., 122.
29. A study of this archive is obviously outside the scope of my chapter and is beyond the ken of my own expertise. Again, I point readers to Sun's *Transforming Monkey* for a detailed analysis of this cultural institution.
30. Anthony C. Yu, 'Introduction', 69.
31. Zhang Zhen, *An Amorous History of the Silver Screen*, 199.
32. Ibid., 210, 432.
33. *A Chinese Odyssey* is now a film trilogy, with *A Chinese Odyssey: Part Two – Cinderella* (*Xiyou ji zhi xianlü qiyuan*, Jeffrey Lau, 1995) released in the same year as the first film and *A Chinese Odyssey: Part Three* (*Dahua xiyou 3*, Jeffrey Lau) appearing in 2016, during a time when *Xiyou ji* adaptations are experiencing a revival.

34. Wu, *The Journey to the West*, vol. 3, 340.
35. Zhang, *An Amorous History of the Silver Screen*, 204–5.
36. Ibid., 210.
37. Ibid., 211.
38. The film was also entitled *Immortal Demon Slayer* for its US release. Coincidentally, Derek Kwok is credited as the co-director of Chow's earlier film, which again exemplifies the enchantment that the *Xiyou ji* story must have had on filmmakers. It is unfortunate that, like Jeffrey Lau's poorly conceived tripartite film series *A Chinese Odyssey*, Kwok's entry in the cinematic œuvre of *Xiyou ji* adaptations is an aesthetically inferior one, hence further justifying the critical lamentation that the *Journey to the West* story has been overused in Chinese cinema.
39. During the writing of this chapter, I have encountered three other titles that are not available in the US: *The Monkey King Caused Havoc in Dragon Palace* (*Danao longgong*, Chen Zhihong, 2019), *Monkey King: The Volcano* (*Qitian dasheng zhi huoyanshan*, Lin Zhenzhao, 2019) and *Monkey King: Cave of the Silk Web* (*Sun Wukong dazhan pansi dong*, Keung Kwok-Man and Jing Wong, 2020).
40. Zhang, *An Amorous History of the Silver Screen*, 211–12.
41. In Chapter 6 of this book, Shi-Yan Chao discusses in greater detail Ho Meng-hua's career and techniques.
42. I am describing this series of films as prestigious not only because the studio permitted Ho to make four films in a period of about two years, but also because they granted the director permission to location shoot outside of the Shaw soundstages; this was quite a privilege in view of how, as Poshek Fu notes, the Hong Kong Clear Water Bay studio 'Movietown was run like an assembly line . . . that was operated on the principles of rational management, cost efficiency, professionalization, and standardization of the production process in pursuit of maximum profit' ('Introduction: the Shaw Brothers diasporic cinema', 5–6). Ho himself describes how 'under the Shaws system, everything needs prior application. And you simply cannot ask for anything on the spot, however trivial. Sometimes it borders on the ridiculous' (quoted in Stephanie Chung Po-yin, 'The industrial evolution of a fraternal enterprise', 9). My point here is that the *Xiyou ji* adaptations were clearly privileged in the eyes of the studio.
43. It is probably no coincidence that Stephen Chow played the Monkey King character in the first two films of Jeffrey Lau's *A Chinese Odyssey* series, a persistent fascination that, one speculates, must have led him to direct his 2013 film.
44. Gayatri Chakravorty Spivak, *Death of a Discipline*, 72.
45. Ibid., 73.
46. See note 21.
47. All dialogue quotations are taken from the subtitles in the Blu-Ray edition of the film available in the US. *Journey to the West: Conquering the Demons*, Blu-Ray, Stephen Chow. Toronto: Magnolia Home Entertainment, 2014. Any minor edits to the English subtitles for further translational clarity and/or sentence-level correctness are mine.
48. Spivak, *Death of a Discipline*, 73.

49. Sedgwick, *Touching Feeling*, 8. Original emphasis.
50. The song involves a series of simple platitudes: 'My child, my child, why are you so bad? Bullying, cheating, how can you do that? Learn to be good. Learn to be loving. Love is in your heart. Filling your life with warmth. Be good, be good and come home soon. My arms are always ready to embrace you. My child, repent with a sincere heart. You'll always be my dearest child. Be good, be good and come home soon. Study hard for a better future. Turn back and become a filial child again. We were all born pure, like children.'
51. The golden tiara-type headgear that Wukong wears is translated by Anthony Yu as 'a flower cap inlaid with gold' (Wu, *The Journey to the West*, vol. 1, 319). Provided by the Bodhisattva Guanyin, Tripitaka uses this cap by chanting 'the Tight-Fillet Sūtra' to control and discipline his wayward disciple (ibid., 320).
52. Spivak, *Death of a Discipline*, 73.
53. Yu, 'Introduction', 69.
54. Wu, *The Journey to the West*, vol. 1, 428.
55. Donna J. Haraway, *Staying with the Trouble*, 1.

Coda: Sino-Enchantment in a Time of Crisis

Kenneth Chan and Andrew Stuckey

As we, the editors, were putting together the manuscript for this book during the spring of 2020, the world was in a state of unprecedented upheaval as it witnessed in horror the death march of the COVID-19 pandemic, unrelentingly making its way across the globe, unhindered by national boundaries, cultural differences and demographic distinctions.[1] The gravity of the situation definitely gave us pause to reflect upon not just the existential questions of life, but also the epistemological significance of the work in this volume – the raison d'être of the fantastic in contemporary Chinese cinemas. Against the backdrop of the physical, material, emotional and psychic trauma of the immeasurable suffering and rising mortality rate that the viral outbreak has wrought in its wake, our academic preoccupation with the fantastic as a film genre and modality, in deep contrast, *feels* trivial, inane and, even, self-indulgent. But this is, after all, a *feeling*, one that is conditioned not only by the perspective of the comparative scale of the pandemic – a planetary sense of crisis matched historically only by the Spanish flu outbreak and World War II – but also by an individual sense of helplessness.

More than just the COVID-19 emergency, a slightly broader historical framework reveals that a sense of crisis predates spring 2020. Before the coronavirus struck outside Asia (but just as Wuhan was being completely sealed off), Michelle Goldberg asked the important question in her *New York Times* opinion piece 'The darkness where the future should be', 'What happens to a society that loses its capacity for awe and wonder at things to come?' She points out that advanced digital technology has made us numb to the wonders that the world already embodies, driving us to fear and 'pessimism' instead.[2] To restrict our attention to Greater China, the severe repression and incarceration of Muslim ethnicities, most prominently Uighurs, in the western province of Xinjiang has been ongoing for several years. Of even longer duration – with roots stretching back to 2014 – are the social unrest and demonstrations in Hong Kong protesting against the restrictive controls enforced by Beijing, contravening the One Country, Two Systems structure which ostensibly governs the relationship between the two polities. Additionally, it is arguable that the global health crisis of COVID-19 has led the Chinese regime to redouble suppressive and repressive political and social controls.[3]

As this volume has demonstrated, fantastic film has the capacity to reveal both fears and hopes in the face of uncertainty. For example, the 2015 award-winning anthology film *Ten Years* (*Shinian*, Jevons Au, Chow Kwun-Wai, Zune Kwok, Ka-Leung Ng and Fei-Pang Wong) speculates exactly on the progress of the struggle in Hong Kong in the years to come. Therefore, it is essential not to allow this feeling of triviality to diminish or erase the significance of cinema (and, in our case, the fantastic) as a cultural institution of human history and creativity. The fantastic has provided and continues to provide – especially during this moment of social distancing and at-home quarantine – a mediatised space for escape, a moment of magical enchantment, a palliative salve during a time when depressing news reports (of how the pandemic is wreaking havoc with our healthcare system, the economy and our way of life) are ubiquitous. We need to be (re-)enchanted by the spiritual and the utopian, by the uplifting possibilities of the human spirit and the hope of better days to come. If there is any silver lining in this time of crisis, we are taught, for instance, to be re-enchanted by the natural world and nonhuman life, and to be respectful of the life force that this virus embodies. The world is put on pause, hence rupturing (to a degree) anthropocentrism and exposing human hubris. With capitalist activity almost grinding to a halt and the majority of the world's population engaging in self-quarantine, the natural realm has given us a small glimpse of what it means to slow down climate change: it is reported that the Himalayas are visible from parts of northern India 'for the first time in "decades"'[4] and that the Venetian canals are clear enough to unveil aquatic life.[5] Although one must be careful not to fall for fake reports, which usually arise out of an optimistic but desperate desire for a global environmental consciousness,[6] what deserves to be remarked upon is how fantastically cinematic these vistas of hope are, and how hopeful what we see on cinematic, televisual and digital screens can be.

On one hand, as many of the chapters in this collection argue, much of the fantastic in cinema is achieved by means of CGI. On the other hand, several contributors (Wang, Chung and Stuckey) also demonstrate that CGI effects are by no means necessary to convey the fantastic through film. This recognition is reinforced in the news reports cited above, newly revealing pristine natural landscapes that had earlier been veiled by pollution or other collateral effects of capitalist consumption. That is one way to say that the ways of viewing cinema that we develop, describe and practise in the analyses performed in the preceding chapters help prepare us for reading the world at large in the same ways as we do these fantastic films.

From a cultural political standpoint, the coronavirus outbreak has also exposed, unfortunately, the racist propensities of national communities across the globe, as white Europe and America scapegoat their ethnic-Chinese and Asian populations by accusing them not only of being the source of the virus but also of being responsible for spreading it.[7] Over in China and Singapore, African residents and non-Chinese migrant workers, respectively, have borne the racialised brunt of social frustration.[8] Here, in the United States, racial and racist discourses have even manifested themselves in terrifying physical violence against Asians and Asian–Americans[9], reinforced – intentionally or not – by politicians who seek to identify the virus as the 'Chinese' virus.[10] In other words, the invisible enemy of the coronavirus needs a visible face – a fantastical and, even, phantasmagoric one. Yiman Wang, in Chapter 10 of this volume, describes the phantasmagoric as 'a succession of elusive and ghostly visual illusions projected on smoke or other translucent surfaces with a magic lantern'. The 'inscrutable' Chinese mien, in its elusive and ghostly alterity, is thus appropriated as the fantastical monstrous enemy combatant in this fight for humanity's survival. Other chapters (McGrath, Pettigrew, Mei Yang and Chan), too, argue in their own ways for the capacities of the fantastic to reveal ethical responses in the face of suffering. The Sino in Sino-enchantment, hence, becomes particularly urgent in the way we critique, oppose and engage these discourses both on and off the cinematic screen.

Therefore, we wish to close this book with a point of promise and possibility that Sino-enchantment offers as a theoretical lens of cultural analysis. Sino-enchantment has the potential to unveil fears in the face of the unknown – medical or political or something else altogether; it also has the capacity to point out hopeful avenues for progress in human society, ecological preservation or planetary ethical behaviour. It is in this context that we present to our readers Sino-enchantment as the means for us to negotiate the complex matrix of cinema, fantasy, spectacle, digitality, nature and culture, in order to be re-enchanted anew by this beautiful posthuman planet we inhabit and share, and truly celebrate in awe and wonder the things to come.

Notes

1. It is significant to note that racial minorities, particularly African and Hispanic Americans, constituted a high percentage of those who have contracted and died from the virus here in the US. Aria Bendix, 'Black and brown people make up two-thirds of US coronavirus deaths below age 65, a new study found' (last accessed 30 August 2020).
2. Michelle Goldberg, 'The darkness where the future should be' (last accessed 27 April 2020).
3. See Yi-Zheng Lian, 'China has a post-pandemic dream for Hong Kong' (last accessed 28 April 2020).

4. Rob Picheta, 'People in India can see the Himalayas for the first time in "decades," as the lockdown eases air pollution' (last accessed 26 April 2020).
5. John Brunton, '"Nature is taking back Venice"' (last accessed 26 April 2020).
6. This era of Trumpian misinformation, social media memes and deep political division and paranoia is fertile ground for real fake news (pardon the oxymoron) that is perpetuated on both the extreme political right and left. See, for instance, the suspiciously incredible news of dolphins frolicking in Venice: Natasha Daly, 'Fake animal news abounds on social media as coronavirus upends life' (last accessed 26 April 2020).
7. Joyce Lau, 'Coronavirus sparks a rising tide of xenophobia worldwide' (last accessed 30 August 2020). Sabrina Tavernise and Richard A. Oppel, Jr, 'Spit on, yelled at, attacked' (last accessed 26 April 2020).
8. Betsy Joles, 'Complaints of racism mar China's coronavirus response' (last accessed 26 April 2020). Dominique Mosbergen, 'COVID-19 surge exposes ugly truth about Singapore's treatment of migrant workers' (last accessed 26 April 2020).
9. Pilar Melendez, 'Stabbing of Asian–American 2-year-old and her family was a virus-fueled hate crime' (last accessed 26 April 2020). Sheng Peng, 'Smashed windows and racist graffiti' (last accessed 26 April 2020).
10. Katie Rogers, Lara Jakes and Ana Swanson, 'Trump defends using "Chinese virus" label, ignoring growing criticism' (last accessed 26 April 2020). Colby Itkowitz, 'Republican strategy memo advises GOP campaigns to blame China for coronavirus' (last accessed 26 April 2020).

Selected Filmography

13 Going on 30, directed by Gary Winick. USA: Revolution Studios, 2004.

20 Once Again (重返20岁 *Chongfan ershisui*), directed by Leste Chen 陈正道. China and South Korea: Beijing Century Media Culture and CJ Entertainment, 2015.

The 36th Chamber of Shaolin (少林三十六房 *Shaolin sanshiliufang*), directed by Liu Chia-Liang 劉家良. Hong Kong: Shaw Brothers, 1978.

Alien, directed by Ridley Scott. USA: Brandywine Productions and Twentieth Century-Fox Productions, 1979.

All the Wrong Clues (鬼嗎智多星 *Guimazhi duoxing*), directed by Tsui Hark 徐克. Hong Kong: Cinema City, 1981.

Animal World (動物世界 *Dongwu shijie*), directed by Han Yan 韓延. China: Shanghai Ruyi Film Production Co., Shanghai Pitaya Film Production Co. and Enlight Pictures, 2018.

The Assassin (刺客聶隱娘 *Cike Nie Yinniang*), directed by Hou Hsiao-hsien 侯孝賢. Taiwan: Central Motion Pictures, China Dream Film Culture Industry, Media Asia Films, Sil-Metropole Organisation, SpotFilms and Zhejiang Huace Film & TV, 2015.

Avatar, directed by James Cameron. USA and UK: Lightstorm Entertainment, Dune Entertainment and Ingenious Film Partners, 2009.

The Bear (*L'Ours*), directed by Jean-Jacques Annaud. France and USA: Price and Renn Productions, 1988.

Beijing 2008: Complete Opening Ceremony. USA: Ten Mayflower Productions, 2008.

A Better Tomorrow III: Love and Death in Saigon (英雄本色3：夕陽之歌 *Yingxiong bense 3: xiyang zhi ge*), directed by Tsui Hark 徐克. Hong Kong: Golden Princess Film Production, 1989.

Black Magic (降頭 *Jiangtou*), directed by Ho Meng-hua 何夢華. Hong Kong: Shaw Brothers (Hong Kong), 1975.

Born in China (我們誕生在中國 *Women dansheng zai Zhongguo*), directed by Lu Chuan 陸川. UK, China and USA: Chuan Films, Brian Leith Productions and Disneynature, 2016.

Buddha's Palm series (如來神掌 *Rulai shenzhang*), directed by Ling Yun 凌雲. Hong Kong: Foo Wah Film Company, 1964.

The Butterfly Murders (蝶變 *Diebian*), directed by Tsui Hark 徐克. Hong Kong: Seasonal Film Corporation, 1979.

A Chinese Ghost Story (倩女幽魂 *Qiannü youhun*), directed by Ching Siu-Tung 程小東. Hong Kong: Cinema City, 1987.

Crazy Alien (疯狂的外星人 *Fengkuang de waixingren*), directed by Ning Hao 寧浩. China: Huanxi Media Group, 2019.

Crimson Peak, directed by Guillermo del Toro. Canada and USA: Double Dare You (DDY), 2015.

Crouching Tiger, Hidden Dragon (臥虎藏龍 *Wohu canglong*), directed by Ang Lee 李安. Taiwan, Hong Kong, USA and China: Sony Pictures Classics, 2000.

Curse of the Golden Flower (满城尽带黄金甲 *Mancheng jindai huangjinjia*), directed by Zhang Yimou 張藝謀. China: Edko Film, 2006.

Dangerous Encounters of the First Kind (第一類型危險 *Diyi leixing weixian*), directed by Tsui Hark 徐克. Hong Kong: Fotocine Film Production, 1980.

Detective Dee: The Four Heavenly Kings (狄仁杰之四大天王 *Di Renjie zhi sida tianwang*), directed by Tsui Hark 徐克. China and Hong Kong: Huayi Brothers, 2018.

Detective Dee: Mystery of the Phantom Flame (狄仁傑之通天帝國 *Di Renjie zhi tongtian diguo*), directed by Tsui Hark 徐克. China and Hong Kong: China Film Co-Production Corporation, 2010.

Double Team, directed by Tsui Hark 徐克. USA and Hong Kong: Mandalay Entertainment, 1997.

The Emperor and the Assassin (荊軻刺秦王 *Jing Ke ci Qinwang*), directed by Chen Kaige 陳凱歌. China, Japan and France: New Wave Company, Beijing Film Studio, Shin Corporation and Canal+, 1998.

The Emperor's Shadow (秦頌 *Qinsong*), directed by Zhou Xiaowen 周曉文. China: Xi'an Film Studio, 1996.

The Eternal Love (双世宠妃 *Shuangshi chongfei*), directed by Yuen Tak 元德. China: Tencent Video, 2017.

The Eternal Love II (双世宠妃 II *Shuangshi chongfei 2*), directed by Wu Qiang 吳强. China: Tencent Video, 2018.

The Final Test (最後一戰 *Zuihou yizhan*), directed by Lo Kin 盧堅. Hong Kong: Bo Ho Films Co., 1987.

The Flowers of War (金陵十三钗 *Jinling shisanchai*), directed by Zhang Yimou 張藝謀. China and Hong Kong: EDKO Film, Beijing New Picture Film and New Picture Company, 2011.

Freaky Friday, directed by Mark Waters. USA: Casual Friday Productions, 2003.

The Fugitive, directed by Andrew Davis. USA: Warner Bros and Kopelson Entertainment, 1993.

Furious 7, directed by James Wan. USA and China: Universal Pictures, Media Rights Capital, China Film Co., Original Film and One Race Films, 2015.

Fuyao (扶摇), directed by Yang Wenjun 杨文军, Xie Ze 谢泽 and Li Cai 李才. China: Zhejiang Television, 2018.

Game of Thrones, created by David Benioff and D. B. Weiss. USA: HBO and Warner Bros Television Distribution, 2011–19.

Ghostbusters, directed by Paul Feig. USA: Columbia Pictures, 2016.

Go Lala Go! (杜拉拉升职记 *Du Lala shengzhiji*), directed by Xu Jinglei 徐静蕾. China: China Film Group Corporation, 2010.

Godzilla: King of the Monsters, directed by Michael Dougherty. USA: Legendary Pictures, 2019.

The Great Wall (長城 *Changcheng*), directed by Zhang Yimou 張藝謀. USA and China: Legendary and Universal, 2016.

Green Snake (青蛇 *Qingshe*), directed by Tsui Hark 徐克. Hong Kong: Film Workshop, 1993.

Gremlins, directed by Joe Dante. USA: Warner Bros, 1984.

Health Warning (打擂台 *Da lei tai*), directed by Kirk Wong 黃志強. Hong Kong: Verdull (Film Dept), 1983.

Hero (英雄 *Yingxiong*), directed by Zhang Yimou 張藝謀. China and Hong Kong: New Picture Film Co. and Elite Group Enterprises, 2002.

House of Flying Daggers (十面埋伏 *Shimian maifu*), directed by Zhang Yimou 張藝謀. China: Beijing New Picture Film Co., China Film Co., Edko Films, Elite Group Enterprises and Zhang Yimou Studio, 2004.

How Long Will I Love U (超时空同居 *Chaoshikong tongju*), directed by Su Lun 苏伦. China: Youth Enlight Picture, 2018.

I, Robot, directed by Alex Proyas. USA: Davis Entertainment, Laurence Mark Productions, Overbrook Films and Mediastream IV, 2004.

If I Were You (变身男女 *Bianshen nannü*), directed by Li Qi 李旗. 2012. China: Zhejiang New Media, 2012.

Jiang Hu: The Triad Zone (江湖告急 *Jianghu gaoji*), directed by Dante Lam 林超賢. Hong Kong: China Star Entertainment, 2000.

Journey to the West: Conquering the Demons (西游·降魔篇 *Xiyou xiangmopian*), directed by Stephen Chow 周星驰. China: Bingo Movie Development, Huayi Brothers Media, China Film Group Corporation (CFGC), Village Roadshow Pictures Asia, Chinavision Media Group, China Film Co. and Edko Films, 2013.

Junior, directed by Ivan Reitman. USA: Universal Pictures and Northern Lights Entertainment, 1994.

Jurassic World: Fallen Kingdom, directed by J. A. Bayona. USA: Amblin Entertainment, Legendary Pictures, Perfect World Pictures and The Kennedy and Marshall Company, 2018.

Kekexili: The Mountain Patrol (可可西里 *Keke xili*), directed by Lu Chuan 陸川. China and Hong Kong: Columbia Pictures, Huayi Brothers Media and National Geographic World Films, 2004.

Knock-Off, directed by Tsui Hark 徐克. USA and Hong Kong: Knock Films A.V.V., 1998.

Kong: Skull Island, directed by Jordan Vogt-Roberts. USA: Legendary Pictures and Tencent Pictures, 2017.

Kungfu Panda, directed by Mark Osborne and John Stevenson. USA: DreamWorks, 2008.

Kungfu Panda II, directed by Jennifer Yuh Nelson. USA: DreamWorks Animation, 2011.

Lady of Steel (荒江女俠 *Huangjiang nüxia*), directed by Ho Meng-hua 何夢華. Hong Kong: Shaw Brothers (Hong Kong), 1970.

Laugh In (哈哈笑 *Haha xiao*), directed by Lung Kong 龍剛. Hong Kong: Eng Wah, 1976.

League of Gods 3D (封神榜 *Fengshenbang*), directed by Koan Hui 許安 and Vernie Yeung. Hong Kong and China: China Star Entertainment Group and Huayi Brothers Media Group, 2016.

Legend of the Demon Cat (妖貓傳 *Yaomao zhuan*), directed by Chen Kaige 陳凱歌. China: 21 Century Shengkai Film, Emperor Motion Pictures, Kadokawa and New Classics Media, 2017.

Lifeline Express (鴻運當頭 *Hongyun dangtou*), directed by Kirk Wong 黃志強. Hong Kong: Cinema City Company, 1984.

Love Through Different Times (穿越时空的爱恋 *Chuanyue shikong de ailian*), directed by Feng Li 冯俐. China: Jiangsu Television, 2002.

The Mad Monk (濟公 *Ji Gong*), directed by Ching Siu-Tung 程小東 and Johnnie To 杜琪峯. Hong Kong: Cosmopolitan Film Productions, 1993.

The Master of Kung Fu (黃飛鴻 *Huang Feihong*), directed by Ho Meng-hua 何夢華. Hong Kong: Shaw Brothers (Hong Kong), 1973.

The Matrix, directed by The Wachowskis. USA: Warner Bros, 1999.

The Miracle Fighters (奇門遁甲 *Qimen dunjia*), directed by Yuen Woo-Ping 袁和平. Hong Kong: Peace Film Production (HK) Co., 1982.

Miss Granny (수상한 그녀 *Susanghan Geunyeon*), directed by Hwang Dong-hyuk 황동혁. South Korea: Yeinplus Entertainment and CJ Entertainment, 2014.

Miss Granny, directed by Joyce Bernal. Philippines: Viva Films, 2018.

The Monkey Goes West (西遊記 *Xiyou ji*), directed by Ho Meng-hua 何夢華. Hong Kong: Shaw Brothers (Hong Kong), 1966.

Monkey King 2 (西遊記之孫悟空三打白骨精 *Xiyou ji zhi Sun Wukong sanda Baigujing*), directed by Cheang Pou-soi 鄭保瑞. Hong Kong and China: Filmko Entertainment, 2016.

Monster Hunt (捉妖記 *Zhuoyao ji*), directed by Raman Hui 許誠毅. China: BDI Films Inc. and Edko Films, 2015.

Monster Hunt 2 (捉妖記2 *Zhuoyao ji 2*), directed by Raman Hui 許誠毅. China: Edko Films, 2018.

Once Upon a Time in China (黃飛鴻 *Huang Feihong*), directed by Tsui Hark 徐克. Hong Kong: Golden Harvest Company, 1991.

The Opium War (鴉片戰爭 *Yapian zhanzheng*), directed by Xie Jin 謝晉. China: Emei Film Studio and Xie Jin–Heng Tong Film & TV Company, 1997.

Outland, directed by Peter Hyams. UK: Warner Bros, 1981.

Pacific Rim, directed by Guillermo del Toro. USA: Warner Bros, 2013.

Palace (宮 *Gong*), directed by Yu Zheng 于正. China: Hunan Television, 2011.

Peggy Sue Got Married, directed by Francis Coppola. USA: TriStar Pictures and Rastar Pictures, 1986.

Peking Opera Blues (刀馬旦 *Daomadan*), directed by Tsui Hark 徐克. Hong Kong: Cinema City, 1986.

Princess Iron Fan (鐵扇公主 *Tieshan gongzhu*), directed by Ho Meng-hua 何夢華. Hong Kong: Shaw Brothers (Hong Kong), 1966.

The Promise (無極 *Wuji*), directed by Chen Kaige 陳凱歌. China: 21 Century Shengkai Film, Capgen Investment Group, China Film Group Corporation (CFGC), Moonstone Entertainment and Show East, 2005.
Rabbit Test, directed by Joan Rivers. USA: Melvin Simon Productions, 1978.
Raise the Red Lantern (大红灯笼高高挂 *Dahong denglong gaogaogua*), directed by Zhang Yimou 張藝謀. China: ERA International, China Film Co-Production Corporation, Century Communications and Salon Films, 1991.
Red Sorghum (紅高粱 *Honggaoliang*), directed by Zhang Yimou 張藝謀. China: Xi'an Film Studio, 1988.
Scarlet Heart (步步惊心 *Bubu jingxin*), directed by Lee Kwok-lap 李国立. China: Hunan Television, 2011.
Shanghai Triad (搖啊搖，搖到外婆橋 *Yao a yao, yaodao waipoqiao*), directed by Zhang Yimou 張藝謀. China and France: Alpha Films, La Sept Cinéma and Shanghai Film Studio, 1995.
Shrek, directed by Andrew Adamson and Vicky Jenson. USA: DreamWorks, 2001.
Shrek 2, directed by Andrew Adamson, Kelly Asbury and Conrad Vernon. USA: DreamWorks, 2004.
Shrek the Third, directed by Chris Miller and Raman Hui. USA: DreamWorks, 2007.
Sing My Life (あやしい彼女 *Ayashii Kanojo*), directed by Nobuo Mizuta 水田伸生. Japan: CJ Entertainment, 2016.
A Slightly Pregnant Man (*L'Événement le plus important depuis que l'homme a marché sur la Lune*), directed by Jacques Demy. France: Lira Films and Roas Produzioni, 1973.
The Sorcerer and the White Snake (白蛇傳說之法海 *Baishe chuanshuo zhi fahai*), directed by Ching Siu-Tung 程小東. China and Hong Kong: Juli Entertainment Media, 2011.
Sweet 20 (*Em là bà nội của anh*), directed by Phan Gia Nhat Linh. Vietnam and South Korea: HKFilm and CJ Entertainment, 2015.
Tai Chi Master (太極張三豐 *Taiji Zhang Sanfeng*), directed by Yuen Woo-Ping 袁和平. Hong Kong: Eastern Productions, 1993.
Temptress Moon (風月 *Fengyue*), directed by Chen Kaige 陳凱歌. China and Hong Kong: Shanghai Film Studio and Tomsen Films, 1996.
A Terra-Cotta Warrior (古今大戰秦俑情 *Gujin dazhan qinyong qing*), directed by Ching Siu-Ting 程小東. Hong Kong: Art & Talent Group, 1989.
The Thousand Faces of Dunjia (奇門遁甲 *Qimen dunjia*), directed by Yuen Woo-Ping 袁和平. China: Le Vision Pictures, Acme Image, Beijing Jinhui Yinghua Entertainment and Star Century Picture, 2017.
Time and Tide (順流逆流 *Shunliu niliu*), directed by Tsui Hark 徐克. Hong Kong and China: Columbia Pictures Film Production Asia, 2000.
Time to Love (新步步惊心 *Xin bubu jingxin*), directed by Song Di 宋迪. China: Huashi Media Investment, 2015.
Titanic, directed by James Cameron. USA: Lightstorm Entertainment, Twentieth Century-Fox and Paramount Pictures, 1997.
A Touch of Zen (俠女 *Xianü*), directed by King Hu 胡金銓. Hong Kong and Taiwan: International Film Company, 1971.

True Lies, directed by James Cameron. USA: Twentieth Century–Fox and Lightstorm Entertainment, 1994.

Twinkle Twinkle Little Star (星際鈍胎 *Xingji chuntai*), directed by Alex Cheung 章國明. Hong Kong: Shaw Brothers, 1983.

Two Brothers (*Deux frères*), directed by Jean-Jacques Annaud. France and UK: Pathé, Pathé Renn Productions, Two Brothers Productions, TF1 Films Production, Canal+ and Allied Filmmakers, 2004.

Ultra Reinforcement (超時空救兵 *Chaoshikong jiubing*), directed by Lam Tze Chung 林子聪. China: Beijing Starlit Entertainment Co., 2012.

The Wandering Earth (流浪地球 *Liulang diqiu*), directed by Frant Gwo 郭帆. China: China Film Group Corporation, 2019.

Warcraft: The Beginning, directed by Duncan Jones. USA: Legendary Pictures, Blizzard Entertainment and Atlas Entertainment, 2016.

Wolf Totem (狼圖騰 *Lang tuteng*), directed by Jean-Jacques Annaud. China and France: China Film Group Corporation, Reperage, Beijing Forbidden City Film, Mars Films, China Movie Channel, Beijing Phoenix Entertainment Co., Chinavision Media Group, Groupe Hérodiade, Loull Productions and Edko Films, 2015.

Yellow Earth (黄土地 *Huangtudi*), directed by Chen Kaige 陳凱歌. China: Guangxi Film Studio, 1984.

Young Detective Dee: Rise of the Sea Dragon (狄仁杰之神都龍王 *Di Renjie zhi shendu longwang*), directed by Tsui Hark 徐克. China and Hong Kong: Film Workshop, 2013.

Zhong Kui: Snow Girl and the Dark Crystal (钟馗伏魔：雪妖魔灵 *Zhong Kui fumo: xueyao moling*), directed by Peter Pau 鮑德熹 and Tianyu Zhao 趙天宇. China, Hong Kong and USA: Village Roadshow Pictures Asia, Warner Bros, Beijing Enlight Pictures, Desen International Media, K. Pictures and Shenzhen Wus Entertainment, 2015.

Zu: Warriors from the Magic Mountain (新蜀山劍俠 *Xin Shushan jianxia*), directed by Tsui Hark 徐克. Hong Kong: Golden Harvest Company, 1983.

Bibliography

Abbas, Ackbar, *Hong Kong: Culture and the Politics of Disappearance* (Minneapolis: University of Minnesota Press, 1997).
Acland, Charles R., 'Senses of success and the rise of the blockbuster', *Film History* 25, 1–2, 2013, 11–18.
Allen, Sarah M., *Shifting Stories: History, Gossip, and Lore in Narratives from Tang Dynasty China* (Cambridge, MA: Harvard University Asia Center, 2014).
Altman, Rick, *Film/Genre* (London: BFI, 1999).
——, 'A semantic/syntactic approach to film genre', *Cinema Journal* 23.3, Spring 1984, 6–18.
Appadurai, Arjun, 'Disjuncture and difference in the global cultural economy', in Patrick Williams and Laura Chrismen (eds), *Colonial Discourse and Postcolonial Theory* (New York: Columbia University Press, 1994), 324–39.
Associated Press, 'China's state broadcaster CCTV rebrands international networks as CGTN in global push', *South China Morning Post*, 31 December 2016, <https://www.scmp.com/news/china/policies-politics/article/2058429/chinas-state-broadcaster-cctv-rebrands-international>.
Attebery, Brian, *Strategies of Fantasy* (Bloomington: Indiana University Press, 1992).
Aytes, Ayhan, 'Return of the crowds: mechanical Turk and neoliberal states of exception', in Trebor Scholz (ed.), *Digital Labor: The Internet as Playground and Factory* (New York: Routledge, 2013), 79–97.
Bao, Weihong, *Fiery Cinema: The Emergence of an Affective Medium in China, 1915–1945* (Minneapolis: University of Minnesota Press, 2015).
Barlow, Tani E., *The Question of Women in Chinese Feminism* (Durham, NC: Duke University Press, 2004).
Barthes, Roland, 'Myth today', in *Mythologies* (New York: Hill and Wang, 2012), 216–74.
Batchelor, Stephen, *After Buddhism: Rethinking the Dharma for a Secular Age* (New Haven, CT: Yale University Press, 2015).
——, *Buddhism without Beliefs: A Contemporary Guide to Awakening* (New York: Riverhead Books, 1997).
Bauman, Zygmunt, *Postmodern Ethics* (Oxford: Blackwell, 1993).
Bays, Daniel H., *A New History of Christianity in China* (Chichester: Wiley–Blackwell, 2012).

Beach, Sophie, 'Zhang Yimou and state aesthetics', *China Digital Times*, 6 August 2008, <http://chinadigitaltimes.net/2008/08/zhang-yimou-and-state-aesthetics>.

Beech, Hannah, 'How China is remaking the global film industry', *Time*, 26 January 2017, <https://time.com/4649913/china-remaking-global-film-industry/>.

Behlil, Melis, *Hollywood Is Everywhere: Global Directors in the Blockbuster Era* (Amsterdam: Amsterdam University Press, 2016).

Bellin, Joshua David, *Framing Monsters: Fantasy Film and Social Alienation* (Carbondale, IL: Southern Illinois University Press, 2005).

Bendix, Aria, 'Black and brown people make up two-thirds of US coronavirus deaths below age 65, a new study found', *Business Insider*, 11 July 2020, <https://www.businessinsider.com/black-hispanic-people-coronavirus-deaths-under-65-cdc-report-2020-7>.

Benjamin, Walter, 'The work of art in the age of its technological reproducibility – second version', in *Walter Benjamin: Selected Writings*, vol. 3. (Cambridge, MA: Harvard University Press, 2006), 101–33.

Bennett, Jane, *The Enchantment of Modern Life: Attachments, Crossings, and Ethics* (Princeton: Princeton University Press, 2001).

Berry, Chris, '"What's big about the big film?": "de-Westernizing" the blockbuster in Korea and China', in Julian Stringer (ed.), *Movie Blockbusters* (London: Routledge, 2003), 217–29.

Berry, Chris, and Mary Farquhar, *China on Screen: Cinema and Nation* (New York: Columbia University Press, 2006).

Berry, Michael, 'Chinese cinema with Hollywood characteristics, or how *The Karate Kid* became a Chinese film', in Carlos Rojas (ed.), *The Oxford Handbook of Chinese Cinemas* (New York: Oxford University Press, 2013), 170–89.

———, *Speaking in Images: Interviews with Contemporary Chinese Filmmakers* (New York: Columbia University Press, 2005).

Berry-Flint, Sarah, 'Genre', in Toby Miller and Robert Stam (eds), *A Companion to Film Theory* (Oxford: Blackwell, 2004), 25–44.

Bierly, Mandi, '*Robin Hood* and the great arrow POV shot debate', *Entertainment Weekly*, 10 May 2010, <https://ew.com/article/2010/05/10/robin-hood-trailer-arrow-pov-shot/>.

Bloechl, Jeffrey, *The Face of the Other and the Trace of God: Essays on the Philosophy of Emmanuel Levinas* (New York: Fordham University Press, 2009).

Boedeker, Hal, 'Olympic opening ceremony: staggering spectacle, troubling symbolism', *Orlando Sentinel*, 9 August 2008, <http://blogs.orlandosentinel.com/tvguy/2008/08/09/olympic-opening>.

Bond, Paul, 'China film market to eclipse U. S. next year: study', *The Hollywood Reporter*, 5 June 2019, <https://www.hollywoodreporter.com/news/china-film-market-eclipse-us-next-year-study-1215348>.

Bordwell, David, *Planet Hong Kong*, 2nd edn (Madison, WI: Irvington Way Institute Press, 2011).

———, *The Way Hollywood Tells It: Story and Style in Modern Movies* (Berkeley: University of California Press, 2006).

Bousé, Derek, 'False intimacy: close-ups and viewer involvement in wildlife films,' *Visual Studies* 18.2, 2003, 123–32.

———, *Wildlife Films* (Philadelphia: University of Pennsylvania Press, 2000).

Braswell, Jim, 'How to use a photographic blind', Photonaturalist.net, 23 February 2015, <http://photonaturalist.net/use-photographic-blind/>.

Briggs, David, 'Study: rising religious tide in China overwhelms atheist doctrine', *The Huffington Post*, 22 January 2011, <https://www.huffingtonpost.com/david-briggs/study-rising-religious-ti_b_811665.html>.

Brunton, John, '"Nature is taking back Venice": wildlife returns to tourist-free city', *The Guardian*, 20 March 2020, <https://www.theguardian.com/environment/2020/mar/20/nature-is-taking-back-venice-wildlife-returns-to-tourist-free-city>.

Brzeski, Patrick, 'China box office: Matt Damon epic The Great Wall scores $24.3M on Friday', *The Hollywood Reporter*, 16 December 2016, <https://www.hollywoodreporter.com/news/china-box-office-matt-damon-epic-great-wall-scores-243m-friday-956905>.

Bukatman, Scott, *Matters of Gravity: Special Effects and Supermen in the 20th Century* (Durham, NC: Duke University Press, 2003).

Burkitt, Laurie, 'Made in China: visual effects for big-budget movies', *The Wall Street Journal*, 14 January 2016, <https://blogs.wsj.com/chinarealtime/2016/01/14/made-in-china-visual-effects-for-big-budget-movies/>.

Butler, David, *Fantasy Cinema: Impossible Worlds on Screen* (London: Wallflower Press, 2009).

Cain, Rob, '"Coco" got all of its ghosts past China's superstition-hating censors', *Forbes*, 27 November 2017, <https://www.forbes.com/sites/robcain/2017/11/27/how-coco-got-all-those-ghosts-past-chinas-superstition-hating-censors/>.

Campany, Robert Ford, *Strange Writing: Anomaly Accounts in Early Medieval China* (Albany, NY: State University of New York Press, 1996).

Campbell, Joseph, *The Hero with a Thousand Faces*, 2nd edn (Princeton: Princeton University Press, 1968).

Cardullo, Bert, *Out of Asia: The Films of Akira Kurosawa, Satyajit Ray, Abbas Kiraostami, and Zhang Yimou: Essays and Interviews* (Newcastle upon Tyne: Cambridge Scholars, 2008).

Cartmell, Deborah, and Imelda Whelehan (eds), *The Cambridge Companion to Literature on Screen* (Cambridge: Cambridge University Press, 2007).

CCTV Jingji banxiaoshi, '*Yingxiong* xiao'ao shichang《英雄》笑傲市场' (Hero triumphs over the market), Sina.com, 23 December 2002, <http://finance.sina.com.cn/jjbxs/news/348.shtml>.

Celestino, Mike, 'Interview: longtime Disney producer Roy Conli talks importance of DisneyNature's "Born in China", especially during first release week', Inside the Magic, 16 March 2017, <https://insidethemagic.net/2017/03/interview-longtime-disney-producer-roy-conli-talks-imporance-disneynatures-born-china-especially-first-release-week/>.

Chan, Evans, 'Zhang Yimou's *Hero* and the temptations of fascism', *Film International* 2.2, 2004, 14–23.

Chan, Kenneth, *Remade in Hollywood: The Global Chinese Presence in Transnational Cinemas* (Hong Kong: Hong Kong University Press, 2009).

———, 'The contemporary *wuxia* revival: genre remaking and the Hollywood transnational factor', in Song Hwee Lim and Julian Ward (eds), *The Chinese Cinema Book* (London: BFI/Palgrave Macmillan, 2011), 150–7.

———, 'Tsui Hark's *Detective Dee* films: police procedural colludes with supernatural-martial arts cinema', in Gary Bettinson and Daniel Martin (eds), *Hong Kong Horror Cinema* (Edinburgh: Edinburgh University Press, 2018), 133–46.

Chang Cheh 張徹, *Zhang Che tan Xianggang dianying* 張徹談香港電影 (*Chang Cheh Remarks on Hong Kong Cinema*), ed. Wei Junzi 魏君子 (Hong Kong: Joint Publishing, 2012).

Chaudhuri, Una, *The Stage Lives of Animals: Zooesis and Performance* (New York: Routledge, 2016).

Chen, Edwin W., 'Musical China, classical impressions: a preliminary study of Shaws' *Huangmei Diao* film', in Wong Ain-ling (ed.), *The Shaw Screen: A Preliminary Study* (Hong Kong: Hong Kong Film Archive, 2003), 51–73.

Chen Kaige 陈凯歌, 'Chen Kaige jiu *Jing Ke ci Qinwang* da jizhe wen 陈凯歌就《荆轲刺秦王》答记者问' (Chen Kaige answers questions about *The Emperor and the Assassin*), 23 October 1998, <http://news.sina.com.cn/richtalk/news/9810/102351.html>.

Chen Xihe 陈犀禾, 'Shadowplay: Chinese film aesthetics and their philosophical and cultural fundamentals', in George S. Semsel, Xia Hong and Hou Jianping (eds), *Chinese Film Theory: A Guide to a New Era* (London: Praeger, 1990), 194–204.

———, 'Xuni xianshizhuyi he houdianying lilun 虚拟现实主义和后电影理论' (Virtual realism and post-filmic theory), *Dangdai dianying* 当代电影 (*Contemporary Cinema*) 2, 2001, 84–8.

Chen Xuguang 陈旭光, 'Lun "Chaoji dapian leixing" de zhongguo dianying dapian 论超级大片类型的中国电影大片' (On Chinese mega-blockbusters), 电影文学 (*Movie Literature*) 8, 2009, 4–6.

Chen Yanjiao 陈琰娇, '*Zhuoyao ji*: yibu baoshou de lixiang zhuyi xiju 捉妖记：一部保守的理想主义喜剧' (Monster Hunt: a conservative idealistic comedy), *Dianying yishu* (*Film Art*) 5, 2015, 31–3.

Cheng, Matthew, 'Destroy the old to establish the new: Wong Fei-hung films of the 1970s', in Po Fan and Lau Yam (eds), *Mastering Virtue: The Cinematic Legend of a Martial Artist* (Hong Kong: Hong Kong Film Archive, 2012), 78–84.

Cheuk Pak Tong, *Hong Kong New Wave Cinema (1978–2000)* (Bristol: Intellect Books, 2008).

'Chi 4.5 yi paozhi gangchan kehuanpian "Mingri zhanji" 斥4.5億炮製港產科幻片《明日戰記》' (Splashing 450 million on Hong Kong produced science fiction film *Warriors of Future*), *Apple Daily*, 17 March 2019.

Chiefeditor (pseudonym), 'A foreign film producer's experience in China – dialogue with John Dietz', *The Chinese Film Market*, 9 February 2017, <http://mag.chinesefilmmarket.com/en/article/a-foreign-film-producers-experience-in-china/>.

Child, Ben, 'Will China's growing box office dominance change Hollywood for ever?', *The Guardian*, 10 September 2015, <https://www.theguardian.com/film/filmblog/2015/sep/10/will-china-box-office-dominance-change-hollywood>.

'China bans time travel', *The New Yorker*, 8 April 2011, <https://www.newyorker.com/culture/richard-brody/china-bans-time-travel>.
'China becomes world's second-biggest movie market', *BBC News*, 22 March 2013, <https://www.bbc.com/news/business-21891631>.
Chow, Rey, 'Film and cultural identity', in John Hill and Pamela Church Gibson (eds), *The Oxford Guide to Film Studies* (New York: Oxford University Press, 1998), 169–75.
———, *Sentimental Fabulations, Contemporary Chinese Films: Attachment in the Age of Global Visibility* (New York: Columbia University Press, 2007).
———, *Woman and Chinese Modernity: The Politics of Reading Between West and East* (Minneapolis: University of Minnesota Press, 1991).
Chris, Cynthia, *Watching Wildlife* (Minneapolis: University of Minnesota Press, 2006).
Chu, Yingchi, *Hong Kong Cinema: Coloniser, Motherland and Self* (London: Routledge, 2003).
Chung, Elaine W., 'Post-2014 Chinese–Korean film co-production: nation branding via online film publicity', in Dal Yong Jin and Wendy Su (eds), *Asia-Pacific Film Co-Productions: Theory, Industry and Aesthetics* (New York: Routledge, 2019), 78–95.
Chung, Hye Jean, 'Media heterotopia and transnational filmmaking: mapping real and virtual worlds', *Cinema Journal* 51.4, Summer 2012, 87–109.
———, *Media Heterotopias: Digital Effects and Material Labor in Global Film Production* (Durham, NC: Duke University Press, 2018).
Chung Po-yin 鍾寶賢, 'Da pianchang, xiao gushi: daoyan He Menghua shou Shaoshi yingcheng de xingshuai 大片廠，小故事：導演何夢華說邵氏影城的興衰' (Big studio, minor story: director Ho Meng-hua remarks on the rise and fall of Shaws Studio), in Liu Hui 劉輝 and Poshek Fu 傅葆石 (eds), 香港的「中國」：邵氏電影 (*Hong Kong's 'China': Shaws Cinema*) (Hong Kong: Oxford University Press, 2011), 105–20.
Chung Po-yin, Stephanie, 'The industrial evolution of a fraternal enterprise: the Shaw Brothers and the Shaw organisation', in Wong Ain-ling (ed.), *The Shaw Screen: A Preliminary Study* (Hong Kong: Hong Kong Film Archive, 2003), 1–17.
Colman, Chris, '"Feng Shen Bang": blockbusting VFX in China', *Animation World Network*, 29 July 2016, <https://www.awn.com/vfxworld/feng-shen-bang-blockbusting-vfx-china>.
Conan Doyle, Arthur, *Sherlock Holmes: The Complete Novels and Stories* (New York: Bantam Dell, 2003).
Confucius, *The Analects*, trans. D. C. Lau (London: Penguin Books, 1979).
Coonan, Clifford, 'ILM to pact with China's Base FX', *Variety*, 18 April 2013, <https://variety.com/2013/film/news/ilm-to-pact-with-chinas-base-fx-1200383782/>.
Cowie, Elizabeth, 'Documenting fictions', *Continuum, Australian Journal of Media & Culture* 11.1, 1997, 54–66.
———, *Representing the Woman: Cinema and Psychoanalysis* (Basingstoke: Macmillan, 1997).
Creed, Barbara, 'Horror and the monstrous-feminine: an imaginary abjection', in James Donald (ed.), *Fantasy and the Cinema* (London: BFI, 1989), 63–89.

Crenshaw, Kimberle, 'Demarginalizing the intersection of race and sex: a black feminist critique of antidiscrimination doctrine, feminist theory and antiracist politics', *University of Chicago Legal Forum*, 1, 1989, 139–66.
Cubitt, Sean, *EcoMedia* (Amsterdam and New York: Rodopi, 2005).
Curtin, Michael, *Playing to the World's Biggest Audience: The Globalization of Chinese Film and TV* (Berkeley: University of California Press, 2007).
Dai Jinhua 戴锦华, '"Ciqin" bianzouqu 刺秦变奏曲' (Variations on the assassination of the King of Qin), in *Zuori Zhidao: Dai Jinhua Dianying Wenzhang Zixuanji* 昨日之岛：戴锦华电影文章自选集 (*Yesterday's Island: Dai Jinhua's Own Selected Essays on Film*) (Beijing: Beijing daxue chubanshe, 2015), 327–50.
Daly, Natasha, 'Fake animal news abounds on social media as coronavirus upends life', *National Geographic*, 20 March 2020, <https://www.nationalgeographic.com/animals/2020/03/coronavirus-pandemic-fake-animal-viral-social-media-posts/>.
Debord, Guy, *Society of the Spectacle* (Detroit: Black & Red, 1983).
de Lauretis, Teresa, 'Culture, public and private fantasies: femininity and fetishism in David Cronenberg's *M. Butterfly*', *Signs* 24.2, Winter 1999, 303–34.
Deppman, Hsiu-Chuang, *Adapted for the Screen: The Cultural Politics of Modern Chinese Fiction and Film* (Honolulu: University of Hawaii Press, 2010).
Derrida, Jacques, and Elisabeth Weber, *Points: Interviews, 1974–1994* (Stanford, CA: Stanford University Press, 1995).
Des Forges, Alexander, *Mediasphere Shanghai: The Aesthetics of Cultural Production* (Honolulu: University of Hawaii Press, 2007).
Desser, David, 'The kung fu craze: Hong Kong cinema's first American reception', in Poshek Fu and David Desser (eds), *The Cinema of Hong Kong: History, Arts, Identity* (New York: Cambridge University Press, 2000), 19–43.
Dillon, Mark, 'Production slate: East meets West', *American Cinematographer*, March 2017, 20–4.
Donald, James, 'Introduction', in James Donald (ed.), *Fantasy and the Cinema* (London: BFI, 1989), 10–21.
Du, Daisy Yan, 'Suspended animation: the Wan brothers and the (in)animate Mainland–Hong Kong encounter, 1947–1956', *Journal of Chinese Cinemas* 11.2, 2017, 140–58.
Dupont, Joan, 'Zhang Yimou, keeping cool in the face of censorship', *The New York Times*, 20 August 1997, <https://www.nytimes.com/1997/08/20/style/IHT-zhang-yimou-keeping-cool-in-the-face-of-censorship.html>.
Edwards, Graham, 'Zhong Kui VFX Q&A', *Cinefex*, 4 August 2015, <http://cinefex.com/blog/zhong-kui/>.
Elberse, Anita, *Blockbusters: Hit-Making, Risk-Taking, and the Big Business of Entertainment* (Victoria, Australia: Scribe, 2014).
'Emmy winner taps Chinese film market', Chinese Films.com, 2 May 2012, <http://www.chinesefilms.cn/141/2012/05/02/141s9123.htm>.
Eng, Robert Y, 'Is *Hero* a paean to authoritarianism?', *AsiaMedia*, 2004, <https://lists.h-net.org/cgi-bin/logbrowse.pl?trx=vx&list=h-asia&month=0408&week=d&msg=6SwOL7U2EEdwHd4Udi2Hww&user=&pw=?>.

Fan, Victor, *Cinema Approaching Reality: Locating Chinese Film Theory* (Minneapolis: University of Minnesota Press, 2015).
Farquhar, Mary, 'Visual effects magic: *Hero*'s Sydney connection', in Gary D. Rawnsley and Ming-Yeh T. Rawnsley (eds), *Global Chinese Cinema: The Culture and Politics of Hero* (London: Routledge, 2010), 184–97.
Feng, Jin, 'Jinjiang', *Journal of Popular Romance Studies* (blog), 31 March 2011, <http://jprstudies.org/tag/jinjiang/>.
Feng Yingxin 冯应馨, 'Xiushou pangguan jiushi zuihao de guanzhu 袖手旁观就是最好的关注' (Observation and inaction offer the best attention), *Chinese Environmental Studies Network* 中华环境网, 20 September 2016, <http://www.zhhjw.org/a/qkzz/zzml/201609/ys/2016/0920/6146.html>.
Ferriss, Suzanne, 'Fashioning femininity in the makeover flick', in Suzanne Ferriss and Mallory Young (eds), *Chick Flicks: Contemporary Women at the Movies* (New York: Routledge, 2007), 41–57.
Ferriss, Suzanne, and Mallory Young. 'Introduction: chick flick and chick culture', in Suzanne Ferriss and Mallory Young (eds), *Chick Flicks: Contemporary Women at the Movies* (New York: Routledge, 2007), 1–25.
Fowkes, Katherine A., *The Fantasy Film* (Malden, MA: Wiley–Blackwell, 2010).
Franklin, Bruce H., 'Visions of the future in science fiction films from 1970 to 1982', in Annette Kuhn (ed.), *Alien Zone: Cultural Theory and Contemporary Science Fiction Cinema* (London: Verso, 1990), 19–32.
Freud, Sigmund, David McLintock and Hugh Haughton, *The Uncanny* (New York: Penguin Books, 2003).
Fu, Poshek, 'Imagining China: Shaws cinema', in Liu Hui and Poshek Fu (eds), *Hong Kong's 'China': Shaws Cinema* (Hong Kong: Oxford University Press, 2011), 3–26.
Gao Quanzhi 高全之, *Chongtan Xiyou ji: shen fo yao mo renjianshi* 重探《西遊記》：神佛妖魔人間事 (*Journey to the West Reconsidered*) (Taipei: Linking Books, 2018).
Garcia, Roger, 'Dialogue 1: Kirk Wong–Roger Garcia', in Jerry Liu (ed.), *Hong Kong Cinema '83* (Hong Kong: Urban Council, 1983), 2–7.
———, 'Dialogue 3: Evans Chan–Roger Garcia', in Jerry Liu (ed.), *Hong Kong Cinema '83* (Hong Kong: Urban Council, 1983), 10–15.
Gardner, Daniel K., *Confucianism: A Very Short Introduction* (Oxford: Oxford University Press, 2014).
Gateward, Frances (ed.), *Zhang Yimou: Interviews* (Jackson: University Press of Mississippi, 2001).
Genette, Gérard, *Palimpsests: Literature in the Second Degree*, trans. Channa Newman and Claude Doubinski (Lincoln: University of Nebraska Press, 1997).
Giles, A. Herbert, and Sung-ling P'u, *Strange Stories from a Chinese Studio* (Taibei Shi: Dunhuang Shuju, 1968).
Gill, Rosalind, and Christina Scharff (eds), *New Femininities: Postfeminism, Neoliberalism and Subjectivity* (New York: Palgrave Macmillan, 2011).
Gledhill, Christine, 'Prologue: the reach of melodrama', in Christine Gledhill and Linda Williams (eds), *Melodrama Unbound: Across History, Media, and National Cultures* (New York: Columbia University Press, 2018), iv–xxv.

———, 'Rethinking genre', in Christine Gledhill and Linda Williams (eds), *Reinventing Film Studies* (London: Arnold, 2000), 221–43.

Glynn, Basil, and Jeongmee Kim, 'International circulation and local retaliation: East Asian television drama and its Asian connotations', in Jeongmee Kim (ed.), *Reading Asian Television Drama: Crossing Borders and Breaking Boundaries* (New York: I. B. Tauris, 2014), 27–46.

Goldberg, Michelle, 'The darkness where the future should be', *New York Times*, 24 January 2020, <https://www.nytimes.com/2020/01/24/opinion/sunday/william-gibson-agency.html?smid=nytcore-ios-share>.

Goldstein, Joseph, *Mindfulness: A Practical Guide to Awakening* (Boulder, CO: Sounds True, 2013).

Goossaert, Vincent, and David A. Palmer, *The Religious Question in Modern China* (Chicago: University of Chicago Press, 2011).

Guido, Laurent, 'Rhythmic bodies/movies: dance as attraction in early film culture', in Wanda Strauven (ed.), *The Cinema of Attractions Reloaded* (Amsterdam: Amsterdam University Press, 2006), 139–56.

Gunning, Tom, 'The cinema of attraction[s]: early film, its spectator, and the avant-garde', *Wide Angle* 8.3–4, 1986, 63–70; reprinted in Wanda Strauven (ed.), *The Cinema of Attractions Reloaded* (Amsterdam: Amsterdam University Press, 2006), 381–8.

Gwynne, Joel, 'The girls of Zeta: sororities, ideal, femininity and the makeover paradigm in *The House Bunny*', in Joel Gwynne and Muller Nadine (eds), *Postfeminism and Contemporary Hollywood Cinema* (Hampshire: Palgrave Macmillan, 2013), 60–73.

Gwynne, Joel, and Nadine Muller (eds), *Postfeminism and Contemporary Hollywood Cinema* (Hampshire: Palgrave Macmillan, 2013).

Hall, Sheldon, 'Tall revenue features: the genealogy of the modern blockbuster', in Steve Neale (ed.), *Genre and Contemporary Hollywood* (London: British Film Institute, 2002), 11–26.

Haraway, Donna J., *Staying with the Trouble: Making Kin in the Chthulucene* (Durham, NC: Duke University Press, 2016), Kindle edn.

Harrison, Simon, 'Cultural boundaries', *Anthropology Today* 15.5, 1999, 10–3.

Hartwell, David, 'Introduction: the return of the fantasy', in Neil Barron (ed.), *Fantasy and Horror: A Critical and Historical Guide to Literature, Illustration, Film, TV, Radio, and the Internet* (Lanham, MD: Scarecrow Press, 1999).

Hassel, Holly, 'Fantasy film: nineteenth and twentieth centuries', in Robin Anne Reid (ed.), *Women in Science Fiction and Fantasy* (Westport, CT: Greenwood Press, 2009), 101–11.

Henderson, John, *The Development and Decline of Chinese Cosmology* (New York: Columbia University Press, 1984).

Hennock, Mary, 'Wolf Totem animal trainer sees risks for Hollywood in China', China Dialogue, 27 March 2015, <https://www.chinadialogue.net/culture/7813-Wolf-Totem-animal-trainer-sees-risks-for-Hollywood-in-China/en>.

Higbee, Will, and Song Hwee Lim, 'Concepts of transnational cinema: towards a critical transnationalism in film studies', *Transnational Cinemas* 1.1, January 2010, 7–21.

Hillenbrand, Margaret, 'Hero, Kurosawa and a cinema of the senses', *Screen* 54.2, 2013, 127–51.
Hinsch, Bret, *Masculinities in Chinese History* (Lanham: Rowman & Littlefield, 2013).
Hinton, David, *The Four Chinese Classics: Tao Te Ching, Chuang Tzu, Analects, Mencius* (Washington: Counterpoint, 2016).
Hoberman, J., 'Man with no name tells a story of heroics, color coordination', *Village Voice*, 17 August 2004, <https://www.villagevoice.com/2004/08/17/man-with-no-name-tells-a-story-of-heroics-color-coordination/>.
Honig, Emily, 'Maoist mappings of gender: reassessing the red guards', in Susan Brownell (ed.), *Chinese Femininities/Chinese Masculinities: A Reader* (Berkeley: University of California Press, 2002), 255–68.
Hu Shih, 'The right to doubt in ancient Chinese thought', *Philosophy East and West* 12.4, 1963, 295–300.
Hu Wenhuan 胡文焕, *Xin ke Shanhai jing: fu xinke Shanhai jing tu* 新刻山海经：附新刻山海经图 (*Newly Printed Shanhai jing and Shanhai jing Illustrations*) (Beijing: Zhongguo shudian, 2013).
Hume, Kathryn, *Fantasy and Mimesis: Responses to Reality in Western Literature* (New York: Methuen, 1984).
Hunt, Leon, *Kung Fu Cult Masters: From Bruce Lee to Crouching Tiger* (London: Wallflower Press, 2003).
Hunter, I. Q., 'Post-classical fantasy cinema: *The Lord of the Rings*', in Deborah Cartmell and Imelda Whelehan (eds), *The Cambridge Companion to Literature on Screen* (Cambridge: Cambridge University Press, 2007).
Huters, Theodore, *Bringing the World Home: Appropriating the West in Late Qing and Early Republican China* (Honolulu: University of Hawaii Press, 2005).
Itkowitz, Colby, 'Republican strategy memo advises GOP campaigns to blame China for coronavirus', *Washington Post*, 25 April 2020, <https://www.washingtonpost.com/politics/2020/04/25/senate-gop-talking-points-coronavirus-blame-china-not-trump/>.
Jackson, Rosemary, *Fantasy: The Literature of Subversion* (London: Methuen, 1981).
Jenkins, Eric S., *Special Affects: Cinema, Animation and the Translation of Consumer Culture* (Edinburgh: Edinburgh University Press, 2014).
Joles, Betsy, 'Complaints of racism mar China's coronavirus response', *Al Jazeera*, 26 April 2020, <https://www.aljazeera.com/news/2020/04/african-china-coronavirus-racism-200424020525672.html>.
Juvan, Marko, *History and Poetics of Intertextuality*, trans. Timothy Pogačar (West Lafayette, IN: Purdue University Press, 2008).
Kearney, Richard, *Strangers, Gods and Monsters: Interpreting Otherness* (London: Routledge, 2007).
Khoo, Olivia, 'Remaking the past, interrupting the present: the spaces of technology and futurity in contemporary blockbusters', in Olivia Khoo and Sean Metzger (eds), *Futures of Chinese Cinema: Technologies and Temporalities in Chinese Screen Cultures* (Chicago: University of Chicago Press, 2009), 241–62.

Kim, Jeongmee, 'Say Hallyu, wave goodbye: the rise and fall of Korean Wave drama', in Jeongmee Kim (ed.), *Reading Asian Television Drama: Crossing Borders and Breaking Boundaries* (New York: I. B. Tauris, 2014), 1–26.

Kim, Seung-kyung, and Kyounghee Kim, *The Korean Women's Movement and the State: Bargaining for Change* (New York: Routledge, 2014).

Knight, Sabina, 'Scar literature and the memory of trauma', in Kirk Denton (ed.), *The Columbia Companion to Modern Chinese Literature* (New York: Columbia University Press, 2016).

Kokas, Aynne, *Hollywood Made in China* (Oakland: University of California Press, 2017).

Koo, Siu-fung, 'Philosophy and tradition in the swordplay film', in Leung Mo-ling (ed.), *A Study of the Hong Kong Swordplay Film* (Hong Kong: Urban Council, 1981), 25–32.

Kracauer, Siegfried, 'Basic concepts', in Timothy Corrigan, Patricia White and Meta Mazaj (eds), *Critical Visions in Film Theory: Classic and Contemporary Readings* (Boston: Bedford/St Martin's, 2011), 291–9.

——, *From Caligari to Hitler: A Psychological History of the German Film* (Princeton: Princeton University Press, 2004).

——, *The Mass Ornament: Weimer Essays* (Cambridge, MA: Harvard University Press, 2005).

Kristeva, Julia, *Desire in Language: A Semiotic Approach to Literature and Art*, ed. Leon S. Roudiez, trans. Thomas Gora, Alice Jardine and Leon S. Roudiez (New York: Columbia University Press, 1980).

——, *Strangers to Ourselves* (New York: Harvester Wheatsheaf, 1996).

Kuhn, Annette, 'Introduction: cultural theory and science fiction cinema', in Annette Kuhn (ed.), *Alien Zone: Cultural Theory and Contemporary Science Fiction Cinema* (London: Verso, 1990), 1–15.

Kwok, Huen Ching, 'Hong Kong produced sci-fi movies and series are difficult to succeed', *Ming Pao Daily*, 12 July 2003.

Kwong Kin-Ming 鄺健銘, *Gang Ying shidai: Yingguo zhimin guanzhishu* 港英時代：英國殖民管治術 (*The British Hong Kong Era: The Governance of British Colonisation*) (Hong Kong: Enrich, 2015).

Lam, Keeto, 'Film workshop: training filmmakers & treating cinema', in Li Cheuk-to (ed.), *A Tribute to Romantic Visions: 25th Anniversary of Film Workshop* (Hong Kong: Hong Kong International Film Festival Society, 2009), 11–16.

Lam, Tong, *A Passion for Facts: Social Surveys and the Construction of the Chinese Nation-State, 1900–1949* (Berkeley: University of California Press, 2011).

Landy, Joshua, and Michael Saler, 'Introduction: the varieties of modern enchantment', in Joshua Landy and Michael Saler (eds), *The Re-Enchantment of the World: Secular Magic in a Rational Age* (Stanford: Stanford University Press, 2009), 1–14.

—— (eds), *The Re-Enchantment of the World: Secular Magic in a Rational Age* (Stanford: Stanford University Press, 2009).

Lang, Brent, '*Warcraft* opens to massive $46 million in China', *Variety*, 8 June 2016, <https://variety.com/2016/film/box-office/warcraft-china-box-office-1201791346/>.

Laplanche, Jean, and Jean-Bertrand Pontalis, 'Fantasy and the origins of sexuality', in Victor Burgin, James Donald and Cora Kaplan (eds), *Formations of Fantasy* (New York: Routledge, 1986), 5–34.

Larson, Wendy, *Zhang Yimou: Globalization and the Subject of Culture* (Amherst, NY: Cambria Press, 2017).

Lau, Jenny Kwok Wah, '*Hero*: China's response to Hollywood globalization', *Jump Cut: A Review of Contemporary Media*, Spring 2007, <http://www.ejumpcut.org/archive/jc49.2007/Lau-Hero/text.html>.

—— (ed.), *Multiple Modernities: Cinemas and Popular Media in Transcultural East Asia* (Philadelphia: Temple University Press, 2003).

Lau, Joyce, 'Coronavirus sparks a rising tide of xenophobia worldwide', *Times Higher Education*, 23 March 2020, <https://www.timeshighereducation.com/news/coronavirus-sparks-rising-tide-ofxenophobia-worldwide#>.

Lau Shing-hon 劉成漢, *Dianying fubixing* 電影賦比興 (*Exposition, Comparison and Affective Imagery in Film*) (Hong Kong: Tiandi tushu, 1992).

Law, Fiona Yuk-wa, 'Fabulating animals–human affinity: towards an ethics of care in *Monster Hunt* and *Mermaid*', *Journal of Chinese Cinemas* 11.1, 2017, 69–95.

Law Kar, 'The origin and development of Shaws' colour *wuxia* century', in Wong Ain-ling (ed.), *The Shaw Screen: A Preliminary Study* (Hong Kong: Hong Kong Film Archive, 2003), 129–43.

Law Kar 羅卡, Ng Ho 吳昊, and Cheuk Pak Tong 卓伯棠 (eds), *Xianggang dianying leixing lun* 香港電影類型論 (*On Hong Kong Film Genres*) (Hong Kong: Oxford University Press, 1997).

Law, Wing-sang, *Collaborative Colonial Power: The Making of the Hong Kong Chinese* (Hong Kong: Hong Kong University Press, 2009).

——, 'Hong Kong undercover: an approach to "collaborative colonialism"', *Inter-Asia Cultural Studies* 9.4, 2008, 522–42.

——, 'The violence of time and memory undercover: Hong Kong's *Infernal Affairs*', *Inter-Asia Cultural Studies* 7.3, 2006, 383–402.

Lazar, Michelle M., 'Entitled to consume: postfeminist femininity and a culture of post-critique', *Discourse & Communication* 3.4, 2009, 371–400.

Ledderose, Lothar, *Ten Thousand Things: Module and Mass Production in Chinese Art* (Princeton: Princeton University Press, 2000).

Lee, Haiyan, *Revolution of the Heart : A Genealogy of Love in China, 1900–1950* (Stanford: Stanford University Press, 2010).

Leung, Noong-kong, 'Golden years: past & future', in Jerry Liu (ed.), *Hong Kong Cinema '82* (Hong Kong: Hong Kong Urban Council, 1982), 12–14.

Lev, Peter, '*Vertigo*, novel and film', in James M. Welsh and Peter Lev (eds), *The Literature/Film Reader: Issues of Adaptation* (Lanham, MD: Scarecrow Press, 2007).

Levina, Marina, and Diem-My T Bui (eds), *Monster Culture in the 21st Century: A Reader* (London: Bloomsbury, 2013).

Levinas, Emmanuel, *Totality and Infinity: An Essay on Exteriority* (Pittsburgh: Duquesne University Press, 2013).

Li, Jinhua, 'Consumerism and Chinese postfeminism: visual economy, chick flicks, and the politics of cultural (re)production', *Forum for World Literature Studies* 6.4, 2014, 564–74.

——, '*Mulan* (1998) and *Hua Mulan* (2009): national myth and trans-cultural intertextuality', in Karen A. Ritzenhoff and Jakub Kazecki (eds), *Heroism and Gender in War Films* (New York: Palgrave Macmillan, 2014), 187–205.

——, 'National cuisine and international sexuality: cultural politics and gender representation in the transnational remake from *Eat Drink Man Woman* to *Tortilla Soup*', *Transnational Cinemas* 8.2, 18 May 2016, 128–44.

——, 'You won't believe her eyes: gender politics, cultural reiteration and the cinematic other in the transnational remake from *Gin Gwai* (the eye) (2002) to *The Eye* (2008)', *Asian Cinema* 28.2, 2017, 181–97.

Li, Pei, and Adam Jourdan, 'China's Hollywood romance sours amid trade war, debt fears', Reuters, 27 April 2018, <https://www.reuters.com/article/us-china-wanda-hollywood/chinas-hollywood-romance-sours-amid-trade-war-debt-fears-idUSKBN1HY0PV>.

Li, Siu Leung, 'The myth continues: cinematic kung fu in modernity', in Meaghan Morris, Siu Leung Li and Stephen Chan Ching-kiu (eds), *Hong Kong Connections: Transnational Imagination in Action Cinema* (Hong Kong: Hong Kong University Press, 2005), 49–63.

Lian, Yi-Zheng, 'China has a post-pandemic dream for Hong Kong', *New York Times*, 25 April 2020, <https://www.nytimes.com/2020/04/25/opinion/china-hong-kong-coronavirus.html>.

Lim, Bliss Cua, *Translating Time: Cinema, the Fantastic, and Temporal Critique* (Durham, NC: Duke University Press, 2009).

Link, E. Perry, Jr, *Mandarin Ducks and Butterflies: Popular Fiction in Early Twentieth-Century Chinese Cities* (Berkeley: University of California Press, 1981).

Liu Chengyu 刘成瑜, 'You *Zhuoyao ji* kan guochan qihuan dianying 由《捉妖记》看国产奇幻电影' (A look at domestic fantasy films from *Monster Hunt*), *Dianying wenxue (Film Literature)*, December 2016, 93–5.

Liu, James J. Y., *The Chinese Knight-Errant* (Chicago: University of Chicago Press, 1967).

Liu, JeeLoo, *An Introduction to Chinese Philosophy: From Ancient Philosophy to Chinese Buddhism* (Malden, MA: Blackwell, 2006).

Lo, Kwai-Cheung, 'Tech-noir: a sub-genre may not exist in Hong Kong science fiction films', in Esther C. M. Yau and Tony Williams (eds), *Hong Kong Neo-Noir* (Edinburgh: Edinburgh University Press, 2017), 140–55.

Loughrey, Clarisse, 'China responds to poor performance of its films by censoring bad reviews', *The Independent*, 30 December 2016, <https://www.independent.co.uk/arts-entertainment/films/news/china-censor-bad-film-reviews-box-office-matt-damon-great-wall-a7501966.html>.

Lu, Sheldon Hsiao-peng, 'National cinema, cultural critique, transnational capital: the films of Zhang Yimou', in Sheldon Hsiao-peng Lu (ed.), *Transnational Chinese Cinemas: Identity, Nationhood, Gender* (Honolulu: University of Hawaii Press, 1997), 105–36.

Lu, Sheldon, and Jiayan Mi (eds), *Chinese Ecocinema: In the Age of Environmental Challenge* (Hong Kong: Hong Kong University Press, 2009).

Luo, Liang, *The Avant-Garde and the Popular: Tian Han and the Intersection of Performance and Politics* (Ann Arbor: University of Michigan Press, 2014).
Lupke, Christopher, *The Sinophone Cinema of Hou Hsiao-Hsien: Culture, Style, Voice, and Motion* (Amherst, NY: Cambria Press, 2016).
McClintock, Pamela, and Stephen Galloway, 'Matt Damon's *The Great Wall* to lose $75 million; future US–China productions in doubt', *The Hollywood Reporter*, 2 March 2017, <https://www.hollywoodreporter.com/news/what-great-walls-box-office-flop-will-cost-studios-981602>.
MacDonald, Scott, 'Toward an eco-cinema', *Interdisciplinary Studies in Literature and Environment* 11.2, Summer 2004, 107–32.
McFarlane, Brian, *Novel to Film: An Introduction to the Theory of Adaptation* (Oxford: Oxford University Press, 1996).
McGrath, Jason, 'Heroic human pixels: mass ornaments and digital multitudes in Zhang Yimou's spectacles', *Modern Chinese Literature and Culture* 25.2, 2013, 51–79.
———, *Postsocialist Modernity: Chinese Cinema, Literature, and Criticism in the Market Age* (Stanford: Stanford University Press, 2008).
McKenna, A. T., and Kiki Tianqi Yu, 'Internationalising memory: traumatic histories and the PRC's quest to win an Oscar', in Felicia Chan and Andy Willis (eds), *Chinese Cinemas: International Perspectives* (London: Routledge, 2016), 21–36.
McMullen, David, 'The real Judge Dee: Ti Jen-chieh and the T'ang restoration of 705', *Asia Major* 6.1 1993, 1–81.
McRobbie, Angela, 'Post-feminism and popular culture', *Feminist Media Studies* 4, November 2004, 255–64.
Majumdar, Samirah, 'Recent Chinese dealings with faith groups reflect a pattern of government restrictions on religion', *The Pew Research Center*, 11 October 2018, <http://www.pewresearch.org/fact-tank/2018/10/11/recent-chinese-dealings-with-faith-groups-reflect-a-pattern-of-government-restrictions-on-religion/>.
Manovich, Lev, *The Language of New Media* (Cambridge, MA: MIT Press, 2001).
Mazdon, Lucy, *Encore Hollywood: Remaking French Cinema* (London: British Film Institute, 2000).
Melendez, Pilar, 'Stabbing of Asian–American 2-year-old and her family was a virus-fueled hate crime: Feds', *Daily Beast*, 31 March 2020, <https://www.thedailybeast.com/stabbing-of-asian-american-2-year-old-and-her-family-was-a-coronavirus-fueled-hate-crime-feds-say?via=FB_Page&source=TDB&fbclid=IwAR32mPGaABjJsnn1RmGHLUoW8NQjbggbF3mj8CTHa0i_BD_gEaCdtV25unM>.
Mendelson, Scott, 'Box office: *Warcraft* bombs in America, is huge in China', *Forbes*, 12 June 2016, <https://www.forbes.com/sites/scottmendelson/2016/06/12/box-office-warcraft-bombs-in-america-outgrosses-star-wars-in-china/#3090edda299e>.
Michelson, Annette, 'Bodies in space: "film as carnal knowledge"', *Artforum*, February 1969, 54–63.
Mo Hong'e, 'Qingdao set for "city of film"', ECNS.cn, 11 May 2018, <http://www.ecns.cn/cns-wire/2018/05-11/302269.shtml>.
Moine, Raphaelle, *Cinema Genre* (Oxford: Blackwell, 2008).

Morton, Lisa, *The Cinema of Tsui Hark* (Jefferson, NC: McFarland & Company, 2001).
Mosbergen, Dominique, 'COVID-19 surge exposes ugly truth about Singapore's treatment of migrant workers', *Huffington Post*, 24 April 2020, <https://www.huffpost.com/entry/singapore-coronavirus-migrant-worker_n_5ea15e27c5b69150246df77f>.
Moskowitz, Marc L., *The Haunting Fetus: Abortion, Sexuality, and the Spirit World in Taiwan* (Honolulu: University of Hawaii Press, 2001).
Mottram, James, 'Zhang Yimou talks *The Great Wall*, China's most expensive movie ever, and again defends Matt Damon's casting', *South China Morning Post*, 16 December 2016, <https://www.scmp.com/culture/film-tv/article/2055100/zhang-yimou-talks-great-wall-chinas-most-expensive-movie-ever-and>.
Moya, Ana, 'Neo-feminism in-between: female cosmopolitan subjects in contemporary American film', in Joel Gwynne and Muller Nadine (eds), *Postfeminism and Contemporary Hollywood Cinema* (Hampshire: Palgrave Macmillan, 2013), 13–26.
Mulvey, Laura, 'Visual pleasure and narrative cinema', *Screen* 16.3, 1 October 1975, 6–18.
Naficy, Hamid, *An Accented Cinema: Exilic and Diasporic Filmmaking* (Princeton: Princeton University Press, 2001).
Neale, Steve, *Genre and Hollywood* (London: Routledge, 2000).
———, 'Questions of genre', in Barry Keith Grant (ed.), *Film Genre Reader IV* (Austin: University of Texas Press, 2012), 159–83.
'Neidi zongpiaofang paiming 内地总票房排名' (Mainland China historical highest box office rankings), CBO zhongguo piaofang, Entgroup, <http://www.cbooo.cn/Alltimedomestic>.
Ng Ho 吳昊, *Disanleixing dianying* 第三類型電影 (*Alternate Cult Films*) (Hong Kong: Joint Publishing, 2005).
'Ni Kuang', *The Encyclopaedia of Science Fiction*, <http://www.sf-encyclopedia.com/entry/ni_kuang>.
Ni Zhen 倪震, *Gaige yu Zhongguo dianying* 改革與中國電影 (*Reform and Chinese Film*) (Beijing: Zhongguo dianying chubanshe, 1994).
Nichols, Bill, 'Film theory and the revolt against master narratives', in Christine Gledhill and Linda Williams (eds), *Reinventing Film Studies* (London: Bloomsbury Academic, 2011), 34–52.
Niu Mengdi 牛梦笛, '*Chongfan 20 sui* Zhong Han hepai xin changshi dianying juben huhuan bentu yuanchuang 重返20岁中韩合拍新尝试 电影剧本呼唤本土原创' (*20 Once Again*: China–Korea new co-production format, calling for made-in-China script), *Guang Ming Daily*, 2 February 2015, <http://media.people.com.cn/n/2015/0202/c40606-26488540.html>.
North, Dan, Bob Rehak and Michael S. Duffy, 'Introduction', in Dan North, Bob Rehak and Michael S. Duffy (eds), *Special Effects: New Histories/Theories/Contexts* (London: BFI/Palgrave, 2015), 1–13.
O'Meara, Radha, 'Inventing rituals: cultural politics in Zhang Yimou's historical films', *Senses of Cinema* 88, October 2018, <http://sensesofcinema.com/2018/feature-articles/zhang-yimou-cultural-politics/>.

Paige, Nicholas, 'Permanent re-enchantments: on some literary uses of the supernatural from early empiricism to modern aesthetics', in Joshua Landy and Michael Saler (eds), *The Re-Enchantment of the World: Secular Magic in a Rational Age* (Stanford: Stanford University Press, 2009), 159–80.

Pang, Laikwan, 'The state against ghosts: a genealogy of China's film censorship policy', *Screen* 52.4, 2011, 461–76.

'Patriotic movie *Monster Hunt* passes *Furious 7*, becomes first Chinese film to take domestic box office crown in two decades', *South China Morning Post*, 13 September 2015, <https://www.scmp.com/news/china/article/1857534/patriotic-chinese-movie-monster-hunt-passes-furious-7-take-china-box>.

Peng Hsiao-yen (ed.), *The Assassin: Hou Hsiao-hsien's World of Tang China* (Hong Kong: Hong Kong University Press, 2019).

Peng, Sheng, 'Smashed windows and racist graffiti: vandals target Asian Americans amid coronavirus', *NBC News*, 10 April 2020, <https://www.nbcnews.com/news/asian-america/smashed-windows-racist-graffiti-vandals-target-asian-americans-amid-coronavirus-n1180556?fbclid=IwAR2S31o5kzjunyj4_DBxp7pKzb9iGyFUX-1W9Vh9vDgrYFfIx1NhlwHvt5ZE>.

Pérez, A. Márquez, '*Shrek*: the animated fairy-tale princess reinvented', in *Fifty Years of English Studies in Spain* (1952–2002) (Santiago de Compostela: Universidad de Santiago de Compostela, 2003), 281–6.

Pettigrew, Ian, 'Entering the cinema of attractions' Matrix: Yuen Wo-Ping's merging of Hollywood spectacle with kungfu choreography', *Asian Cinema* 29.1, 2018, 81–97.

Picheta, Rob, 'People in India can see the Himalayas for the first time in "decades," as the lockdown eases air pollution', *CNN*, 9 April 2020, <https://www.cnn.com/travel/article/himalayas-visible-lockdown-india-scli-intl/index.html>.

Pickert, Kate, 'The mindful revolution', *Time*, 3 February 2014, <http://content.time.com/time/magazine/article/0,9171,2163560,00.html>.

Pines, Yuri, 'A hero terrorist: adoration of Jing Ke revisited', *Asia Major* 21.2, 2008, 1–34.

'Pinewood presents accreditation to Wanda Studios Qingdao', PinewoodGroup.com, 30 April 2018, <https://www.pinewoodgroup.com/pinewood-today/news/pinewood-presents-accreditation-to-wanda-studios-qingdao>.

Plate, S. Brent, 'Religion and world cinema', in William L. Blizek (ed.), *The Continuum Companion to Religion and Film* (London: Continuum, 2009).

Price, Monroe E., 'Introduction', in Monroe E. Price and Daniel Dayan (eds), *Owning the Olympics: Narratives of the New China* (Ann Arbor: University of Michigan Press, 2008), 1–16.

Prince, Stephen, 'Introduction: world filmmaking and the Hollywood blockbuster', *World Literature Today* 77.3–4, 2003, 3–7.

Pu Songling 蒲松齡, *Quanben xinshu Liaozhaizhiyi* 全本新書聊齋誌異 (*A New Anthology of Liaozhai zhiyi*) (Beijing: Renmin wenxue chubanshe, 2010).

Purse, Lisa, 'Layered encounters: mainstream cinema and the disaggregate digital composite', *Film-Philosophy* 22.2, 2018, 148–67.

Purser, Ronald E., *McMindfulness: How Mindfulness Became the New Capitalist Spirituality* (London: Repeater Books, 2019).

Radner, Hilary, *Neo-Feminist Cinema: Girly Films, Chick Flicks, and Consumer Culture* (New York: Routledge, 2010).

Rawnsley, Gary D., 'The political narrative(s) of *Hero*', in Gary D. Rawnsley and Ming-Yeh T. Rawnsley (eds), *Global Chinese Cinema: The Culture and Politics of* Hero (London: Routledge, 2010) 13–26.

Rawnsley, Gary D., and Ming-Yeh T. Rawnsley (eds), *Global Chinese Cinema: The Culture and Politics of* Hero (London: Routledge, 2010).

Rea, Christopher, *The Age of Irreverence: A New History of Laughter in China* (Oakland: University of California Press, 2015).

Rehak, Bob, *More Than Meets the Eye: Special Effects and the Fantastic Transmedia Franchise* (New York: New York University Press, 2018).

Rickitt, Richard, *Special Effects: The History and Technique* (New York: Billboard Books, 2007).

Rodowick, D. N., *The Virtual Life of Film* (Cambridge, MA: Harvard University Press, 2007).

Rogers, Katie, Lara Jakes and Ana Swanson, 'Trump defends using "Chinese virus" label, ignoring growing criticism', *New York Times*, 18 March 2020, <https://www.nytimes.com/2020/03/18/us/politics/china-virus.html>.

Ross, Andrew, 'In search of the lost paycheck', in Trebor Scholz (ed.), *Digital Labor: The Internet as Playground and Factory* (New York: Routledge, 2013), 13–32.

Sarto, Dan, 'ILM Singapore hubs its first feature with Zhang Yimou's *The Great Wall*', <https://www.awn.com/vfxworld/ilm-singapore-hubs-its-first-feature-zhang-yimous-great-wall>.

Schatz, Thomas, *Hollywood Genres: Formulas, Filmmaking, and the Studio System* (New York: Random House, 1981).

———, 'New Hollywood', in Julian Stringer (ed.), *Movie Blockbusters* (London and New York: Routledge, 2003), 15–42.

———, 'The studio system and conglomerate Hollywood', in Paul MacDonald and Janet Wasko (eds), *The Contemporary Hollywood Industry* (Oxford: Blackwell, 2008), 13–42.

Schreiber, Michele, *American Postfeminist Cinema: Women, Romance and Contemporary Culture*, reprint (Edinburgh: Edinburgh University Press, 2015).

Sedgwick, Eve Kosofsky, *Touching Feeling: Affect, Pedagogy, Performativity* (Durham, NC: Duke University Press, 2003).

Sek Kei 石琪, 'Haha xiao: ticai xinxian, shihe ertong 《哈哈笑》：題材新鮮，適合兒童' (*Laugh In*: fresh theme suitable for children), *Mingbao wanbao* 明報晚報 (*Mingpao Evening News*), 3 July 1976. Reprinted in Sek Kei 石琪 (ed.), *Shi Qi ying hua ji: ba damingjia fengmao* 石琪影話集：八大名家風貌 (*Conversations on Cinema: Styles of Eight Masters*) (Hong Kong: Ciwenhua tang, 1999), 141–2.

Shambaugh, David, 'China's soft-power push: the search for respect', *Foreign Affairs*, 6 June 2015, <https://www.foreignaffairs.com/articles/china/2015-06-16/chinas-soft-power-push>.

Shek, Kei, 'Shaw Movie Town's "China dream" and "Hong Kong sentiments"', in Wong Ain-ling (ed.), *The Shaw Screen: A Preliminary Study* (Hong Kong: Hong Kong Film Archive, 2003), 37–47.

Shih, Shu-mei, 'Toward an ethics of transnational encounters, or, "when" does a "Chinese" woman become a feminist?', in Françoise Lionnet and Shu-mei Shih (eds), *Minor Transnationalism* (Durham, NC: Duke University Press, 2005), 73–108.

———, *Visuality and Identity: Sinophone Articulations across the Pacific* (Berkeley: University of California Press, 2007).

Sima Qian 司馬遷, *Shiji* 史記 (*Records of the Grand Historian*) (Beijing: Zhonghua shuju, 1996).

———, *The First Emperor: Selections from the* Historical Records, trans. Raymond Dawson (Oxford: Oxford University Press, 2007).

Singer, Ben, *Melodrama and Modernity: Early Sensational Cinema and its Contexts* (New York: Columbia University Press, 2001).

Sobchack, Vivian, 'The fantastic', in Geoffrey Nowell-Smith (ed.), *The Oxford History of World Cinema* (Oxford: Oxford University Press, 1996), 312–21.

Soh, Kai, and Brian Yecies, 'Korean–Chinese film remakes in a new age of cultural globalisation: *Miss Granny* (2014) and *20 Once Again* (2015) along the digital road', *Global Media and China* 2.1, 1 March 2017, 74–89.

Sontag, Susan, 'Fascinating fascism', *The New York Review of Books*, 6 February 1975, <http://www.nybooks.com/articles/archives/1975/feb/06/fascinating-fascism>.

Spivak, Gayatri Chakravorty, *Death of a Discipline* (New York: Columbia University Press, 2003).

———, *Outside in the Teaching Machine* (London and New York: Routledge, 1993).

Stam, Robert, *François Truffaut and Friends: Modernism, Sexuality, and Film Adaptation* (New Brunswick: Rutgers University Press, 2006).

Stam, Robert, and Toby Miller, *Film Theory: An Anthology* (Oxford: Blackwell, 2000).

Strassberg, Richard E., *A Chinese Bestiary: Strange Creatures from the Guideways through Mountains and Seas [Shan Hai Jing]* (Berkeley: University of California Press, 2002).

Stuckey, G. Andrew, *Metacinema in Contemporary Chinese Film* (Hong Kong: Hong Kong University Press, 2018).

Sun, Hongmei, *Transforming Monkey: Adaptation and Representation of a Chinese Epic* (Seattle: University of Washington Press, 2018).

Taiping guangji 太平廣記 (*The Taiping Anthology*) (Harbin: Harbin Press, 1995).

Tally, Margaret, '"She doesn't let age define her": sexuality and motherhood in recent "middle-aged chick flicks"', *Sexuality and Culture* 10.2, 1 June 2006, 33–55.

Tan See-Kam, 'Surfing with the surreal in Tsui Hark's wave: collage practice, diasporic hybrid texts, and flexible citizenship', in Esther M. K. Cheung, Gina Marchetti and Tan See-Kam (eds), *Hong Kong Screenscapes: From the New Wave to the Digital Frontier* (Hong Kong: Hong Kong University Press, 2011).

Tan See-Kam and Annette Aw, '*The Love Eterne*: almost a (heterosexual) love story', in Chris Berry (ed.), *Chinese Films in Focus II* (London: BFI, 2008), 160–6.

Tanimoto, Steven L., *An Interdisciplinary Introduction to Image Processing: Pixels, Numbers, and Programs* (Cambridge, MA: MIT Press, 2012).
Tavernise, Sabrina, and Richard A. Oppel, Jr, 'Spit on, yelled at, attacked: Chinese–Americans fear for their safety', *New York Times*, 23 March 2020, <https://www.nytimes.com/2020/03/23/us/chinese-coronavirus-racist-attacks.html?fbclid=IwAR1U06Afu1ACCHVw7GkqvoUN3qCioFI1DPmXrxA61TkPnXImY9NBjQYMgcw#click=https://t.co/L5sjq5bTzX>.
Taylor, Charles, 'Hero', Salon.com, 27 August 2004, <http://www.salon.com/2004/08/27/hero_2>.
Telotte, J. P., 'Editor's note', *Film Criticism* 7, 1982, 2–3.
——, *Science Fiction Film* (Cambridge: Cambridge University Press. 2004).
Teo, Stephen, *Chinese Martial Arts Cinema: The Wuxia Tradition*, 2nd edn (Edinburgh: University of Edinburgh Press, 2016).
——, 'Chinese melodrama: the *wenyi* genre', in Linda Badley, R. Barton Palmer and Steven Jay Schneider (eds), *Traditions in World Cinema* (New Brunswick, NJ: Rutgers University Press, 2006), 203–13.
——, *Hong Kong Cinema: The Extra Dimensions* (London: British Film Institute, 1997).
——, 'Tsui Hark: national style and polemic', in Esther C. M. Yau (ed.), *At Full Speed: Hong Kong Cinema in a Borderless World* (Minneapolis: University of Minnesota Press, 2001), 143–58.
Theweleit, Klaus, *Male Fantasies*, vol. 2 (Minneapolis: University of Minnesota Press, 1989).
Todorov, Tzvetan, *The Fantastic: A Structural Approach to a Literary Genre*, trans. Richard Howard (Ithaca, NY: Cornell University Press, 1975).
'Trained wolves steal the show in "Wolf Totem" film adaptation', *New York Post*, 10 September 2015, <http://nypost.com/2015/09/10/trained-wolves-steal-the-show-in-wolf-totem-film-adaptation/>.
Tsang, Raymond, 'Wuxia fantasy: abstract humanism and the fear and anxiety in the Cold War', unpublished paper.
Tsui Hark, interview by Stephen Short, 'Tsui Hark: "you have to touch people with film": the Hong Kong film director on sex, violence and leading ladies', *Time*, 3 May 2000, <http://edition.cnn.com/ASIANOW/time/features/interviews/int.tsuihark05032000.html>.
Turnock, Julie, *Plastic Reality: Special Effects, Technology, and the Emergence of 1970s Blockbuster Aesthetics* (New York: Columbia University Press, 2015).
Udden, James, *No Man an Island: The Cinema of Hou Hsiao-hsien*, 2nd edn (Hong Kong: Hong Kong University Press, 2017).
Van Dover, J. K., *The Judge Dee Novels of R. H. van Gulik: The Case of the Chinese Detective and the American Reader* (Jefferson: McFarland & Company, 2015).
van Gulik, Robert, *The Chinese Gold Murders* (New York: Harper Perennial, 2004).
van Zoonen, Liesbet, *Feminist Media Studies* (London: SAGE, 1994).
Variety Staff, 'ILM teams with China's Base FX', *Variety*, 22 May 2012, <https://variety.com/2012/film/news/ilm-teams-with-china-s-base-fx-1118054498/>.

Vukovich, Daniel, *China and Orientalism: Western Knowledge Production and the P.R.C.* (London: Routledge, 2012).
Wang, Chi-Chen (trans.), *Traditional Chinese Tales* (New York: Greenwood Press, 1944).
Wang, Haizhou, and Ming-Yeh T. Rawnsley, '*Hero*: rewriting the Chinese martial arts film genre', in Gary D. Rawnsley and Ming-Yeh T. Rawnsley (eds), *Global Chinese Cinema: The Culture and Politics of* Hero (London: Routledge, 2010), 90–105.
Wang Jianlin, 'Welcome remarks', Qingdao, 22 September 2013, Wanda-Group.com, <http://www.wanda-group.com/2013/chairmannews_0922/497.html>.
Wang, Yiman, 'Of animals and men: towards a theory of docu-ani-mentary', in Matthew D. Johnson, Luke Vulpiani, Keith B. Wagner and Kiki Tianqi Yu (eds), *China's iGeneration: Cinema and Moving Image Culture for the Twenty-First Century* (New York: Bloomsbury Academic, 2014), 167–80.
——, *Remaking Chinese Cinema: Through the Prism of Shanghai, Hong Kong, and Hollywood* (Honolulu: University of Hawaii Press, 2013).
Wang, Yiwen, 'An analysis of the cultural elements and international reach of *The Great Wall*', *International Communication of Chinese Culture* 5.4, 2018, 309–12.
Welsh, James M., and Peter Lev (eds), *The Literature/Film Reader: Issues of Adaptation* (Lanham, MD: Scarecrow Press, 2007).
Wetering, Janwillem van de, *Robert Van Gulik: His Life His Work* (New York: Soho Press, 1998).
Whissel, Kristen, *Spectacular Digital Effects: CGI and Contemporary Cinema* (Durham, NC: Duke University Press, 2014).
——, 'The digital multitude', *Cinema Journal* 49.4, Summer 2010, 90–110.
Williams, Linda, 'Melodrama revised', in Nick Browne (ed.), *Refiguring American Film Genres: Theory and History* (Berkeley: University of California Press, 1998), 42–88.
Williams, Trey, 'Universal no longer needs Legendary's help in China, studio's filmed group chairman says', *The Wrap*, 6 September 2018, <https://www.thewrap.com/universal-no-longer-needed-legendarys-help-in-china-filmed-group-head-jeff-shell-says/>.
Wong Ain-ling, 'Ho Meng-hua', in Wong Ain-ling (ed.), *The Shaw Screen: A Preliminary Study* (Hong Kong: Hong Kong Film Archive, 2003), 316–17.
Woo, John, 'Interview with John Woo: the carrier's flight from concept to creation', special feature in *Red Cliff, Part I & Part II*, Original International Version DVD, Magnolia Home Entertainment, 2010.
Woodland, Sarah, *Remaking Gender and the Family* (Leiden: Brill, 2018).
Worley, Alec, *Empires of the Imagination: A Critical Survey of Fantasy Cinema from Georges Méliès to* The Lord of the Rings (Jefferson, NC: McFarland & Company, 2005).
Wright, Arthur F., *Buddhism in Chinese History* (Stanford, CA: Stanford University Press, 1959).
Wright, Robert, *Why Buddhism Is True: The Science and Philosophy of Meditation and Enlightenment* (New York: Simon & Schuster, 2017).
Wu Cheng'en, *The Journey to the West*, trans. and ed. Anthony C. Yu, revised edn, 4 vols (Chicago: University of Chicago Press, 2012).

Wu, Hung, *Wu Liang Shrine: The Ideology of Early Chinese Pictorial Art* (Stanford, CA: Stanford University Press, 1992).

'*Wu ji*: Chen Kaige dianying 无极: 陈凯歌电影' (*The Promise*: a film by Chen Kaige), www.sina.com.cn, 15 December 2005, <http://ent.sina.com.cn/f/thepromise/index.shtml>.

Wyatt, Justin, *High Concept: Movies and Marketing in Hollywood* (Austin: University of Texas Press, 1994).

Xi Ling 西岭, 'Shi xi haishi you? guochan dapianfeng toushi 是喜还是忧？国产大片风透视' (Comedy or tragedy? clearly viewing the trend for domestic blockbusters), 电影评介 (*Movie Review*) 4, 1996, 4.

Xie Haimeng 謝海盟, *Xingyun ji*: Cike Nie Yinniang *paishe celu* 行雲級：刺客聶隱娘拍攝側錄 (*Records of Flying with the Clouds: Memories of Filming* The Assassin) (Taipei: INK, 2015).

Xu, Gary, 'Remaking East Asia, outsourcing Hollywood', in Leon Hunt and Leung Wing-fai (eds), *East Asian Cinemas: Exploring Transnational Connections on Film* (New York: I. B. Tauris, 2008), 191–202.

Yan, Haiping, 'Inhabiting the city: tropes of "home" in contemporary Chinese cinema', *China Review* 13.1, Spring 2013, 93–135.

Yang, Chi-ming, *Performing China: Virtue, Commerce, and Orientalism in Eighteenth-Century English 1660–1670* (Baltimore: Johns Hopkins University Press, 2011).

Yang, Fenggang, *Religion in China: Survival & Revival Under Communist Rule* (Oxford: Oxford University Press, 2012).

Yang Jialuo 楊家駱 and Liu Yanong 劉雅農 (eds), *Tangren chuanqi xiaoshuo* 唐人傳奇小說 (*Tang Chuanqi Tales*) (Taipei: Shijie shuju, 1982).

Yang, Li, *The Formation of Chinese Art Cinema: 1990–2003* (New York: Palgrave Macmillan, 2018).

Yang, Wenqi, and Fei Yan, 'The annihilation of femininity in Mao's China: gender inequality of sent-down youth during the Cultural Revolution', *China Information* 31.1, 1 March 2017, 63–83.

Yeh, Emilie Yueh-yu, 'Poetics and politics of Hou Hsiao-hsien's films', in Sheldon H. Lu and Emilie Yueh-yu Yeh (eds), *Chinese-Language Film: Historiography, Poetics, Politics* (Honolulu: University of Hawaii Press, 2005), 163–85.

Yeh, Emilie Yueh-yu, and Neda Hei-tung Ng, 'Magic, medicine, cannibalism: the China demon in Hong Kong horror', in Jinhee Choi and Mitsuyo Wada-Marciano (eds), *Horror to the Extreme: Changing Boundaries in Asian Cinema* (Hong Kong: Hong Kong University Press, 2009), 145–59.

Yin Hong 尹鸿, 'Zhongguo dianying chanyebeiwanglu 2012 中国电影产业备忘录 2012' (A memo on the Chinese film industry in 2012), 电影艺术 (*Film Art*) 2, 2013, 5–19.

Yin Yijun, 'Building the industry behind China's unbelievable TV shows', *Sixth Tone*, 20 September 2017, <http://www.sixthtone.com/news/1000853/building-the-industry-behind-chinas-unbelievable-tv-shows>.

Yu, Anthony C., 'Introduction', in Wu Cheng'en, *The Journey to the West*, trans. and ed. Anthony C. Yu, revised edn, 4 vols (Chicago: University of Chicago Press, 2012), 1–96.

Yu, Sabrina Qiong, 'Camp pleasure in an era of Chinese blockbusters: internet reception of *Hero* in mainland China', in Gary D. Rawnsley and Ming-Yeh T. Rawnsley (eds), *Global Chinese Cinema: The Culture and Politics of* Hero (London: Routledge, 2010), 135–51.

Yuan, Ke 袁珂, *Shanhai jing jiaozhu* 山海經校注 (*Annotated* Shanhai jing) (Shanghai: Shanghai guji chubanshe, 1980).

Zeitlin, Judith T., *Historian of the Strange: Pu Songling and the Chinese Classical Tale* (Stanford, CA: Stanford University Press, 1993).

Zhang, Lijia, 'How can I be proud of my China if we are a nation of 1.4bn cold hearts?', *The Guardian*, 22 October 2011, <https://www.theguardian.com/commentisfree/2011/oct/22/china-nation-cold-hearts>.

Zhang Qian, 'The "Four Evils" are still out there', *Shanghai Daily*, 2 April 2017, <https://archive.shine.cn/sunday/now-and-then/The-four-evils-are-still-out-there/shdaily.shtml>.

Zhang, Xiaoqun, 'Business, soft power, and whitewashing: three themes in the US media coverage of "The Great Wall" film', *Global Media and China* 2.2, September 2017, 317–32.

Zhang, Yingjin, *Chinese National Cinema* (New York: Routledge, 2004).

———, *Cinema, Space, and Polylocality in a Globalizing China* (Honolulu: University of Hawaii Press, 2012).

Zhang Zhen, *An Amorous History of the Silver Screen: Shanghai Cinema, 1896–1937* (Chicago: University of Chicago Press, 2005).

Zhao, Yuezhi, 'Whose *Hero*? the "spirit" and "structure" of a made-in-China global blockbuster', in Michael Curtin and Hemant Shah (eds), *Reorienting Global Communication: Indian and Chinese Media Beyond Borders* (Chicago: University of Illinois Press, 2010), 161–82.

Zheng, Jiaran, *New Feminism in China: Young Middle-Class Chinese Women in Shanghai* (Singapore: Springer Singapore, 2016).

Zhong Acheng, Zhu Tianwen and Xie Haimeng, '*Cike Nie Yinniang* juben' (Script for *The Assassin*), in Xie Haimeng, *Xingyun ji: Cike Nie Yinniang paishe celu* (*Records of Flying with the Clouds: Memories of Filming* The Assassin) (Taipei: INK, 2015).

Zhou Nanyan 周南焱, '*Chongfan 20 Sui* zhanhuo 3.5yi Zhong Han hepaipian mishang "yiji liangchi"《重返20岁》斩获3.5亿 中韩合拍片 迷上"一鸡两吃"' (*20 Once Again* gained 350 million, China–Korea co-production obsessed with "one script two versions"), *Beijing Daily*, 3 February 2015, <http://ent.people.com.cn/n/2015/0203/c1012-26496354.html>.

Zhou Xing 周星, 'Zai wenhua hongguan yu yishu weiguan shang kandai Zhuo yao ji de shidai yiyi 在文化宏观与艺术微观上看待《捉妖记》的时代意义' (Contemporary significance of *Monster Hunt* from the perspective of culture and art), *Yishu baijia* (*The Hundred Schools of the Arts*), 5, 2015, 37–42.

Zhuangzi, 'Shuo jian – delight in the sword-fight', trans. James Legge, *Chinese Text Project*, <https://ctext.org/zhuangzi/delight-in-the-sword-fight>.

'Zhuoyao ji: guochan dapian de xin biaogan yu xin shidai zhutiyantaohui 《捉妖记》：国产大片的新标杆与新世代主题研讨会' (A symposium on *Monster Hunt*: a new benchmark and new era for Chinese blockbusters), *Dianying yishu* 电影艺术 (*Film Art*), 7 August 2015, <http://www.chinafilm.org.cn/Item/Show.asp?m=1&d=8340>.

Žižek, Slavoj, *Looking Awry: An Introduction to Jacques Lacan through Popular Culture* (Cambridge, MA: MIT Press, 1991).

Index

3D, 58
13 Going on 30 (Winick, 2004), 151
20 Once Again (*Chongfan ershisui*, Chen, 2015), 19, 149, 152–63
36th Chamber of Shaolin, The (*Shaolin sanshiliufang*, Liu, 1978), 170
2046 (Wong, 2004), 146

Abbas, Ackbar, 13
Academy Awards, 55
action films, 77, 172
adaptations, 97–101, 102, 104–8, 228–31
Adorno, Theodor, 16
Aesop, 8
aesthetics, 5, 85
Alien (Scott, 1979), 212
aliens, 135, 137, 139, 153
All the Wrong Clues (*Guimazhi duoxing*, Tsui, 1981), 172
Altman, Rick, 101, 130
American cinema *see* Hollywood
amusement venues, 9–10
Animal Logic, 45
animation, 11, 12, 14
Annaud, Jean-Jacques, 186, 191, 192–3, 196
anomaly tales, 8
anthropocentrism, 187–9, 190–9, 200–1, 202n22, 207, 208

Appadurai, Arjun, 200
art films, 75, 78, 169
Assassin, The (*Cike Nie Yinniang*, Hou, 2015), 19, 95–7, 102–8
and adaptation, 98, 99–100, 100–1
Attebery, Brian, 4, 5
authoritarianism, 18, 44, 46, 65, 72, 82, 140
Avatar (Cameron, 2009), 22n65, 45, 56
Avengers: Infinity War (Russo, 2018), 77

B-movies, 5, 6
Bao, Weihong, 12, 97
Barbarella (Vadim, 1968), 136
Barlow, Tani, 160
Barthes, Roland, 81
Base FX, 61
Batchelor, Stephen, 224, 226, 227
Bear, The (*L'Ours*, Annaud, 1988), 191
Behlil, Melis, 60
Beijing Olympics (2008), 27–9, 37–9, 56
and mass ornament, 40, 41–2, 43–4
Bellin, Joshua, 4, 6
Benjamin, Walter, 39
Bennett, Jane, 18
Berry, Chris, 10, 75
Better Tomorrow III: Love and Death in Saigon, A (*Yingxiong bense 3: xiyang zhi ge*, Tsui, 1989), 172
Bible, the, 8

Black Magic (*Jiangtou*) trilogy
  (Ho, 1975–6), 116, 124–5
Bleeding Steel (*Jiqi zhi xue*, Zhang,
  2017), 14
blockbusters, 5, 29, 52, 67, 73–5
  and *The Assassin*, 102–3
  and China, 71
  and genre, 77–8
  and martial arts, 101–2
  see also *Hero*
body-swaps, 7, 19, 149, 151, 154–60
Bordwell, David, 172
Born in China (*Women dansheng zai
  Zhongguo*, Lu, 2016), 185, 186–7,
  189–93, 195–201
Bousé, Derek, 195, 197
Brain Stealers, The (*Diehaihua*, Inoue,
  1968), 135
Bremble, Christopher, 61
Buddha's Palm (*Rulai shenzhang*, Ling,
  1964), 131, 132, 139
Buddhism, 10, 13, 19, 116
  and CGI, 30
  and global, 222–8
  and *Journey to the West*, 232–3, 235,
    237–8, 240–1
  and martial arts, 170
budgets, 75–9, 103
Bukatman, Scott, 180
Burning of the Red Lotus Temple (*Huoshao
  hongliansi*, Zhang, 1928), 97, 178
Bush, George W., 41
Butler, David, 5, 7
Butterfly Murders, The (*Diebian*, Tsui,
  1979), 12, 129, 135–8, 147, 172

camera shots
  and *The Assassin*, 107
  and CGI, 34–5
  and fly-bys, 57
  and *Hero*, 46, 85–6, 88–9
  and *Journey to the West*, 233, 237–8
  and wildlife, 194–5, 196

Cameron, James, 45
Campbell, Joseph, 81
Cao Cao, 30, 32
Cao Yu, 115
Cao Zhi
  'Luo shen fu' ('Rhapsody on the
    Goddess of the Luo River'), 21n34
capitalism, 29, 42–3, 45, 146
Cave of the Silken Web (*Pansidong*, Ho,
  1967), 115–16, 229, 231
Cave of the Spider Spirit, The (*Pansidong*,
  Dan, 1927), 229–30
censorship, 10, 78, 160, 162, 169
CGI *see* computer-generated imagery
Chan, Charlie, 174
Chan, Kenneth, 7, 19, 174
Chan, Peter
  Dragon (2011), 13
Chang Cheh, 12, 122–3, 124
Chang Chen, 102
Chao, Shi-Yan, 19
Chapman, Phil, 186
Chen Duxiu, 8
Chen, Edwin, 119
Chen Kaige, 55, 77
  The Promise (2005), 13, 209
  see also *Emperor and the Assassin, The*
Cheng, Matthew, 123
Cheuk, Pak Tong, 137, 142
Cheung, Alex, 138
chick flick fantasy, 149–63
children, 5, 186, 191, 233
  and monsters, 208, 209, 211, 216, 218
China, 1, 11, 18
  and Beijing Olympics, 27–9, 37–9, 40,
    41–2, 43–4, 56
  and Buddhism, 222
  and coronavirus, 247
  and culture, 119–20
  and Hong Kong, 245–6
  and landscapes, 81
  and literature, 8–9
  and religion, 17, 166, 167–8, 180n1

and Warring States, 76–7
and wildlife, 197–8, 199
see also Chinese cinema
China Film Co. Ltd, 186, 193
China Film Corporation, 74
Chinese cinema, 1–3
   and blockbusters, 71, 74–5, 90–1
   and CGI, 29–31
   and chick flick fantasy, 149, 151, 152, 160–3
   and co-production, 49–58, 66–7
   and fantastic, 6–7, 8–14, 59
   and Hollywood, 6–7
   and Korea, 153
   and religion, 166–7, 168–71
   see also Sino-enchantment
Chinese Civil War, 11
Chinese Communist Party (CCP), 11, 166, 168, 169
'Chinese Dream' (*Zhongguo Meng*), 54
Chinese Ghost Story, A (*Qiannü youhun*, Ching, 1987), 13, 171
Chinese Odyssey: Part One – Pandora's Box, A (*Xiyou ji zhi yueguang baohe*, Lau, 1995), 229, 242n33
Ching "Tony" Siu-Tung, 171
Chow, Rey, 53, 211–12
Chow, Stephen, 19, 30, 226–7, 231–2, 233
Christianity, 167, 168, 182n36
Chu T'ien-wen, 98
Chung, Elaine, 7, 19
Chung, Hye Jean, 54, 56
Cinderella Chef (*Mengqi shishen*, Zhao/Zhang, 2017), 162
cinema, 3–4, 5; *see also* Chinese cinema; Hollywood
cinema of attractions, 2, 9–11, 14, 63
   and *Hero*, 89, 90
   and Ho Meng-hua, 118–20, 127n30
   and Tsui Hark, 177, 179–80, 182n41
cinematography, 30, 88, 107–8

City of Sadness (*Beiqing chengshi*, Hou, 1989), 107
Classic of Mountains and Seas, The (*Shanhai jing*), 8, 62, 204, 205–7, 212–13, 216
climate change, 246
Close Encounters of the Third Kind (Spielberg, 1977), 138
close-ups, 194–5
Cloud Atlas (Tykwer/Wachowski, 2012), 45
co-production, 49–58, 66–7
Cold War, 27, 223
colonialism, 16, 128–9, 131, 146
colour, 83–4
comedies, 77, 135, 138–9, 172
communism, 27, 28, 226; *see also* Chinese Communist Party; Mao Zedong
computer-generated imagery (CGI), 6, 14, 18, 29–31, 53, 246
   and *The Assassin*, 103
   and digital multitudes, 31–5
   and *The Great Wall*, 50, 57–8, 59
   and *Hero*, 45, 86–7
Confucius, 8, 9, 28, 80, 168
   and monsters, 205, 206, 219n10
Conli, Roy, 196–7
coronavirus *see* COVID-19 pandemic
costume, 56, 118–19
costume drama (*guzhuang pian*), 12, 97, 102, 172, 229–30
COVID-19 pandemic, 245, 246, 247
Cowie, Elizabeth, 188, 198
CPC *see* Chinese Communist Party
Crazy Alien (*Fengkuang de waixingren*, Ning Hao, 2019), 67
Creed, Barbara, 124
Crimson Peak (Del Toro, 2015), 169
Crouching Tiger, Hidden Dragon (*Wohu canglong*, Lee, 2000), 13, 30, 78, 79, 81, 98
Cubitt, Sean, 189–90

Cui Weiping, 35–6
Cultural Revolution, 167–8, 170, 180n1, 209
culture, 1–3, 5, 6–7, 119–20
　and fantastic, 8–14
　and Hong Kong, 18
　see also popular culture
Cunliffe, Tom, 7, 19
Curse of the Golden Flower (*Mancheng jindai huangjinjia*, Zhang, 2006), 32, 37, 56, 73

Dai Jinhua, 76–7
Dalai Lama, 168, 176, 223
Damon, Matt, 50, 57, 102
Dan, Prince of Yan, 76
Dangerous Encounters of the First Kind (*Diyi leixing weixian*, Tsui, 1980), 172
Daoism, 10, 13, 107, 111n47, 134
　and *Hero*, 84–5, 49
　and *Journey to the West*, 222, 224, 229
　and Tsui Hark, 166, 167, 170, 175, 176, 177, 178, 181n32
DC universe, 4
Dead and the Deadly, The (*Ren xia ren*, Wu Ma, 1982), 133
Dead End (*Sijiao*, Chang, 1969), 124
Dead or Alive: Final (Miike, 2002), 131–2
Deadly Breaking Sword, The (*Fengliu duanjian xiaoxiaodao*, Sun, 1979), 133
Debord, Guy, 16, 44
Dee (Di Renjie), 173–4
demon stories, 10
D'entre les morts (Boileau/Narcejac), 100
Des Forges, Alexander, 9
Detective Dee films, 19, 167, 173, 174–80; *see also* Dee (Di Renjie)
Detective Dee: The Four Heavenly Kings (*Di Renjie zhi sida tianwang*, Tsui, 2018), 174, 175–6, 177, 180, 203

Detective Dee: The Mystery of the Phantom Flame (*Di Renjie zhi tongtian diguo*, Tsui, 2010), 174–5
Dietz, John, 59
digital cinema, 18–19
Digital Domain, 45
digital multitudes, 29, 31–5, 45–6, 56–7
　and *The Great Wall*, 63–4
　and *Hero*, 86–7
　see also mass ornament
Dijiang (Thearch Long River), 205, 206, 212–13, 216
disenchantment, 15–17, 19, 23n71, 132, 137, 225, 230
Disney, 7, 66
Disneynature, 186, 190, 192, 196–7, 198
DJI, 57
documentary, 3, 4, 19, 36, 186–7, 190–2, 196–8
domesticity, 204–5, 208–9, 211
Donald, James, 4
Double Team (Tsui, 1997), 172
Dragon (*Wuxia*, Chan, 2011), 13
Dream of the Red Chamber (*Hongloumeng*), 8
DreamWorks, 7
Du Liniang, 8
Duel, The (*Dajuedou*, Chang, 1971), 124
Duel of the Fists (*Quanji*, Chang, 1971), 124
Duffy, Michael, 13

ecocinema, 185, 189–93
economics, 28–9
Elberse, Anita
　Blockbusters, 74
Emperor and the Assassin, The (*Jing Ke ci Qinwang*, Chen, 1998), 71, 77, 79, 82, 83, 86
Emperor's Shadow, The (*Qinsong*, Zhou, 1996), 71, 77
enchantment *see* Sino-enchantment
Eng, Robert, 44–5

enlightenment, 16
environmentalism, 190–1
epics, 6, 8
escapism, 5
Eternal Love, The series (*Shuangshi chongfei*, Yuen/Wu, 2017–20), 162
Ewers, Heinz, 90
extras, 81

fables, 8
Fairbanks, Douglas, Sr, 7
fairy tales, 6, 8, 203–4
fake news, 246, 248n6
Falun Gong sect, 17, 168, 176, 177
family, 19, 220n22, 233–4
 and *Monster Hunt*, 204–5, 208–9, 211–12, 214–18
Fan Yuqi, General, 82
fantastic, 1–2, 246
 and *The Assassin*, 95, 108
 and blockbusters, 77–8
 and Chinese culture, 8–14
 and classical tales, 203–4
 and definition, 187–90
 and genre, 2–7, 112–14
 and *Hero*, 72, 79–90
 and Ho Meng-hua, 115–26
 and Hong Kong, 171
 and modernity, 14–17
 and *Monster Hunt*, 204–5
 and science fiction, 22n65
 and wildlife, 200–1
 see also chick flick fantasy; science fiction; Sino-enchantment
fantasy *see* fantastic
Farquhar, Mary, 10, 30, 34–5
fascism, 29, 35–9, 41
feminism, 150
Fifth-Generation, 55
film blanc, 6, 7, 19
film noir, 172
Final Test, The (*Zuihou yizhan*, Lo, 1987), 129, 140, 143–6, 147

Five Shaolin Masters (*Shaolin wuzu*, Chang, 1974), 124
Flowers of War (*Jinling shisanchai*, Zhang, 2011), 61
Flying Guillotine, The (*Xuedizi*, Ho, 1975), 116
folk tales, 203–4
Forbidden Kingdom, The (Minkoff, 2008), 226
Fowkes, Katherine, 5
fox spirit stories, 8
Foxconn, 42
franchises, 4, 51, 52, 59, 60, 66
Frankfurt School, 16
Freaky Friday (Waters, 2003), 151
French cinema, 3
Freud, Sigmund, 187–8
Fugitive, The (Davis, 1993), 71

Galloping Horse, 45
Game of Thrones (TV series, 2011–19), 64
Garcia, Roger, 131
gender, 214–15, 221n40; *see also* women
Genette, Gérard
 Palimpsests, 96–7, 98–9, 101
genres, 2–7, 75–9, 96–7, 101, 112–15, 172; *see also* chick flick fantasy; horror films; martial arts; science fiction
Germany *see* Nazi Germany
Ghost in the Shell (*Kokaku kidotai*, Oshii, 1995), 131, 140
Ghostbusters (Feig, 2016), 169
ghosts, 8, 10, 133–4, 169
Gill, Rosalind, 150
Gledhill, Christine, 3, 113
global cinema, 2, 3
globalisation, 45, 200, 223
Go Lala Go! (*Du Lala shengzhiji*, Xu, 2010), 152
Goddess, The (*Shennü*, Wu, 1932), 10–11
Godzilla (Edwards, 2014), 51

Godzilla: King of the Monsters (Dougherty, 2019), 67
Goldberg, Michelle, 245
Good Men, Good Women (*Haonan haonü*, Hou, 1995), 107
Goossaert, Vincent, 167, 170
Grandmaster, The (*Yidai zongshi*, Wong, 2013), 13
Great Wall, The (*Changcheng*, Zhang, 2016), 13–14, 19, 50–2, 54, 67
    and genre, 102
    and politics, 64–6
    and visual effects, 57, 58, 59, 61, 62–4
    and Zhang Yimou, 55–6
Great Wall of China, 50–8, 55, 57
Great World (Shanghai), 9–10
Green Snake (*Qingshe*, Tsui, 1993), 167
Gremlins, The (Dante, 1984), 177
grotesque, 1
Gua, Grace, 157
Guan Mingjie, 53
Guan Yu, 170
Gunning, Tom, 2, 9, 79, 90, 118; see also cinema of attractions
Guo Pu, 206, 207

Hall, Sheldon, 73, 77
Haraway, Donna, 240, 241
Harry Potter series (Rowling), 6, 228
Hartwell, David, 80–1
Havoc in Heaven (*Danao tiangong*, Wan, 1961–4), 226
Health Warning (*Da lei tai*, Wong, 1983), 129, 131, 140–3, 147
Healthy Realism, 11
Hengdian World Studios (Zhejiang Province), 67
Hero (*Yingxiong*, Zhang, 2002), 13, 19, 29, 44–6, 55, 75
    and blockbuster model, 90–1
    and budget, 75–6
    and CGI, 30–1, 32–5
    and crowds, 56
    and fantastic, 79–90
    and ideology, 72–3
    and martial arts, 78–9
    and mass ornament, 35–7, 40
    and story, 77
high fantasy, 81
Hillenbrand, Margaret, 35, 45
Hinduism, 8
Hitchcock, Alfred, 100
Hitler, Adolf, 36, 37, 40
Ho Meng-hua, 6, 19, 114–26, 231
Hoberman, J., 36
Hollywood, 2, 3, 5
    and blockbusters, 73–5, 77
    and chick flick fantasy, 155
    and Chinese cinema, 6–7, 49–58
    and fantasy, 78
    and science fiction, 131, 132
    and women, 150
Holmes, Sherlock, 174
Hong Kong, 1, 6, 10, 11–12
    and autonomy, 35
    and *Butterfly Murders*, 135–8
    and China, 78, 245–6
    and colonialism, 128–9
    and culture, 18
    and fantasy, 171
    and *The Final Test*, 143–6
    and genres, 164n21
    and *Health Warning*, 140–3
    and horror films, 13–14
    and martial arts, 169–70
    and religion, 17
    and science fiction, 7, 19, 129–35, 139–40, 146–7
    and *Twinkle Twinkle Little Star*, 138–9
    see also Ho Meng-hua; Tsui Hark
'Hongxian' (Red Thread), 98, 100
Hoon, Samir, 64
Horn, Alan, 74
horror films, 6, 10, 13–14, 16, 78
    and Ho Meng-hua, 116, 120–6
Hou Hsiao-hsien, 6; see also *Assassin, The*

House of Flying Daggers (*Shimian maifu*, Zhang, 2004), 30, 55, 73
How Long Will I Love U (*Chaoshikong tongju*, Su, 2018), 149
Hu Jintao, 41
Hu, King 12, 122–3
Hu Shih, 8, 173
Hui, Raman, 212
Hui Brothers, 139
Hume, Kathryn
  Fantasy and Mimesis, 112–13
Hutchinson, Tom, 113
hybridity, 205–6, 213

I Love Maria (*Tiejia wudi*, Chung/Tsui, 1988), 148n30
I, Robot (Proyas, 2004), 64
ideology, 1–2, 6, 35–9
If I Were You (*Bianshen nannü*, Li, 2012), 149
Industrial Light and Magic (ILM), 61–2, 66
intermediality, 95, 97
intertextuality, 95–7

Jackson, Peter, 99
Jackson, Rosemary, 4
Jade Raksha, The (*Yuluocha*, Ho, 1968), 116
Japan, 11, 102, 163
Jaws (Spielberg, 1975), 73–4, 77, 234
Jenkins, Eric, 89–90
Jiang Hu: The Triad Zone (*Jianghu gaoji*, Lam, 2000), 170
Jiang Rong, 186, 191, 193
jianghu ('rivers and lakes'), 35, 44
Jin Yong, 98, 99
Jing Ke, 76, 77, 79, 79–80, 82
Jing Tian, 50
John Carter (Stanton, 2012), 56, 64
Journey to the West (*Xiyou ji*, c. 16th century), 7, 11, 19, 98
  and Stephen Chow, 19, 224–8, 231–41

  and film adaptations, 228–31
  and Ho Meng-hua, 115–16, 119–20, 123, 127n29
  and Hong Kong, 135
Journey to the West: Conquering the Demons (*Xiyou xiangmopian*, Chow, 2013), 149, 203, 224–8, 230, 231–41
Journey to the West: The Demons Strike Back (*Xiyou fuyaopian*, Tsui, 2017), 230
Jurassic World: Fallen Kingdom (Bayona, 2018), 51

Kearney, Richard, 213
Kekexili: The Mountain Patrol (*Keke xili*, Lu, 2004), 186
Kennedy, Kathleen, 61
Kill Bill films (Tarantino, 2003–4), 7
Killer Darts (*Zhuihunbiao*, Ho, 1968), 116, 120
King Kong (Guillermin, 1976), 116
kinship, 211–12
Knock-Off (Tsui, 1998), 172
Kokas, Aynne, 53, 54
Kong: Skull Island (Vogt-Roberts, 2017), 51
Koo, Louis, 146
Koo, Siu-fung, 133
Korea *see* South Korean film
Kracauer, Siegfried, 29, 37, 39–41, 41–2, 44, 112
Kristeva, Julia, 95
Kundun (Scorsese, 1997), 223
kung fu, 79, 120, 123–5, 172
  and science fiction, 131, 140–3
Kung Fu Hustle (*Gongfu*, Chow, 2004), 30
Kurosawa, Akira, 45, 46n11
Kwok, Huen Ching, 131, 132

Lady Hermit, The (*Zhong Kui niangzi*, Ho, 1971), 116
Lady of Steel (*Huangjiang nüxia*, Ho, 1970), 116, 120–3
Lam, Tong, 28

Land of Many Perfumes, The (*Nüerguo*, Ho, 1968), 116, 231, 243n42
landscapes, 81, 84, 107
Landy, Joshua
   The Re-Enchantment of the World, 16
Lang, Fritz, 6
Larson, Wendy, 35, 44
Lau, Jenny Kwok Wah, 72, 75
Laugh In (*Haha xiao*, Lung, 1976), 135
Law, Wing-sang, 128
League of Gods (*Fengshenbang*, Hui, 2016), 14, 59–60, 62, 102
Lee, Ang, 79; see also *Crouching Tiger, Hidden Dragon*
Lee, Bruce, 122
Lee, Haiyan, 208
Lee Ping Bing, Mark, 107–8
Legend of Fuyao (*Fuyao*, Yang/Xie/Li, 2018), 162
Legend of the Demon Cat (*Yaomao zhuan*, Chen, 2017), 203
Legendary Pictures, 51, 67, 68n5
Leith, Brian, 186
Leung, Noong-kong, 133–4
Leung, Tony, 203
Lev, Peter, 100
Levinas, Emmanuel, 213
Li, Jinhua, 151
Li, Siu Leung, 132
Liang Qichao, 8
Life is a Moment (*Zhaohua xishi*, Woo, 1987), 148n30
Lifeline Express (*Hongyun dangtou*, Wong, 1984), 134
Lim, Bliss Cua, 15–17, 188, 217
literature, 7, 8–9, 10
   and adaptations, 98–101
   and Dee, 173–4
   and martial arts, 97–8
   and religion, 232–3
   and science fiction, 130–1
   and supernatural, 178
   and *zhiguai* tradition, 204

Little Buddha (Bertolucci, 1993), 223
Liu Cixin
   The Three-Body Problem (*Santi*), 14
Lo, Kwai-Cheung, 142, 146
Lord of the Rings trilogy (Jackson, 2001–3), 6, 32, 44, 64, 99
   and mass ornament, 36, 37, 39–40
Love Eterne, The (*Liang Shanbo yu Zhu Yingtai*, Li, 1963), 12, 119
Love Through Different Times (*Chuanyue shikong de ailian*, Feng, 2002), 151
Lovecraftian fantasy, 80–1
Lu Chuan, 186, 191–3, 196, 198
Lu, Sheldon Hsiao-peng, 55
Lu Xun, 8
Lumière brothers, 3, 112
Lung Kong, 135
Luo Guanzhong
   Romance of the Three Kingdoms, 30
Lupke, Christopher, 104

MacDonald, Scott, 189
McGrath, Jason, 18, 56–7, 60
McKenna, A. T., 54–5
Mad Monk, The (*Ji Gong*, Ching, 1993), 171
magic, 1, 6, 11
magic realism, 6
main melody films, 75, 78, 91n14
Malaysia, 124
male fantasy films, 164n22
Mandarin Ducks and Butterfly literature, 9, 208, 209
Manovich, Lev, 30
Mao Zedong, 27, 28, 41, 159–60, 168, 180n1
martial arts, 1, 7, 9
   and adaptations, 97–8, 99–100
   and ban, 168–70
   and blockbusters, 101–2
   and CGI, 29–30
   and Detective Dee films, 177–80
   and digital multitudes, 31–5

and Ho Meng-hua, 116, 120–6
and Hong Kong, 12, 133
and *Journey to the West*, 229
and science fiction, 136–7
and special effects, 10
and Taiwan, 11
and transnationalism, 13
see also *Assassin, The*; *Hero*; *kung fu*
Marvel Cinematic Universe (MCU), 4, 66
mass ornament, 29, 35–43, 45
MASSIVE (Multiple Agent Simulation System in Virtual Environment), 40, 64
Master of Kung Fu, The (*Huang Feihong*, Ho, 1973), 116, 120–4, 125
Matrix, The (Wachowskis, 1999), 7, 89, 179–80
Maxu Weibang, 13
  Song at Midnight (1937), 10
May Fourth Movement, 10
media, 9, 53
Media Asia Group, 45
Méliès, Georges, 3, 112
melodrama, 115
merchandise, 52
Mermaid, The (*Meirenyu*, Chow, 2016), 77
Metropolis (Lang, 1927), 136
Michelson, Annette, 136
Mighty Peking Man, The (*Xingxingwang*, Ho, 1977), 116
Miike, Takashi, 131–2
Miller, Toby, 58
mimesis, 112–13
Ming Dynasty, 57, 151
Ming Pao (newspaper), 130–1
Minkoff, Rob, 226
Miramax, 76
mise-en-scène, 81, 176, 188
  and desire, 114, 115, 118, 120, 124, 126
Miss Granny (*Susanghan Geunyeon*, Hwang, 2014), 149, 153–63
modernity, 2, 11, 15–16, 18, 242n15

Moine, Raphaelle, 130
Monkey Goes West, The (*Xiyou ji*, Ho, 1966), 115, 116, 118–19, 125, 231, 243n42
Monkey in Hong Kong (*Sun Wukong danao Xianggang*, Tang, 1969), 135
Monkey King, 228
Monkey King trilogy (Cheang, 2014–18), 230
monster films, 6, 7, 13–14, 62, 220n22; see also *Monster Hunt*
Monster Hunt (*Zhuoyao ji*, Hui, 2015), 7, 13, 19, 149, 203, 204–12
  and otherness, 212–18
Monster Hunt 2 (*Zhuoyao ji 2*, Hui, 2018), 203
Moskowitz, Marc L., 169
Mummy, The (Sommers, 1999), 32
Münsterberg, Hugo, 90
mysticism, 19
mythology, 8, 81–3, 136, 203–4, 212–13

Na Moon-hee, 157
Naficy, Hamid, 172
narrative, 79–83
nationalism, 29, 72, 128–9, 171–3
Nationalist Party, 10, 11
Nazi Germany, 35, 36, 37, 39, 44, 140–1
Neale, Steve, 5, 112–13
New Dragon Inn (*Xin longmen kezhan*, Lee/Ching/Tsui, 1992), 81
New Life Movement, 10, 11
New Wave, 12, 13, 172
Ni Kuang
  Wisely series, 130–1, 133
Ni Zhen, 75
Nichols, Bill, 211
'Nie Yinniang', 98, 99–101, 104–8
North, Dan, 13, 19

on-location shooting, 30–1
Once Upon a Time in China (*Huang Feihong*, Tsui, 1991), 142, 172

opera, 7, 10, 11, 12, 56, 119
Opium War, The (*Yapian zhanzheng*, Xie, 1997), 71, 75, 78, 83, 86
Oriental Movie Metropolis (Qingdao), 49–50, 57, 67
Oscars *see* Academy Awards
otherness, 197, 204–5, 212–18
Outland (Hyams, 1981), 143–6

Pacific Rim (Del Toro, 2013), 177
Palace (*Gong*, Yu, 2011), 152, 162
Palmer, David A., 167, 170
Pang, Laikwan, 169, 181n11
Pascal, Pedro, 50
pastiche, 96, 101
Peggy Sue Got Married (Coppola, 1986), 151
Peking Opera Blues (*Daomadan*, Tsui, 1986), 172
Peony Pavilion, The (*Mudan ting*), 8
People's Liberation Army, 32
People's Republic of China (PRC) *see* China
Pettigrew, Ian, 19
Phantom of the Opera (Julian, 1925), 10
Philippines, the, 163
photogrammetry, 61
photography *see* cinematography
Pines, Yuri, 76–7
pixels, 36, 37–8, 39, 43, 65
planetarity, 232, 234, 237–9
Plate, S. Brent, 169
playfulness, 5
politics, 1–2, 5, 11, 17
  and *The Great Wall*, 64–6
  and *Hero*, 35–9, 72–3
  see also communism; socialism
popular culture, 214, 219n8, 221n40
postfeminism, 19, 150–3, 155, 160
PRC *see* China
Prince, Stephen, 77–8

Princess Iron Fan (*Tieshan gongzhu*, Ho, 1966), 115, 116–17, 118–19, 125, 231, 243n42
Princess Iron Fan (*Tieshan gongzhu*, Wan/Wan, 1941), 11
Promise, The (*Wuji*, Chen, 2005), 13, 209
propaganda, 29, 53
Pu Songling *see Strange Stories from a Chinese Studio* (*Liaozhai zhi yi*)
Puppetmaster, The (*Ximeng rensheng*, Hou, 1993), 107
Purse, Lisa, 57–8
Purser, Ronald
  McMindfulness, 224

Qin, 76
Qin Dynasty, 32–6, 37, 44, 47n15, 151–2
qing (feeling), 208–9
Qingdao *see* Oriental Movie Metropolis

racism, 27, 247
Raise the Red Lantern (*Dahong denglong gaogaogua*, Zhang, 1991), 46, 55
Rashomon (Kurosawa, 1950), 46n11
Rawnsley, Gary D., 44
Rawnsley, Ming-Yeh T., 44
re-enchantment, 16–17, 108, 188, 246
  and *Journey to the West*, 231, 233
  and religion, 171, 225–6
realism, 3, 4, 9, 10, 11
  and *The Great Wall*, 62
  and main melody, 78
Red Cliff (*Chibi*, Woo, 2008), 13, 30, 31–2
Red Sorghum (*Honggaoliang*, Zhang, 1988), 55
Rehak, Bob, 13, 54, 58, 63
religion, 8, 10, 17, 19, 166–71
  and Detective Dee films, 174–80
  and *Journey to the West*, 229
  and literature, 232–3
  see also Buddhism; Christianity; Daoism; Uighur Muslims
remakes, 5, 149, 153–60

Riefenstahl, Leni, 35, 36–7, 39, 40, 41
Riots in Outer Space (*Liangsha danao taikong*, Wong, 1959), 135
Robin Hood (Scott, 2010), 46n12
Robocop (Verhoeven, 1987), 133
Rodowick, D. N., 14
Rogge, Jacques, 41
Romance of the Three Kingdoms (*Sanguo yanyi*), 30
romantic comedy, 6
romantic love, 208, 209–10, 239–40
Rowling, J. K., 4, 6, 228
Rubio, Mayes C., 56

Saler, Michael
The Re-Enchantment of the World, 16
SARFT (State Administration of Radio, Film and Television), 169, 176
Scarlet Heart (*Bubu jingxin*, Lee, 2011), 152, 162
Scharff, Christina, 150
Schatz, Thomas, 74
Schreiber, Michele, 155
science fiction, 6, 7, 14, 22n65, 78
    and *Butterfly Murders*, 135–8
    and *The Final Test*, 143–6
    and *Health Warning*, 140–3
    and Hong Kong, 19, 128, 129–35, 139–40, 146–7
    and *Twinkle Twinkle Little Star*, 138–9
SCO Film Festival, 67
Second Sino-Japanese War, 11, 12
Security Unlimited (*Modeng baobiao*, Hui, 1981), 139
Sedgwick, Eve Kosofsky
Touching Feeling, 227, 234
Sek Kei, 135
self-sacrifice, 82
sentimentality, 204–5, 208–12, 219n9
sets, 81, 102
Seven Years in Tibet (Annaud, 1997), 186, 223
shadowplay (*yingxi*), 9

shamanism, 8, 21n34
Shambaugh, David, 53, 54
Shanghai, 10, 11, 97, 229
Shanghai Fortress (*Shanghai baolei*, Teng, 2019), 14
Shanghai Triad (*Yao a yao, yaodao waipoqiao*, Zhang, 1995), 71
Shanshan (Ho, 1967), 115
Shaolin Temple (*Shaolinsi*, Chang, 1976), 124
Shaw Brothers, 19
    and Ho Meng-hua, 115–16, 119, 122–3, 126
    and science fiction, 135, 138–9
Shek Kei, 119
Shih, Shu-mei, 17
Shim Eun-kyung, 157
Shrek series (2001–7), 212
Shu Qi, 102
Sima Qian
    'Biography of Assassins' (*Cike liezhuan*), 104
Simpson, Andrew, 193–4, 199
Singapore, 18, 61
Sino-enchantment, 1–2, 3, 17–20, 247
    and *Journey to the West*, 224, 225–8
Sinophone, 17–18
Six Fingered Lord of the Lute, The (*Liuzhi qinmo*, Chen, 1965), 133
Slaby, Adolph, 90
slow motion, 89
snow leopards, 191–2, 198
Sobchack, Vivian, 113
socialism, 11, 18, 74
Song at Midnight (*Yeban gesheng*, Maxu, 1937), 10
Song Dynasty, 50, 57, 122, 123
Songs of Chu (*Chuci*, c. Warring States Period), 21n34
Sontag, Susan, 29, 36
Sorcerer and the White Snake, The (*Baishe chuanshuo zhi fahai*, Ching, 2011), 171, 203
sound effects, 118–19

South Korean film, 7, 149, 153–60
spatiality, 236–7
special effects, 5, 10, 12, 13
   and martial arts, 29–30
   and meaning, 53–4
   and outsourcing, 45
   see also computer-generated imagery
spectacles, 6, 83–90
Spielberg, Steven, 73–4
spirits, 8, 9, 133–4
Spivak, Gayatri Chakravorty
   Death of a Discipline, 232, 234, 239
Stam, Robert, 58
Star Wars (Lucas, 1977), 138, 139
Star Wars: Attack of the Clones (Lucas, 2002), 36
Starling by Each Step (*Bubu jingxin*, 2005–6), 151–2
stereotypes, 28
storytelling, 8, 75–9
Strange Stories from a Chinese Studio (*Liaozhai zhi yi*), 8, 10, 11, 13
   and *Monster Hunt*, 205, 206, 207
Strategies of the Warring States (*Zhanguo ce*), 76
Street Angel (*Malu tianshi*, Yuan, 1937), 11
Stuckey, Andrew, 19, 225, 227
Sun, Hongmei, 226
Sun Yat-sen, 28
Super Inframan, The (*Zhongguo chaoren*, Hua, 1975), 131, 135
supernatural, 6, 8, 15, 169, 177–8
superstition, 19, 168–9
swashbucklers, 7
sword and sorcery, 6, 7

Tai Chi Master (*Taiji Zhang Sanfeng*, Yuen, 1993), 170
Taiwan, 1, 6, 11, 18, 35
   and *The Assassin*, 102
   and Foxconn, 42
   and martial arts, 169–70
   and religion, 17

Tales of Wu Kong, The (*Wukong zhuan*, Kwok, 2017), 230
Tan See-Kam, 167, 172
Tang Dynasty, 98, 104–5, 123, 173, 222
Taotie, 62–5
Tarantino, Quentin
   Kill Bill films, 7
television, 153, 162
temporality, 15–16
Temptress Moon (*Fengyue*, Chen, 1996), 71
Ten Years (*Shinian*, Au/Chow/Kwok/Ng/Wong, 2015), 246
Teng, Teresa, 153
Teo, Stephen, 7, 10
   and *kung fu*, 120, 121
   and martial arts, 79, 97, 101–3, 169
   and religion, 177–8
   and science fiction, 138
   and Tsui Hark, 12, 13, 171
Terminator, The (Cameron, 1984), 133
Terra-Cotta Warrior, A (*Gujin dazhan qinyong qing*, Ching, 1989), 171
terracotta warriors, 32, 34
Thousand Faces of Dunjia, The (*Qimen dunjia*, Yuen, 2017), 59, 60
Three Teachings see religion
Ti Lung, 123–4
Tian Han, 115
Tibet, 35, 168, 223
Tiller Girls, 39, 40, 41
Time and Tide (*Shunliu niliu*, Tsui, 2000), 172
time-slip dramas, 151–2
Time to Love (*Xin bubu jingxin*, Song, 2015), 152
time travel, 149, 162
Titanic (Cameron, 1997), 45, 71
Todorov, Tzvetan, 4–5, 15, 113, 188
Tolkien, J. R. R., 4, 6
   The Lord of the Rings, 81, 228
totalitarianism, 29, 35–6, 44, 45
Touch of Zen, A (*Xianü*, Hu, 1971), 7, 11, 169–70

tradition, 2, 18
transnationalism, 2–3, 13
　and *20 Once Again*, 153–60
　and *The Assassin*, 102–3
　and Buddhism, 223
　and *Hero*, 72
　and visual effects, 60–1
　see also co-production
transtexts, 98–9
Triumph of Will (Riefenstahl, 1935), 36–7, 39, 44
Tron (Lisberger, 1982), 133
Troy (Petersen, 2004), 32
True Lies (Cameron, 1994), 71
Tsang, Raymond, 133
Tsui Hark, 12, 13, 135–8, 142, 166–7, 171–3; *see also* Detective Dee films
Tsumabuki Satoshi, 102, 105
Turandot (Puccini), 56
Turnock, Julie, 62
Twinkle Twinkle Little Star (*Xingji chuntai*, Cheung, 1983), 129, 138–9, 147
Two Brothers (*Deux frères*, Annaud, 2004), 191

Udden, James, 103
UFOs, 135, 138–9
Uighur Muslims, 17, 168, 176, 245
Ultra Reinforcement (*Chaoshikong jiubing*, Lam, 2012), 149
Under the Dome (*Qiongding zhi xia*, Chai, 2015), 190
United States of America (USA), 223, 247; *see also* Hollywood
Universal Pictures, 51

Van Damme, Jean-Claude, 172
Van Dover, J. K., 173
Van Gulik, Robert, 173–4, 181n32
Vengeance (*Baochou*, Chang, 1970), 124
verisimilitude, 112–13
Vertigo (Hitchcock, 1958), 100
Vietnam, 163

visual effects (VFX), 53–4, 55, 56–66, 66–7; *see also* special effects; spectacles
Vukovich, Daniel, 28

Walsh, Raoul, 6
Wanda, Dalian, 49–50, 51, 52, 57
Wandering Earth, The (*Liulang diqiu*, Gwo, 2019), 14, 67, 73, 146
Wang Dulu, 98
Wang, Haizhou, 44
Wang Jianlin, 49, 67
Wang Weiyi
　Cloudy the Star Wolf (*Mingxing lang*), 193
Wang, Yiman, 4, 19
Warcraft: The Beginning (Jones, 2016), 51, 56
warfare *see* warriors
Warner Bros, 51, 74
Warring States period, 8, 76–7, 104
warriors, 31–5, 37, 44, 56, 86–7
Warriors of Future (*Mingri zhanji*, Koo, 2019), 146–7
wealth, 210–11
wenqing (warm sentimentality), 211
West, the, 27–9
Weta, 60, 69n34
Whissel, Kristen, 29, 32, 33, 36–7, 62–3, 65
Wild Girl, The (*Ye guniang*, Ho, 1957), 115
wildlife, 185–7, 189, 191–201, 202n22
Williams, Linda, 113
Wolf Totem (*Lang tuteng*, Annaud, 2015), 185, 186, 187, 189–96, 198–201
Wolf Warrior 2 (*Zhanlang 2*, Wu, 2017), 73, 77
wolves, 186, 187, 191, 192, 193–4, 195–6, 198, 199, 201n15
women, 99–100, 230–1, 239; *see also* chick flick fantasy
wonder films, 6
Wong Fei-hung, 121, 122, 123

Wong Kar-wai
  The Grandmaster (2013), 13
Woo, John
  Red Cliff (2008), 13, 30, 31–2
world-building, 80–1, 84
worlding, 200, 201
Wright, Arthur, 222
Wright, Robert
  Why Buddhism is True, 225
Wu Cheng'en, 228–31
Wu Zetian, Empress, 173, 174–5, 180
Wuba, 206, 208, 212, 214, 215–18
wuxia see martial arts
Wyatt, Justin, 83

Xi Jinping, 53, 54
xia (martial artists), 104–5
Xiao Wu (Jia, 1997), 78
Xie Haimeng, 98
Xinhua, 53
Xinjiang, 35
Xiyou ji see Journey to the West

Yan, 76
Yang, Fenggang, 168, 177
Yang, Li, 19
Yang, Mei, 7, 19
Yang Zishan, 157
Yee Chau-sui, 139
Yellow Earth (*Huang tudi*, Chen, 1984), 55
Yi Lui, James, 139

Ying Zheng, King of Qin, 76–7, 79–80, 82, 83
Yingling (Ding Shanxi, n.d.), 169
Young Detective Dee: Rise of the Sea Dragon (*Di Renjie zhi shendu longwang*, Tsui, 2013), 174, 175, 177, 178–9
Yu, Anthony, 228–9, 240
Yu, Kiki Tianqi, 54–5
Yu, Sabrina Qiong, 44
Yuen Woo-ping, 7, 59
Yunnan Qinghai Rural Moving Image Project, 185

Zen Buddhism, 222
Zhang, Xiaoqun, 52–3
Zhang Yimou, 13, 18–19, 29, 32
  and Beijing Olympics, 27, 28, 37–9, 41, 42–3, 43, 44
  see also *The Great Wall* (*Changcheng*), *Hero* (*Yingxiong*)
Zhang, Yingjing, 52
Zhang Zhen, 97, 229–30
Zhong Acheng, 98
Zhong Kui (*Zhong Kui fumo: xueyao moling*, Pau/Zhao, 2015), 60
Zhou Dynasty, 213
Zhou Xiaowen, 77
Zhuangzi, 8
Zu: Warriors of the Magic Mountain (*Xin Shushan jianxia*, Tsui, 1983), 12, 135–6, 167, 172

EU representative:
Easy Access System Europe
Mustamäe tee 50, 10621 Tallinn, Estonia
Gpsr.requests@easproject.com

www.ingramcontent.com/pod-product-compliance
Lightning Source LLC
Chambersburg PA
CBHW052054230426
43671CB00011B/1901